Chaplin: Genius of the Cinema

Chaplin: Genius of the Cinema

Jeffrey Vance

Manoah Bowman, Photographic Editor

Introduction by David Robinson

Harry N. Abrams, Inc., Publishers

Contents

Page 2: Chaplin, dressed in a prison uniform, applies makeup during production of MODERN TIMES (1936).

Opposite: Chaplin reads the POLICE GAZETTE while lying fully clothed in a bathtub on the set during a break in the filming of PAY DAY (1922).

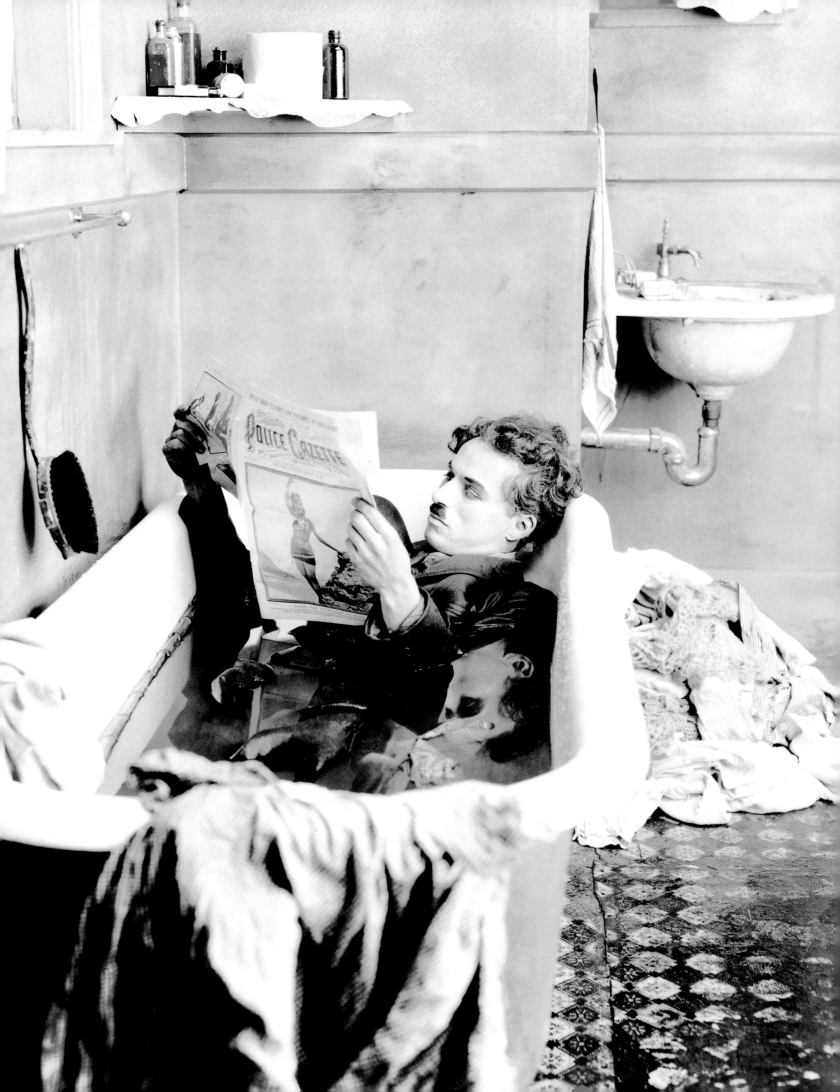

Introduction

David Robinson

Charlie Chaplin began his professional career in the nineteenth century and achieved world fame in the second decade of the twentieth century, before the cinema had even come of age. At the start of the twenty-first century his work is attracting renewed recognition and devotion, as generations that have grown up long since he ceased creative activity discover how much he has still to tell about our lives and society, and about the workings of the human heart. His films are once again being made internationally available in theaters and on new digital formats. In collaboration with the Chaplin family's Association Chaplin, the Cineteca di Bologna has a continuing program to restore his films and is in the process of making the vast documentation contained within the Chaplin Archives universally accessible via the Internet. The Academy of Motion Picture Arts and Sciences, working with Association Chaplin, has performed important work to preserve the precious Chaplin photograph collection. The British Film Institute has inaugurated the Chaplin Foundation to bring together British collections of films, documents, and artifacts and to promote the study of the country's most celebrated native filmmaker. The Manoir de Ban, Chaplin's home for the last twenty-five years of his life, is currently being transformed into a museum to be known as the Charlie Chaplin Heritage Site. Chaplin, in 2003, is once again at a peak of esteem.

Historically, though, like most artists, his reputation has suffered vicissitudes, in his case dramatic. In the 1920s and 1930s he was, in his character of the Tramp, the best-known and best-loved figure the world had ever known. In the 1940s, as he abandoned the Tramp for new characters in *The Great Dictator* and *Monsieur Verdoux*, some of his old public were bewildered; meanwhile, with the onset of America's political paranoia in the Cold War era, Chaplin, as a foreigner and free-thinker, became the target of powerful elements of the far right.

When in the early 1950s he felt himself forced into exile from the country where he had achieved fame and fortune, Chaplin was enthusiastically welcomed home by Europe. The British, in particular, stoutly defended their own son against the transatlantic ingrates. Yet in turn the British critics—perhaps on the "prophet in his own land" principle, or as a delayed response to the pervasive smears he had suffered in the United States— turned against him. Jeffrey Vance reminds me that in 1968, reporting on the reception of his last film, *A Countess from Hong Kong,* I reflected sadly that "The eclipse of Charles Chaplin's critical reputation is practically complete."

Chaplin lived to see the reaction, and suffered acutely, because he loved Britain deeply, and in later years constantly returned to those South London streets where he had passed his toughest years. Oona Chaplin rationalized his unpopularity in her own way as a kind of perverted romanticism in the English: "If Charlie had died broke, drunk, and miserable they would love him; but they can never forgive him for dying happy, rich, and living in Switzerland." Another explanation in terms of national temperament is that Britain's political history in the postwar half-century tended to exacerbate the national taste for satire into an acute, pervasive cynicism; and it is impossible to be cynical or mean-spirited and appreciate the director of *The Kid.* The signs now though are that even Britain has come around, in the atmosphere of renewed appreciation to which this book will make a substantial contribution.

Of the making of books on Chaplin there is no end. It long ago became impossible to keep count of the hundreds of titles, in languages from Armenian to Yiddish. From experience as a Chaplin biographer, I do not envy anyone embarking on a book today. Having written in the early 1980s, I count myself the last lucky one, as the beneficiary of an extraordinary concatenation of then-new documentation. I was given access to the hitherto unseen treasures of the Chaplin Archives, and to the groundbreaking discoveries of Harold Manning, David Clegg, and Alan Neate in their researches on Chaplin's childhood and early professional years. There were even survivors of Chaplin's Karno years living and communicative. The Freedom of Information Act had just revealed the absurdity and horror of the FBI's machinations. All of this I was privileged to garner, greedily, into *Chaplin: His Life and Art.*

If I cannot hope for such good fortune for successive biographers, at least it is a pleasant obligation to share my luck with them, if they can make use of it. Jeffrey Vance has marshaled the whole story succinctly, and is particularly perceptive on Chaplin's political and amorous associations as well as on a key—and often neglected—work, *The Circus*. He has been fortunate enough to have had access to the documentation contained within the Chaplin Archives and has drawn upon an impressive array of interviews he has conducted with Chaplin collaborators, friends, and family. The publication in this volume of a significant portion of Richard Meryman's 1966 interview with Chaplin is also a terrific addition to the Chaplin canon.

But the raison d'être of this book is not so much the text as the photographs, an unprecedented collection for which Jeffrey Vance and Manoah Bowman began with the original collection of Chaplin's own studio negatives, and were thereafter indefatigable in taking images from 35mm film frames or seeking out obscure press photos, family snapshots, images by great photographers and unknowns, the portraits by Baron de Meyer and Edward Steichen, and W. Eugene Smith's long-overlooked record of Chaplin at work on *Limelight*. Some are quite new, others are familiar, but, even with the old friends, Vance's probing and perceptive captions often reveal new significance and identify hitherto anonymous people. The inquisitive will discover nuggets such as that in 2002 there was still a living survivor from *Shoulder Arms*, the ninety-two-year-old True Boardman (even though his scenes were cut from the finished film).

There are rare glimpses of Chaplin at work. The endless studio discussions about gags and scenarios are legend; but here for the first time is a picture that shows us how it looked—the Chaplin unit in 1916, their crazy screen costumes decently replaced by neat ties and boater hats, sitting around the boss in cane chairs, solemn as owls in the deeply serious business of how to get a laugh. Here too is Chaplin in 1923 demonstrating to Edna Purviance the precise gestures and facial play with which she should mourn over her dead love in *A Woman of Paris*.

Everyone who visited Hollywood in the golden years—Churchill, the Mountbattens, Pavlova—made a pilgrimage to the Chaplin Studios, with their absurd exterior simulating (out of deference to local Good Taste) an Olde Englyshe village street. Until now I was always a little skeptical of Chaplin's stories about his and Nijinsky's mutual admiration of each other's terpsichorean accomplishments, and how the dancer kept his Los Angeles public waiting for half an hour while the two chatted, but here is the proof: an enchanting picture of the Russian Ballet visiting the set of *Easy Street*. Nijinsky, his arm around Chaplin, never looked so joyful.

Brought together in new combinations, these five hundred photographs provide an infinitely fascinating study. We all think, for example, that we know the Chaplin costume. Look closely and you will discover how it varied: sometimes the tie is a bow, sometimes a cravat, sometimes absent. Often a picture can be dated from the tie alone. And then there is Chaplin's gaze. In portraits he looks directly, challengingly at the camera, and equally, quite often, when he is in character in *The Fireman* or *The Pilgrim*. The Tramp though is much more elusive, generally looking off, somewhere to the side, avoiding our gaze, perhaps apprehensive of something, someone in the world within the picture. This is not a collection to skim through once.

Then there are the famous pictures we know so well. Seeing them again, all together, big and beautifully reproduced in duotone, is startling. Though they are just fleeting moments—fractions of seconds—from the last century's cinema, these pictures are permanently inscribed in a universal iconography.

For Jeffrey Vance, "What Shakespeare is to Elizabethan theater, Dickens to the Victorian novel, and Picasso to modern art, Chaplin is to twentieth-century cinema." Paradoxically, we have another, grand appreciation of Chaplin as man and artist from Marlon Brando, who so hated the experience of working with Chaplin on *A Countess from Hong Kong* that communication between the two men ceased altogether. At his most exasperated, the actor thought him "probably the most sadistic man I'd ever met . . . an egotistical tyrant and a penny-pincher"; and yet, "I still look up to him as perhaps the greatest genius that the medium has ever produced. I don't think anyone has ever had the talent he did; he made everyone else look Lilliputian. But as a human being he was a mixed bag, just like all of us." Perhaps that "just like all of us" was, in fact, the ultimate secret of Chaplin's unequaled gift of seeing and comprehending and showing the human heart in all its unpredictability.

The Chaplin Image

Manoah Bowman

There is nothing more poignant than the passage of time. In the realm of the motion picture this fact is made even more evident by watching many successful actors age onscreen. Year after year and film after film, the spectator witnesses the evolution of these individuals, most of whom the viewer will never know or meet. Often these actors become touchstones of the very period in which they lived. Relics, perhaps, of days gone by. Most out live their popularity, and few ever regain a semblance of it. Even more uncommon are those individuals who become legends in their own lifetime. Of course, there are exceptions to the rule. Charlie Chaplin was the exception to every rule. Love him or hate him, Chaplin is the cinema's first immortal.

The Chaplin image in photography is best exemplified in the eight famous photographs reproduced in this section. Significantly, the most famous stills of Chaplin incorporate the pervasive themes of his films: everyman vs. authority *(The Kid)*, loneliness *(The Gold Rush)*, the unwanted presence *(The Gold Rush)*, the eternal outsider looking in *(The Circus)*, everyman vs. "the system" *(Modern Times)*, comedy that borders on tragedy *(The Great Dictator)*, and resilience in the face of defeat *(Limelight)*.

Tracing Chaplin's history through photography is a most unusual and exciting journey. The photographs in this volume cover his early years, beginning in 1897 all the way through his final days in 1977; thus, the book aspires to be the definitive photographic overview of Chaplin's complete life and career. Some of the most interesting images uncovered were the fascinating press photos from photo agencies and archives in the United States and Great Britain. The sheer quantity of news photography on Chaplin is colossal. One can ascertain that while Chaplin was not always making movies, he was always making headlines—everything from his birthdays to his vacations, politics, love life, and new film projects kept him constantly in the public eye.

More exciting than the press photography, however, was the extraordinary collection of film and personal photography held by the Chaplin Archives in Paris and in Switzerland, only a fraction of which was used in the filmmaker's own illustrated book, *My Life in Pictures*, published in 1974.

Chaplin was also photographed throughout his career by many noted portrait photographers, such as Witzel, Hartsook, Homer Peyton, Edward Steichen, Nickolas Muray, John Engstead, Lord Snowdon, Horst Tappe, and Richard Avedon, and by actor/photographers Roddy McDowall and Candice Bergen. Beyond the work of the unit still photographers (credited when known, many for the first time in this book), some of Chaplin's later films were documented with special photographic records. Robert Florey, associate director of *Monsieur Verdoux*, took many pictures with his still camera for his own private record of the production. Florence Homolka did a special shoot of *Limelight*, and W. Eugene Smith covered the film for a *Life* magazine pictorial entitled "Chaplin at Work." A plethora of photographers covered Chaplin's final film, *A Countess from Hong Kong*, including Hatami, Douglas Kirkland, Norman Gryspeerdt, and Alfred Eisenstadt.

The primary photographers who covered Chaplin's private life in later years were his wife, Oona, and family friend Jerry Epstein. Oona Chaplin shot almost exclusively 35mm black-and-white negative throughout the years 1953 to 1977. Geraldine Chaplin recalled, "My mother was an avid photographer and in her pictures my father acts up and strikes funny poses. Fortunately, she carefully stored away all the negatives to her pictures. . . . She loved mechanical things and gadgets. In the early 1970s she began to take pictures in color on her Polaroid instant

The Tramp and the Kid (Jackie Coogan) are pursued by a cop (Tom Wilson) in THE KID (1921). Perhaps no other Chaplin image better illustrates the filmmaker's pervasive theme of everyman up against authority than this beautifully rendered image, which captures humor and emotion as well as the simplicity of a comic strip brought gloriously to life.

camera." These photographs allow an intimate glimpse and insight into this complex man and his family.

Within the Chaplin Archives are thousands of original nitrate, glass, and safety still negatives, signed portraits, personal photo albums, loose vintage prints of various sizes, and still photo keybooks for several of the feature films; the rarest item of all is Chaplin's personal Mutual-Chaplin Specials photo album, containing more than 170 original prints that cover all of Chaplin's twelve comedies made for Mutual in 1916–17. Most of these are unique vintage prints.

At the onset of this book project, an agreement was made between the Chaplin family's Roy Export Company Establishment and the Academy of Motion Picture Arts and Sciences'

Margaret Herrick Library to perform urgent preservation and conservation work on the Mutual album and other photographic materials being considered for this volume. The first project, undertaken by the Academy's photographic curator Robert Cushman, was the dismantling, rewashing, and redrying of the photographs from this fragile album in order to free the prints from the potentially damaging glues and old, acidic black scrapbook paper. Next, author Jeffrey Vance made several trips to Paris to select hundreds of the best original negatives, which he hand-carried back and forth from Paris to Beverly Hills so that the Academy could produce new archival custom fiber preservation prints. The outgrowth of this work has been the establishment of a Charles Chaplin/Roy Export Co. Est. Collection at the Academy

Left: Handsome devil: Chaplin's portrait for VANITY FAIR, *taken in New York City in the summer of 1925, is his single most important portrait. Like many great works of art, it is open to several interpretations. Photographer Edward Steichen succeeds brilliantly in capturing the satyr quality of the man while his comic spirit—the Tramp—looms large behind him, on a white backdrop representing a motion-picture screen. Photograph by Edward Steichen*

Opposite: Charlie peers through a hole in the circus tent to catch a glimpse of the pretty bareback rider in THE CIRCUS (1928). *The character of the eternal outsider looking in became synonymous with Chaplin. This often-imitated image not only was used on posters advertising the film but also made the cover of* TIME *magazine in 1931. The image is a testament to the fact that the Tramp had become as instantly recognizable from the back as he was from the front.*

Above: Charlie becomes literally caught up in the machine age in MODERN TIMES (1936), one of Chaplin's most iconic images, as he goes crazy trying to retain his individuality and humanity in a mechanized world. Photograph by Stern

Opposite: Adenoid Hynkel, Chaplin's devastating lampoon of Adolf Hitler, contemplates global domination in THE GREAT DICTATOR (1940). This image was used as poster art for the film. The still expertly portrays the absurdity of Hitler's desire to conquer the world and is a testament to Chaplin's ability to explore tragedy as well as controversial subject matter in his films. Photograph by William Wallace

Resilience in the face of defeat: Calvero and his partner (Buster Keaton) at their dressing tables prepare to launch a comeback in LIMELIGHT (1952). This melancholy photograph could stand on its own as a work of art. The image is poignant for the knowledge that the two great silent comics are paired for the first and only time to bid farewell to the visual-comedy art they had perfected more than twenty years earlier. Notice how the stone-faced Keaton is drawn to Chaplin, while Chaplin is drawn to himself. Photograph by Hommel

Library. A large quantity of these new first-generation prints were sent to Harry N. Abrams, Inc. for making the reproductions seen in this book.

Of all the images sought out for this volume, still photographs from the Essanay, and especially the Keystone, films were the most difficult to find. For these early films, 35mm frame enlargements have occasionally been used, obtained in many cases by accessing original nitrate motion-picture elements.

Perhaps the most touching discoveries made were the images documenting Chaplin's early life. Many of these photographs, including shots from his music-hall days and a handful of candid pictures from his early career in films, are inscribed with Chaplin's own writing and remembrances. It is somewhat jarring to see how unsure his handwriting and spelling were during this period. The inscriptions stand in stark contrast to the urbane and sophisticated personal image that Chaplin perpetuated throughout his life during his many years of self-education. These photographs, highlighted by his wayward spelling, are a testament to his phenomenal effort and ambition to rise above his impoverished Cockney beginnings.

Even with the thousands of images of Chaplin to choose from, there were still a few gaps. Because Chaplin did not allow still photos to document some of his most famous set pieces, for fear that seeing the stills in advance would spoil key moments in the films, no stills were taken of the eating of the shoe or the dance of the rolls from *The Gold Rush*, the heartbreaking ending of *City Lights*, or the gibberish song from *Modern Times*. Also, there are very few stills—and of only marginal quality—that exist from the abandoned film *The Professor*. Therefore, in such instances, 35mm frame enlargements were made from the films themselves.

Over twenty-five years since his death and at least seventy-five years past his most prolific period in film, Chaplin has become an icon for the ages. This is in no small part due to the marketing of Chaplin's famous Tramp image, first in photographs and artwork publicizing his films and soon after in product merchandizing. This merchandizing has become a small industry in itself, as Chaplin's Tramp persona has appeared on everything from coffee mugs to postage stamps and has helped sell items as varied as cigarettes and personal computers. Moreover, the public has also been inundated with innumerable Chaplin imitators, not only in the silent era but also in everything from *Sunset Boulevard* to *Sesame Street* since the advent of sound film and television. While the term *oversaturation* leaps to mind, one must remember that it is precisely because of this marketing that Chaplin is continually reintroduced to new generations. One could argue that this has also cheapened his image and encouraged cineastes to seek out other masters of silent-film comedy, such as Buster Keaton and Harold Lloyd, whose films and onscreen personae had formerly not received the same recognition or scrutiny allotted to Chaplin. However, a significant difference between Chaplin and the other great silent clowns is that he was never forgotten in the first place; and, while he might not win the current popularity contests among them, he will always be more famous. Ironically, Chaplin runs the risk of posterity defining him solely by the enduring icon (the instantly recognizable Tramp), as only a small segment of the population has seen his greatest films. Hopefully this book—and greater access to the Chaplin films—will provide a more well-rounded picture of his life and art, his legacy to the world.

The Early Years

No human being is more responsible for the development and popularization of cinema as the dominant form of art and entertainment in the twentieth century than Charlie Chaplin. Yet, Chaplin's importance as a historic figure is eclipsed by the universality of his screen character, the Little Tramp, which transcended cinema almost from its inception and became a towering figure in world culture. Building on traditions forged in the *commedia dell'arte* and the British music halls, Chaplin brought traditional art forms into an emerging medium

and changed both cinema and culture in the process. The birth of modern comedy occurred when Chaplin donned his derby hat, affixed his toothbrush mustache, and stepped into his impossibly large shoes for the first time. Chaplin and

the Tramp, like certain characters or turns of phrase in Shakespeare and Dickens, have remained firmly embedded in the collective artistic consciousness ever since.

Chaplin enjoys iconic status not just because of the Tramp's universally rec-

Opposite from top to bottom:

Chaplin at the time he was touring with the Eight Lancashire Lads, c. 1899

Charles Chaplin Sr., c. 1885. Photograph by H. T. Reed

Hannah Chaplin, c. 1885

Left: Chaplin, age seven (circled), at the Central London Poor Law School at Hanwell, 1897. Chaplin reflected in 1966 that the unhappiness of his youth was "not so much from being deprived of any-thing—never very hungry at any time—of course, there was always plenty of bread and butter around. It is the humiliation of poverty which is so distressing."

ognized appearance or the most analyzed, sublime moments from his films, regarded among cinema's finest achievements, but also because of the Tramp's universal values. Audiences around the world still relate to the Tramp as they did in cinema's early years because of his relentless, indefatigable pursuit of the fruits of abundance and happiness and his righteous struggle against those in power who bar his way. Chaplin embraced these same values to survive in the squalor of his South London youth; they reflect the same endeavor that consumed him, often to his detriment, throughout most of his life. There is hardly a soul who cannot relate to the Tramp, who is repeatedly knocked down yet picks himself up time and time again, dusts himself off, and genially wanders off in search of a better life. It is this shared human connection with the Tramp that will perpetuate Chaplin's legacy for as long as travails and triumphs, passion and tears, animate the human condition.

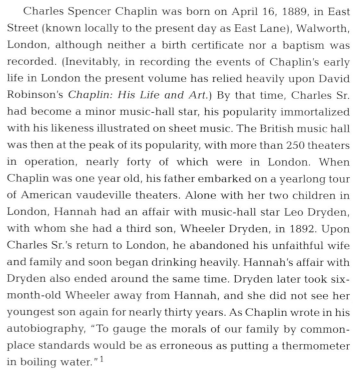

The life of Charlie Chaplin is one of the greatest rags-to-riches stories ever told. The man who became one of the most famous and best-loved men of the twentieth century began his life as one of the poorest children of late Victorian South London. In the boroughs of Lambeth and Southwark, the city still retained the atmosphere portrayed by Charles Dickens.

His parents were both entertainers. The Chaplin family, who for generations lived in Suffolk, England, descended from Huguenots, and the name "Chaplin" originates from the French word *capeline* (a mailed hood). His father, Charles Chaplin Sr., was born in London in 1863. At the time of his marriage in 1885 he was a professional singer with a fine baritone voice. Charles Sr.'s wife, Hannah Harriet Pedlingham (née Hill), was born in London in 1865, daughter of a poor, journeyman boot maker. A soubrette who appeared in the British music halls under the stage name Lily Harley, Hannah gave birth to a boy named Sidney John fourteen weeks prior to her marriage. The paternity of Sidney (who alternated the spelling of his name as both "Sidney" and "Sydney" and is hereafter referred to as Sydney) remains uncertain, although the Chaplin brothers knew for sure that they did not share the same father. His reputed father was an Anglo-Jew named Sidney Hawkes, but Sydney adopted the name Chaplin early in life. However, for the sake of simplicity Sydney is hereafter called Chaplin's brother, which is how Chaplin himself referred to him.

Charles Spencer Chaplin was born on April 16, 1889, in East Street (known locally to the present day as East Lane), Walworth, London, although neither a birth certificate nor a baptism was recorded. (Inevitably, in recording the events of Chaplin's early life in London the present volume has relied heavily upon David Robinson's *Chaplin: His Life and Art.*) By that time, Charles Sr. had become a minor music-hall star, his popularity immortalized with his likeness illustrated on sheet music. The British music hall was then at the peak of its popularity, with more than 250 theaters in operation, nearly forty of which were in London. When Chaplin was one year old, his father embarked on a yearlong tour of American vaudeville theaters. Alone with her two children in London, Hannah had an affair with music-hall star Leo Dryden, with whom she had a third son, Wheeler Dryden, in 1892. Upon Charles Sr.'s return to London, he abandoned his unfaithful wife and family and soon began drinking heavily. Hannah's affair with Dryden also ended around the same time. Dryden later took six-month-old Wheeler away from Hannah, and she did not see her youngest son again for nearly thirty years. As Chaplin wrote in his autobiography, "To gauge the morals of our family by commonplace standards would be as erroneous as putting a thermometer in boiling water."[1]

Hannah Chaplin was left alone to raise her two remaining sons; her estranged husband was ordered by the court to pay child support, but his remittances were infrequent. At first Hannah attempted to support her two children by working in the music halls. However, her voice—which was never strong—grew progressively weaker. It would sometimes even crack or disappear in performance, and it was at such a moment that the stage manager at the Canteen at Aldershot, who had seen the young Charlie perform before Hannah's friends, substituted the five-year-old boy for Hannah. He sang a popular song titled "'E Dunno Where 'E Are," and the rowdy audience—delighted by the precocious child—tossed coins onto the stage. "That night

Opposite top: Sydney Chaplin, Charlie's elder brother, 1902

Opposite middle: Chaplin as Billy the pageboy in a touring company of the play SHERLOCK HOLMES, 1903. He toured with various companies for two and a half years and learned much about stagecraft from the two actors who had the leading role of Holmes: H. A. Saintsbury and William C. Gillette. Chaplin played with Gillette (coauthor of the play and creator of the role of Holmes on stage) during a London revival at the Duke of York's Theatre in 1905, making Chaplin a West End actor at age sixteen.

Opposite bottom: The CASEY'S CIRCUS company, 1906. Chaplin is in the middle row, wearing a derby hat; comedian Will Murray, the lead artist and general director, is on Chaplin's right. Chaplin was the star of the company and had two solo turns. In one of these, a burlesque of Dick Turpin (a notorious English robber), Chaplin developed the gag of turning corners on one leg—as the one pivots, the other sticks straight out from his body—which became a signature movement of the Tramp character. He toured with CASEY'S CIRCUS for more than a year.

Above: Chaplin (center, in clownlike makeup) played a plumber's assistant in popular author and playwright Wal Pink's comedy sketch REPAIRS, 1906. Chaplin's brother Sydney is the mustachioed painter on top of the stepladder at rear of the stage. The piece was based on a favorite comedy situation in which incompetent plumbers, painters, and paperhangers wreak havoc on the house they are supposed to repair. Chaplin later introduced paperhanging sketches into his films WORK, THE CIRCUS, and A KING IN NEW YORK.

was my first appearance on the stage and Mother's last," remembered Chaplin in his autobiography.[2] Hannah later earned money through seamstressing. As the family grew poorer, they moved from one garret to another in a quest for less expensive housing. Adding to her misery, Hannah witnessed her own mother, who also lived in South London, become an alcoholic and then be institutionalized as clinically insane.

Chaplin's greatest influence was his mother. She entertained him with anecdotes, songs, and tales of Napoleon. (Hannah's stories of Bonaparte, as well as her comment that Charles Sr. resembled Napoleon, sparked Chaplin's lifelong fascination with the Little Corporal.) During this period, Hannah also became a born-again Christian, regaling Charlie and Sydney with impassioned readings from the Scriptures and stories of Jesus Christ's love and pity for the poor and for little children. During one such reading Hannah performed Christ's suffering at Golgotha with impassioned fervor. Chaplin remembered in his autobiography:

> Mother had so carried me away that I wanted to die that very night and meet Jesus. But Mother was not so enthusiastic. "Jesus wants you to live first and fulfill your destiny here," she said. In that dark room in the basement at Oakley Street [where they were living at the time], Mother illuminated to me the kindliest light this world has ever known, which has endowed literature and the theatre with their greatest and richest themes: love, pity and humanity.[3]

Love, pity, and humanity became important themes of Chaplin's art. Indeed, his compassion for others was instilled in him by his mother, who also imparted to her son an innate sense of dignity despite the threadbare clothes he wore. Chaplin recalled, "Mother always stood outside her environment and kept an alert ear on the way we talked, correcting our grammar and making us feel that we were distinguished."[4] He also learned from her keen observations of people:

> If it had not been for my mother, I doubt if I could have made a success of pantomime. She was one of the greatest pantomime artists I have ever seen. She would sit for hours at a window,

looking down at the people on the street and illustrating with her hands, eyes, and facial expression just what was going on below. At the time, she would deliver a running fire of comment. And it was through watching and listening to her that I learned not only how to express my emotions with my hands and face, but also how to observe and to study people.

> She was almost uncanny in her observations. For instance, she would see Bill Smith coming down the street in the morning, and I would hear her say, "There comes Bill Smith. He's dragging his feet and his shoes are polished. He looks mad, and I'll wager he's had a fight with his wife, and come off without his breakfast. Sure enough! There he goes into the bake shop for a bun and coffee!"

> And inevitably during the day, I would hear that Bill Smith had had a fight with his wife.[5]

In 1895 Hannah began a cycle of periodic confinement for mental instability, which forced Charlie to stay with relatives and Sydney to be sent to the Lambeth Workhouse and later the West Norwood Schools, charity institutions for the very poor. By the summer of 1896 Charles, age seven, and Sydney, age eleven, were first taken to Newington Workhouse and soon thereafter transferred to the Central London Poor Law School at Hanwell, London, an institution for children without families. Sydney was soon sent to the battleship *Exmouth,* used for the training of poor boys for naval service. The sense of isolation and loneliness the sensitive young Charlie experienced was acute. At Hanwell he was taught to write his name, "Chaplin." "The word fascinated me and looked like me, I thought," Chaplin later reflected.[6] He was naturally left-handed but was forced to write with his right hand. In adulthood, Chaplin played string instruments and held a tennis racket in his left hand, but wrote with his right hand. For Christmas at Hanwell, Chaplin—having committed some breach of the rules—received a single orange, and for the rest of his life the holiday reminded him of his early poverty.[7]

In January 1898, after more than a year and a half at Hanwell, Charlie rejoined his mother and Sydney, but the reunion was short-lived. After a few months, Hannah had another relapse and

Chaplin imitates Sir Herbert Beerbohm Tree as Fagin, c. 1906. Tree was Chaplin's idol as a boy of fourteen when he watched the great stage actor/manager's interpretations from the gallery of His Majesty's Theatre in London. Chaplin reflected in 1966, "I loved Tree. Tree is my favorite [actor]—full of mannerisms, but I loved him. He did wonderful things and played impossible parts . . . and he would make it humorous and poetic."

Chaplin impersonating "Dr." Walford Bodie, the famous hypnotist and healer of the music halls, in one of his solo sketches for CASEY'S CIRCUS, 1906

Chaplin, c. 1909, as he looked when he joined Fred Karno's Speechless Comedians. Photograph by Fred, Manchester & Leeds

was committed once again to an infirmary. "Vaguely I felt that she had deliberately escaped from her mind and had deserted us. In my despair I had visions of her looking pathetically at me, drifting away into a void," Chaplin later recalled.[8] For several weeks in 1898 Sydney and Charlie lived with Charles Sr., his mistress, Louise, and their young son at their flat at 287 Kennington Road. Charlie was fascinated with his father, absorbing and studying his every action. Charles Sr. was an alcoholic who was frequently drunk and occasionally violent. Louise resented the imposition of caring for two additional children and made her attitude clearly known to Sydney and Charlie. Chaplin remembered his time on Kennington Road with his father as "the longest and saddest of my life."[9] Everyone was relieved when Hannah, in a period of remission, was discharged and once more took her sons into a precarious existence, moving from lodging to lodging.

The three moved to a room located at 39 Methley Street, where one incident occurred that remained vivid for the rest of Chaplin's life:

> At the end of our street was a slaughter-house, and sheep would pass our house on their way to be butchered. I remember one escaped and ran down the street to the amusement of onlookers. Some tried to grab it and others tripped over themselves. I had giggled with delight at its lambent capering and panic, it seemed so comic. But when it was caught and carried back into the slaughter-house, the reality of the tragedy came over me and I ran indoors, screaming and weeping to Mother: "They're going to kill it! They're going to kill it!" That stark, spring afternoon and that comedy chase stayed with me for days; and I wonder if that episode did not establish the premise of my future films—the combination of the tragic and the comic.[10]

At not quite ten years of age, Chaplin embarked on the career of a professional entertainer that lasted the rest of his life. His father arranged for impresario William Jackson to hire the boy for his troupe of child performers, the Eight Lancashire Lads. Chaplin made his first appearance with the troupe in *Babes in the Wood* at the Theatre Royal, Manchester, on Christmas Eve 1898, and toured Great Britain with the troupe for the next two years. It was while the Lads were appearing as animals in the pantomime *Cinderella* at the London Hippodrome that Chaplin received his first laugh. Appearing as a cat, Chaplin improvised raising his

back leg against the side of the proscenium arch. The canine behavior received a roar of laughter from the audience.

Providing the young Charlie with his professional start was Charles Sr.'s great legacy to his son. In 1901, at the age of thirty-seven, the elder Chaplin died from the effects of acute alcoholism, the disease of the music halls, where managers encouraged the artistes to socialize with patrons, as theaters depended on the sale of alcohol in large measure for their profits.

Given the realities of poverty and an unstable family life, perhaps an ordinary child of eight or nine years of age would have succumbed and faded away. Not young Charlie. By the age of ten he was working as a professional in the music halls, playing on the same bills as Dan Leno, Marie Lloyd, and Bransby Williams. Williams, who specialized in impressions of Dickens characters, enthralled Chaplin with his performances and ignited in him a curiosity about literature and particularly about Dickens, with whose work he later closely identified. His bleak and unhappy childhood made the vitality and glamour of the music halls appealing to him. The singular spirit of the people of Lambeth as well as the vitality and sordidness of the music halls and public houses made an indelible mark on Chaplin's artistic memory.

In 1901, Hannah was once again discharged from the hospital and arranged for Chaplin to leave the Eight Lancashire Lads; she believed her son was leading an unhealthy life. For the next two years they lived a meager existence in Lambeth and Southwark, where Hannah earned what she could with sewing work. Chaplin rarely went to school and was variously employed as an errand boy, a doctor's boy, a pageboy, a clerk at the newsstand and bookseller W. H. Smith, a glassblower, a printer, and a clog-dance instructor. He also tried selling old clothes and making and selling simple toys from discarded cardboard shoe boxes, twine, cork, and colored paper. Sydney found work as a steward and bugler on passenger boats sailing between London and South Africa. He returned between voyages and shared his earnings with his mother and brother, splurging on breakfast luxuries such as bloaters, kippers, haddocks, and toasted teacakes. Chaplin retained lifelong memories of the bittersweet time spent with his mother and brother in Kennington Park. In later life, he refused to

Chaplin as Archibald in the Karno sketch SKATING, *c. 1909. Photograph by Fred, Manchester & Leeds*

enter London parks, as they were too vivid a reminder of his melancholy boyhood and depressed him.[11]

In May 1903 Chaplin came home to their small garret at 3 Pownall Terrace to discover that Hannah had once again lost her sanity. Chaplin had to lead her through the streets to the local infirmary and give evidence for her committal to a mental institution. Fortunately, Sydney soon returned home from South Africa, and her two sons visited her at the Cane Hill asylum located in the southern outskirts of London. The fourteen-year-old Chaplin was haunted by her remark, "if only you had given me a cup of tea that afternoon, I would have been all right."[12]

Despite their various occupations, the Chaplin brothers never lost their resolve to become actors. Charlie obtained an interview with Blackmore's theatrical agency in London, which later sent him to an audition for the role of Billy the pageboy in a touring production of *Sherlock Holmes,* written by Arthur Conan Doyle and American actor-manager William C. Gillette, who created the title role. Chaplin was given the role, and the star of the tour, H. A. Saintsbury, hired Chaplin to play a newsboy in his own production, *Jim: A Romance of Cockayne.* Interestingly, Chaplin recalled that at this period of time he had great difficulty reading and that his brother Sydney had to coach him with his dialogue.[13] Although *Jim: A Romance of Cockayne* was not a success, Chaplin received favorable reviews. However, for nearly three years, Chaplin toured Great Britain in *Sherlock Holmes.* In many towns the local newspapers praised Chaplin in their reviews of the play. Indeed, he garnered such a reputation for his humorous portrayal of Billy that in October 1905 Gillette sent for him to play Billy in a new one-act *Sherlock Holmes* comedy at the Duke of York's Theatre in the West End of London, followed by a revival of the original play.

At the age of sixteen Chaplin joined Sydney in the cast of Wal Pink's music-hall comedy sketch *Repairs,* as a plumber's assistant, and after ten weeks joined the company of the long-running comedy sketch *Casey's Circus,* which involved Cockney urchins in a slum courtyard. A year later Chaplin became the star of the sketch, going on tour with *Casey's Circus* for more than a year and a half. During this period Chaplin developed his comic run, sticking one leg out sideways and pivoting on the other as he turned a corner, which later became a signature trait of his Tramp character.

Meanwhile, Sydney joined Fred Karno's Speechless Comedians in July 1906 and by 1908 was playing leading comedy roles. He was eager to get Charlie signed to a contract with Karno. Great Britain's greatest impresario of the comedy sketch, Fred Karno was unsure of Charlie Chaplin. He later remembered that Chaplin "seemed undernourished and frightened, as though he expected me to raise my hand to hit him . . . he seemed to me to be much too timid to do anything good on stage, especially in the knockabout comedy shows that were my specialty."[14]

Karno nevertheless gave Charlie a two-week trial. After watching his first performances Karno quickly signed him in February 1908 to a two-year contract with a third year's option. Within a short period of time, Chaplin was playing lead roles in comedy sketches such as *Mumming Birds* (also known as *A Night in an English Music Hall*), *The Football Match, Skating,* and *Jimmy the Fearless.* His greatest success was playing the Inebriated Swell in *Mumming Birds,* and it was ironic that Chaplin, who seldom in his early life drank much liquor owing to his father's bad example, became a comedy star in the British music halls playing a drunk.

Chaplin learned much from Karno about comic pacing, the introduction of pathos into laughter, and the use of elegant music to underscore comic action. Stanley Jefferson, Chaplin's understudy (who later became Stan Laurel of Laurel and Hardy fame), recalled that while rehearsing slapstick situations of a sketch, Karno would frequently shout out, "Keep it wistful, gentlemen, keep it *wistful* as well. That's hard to do but we want sympathy with the laughter. Wistful!"[15] Laurel also remembered an important aspect of Chaplin's unique appeal that set him apart from the others:

> What has to be remembered about Charlie is that though he was essentially a pantomimist—and none better—still, with Charlie, things really began with his face. That may seem strange but it's true. He had those eyes that absolutely forced you to look at them. He had the damnedest way of looking at an audience. He had the damnedest way of looking at *you,* on stage. I don't think anyone has ever written about those eyes of his. They're very dark, the deepest kind of blue, and intense, just like him. And they can dominate anyone they look at. That's part of the secret of his great success—eyes that make you believe him in whatever he does.[16]

In the autumn of 1908, while working for Karno in England, the nineteen-year-old Chaplin fell in love for the first time. Hetty Kelly was a fifteen-year-old dancer with a music-hall troupe called Bert Coutt's Yankee Doodle Girls, "a slim gazelle with a shapely oval face, a bewitching full mouth, and beautiful teeth— the effect was electric," according to Chaplin.[17] Chaplin wrote more than fifty years later, "Although I had met her but five times, and scarcely any of our meetings lasted longer than twenty minutes, that brief encounter affected me for a long time."[18] In fact, with the exception of his mother, Hetty Kelly was the most powerful female attachment of his early life. Its emotional impact later enriched his film work. As Chaplin later explained in 1933, his experience with Kelly "was the beginning of a spiritual development, a reaching out for beauty."[19]

As for Hannah Chaplin, after a brief period of remission when she once again lived with Charlie and Sydney, she was institutionalized at Cane Hill asylum and later in the private care facility of Peckham House. After providing her the basic physical

Chaplin portrait taken in Minneapolis during his first American Karno tour, c. 1911. Photograph by Sussman Photo Studio

Chaplin in front of a poster for A NIGHT IN AN ENGLISH MUSIC HALL *during his first American Karno tour, 1911. With Chaplin are the vaudeville trapeze performers Lohse and Sterling. Ralph Lohse (right) and Chaplin briefly intended to become partners raising hogs. "But for buying a book on scientific hog-raising," remembered Chaplin in his autobiography, "I might have given up show business and become a hog-farmer, but that book, which graphically described the technique of castrating hogs, cooled my ardour and I soon forgot the enterprise."*

comforts during her last remission, Chaplin remembered the news of her relapse "came like a stab in the heart."[20] For the rest of Chaplin's life, his mother was a painful reminder of his unhappy past; and although he did his best to hide this from her, he avoided the pain by avoiding her.[21]

In the autumn of 1910 Chaplin was selected to star in the Karno company sent to tour the United States for nearly two years. He returned to England to find his brother married and life in England less adventuresome than life on the road in America. Five months later, in October 1912, he readily embarked on a second Karno tour of America. Chaplin later reflected, "In England I felt I had reached the limit of my prospects; besides, my opportunities there were circumscribed. With scant educational background, if I failed as a music-hall comedian I would have little chance but to do menial work. In the States the prospects were brighter."[22] His instincts proved accurate: while appearing in Philadelphia in May 1913, the Karno troupe received a telegram that led Chaplin to an offer to appear in motion pictures.

Chaplin's childhood shaped not only his personality but also his art. His story is one of great loneliness, brought on by the estrangement from his father, the institutionalization of his mother, and the later fame he attained, which caused a different type of isolation. An examination of his early life can lead to much psychological speculation, which, unfortunately, far removed from the period, will perhaps never be properly answered. No less an authority of psychology than Sigmund Freud speculated on the Chaplin psyche in 1931:

> He is undoubtedly a great artist; certainly he always portrays one and the same figure; only the weakly, poor, helpless, clumsy youngster for whom, however, things turn out well in the end. Now do you think for this role he has to forget about his own ego? On the contrary, he always plays only himself as he was in his dismal youth. He cannot get away from those impressions and humiliations of that past period of his life. He is, so to speak, an exceptionally simple and transparent case.[23]

Chaplin was, in fact, a complex man and a protean artist. However, Freud's analysis of the connection between Chaplin's work and his psychology correctly suggests that Chaplin was essentially an actor with an actor's need to dominate a particular audience or occasion. (This need for complete control—extending to every aspect of his life and work—stemmed from his childhood and his belief that he had little control over his circumstances.) Paradoxically, Chaplin felt alienated by and anxious about the very audiences whose love he desired. Performance was an essential part of Chaplin the man; a role was always sought to mask his insecurity. His art afforded him a trajectory to stardom virtually without parallel, forcing him to contend with unprecedented mass adoration. That Chaplin was able to retain his humanity during the heights of this fame—as well as the later retraction of that fame and adulation—is one of the most remarkable aspects of his life story.

Above: Chaplin as the inebriated Archibald Binks photographed while on tour with Karno in A NIGHT IN A LONDON CLUB *at the Empress Theatre, Los Angeles, c. 1910. More than fifty years later, Chaplin reflected on his stage career, "On the stage I was a very good comedian in a way. In shows and things like that. [But] I hadn't got that come-hither business that a comedian should have. Talk to an audience—I could never do that. I was too much of an artist for that. My artistry is a bit austere—it is austere." Photograph by Kessler*

Top left: Chaplin with Karno posters, in which he is given star billing, at the Exeter, California, railway depot, November 1911

Left: Karno players photographed on the Continental Divide during the second American Karno tour, c. 1913. Chaplin is standing second from the right; Stanley Jefferson (Stan Laurel) is standing second from the left; Fred Karno Jr. is seated.

Keystone: The Tramp Is Born

It would be easy to mistake the story of how Chaplin stumbled into his first motion-picture contract as the plot of a Chaplin comedy, were it not true. Alf Reeves, manager of the Fred Karno Company touring in America, received a telegram at the Nixon Theatre in Philadelphia on May 12, 1913, which read, "IS THERE A MAN NAMED CHAFFIN IN YOUR COMPANY OR SOMETHING LIKE IT STOP IF SO WILL HE COMMUNICATE WITH KESSEL AND BAUMAN 24 LONGACRE BUILDING BROADWAY."[1]

Reeves, believing the telegram must be referring to Chaplin, showed it to him. When Chaplin discovered that the tenants of the Longacre Building were mostly attorneys, he imagined that his great-aunt, Elizabeth Wiggins, had died and left him an inheritance. He immediately arranged a day trip to New York City.

Chaplin was disappointed to discover that the telegram had been sent by Adam Kessel Jr. and Charles O. Baumann, owners of the New York Motion Picture Company, who wanted to sign him as a comedian with the Keystone Film Company. Keystone's lead comedy player, Ford Sterling, was intending to leave to start his own company, and they needed to find a replacement.

Chaplin at the time he started working for the Keystone Film Company, c. 1914. Photograph by Witzel

comedy. In Europe, Pathé Frères, the great French film company, made trick-and-chase films. America lagged behind Europe in the development of film comedy, and Chaplin was not the first comic star of the cinema. Foremost of the Europeans was Max Linder of France, a gifted artist who had been making films since 1905 for Pathé and the cinema's first international comedy star. His style and technique influenced Chaplin. Linder's character was a resourceful and gallant *boulevardier* who ingeniously managed to extricate himself from the many predicaments that confronted him. Chaplin was not even the first American comic film star. That distinction goes to the fat and genial John Bunny, who made a successful series of comedy films from 1910 to 1915 for the Vitagraph Company. However, Keystone consistently produced the best film comedies of the early silent era.

An official of the New York Motion Picture Company and Mack Sennett, who ran Keystone, had both seen Chaplin in one of his tours and recognized his potential for film comedy. Chaplin was lured to accept the Keystone offer by the large salary: $150 weekly for three months raised to $175 weekly for the rest of the year, which was more than double his Karno salary of $75 a week. In September 1913 he signed his first film contract for a period of one year with the Keystone Film Company, beginning December 13, 1913.[2]

Chaplin had considered appearing in motion pictures before he received the offer from Keystone, wanting to purchase the motion-picture rights to all of Fred Karno's sketches and make films of them. Ironically, Chaplin actually believed that making movies would help his stage career. He had seen some Keystone films and was not particularly impressed. "I was not terribly enthusiastic about the Keystone type of comedy, but I realized their publicity value. A year at that racket and I could return to vaudeville an international star," he had surmised.[3]

Motion-picture comedy began with a simple comic situation, in the Lumière Brothers' *L'Arroseur arrosé* (*Watering the Gardener*, 1895), in which a boy steps on a garden hose as a gardener waters a lawn, cutting off the water, only to step off just as the gardener peers quizzically at the nozzle and is doused with the restored flow of water. Soon the chase developed as the essential element of

The Keystone Film Company was presided over by the man frequently billed in his lifetime as "the king of comedy," Mack Sennett. Irish Canadian-born Sennett worked as a boilermaker before failing as an actor in burlesque and musical comedy. He joined the Biograph Company in New York City in 1908 as an actor and there mastered film craft from the leading American film director, D. W. Griffith. By late 1910 Sennett was the scenarist and director of many of Biograph's comic productions. Two years later, Kessel and Baumann hired Sennett as production

chief of their new comedy studio in California, the Keystone Film Company.

Keystone was based in the former Bison Studios at 1712 Alessandro Street (now Glendale Boulevard), in the Edendale district of Los Angeles, near present-day Echo Park. Relocating to the West Coast, Sennett brought his principal players from Biograph to Keystone: Mabel Normand (with whom Sennett had a long and turbulent intimate relationship), Fred Mace, and Ford Sterling. The original Keystone players were quickly augmented by Roscoe Arbuckle (known as "Fatty"), Chester Conklin (known as "Walrus"), Mack Swain (known as "Ambrose"), and others. At the time Chaplin joined Keystone, the company was producing twelve one-reel comedies plus one two-reel comedy a month. Sennett directed the first unit while Henry "Pathé" Lehrman—a former streetcar conductor whose nickname derived from his fraudulently representing himself to D. W. Griffith as associated with Pathé Frères—directed the second unit.

Sennett possessed an intuitive, almost uncanny understanding of film comedy. He was the creative force behind the Keystone

Above: Charlie encounters Mabel Normand—clad only in her pajamas and accidentally locked out of her room—in the hotel corridor in MABEL'S STRANGE PREDICAMENT *(1914), the first film in which Chaplin donned the Tramp costume.*

Opposite top: Chaplin (right) plays a shifty and seedy dandy, donning a top hat, frock coat, and monocle, in MAKING A LIVING *(1914), his first screen appearance and quite unlike the character that would make him famous. Henry Lehrman (center), who directed the film, plays the dubious dandy's rival for a position at a newspaper office. The actor portraying the newspaper editor (left) is unidentified.*

Opposite bottom: KID AUTO RACES AT VENICE *(1914) was the first film in which the public saw Chaplin's Tramp character. It is built around the simple premise of a cameraman and a director who are trying to film the races but are prevented by a little tramp who continues to get in front of the camera. Frank D. Williams is behind the camera; director Henry Lehrman is on the right.*

Kops (a madcap mockery of the police force), the Sennett Bathing
Beauties, and custard-pie fights in motion pictures. In Sennett's
films, frantic pacing of broad slapstick took precedence over
characterization and story. Although crude and obvious, these
comedies also were simple and joyous affairs, brimming with
ebullience and vitality. Keystone rarely deviated from certain
types of comedies: those set in parks (filmed in Los Angeles's
Echo Park or Westlake Park), those staged at public events (such
as parades), and those filmed exclusively at the studio or in a
combination of studio and location filming. A situation typically
led to some sort of rally or chase, explosion, or the principal characters falling into a lake. The world of the Keystone comedies
embraced the innocent mischief of the comic strips—hurling
bricks, hitting rivals or police officers with mallets, kicking someone in the backside—and was populated with pretty girls, virago
wives, and men with grotesque mustaches and beards.

Chaplin arrived at Keystone in early December 1913 and took
a room at the Great Northern Hotel in downtown Los Angeles (he
would later relocate to the Los Angeles Athletic Club). Sennett
was startled to find Chaplin so young because he had played
older men on the stage. The actor was intimidated by the
Keystone lot and its players:

> Sennett took me aside and explained their method of working.
> "We have no scenario—we get an idea then follow the natural
> sequence of events until it leads up to a chase, which is the
> essence of our comedy." This method was edifying, but person-
> ally I hated a chase. It dissipates one's personality; little as I knew
> about movies, I knew that nothing transcended personality.[4]

Chaplin's first film was aptly titled *Making a Living* (1914), in
which Chaplin plays a sharper dressed in a black silk top hat,

frock coat, and monocle, with the drooping mustache of a typical stage villain and reminiscent of his Karno characters Archibald Binks in *The Wow-Wows* and the drunk in *A Night in a London Club*. The action of the film involves the sharper's efforts to usurp the girlfriend and job of a news photographer (Henry Lehrman). Chaplin was accustomed to months of rehearsing and refining a comedy sketch with Karno. He quickly discovered that at Keystone subtlety always gave way to breakneck speed. Inevitably, friction developed between Chaplin and Lehrman, who also directed *Making a Living*. Chaplin wanted a character-driven film with a slower pace, while Lehrman insisted on the fast knockabout. He was further confused by why scenes were shot out of narrative order. He had no previous film experience and had always rehearsed and performed his theatrical work in the proper sequence. Chaplin was devastated when he saw the final product and discovered what Lehrman had edited, recalling: "Although the picture was completed in three days, I thought we contrived some very funny gags. But when I saw the finished film it broke my heart, for the cutter had butchered it beyond recognition, cutting into the middle of all my funny business."[5]

Despite Chaplin's low opinion of the film, *Making a Living* was well received when it was released on February 2, 1914. *The Moving Picture World,* an important trade magazine, wrote, "The clever player who takes the role of [the] nervy and very nifty sharper in this picture is a comedian of the first water, who acts like one of Nature's own naturals. . . . People out for an evening's good time will howl."[6]

The second film Chaplin made at Keystone, *Mabel's Strange Predicament* (1914), was the first film in which Chaplin donned the costume and character of the Tramp. (However, *Kid Auto Races at Venice* [1914], Chaplin's third film, was the first of these two films to be released.) Sennett brought Chaplin into the cast of *Mabel's Strange Predicament* as an afterthought, wanting him simply to enter a hotel lobby set and provide some comic business. He told Chaplin, "Put on a comedy makeup. Anything will do."[7] Chaplin recalled in his autobiography:

> I had no idea what makeup to put on. I did not like my get-up as the press reporter [in *Making a Living*]. However, on the way to the wardrobe I thought I would dress in baggy pants, big shoes, a cane and a derby hat. I wanted everything to be a contradiction: the pants baggy, the coat tight, the hat small and the shoes large. I was undecided whether to look old or young, but remembering Sennett had expected me to be a much older man, I added a small moustache, which, I reasoned, would add age without hiding my expression.
>
> I had no idea of the character. But the moment I was dressed, the clothes and the makeup made me feel the person he was. I began to know him, and by the time I walked on to the stage he was fully born.[8]

Encouraged by the laughs his Tramp was receiving, Chaplin explained the character to Sennett, "You know this fellow is many-sided, a tramp, a gentleman, a poet, a dreamer, a lonely fellow, always hopeful of romance and adventure. He would have you believe he is a scientist, a musician, a duke, and a polo-player. However, he is not above picking up cigarette-butts or robbing a baby of its candy. And, of course, if the occasion warrants it, he will kick a lady in the rear—but only in extreme anger!"[9] And thus, nearly spontaneously was born the most celebrated character in the history of motion-picture comedy.

In *Mabel's Strange Predicament,* the Tramp is introduced, slightly tipsy, in the lobby of a hotel. In a typical Keystone plot, he becomes involved with a young woman (Mabel Normand) in a bedroom mix-up. Later, the Tramp encounters Mabel in the corridor of the hotel dressed in her pajamas, as she has managed to lock herself out of her room. The favorable reaction to the Tramp by the seasoned Sennett company was a major victory for Chaplin, and Sennett allowed Chaplin's first scene to go the entire seventy-five-foot length (approximately one minute) without any editing—not the usual method at Keystone. Moreover, the Tramp character was reworked into the film's scenario to appear in nearly all of its scenes from beginning to end.

Sennett was pleased, and so was Chaplin. He later explained, "As the clothes had imbued me with the character, I then and there decided I would keep to this costume whatever happened."[10] Yet Chaplin was not entirely accurate. Although he used the costume for the majority of the Keystone films, he frequently deviated from it as well.

The Tramp character was influenced by tramp comedians of the British music hall as well as the real-life tramps Chaplin had

encountered in his childhood. A distinctive costume that fostered immediate recognition was traditionally an integral part of the success of a circus clown or music-hall comedian. The particular mixture Chaplin concocted—derby hat, toothbrush mustache, whangee (a type of bamboo) walking stick, baggy trousers, tight cutaway coat, and oversize boots (Chaplin's actual shoe size was five; he originally wore a size fourteen boot as the Tramp, on the wrong feet, for a splay-foot walk)—was, when combined, his own creation.

Cinema audiences first saw the Tramp in Chaplin's third film for Keystone, *Kid Auto Races at Venice* (also directed by Lehrman), which was filmed on the Saturday afternoon of the same week in which *Mabel's Strange Predicament* was filmed; but *Kid Auto Races at Venice* was edited and delivered to exhibitors first. *Kid Auto Races at Venice,* a Keystone "event" comedy, was a split-reel film (five hundred feet or less, and running approximately seven minutes) filmed in forty-five minutes to take advantage of a children's car race at the oceanside resort of Venice, California. The plot, such as it is, is quite simple: the Tramp makes a nuisance of himself while a camera crew attempts to film the event. Although quite primitive, the film is historic not only because it represents the first appearance of the Tramp on screen, but also because it manages to record the first audience's reaction to the character. The audience, of course, is the throng of spectators at the race who begin to notice this peculiar fellow causing trouble with a "camera crew." At first the audience does not know what to make of the Tramp, then they begin to smile, then titter, and then laugh at his antics. In those brief moments of discovery, recorded for posterity, a comedic revolution was born. Walter Kerr observed:

> He is elbowing his way into immortality, both as a "character" in the film and as a professional comedian to be remembered. And he is doing it by calling attention to the camera as camera.
>
> He would do this throughout his career, using the instrument as a means of establishing a direct and openly acknowledged relationship between himself and his audience. In fact, he is, with this film, establishing himself as *one among the audience,* one among those who are astonished by this new mechanical marvel, one among those who would like to be pho-

tographed by it, and—he would make the most of the implication later—one among those who are invariably chased away. He looked at the camera and went through it, joining the rest of us. The seeds of his subsequent hold on the public, the mysterious and almost inexplicable bond between this performer and everyman, were there.[11]

The genius of the Tramp character is that he is so human and familiar—he is one of us. It is nothing short of remarkable that when directed by Sennett to find something funny to wear, Chaplin invented spontaneously that day in 1914 a symbol of all downtrodden and resilient humanity.

Chaplin took every opportunity he could to learn the business of making films and in his first efforts went beyond what was expected of him. He believed he could be creating the scenarios and directing his films better than the Keystone directors Lehrman, George Nichols, and even Sennett. When he was assigned to take direction from Mabel Normand for the two-reel comedy *Mabel at the Wheel* (1914), and Normand would not take his suggestions for his character's comedy business, Chaplin confronted her and refused to work on the film for the rest of the day in protest.

According to Chaplin, Sennett at that point was on the brink of discharging him, but a telegram from the front office arrived clamoring for more Chaplin pictures. Sennett mollified Chaplin and Normand, and they completed *Mabel at the Wheel* amicably. Chaplin then asked to direct his own films, volunteering to deposit $1,500—his entire savings—as a guarantee if it could not be released. Sennett agreed and promised Chaplin a $25 bonus for each picture he made as a director. From his first films as director, *Twenty Minutes of Love* (1914) and *Caught in the Rain* (1914), to the end of his year at Keystone, Chaplin directed virtually all of the films in which he appeared, the notable exception being *Tillie's Punctured Romance* (1914).[12]

Chaplin's Keystone films fell far short of the gentle, sophisticated comedy that would be the hallmark of his later work. Yet, Chaplin injected into the films and, in turn, into early film come-

Opposite top: Chaplin as the crude, shrewish wife in A BUSY DAY (1914), the first of three times in his motion-picture career in which he is dressed as a woman. The film was photographed in one day—April 11, 1914—with a military parade celebrating the opening of the harbor in San Pedro, California, as its background. (Frame enlargement from 35mm motion-picture film)

Opposite bottom: Charlie is an artist, with Cecile Arnold as Madeline (the model at left) and Vivian Edwards (reclining), in THE FACE ON THE BAR ROOM FLOOR (1914), a parody of the then-popular 1887 poem of love betrayed, by Hugh Antoine D'Arcy.

Left: In THE ROUNDERS (1914), Chaplin plays Mr. Full and Roscoe "Fatty" Arbuckle plays Mr. Fuller, two inebriates-about-town who, by the film's end, take refuge from their angry wives in a rowboat on Echo Park Lake and attempt to sleep, unaware that the boat is slowly sinking. (Frame enlargement from 35mm motion-picture film)

Below: Mabel (Mabel Normand) divides her attentions between Mr. Wow-Wow (Chaplin) and Ambrose (Mack Swain) at the racetrack in GENTLEMAN OF NERVE (1914).

dy an acute understanding of character and movement that he had refined during his years in the British music halls, and a style of comedy that was polished yet appeared spontaneous at the same time.

Within weeks of the Tramp's first appearance, the public had embraced him. Orders for the Chaplin Keystone films grew tremendously. It would only take a few months for Chaplin to be recognized as the most popular comedian in motion pictures, although his great fame and international stardom would not flower until after he signed with the Essanay Film Manufacturing Company in early 1915.

Once Chaplin had control over his own films, he began to enjoy his work at Keystone: "It was this charming alfresco spirit that was a delight—a challenge to one's creativeness. It was so free and easy—no literature, no writers, we just had a notion around which we built gags, then made up the story as we went along,"[13] he recalled in his autobiography. Most of the films were made in a week. A park, a hotel, a café, a dentist's office, a bakery, a racetrack, the backstage of a theater, and even a motion-picture studio were the simple backdrops against which Chaplin's inspired comedies unfolded.

Chaplin reprised his famed, fall-down drunk from his Karno days on several occasions at Keystone (*Mabel's Strange Predicament*, *Tango Tangles*, *His Favorite Pastime*, *Mabel's Married Life*, *The Rounders*, all made in 1914). Indeed, Chaplin's years with Karno prepared him well for the considerable athletic prowess

required to perform the pratfalls and physical clowning of the Keystone comedies.

In the Keystone films, Chaplin imbues the Tramp with some of his famous traits: his waddling shuffle, the way he rounds a corner (making a sharp turn and skidding, holding one foot straight out and balancing on the other foot while holding his hat), his iconoclastic nose-thumbing (known as "cock a snoot") at propriety and authority, and his twitching mustache. He can be seen drop-kicking a cigarette over his shoulder or laughing at the camera, behavior that would reappear in subsequent films. The Tramp's reactions to a situation were often more interesting than the situations themselves.

The New Janitor (1914), a one-reel comedy, was the first appearance of pathos in a Chaplin film. Chaplin later recalled:

> I can trace the first prompting of desire to add another dimension to my films besides that of comedy. I was playing in a picture called *The New Janitor,* in a scene in which the manager of the office fires me. In pleading with him to take pity on me and let me retain my job, I started to pantomime appealingly that I had a large family of little children. Although I was enacting mock sentiment, Dorothy Davenport, an old actress, was on the sidelines watching the scene, and during rehearsal I looked up and to my surprise found her in tears. "I know it's supposed to be funny," she said, "but you just make me weep." She confirmed something I already felt: I had the ability to evoke tears as well as laughter.[14]

Dough and Dynamite (1914), a two-reel comedy directed by Chaplin, was one of the most successful Keystone films. Charlie and Chester Conklin are waiters at a bakery/café who substitute for the bakers when the bakers strike. The film is filled with wonderful comedy touches, such as Charlie balancing a tray of bread loaves on his head and making doughnuts by flinging dough around his wrists like bracelets. In both characterization and structure, *Dough and Dynamite* is much finer than other comedy films of the time. It took nine days to film at a cost of $1,800; because Chaplin went over his prescribed budget of $1,000,

Sennett withheld his $25 directing bonus. Yet, according to Chaplin, the film grossed more than $135,000 in its first year.

Tillie's Punctured Romance was the first feature-length film comedy. It was designed to star the famous stage comedienne Marie Dressler and was based on *Tillie's Nightmare,* the 1910 Broadway hit that gave new impetus to her already impressive and lengthy career. It was the only film in which Chaplin played a supporting role. Yet, when the film was released, *Tillie's Punctured Romance* benefited Chaplin more than anyone else; nearly every motion-picture producer pursued him, wanting to sign him to a contract.

The film's simple story involves Tillie Banks (Marie Dressler), a country girl deceived by a city slicker (Chaplin) to steal her father's money and run away with him to the city. Once there, the slicker takes her money and abandons her for Mabel (Mabel Normand). When it is reported that Tillie is the sole heir to a fortune, the slicker finds Tillie, marries her, and enjoys the good life until the fortune Tillie has inherited proves to be short-lived. A chase ensues when Tillie finds the slicker in a compromising moment with Mabel.

Directed by Mack Sennett and filmed in forty-five days, *Tillie's Punctured Romance* was tremendously popular when released, and Chaplin was singled out for his considerable work in making the film a hit. Chaplin, however, did not think much of the film. In his autobiography he dismissed it: "It was pleasant working with Marie, but I did not think the picture had much merit."[15]

Chaplin's personal life during his time at Keystone was almost nonexistent; he worked long hours, six days a week. Keystone player Peggy Pearce was apparently his first known love in Los Angeles. He met her, he remembered, in the third week at the studio and described her as his "first heart-throb." However, Chaplin recalled, "At that time I had no desire to marry anyone. Freedom was too much an adventure. No woman could measure up to that vague image I had in my mind."[16]

Chaplin's last Keystone release was the two-reeler *His Prehistoric Past* (1914), which proved to be a strain on his concentration with so many business propositions that required his attention. "I suppose that was the most exciting period of my career, for I was on the threshold of something wonderful,"[17] Chaplin later wrote. When Keystone sought to renew Chaplin's contract, he announced to Sennett that he wanted $1,000 a week. Sennett responded that was more than he earned himself, to which Chaplin replied, "I know it, but the public doesn't line up outside the box-office when your name appears [*sic*] as they do for mine."[18] The producer was unwilling to meet his demands.

Chaplin refined Keystone slapstick and film comedy in general by slowing down the frantic pace of the films, giving them a rudimentary structure, and establishing a strong character, which he accomplished by drawing on his knowledge of stagecraft and pantomime. At Keystone he developed film technique and comic pacing for motion pictures that he would employ in some form or fashion for the rest of his career.

soon after throughout the world. It is staggering to consider that not only was there no radio or television to publicize or advertise the Tramp, but also the Keystone Film Company never credited its players by name on the films themselves or on its posters during Chaplin's tenure. To draw a crowd, many exhibitors merely cut out a cardboard figure of the Tramp and placed it outside the cinema with the phrase "I am here to-day."[20]

Chaplin said, "All I need to make a comedy is a park, a policeman and a pretty girl."[21] He was confident in his own ideas. However, despite the advances in film comedy he made at Keystone, his Tramp character was far from fully formed. It would take several years for Chaplin to develop the emotional range and depth that would mark his mature art. Yet the seeds of this art were sown at Keystone. As Mack Sennett remembered, "it was a long time before he abandoned cruelty, venality, treachery, larceny, and lechery as the main characteristics of the tramp. Chaplin shrank his tramp in gradually diminishing sizes and made him pathetic—and lovable."[22] Not until Chaplin's Essanay work does his screen persona fully emerge.

Although Chaplin's relationship with the leader of the Keystone "fun factory" was often rocky, Sennett was a man of great enthusiasm if the work was good (a trait he shared with Fred Karno), and he afforded Chaplin the validation he needed. Ultimately, when Sennett gave Chaplin control over his own films, the men worked well together. Chaplin also admired Sennett's belief in his own taste, a quality he instilled in the actor that helped to stimulate his creative imagination.

Chaplin's tenure at Keystone is legendary because it marks the birth of the Tramp. More than just a great character, the Tramp embodies the heroic age of the cinema. To many, he was film. As Lewis Jacobs wrote in 1939, "To think of Charlie Chaplin is to think of the movies."[19]

An extraordinary aspect of Chaplin's popularity was that he quickly became the most popular film comedian in America and

After completing thirty-five films for Keystone of various lengths—split reels, one-reelers, and two-reelers, plus the feature film *Tillie's Punctured Romance*—Chaplin emerged from his first experience in motion pictures triumphant. Without knowing his name, audiences embraced him as the most popular character in film comedy. Not a bad beginning for a young vaudevillian who thought he was summoned to a lawyer's office to receive an old aunt's inheritance.

Opposite: Charlie the piano mover is offered a drink by Billy Gilbert (center) and Charley Chase (right) at the piano shop in HIS MUSICAL CAREER *(1914).*

Above: Tillie (Marie Dressler) takes hold of her crooked husband (Chaplin) and his accomplice (Mabel Normand) in TILLIE'S PUNCTURED ROMANCE *(1914), the first feature-length comedy film.*

Right: Charlie and Mabel Normand are caught holding hands by their spouses (Phyllis Allen and Mack Swain) in GETTING ACQUAINTED *(1914).*

Essanay-Chaplin Brand

If the early slapstick of the Keystone comedies represents Chaplin's cinematic infancy, the films he made for the Essanay Film Manufacturing Company are his adolescence. The Essanays find Chaplin in transition, taking greater time and care with each film, experimenting with new ideas, and adding flesh to the Tramp character that would become his legacy. Chaplin's Essanay comedies reveal an emerging artist experimenting with his palette and finding his craft.

After the expiration of his one-year contract with the Keystone Film Company, Chaplin was lured to Essanay for the unprecedented salary of $1,250 per week, with a bonus of $10,000 for merely signing with the company. The fourteen films he made for the company were distinctly marked and designated upon release as the "Essanay-Chaplin Brand." The company's headquarters were in Chicago, Illinois, and it had a second studio in Niles, California. The name Essanay was formed from the surname initials, *S* and *A,* of its two founders: George K. Spoor, who provided the financing and managed the company, and G. M. Anderson, better known as "Broncho Billy" Anderson, cinema's first cowboy star.

Essanay began in 1907 and a year later became a member of the powerful Motion Picture Patents Company. Chaplin's one

Three full-length portraits of Chaplin as the Tramp, 1915. Photographs by Witzel

Opposite bottom left: The Essanay stars, c. 1915: leading man Francis X. Bushman (left), Chaplin (center), and Essanay cofounder and cinema's first cowboy star G. M. "Broncho Billy" Anderson (right)

Opposite top right: Chaplin and Edna Purviance at the former Majestic Studio, 1915. Purviance possessed youth, beauty, and a maternal quality that made her attractive to Chaplin.

Right: Essanay producer Jess Robbins, Sydney Chaplin, and Chaplin at the former Majestic Studio, 1915

Below: Chaplin with leading American film director D. W. Griffith (left) and pioneer film producer Thomas H. Ince (right) at the Keystone studio, 1915. Actors Donald Crisp and Edna Purviance are on the far right. Ince's death in 1924 following a pleasure cruise on publishing magnate William Randolph Hearst's yacht (with Chaplin in attendance) is one of Hollywood's great unsolved mysteries. The official version is that Ince died of a heart attack suffered on board. The enduring rumor is that Hearst, in a case of mistaken identity, discovered Ince with Hearst's mistress, actress Marion Davies, below deck and shot him in the back of the head, believing he was Chaplin (Hearst was aware that Chaplin and Davies were having an affair). The story served as the basis of Peter Bogdanovich's film THE CAT'S MEOW (2001).

play more sophisticated plots and involve more textured characters. The maddening pace of producing nearly one new Keystone comedy each week was reflected in the rapid pace and formulaic story lines in the films. However, the pace at Essanay was somewhat slower, allowing Chaplin to take more time and care in creating his films, and more room to experiment. This tempered pace shows in the style of the films, which contain more subtle pantomime and character development. Although the first seven films Chaplin made for Essanay were released over three months, Chaplin slowed the rate of production to one two-reel film (approximately twenty-five minutes in length) per month after that.

Chaplin also wanted to gentrify his films, being very much aware of criticisms that attacked his earlier work as vulgar and crude. More refined comedy was familiar territory for Chaplin, who learned his art in the British music halls, where bringing an audience along as character and story were developed was paramount to getting the big laugh. The great French silent-film comedian Max Linder, whom Chaplin admired, pioneered this method of acting in film. The Tramp's drunken mannerisms in *A Night Out* and *A Night in the Show* borrow heavily from Chaplin's classic music-hall acts, and his female impersonation in *A Woman* reflects the style of masquerade comedy found in many music-hall sketches.

Chaplin's early efforts to pull Essanay in the direction of character-based comedy brought about a certain degree of tension with his employer. After all, the name of the company was the Essanay Film *Manufacturing* Company, and a factory culture

prevailed there. Standardization was actually a goal of the Motion Picture Patents Company, in which Essanay had been participating for seven years by the time Chaplin joined it. Its position in the film industry had been won by series films such as the *Broncho Billys*, the *Alkali Ikes*, the *Snakevilles*, and the *George Ade Fables*. No doubt its expectation was that Chaplin would provide another successful, if predictable, run of more-or-less standardized product. Alarmed when he was instructed at Essanay's Chicago studio to pick up his script from Essanay's head scenario writer, Louella Parsons (who later became a powerful Hollywood gossip columnist), Chaplin snapped, "I don't use other people's scripts, I write my own."[1]

Chaplin had other disagreements with Essanay from the beginning. The company's cofounder, George K. Spoor, had never heard of Chaplin and was reluctant at first to give him his promised $10,000 signing bonus. Chaplin also refused to allow Essanay's practice of projecting the original negative when screening rough film footage, which saved the studio the expense of making a positive copy, insisting that viewing prints had to be made. After Chaplin left Essanay, he despised the company's unscrupulous tactics of reediting his films using discarded material in various forms. It was perhaps because of this acrimony (and the resulting lawsuits) that Chaplin remained bitter about this period in his career for the rest of his life.

Chaplin's dismissive treatment of his Essanay films is unfortunate. Apart from their revelation of the fascinating and subtle evolution of Chaplin's comedy, these films demand a prominent place in the history of film for another, simpler reason—they made Chaplin an icon. Adorned with his instantly recognizable makeup, Chaplin became the most famous man in the world when he worked for Essanay in 1915. An article in *Motion Picture Magazine* stated, "The world has Chaplinitis. . . . Any form of expressing Chaplin is what the public wants. . . . Once in every century or so a man is born who is able to color and influence the world . . . a little Englishman, quiet, unassuming, but surcharged with dynamite is flinching the world right now."[2]

Essanay exploited Chaplin's success to the hilt. The Tramp was the pioneer subject of today's modern multimedia marketing and merchandising tactics, spawning songs as well as toys, postcards, cartoon strips, and statuettes that bore his likeness. Imitation, the sincerest form of flattery, was often upon the Tramp in this period as well, as a host of imitators appeared—from Billie Ritchie to Harold Lloyd's early Lonesome Luke character.

Chaplin's Essanay comedies hold another distinction. For the first time in his career, words that would be applied to Chaplin for the rest of his life—*comic artistry* and *genius*—were written in praise of his work. Indeed, there are moments in these early films that deserve such accolades. Perhaps the greatest joy in watching them is the discovery of many conceits, themes, and devices that would serve the great clown so well in the creation of his mature films.

HIS NEW JOB (1915)

Chaplin's first Essanay comedy—and appropriately titled—was the only film he made at Essanay's Chicago studio. As with his Keystone films *A Film Johnnie* (1914) and *The Masquerader* (1914), Chaplin chose to set the action in a film studio. Charlie is hired as a prop man and is soon demoted to a carpenter's assistant at the Lockstone studio (a play on his former employer, Keystone) before being given the chance to act, which ends in disaster. The film was Chaplin's first pairing with cross-eyed comedian Ben Turpin and features an early appearance by Gloria Swanson as a secretary. It is also notable for several tracking shots, despite Chaplin's reputation for static cinematography, which was seldom used in film comedy of the period.

A NIGHT OUT (1915)

Chaplin's second film for Essanay was the first of five films shot in and around the company's Niles studio in Northern California. The plot is a variation of the teaming of Chaplin and Roscoe "Fatty" Arbuckle in the Keystone film *The Rounders*. This time

he is paired with Ben Turpin, with whom he forms an excellent comedy partnership. Chaplin and Turpin are drunks-about-town, starting at a café and ending in a risqué hotel-room mix-up with a pretty girl, similar to the situation in the Keystone comedies *Mabel's Strange Predicament* and *Caught in the Rain*, but this time with Edna Purviance, in her first film with Chaplin.

THE CHAMPION (1915)

Inspired by the Keystone film *The Knockout* (1914) and Chaplin's interest in boxing, this comedy has Charlie finding employment as a sparring partner who fights in the prize ring and wins the championship match with the help of his pet bulldog. Boxing events were then illegal in most states, and films of boxing matches (including comic takes on them) satisfied a pent-up interest in the subject. The relationship of the Tramp and his dog would be fully developed three years later in *A Dog's Life* (1918), and Chaplin's brilliant choreography in the ring anticipates the boxing match in *City Lights* (1931). G. M. "Broncho Billy" Anderson plays a spectator in the boxing sequence.

Opposite top: Charlie commandeers the unlit cigarette from the mouth of Ben Turpin in HIS NEW JOB *(1915). Turpin made an excellent comedy partner for Chaplin. However, as this still suggests, the two men were fiercely competitive with each other. Indeed, Chaplin was nervous that the cross-eyed comedian was stealing scenes from him by just looking directly into the camera.*

Opposite middle: Charlie is charmed by a statuesque leading lady (Charlotte Mineau) while seeking employment at a motion-picture studio in HIS NEW JOB. *The unidentified player at right holding the ear trumpet portrays the hearing-impaired studio manager.*

Above: The drunken duo of Charlie and Ben Turpin harass a man-about-town Frenchman (Leo White) in a restaurant in A NIGHT OUT *(1915). Photograph by Carl W. Thetford*

Opposite: Charlie the pugilist, with his faithful bulldog, Spike, at his side, prepares for the climactic championship bout in THE CHAMPION.

Right: Charlie takes notice of the revolver pointed at him by a crooked gambler (Leo White) in THE CHAMPION *(1915). This sequence, in which White's villain attempts to bribe Charlie to throw a fight, borrows from a similar scene in the Karno sketch* THE FOOTBALL MATCH.

Middle: Charlie is stopped by a police officer (Ernest van Pelt) while a nursemaid (Edna Purviance) holds the handbag everyone wants in IN THE PARK *(1915), filmed on location in a San Francisco park.*

Bottom: Charlie impersonates Count Chloride de Lime in A JITNEY ELOPEMENT *(1915), with Paddy McGuire as the elderly footman (left), Lloyd Bacon as the butler (center), Edna Purviance as the lovely daughter to whom the nobleman is to be betrothed, and Fred Goodwins as the father. Photograph by Dealey*

Right: Charlie, suffering from a tender backside after falling onto a campfire, prefers to eat standing as the farmer (Fred Goodwins) offers him a cup of coffee and the farmer's daughter (Edna Purviance) is seated at the kitchen table in THE TRAMP *(1915).*

Below: Charlie makes his signature exit, down a metaphorically open-ended road, for the first time in THE TRAMP. *(Frame enlargement from 35mm motion-picture film)*

IN THE PARK (1915)

The first of two one-reel shorts Chaplin made for Essanay, the film was hastily made at the request of the company as result of the prolonged production of his previous film, *The Champion*. The film, which involves Charlie interfering in the lives of two star-crossed lovers, has the same improvisational feel of the simple park comedies made at Keystone, and is nearly a remake of his own Keystone film *Twenty Minutes of Love*.

A JITNEY ELOPEMENT (1915)

Charlie must rescue his sweetheart, Edna, from an arranged marriage by posing as Count Chloride de Lime, the man to whom Edna is betrothed but whom neither she nor her father has ever seen. The film ends with a car chase featuring a Ford automobile, a target of contemporary humor. Impersonation and mistaken identity were devices Chaplin enjoyed. Having used them previously in *Her Friend the Bandit* (1914) and *Caught in a Cabaret* (1914), he would return to them in films such as *The Count* (1916), *The Idle Class* (1921), and *The Great Dictator* (1940). Among the wonderful bits of comic transposition in *A Jitney Elopement* is a bit of business Chaplin had performed in Fred Karno's music-hall sketch *Jimmy the Fearless:* attempting to slice a roll of bread, Charlie continues in a spiral cut, turning the roll into a concertina.

THE TRAMP (1915)

Charlie saves a farmer's daughter from some thieving toughs and subsequently stops their attempt to rob the farm. He falls in love with the girl, but upon the appearance of her sweetheart, the little fellow realizes the true situation. He departs, leaving behind a note to the girl that reads: "I thort your kindness was love but it aint cause I seen him. Goodbye." This prototypical Chaplin film is important for its superb characterization and construction, successfully integrating pathos with comedy. The film's sad ending—new to film comedy—incorporates Chaplin's first use of the classic fade-out, in which the Tramp shuffles away alone into the distance, with his back to the camera.

SHANGHAIED (1915)

Chaplin rented a boat, the *Vaquero*, to inspire the plot of this comedy gem. Charlie is hired to shanghai a crew, only to be shanghaied himself as well. He has to save himself and his sweetheart, who has stowed away, before the boat is sabotaged for the insurance. The film contains some of Chaplin's early playful dancing (dance would be an important part of his mature films), seasickness (one of Chaplin's favorite routines), and a curious homosexual situation involving Chaplin and the cabin boy, highly unusual in mainstream cinema for its time.

BY THE SEA (1915)

The second of two one-reel shorts Chaplin made for Essanay, the film was photographed around the Venice, California, amusement pier in just one day. This extended improvisation includes Chaplin's first use of the flea routine, which he would develop further for his feature film *Limelight* (1952).

WORK (1915)

The havoc created by incompetent laborers had always been prime slapstick material. For example, in 1906 Chaplin had appeared in Wal Pink's music-hall sketch *Repairs*, playing a plumber's assistant. In this comedy, Chaplin plays a paperhanger's assistant hired to wallpaper a mansion (the imposing home was the Bradbury Mansion, one of the biggest homes in Los Angeles). Peace is replaced with anarchy, culminating in a massive explosion. The opening sequence—which shows Charlie pulling a work cart down a busy street and up a steep hill with his boss sitting in the cart's driver seat, hitting Charlie with a whip—is striking for its symbolic portrayal of the exploitation and degradation of human laborers.

Charlie is knocked unconscious with a mallet and forced to be a part of a boat's crew in SHANGHAIED *(1915). Lawrence A. Bowes is the captain at right.*

Right: A candid photograph of Chaplin with a mule on location in Venice Beach, California, during production of BY THE SEA. *Photograph attributed to Jess Robbins*

Middle right: In a momentary reprieve from their fighting, Charlie and his nemesis (Billy Armstrong) enjoy ice cream cones, while the refreshment vendor (Harry Pollard) wonders who will pay the bill, in BY THE SEA *(1915).*

Below: Charlie is an incompetent painter and paperhanger's assistant who is temporarily distracted by the charms of the maid (Edna Purviance) in WORK *(1915).*

Left: Chaplin, Edna Purviance, and Marta Golden surrounded by three unidentified men during production of WORK at the former Majestic Studio in Los Angeles. Photograph by Byken Takagi

Below: Chaplin (sitting on Edna Purviance's lap) with cast and crew members during production of WORK at the former Majestic Studio. Paddy McGuire is standing on the far left, and Charles Insley is seated on the far right. Cameraman Harry Ensign is presumably next to the Pathé camera. Photograph attributed to Jess Robbins

A WOMAN (1915)

Chaplin had twice donned female attire at Keystone, in *A Busy Day* and *The Masquerader*. *A Woman* was Chaplin's last and finest female impersonation, a then-popular device among comedians (Julian Eltinge built a career and fortune on it). The first half of the film is a typical park comedy, in which the Tramp causes havoc as a result of his mischief with a flirtatious woman, soda bottles, and a nearby lake. The second half requires Charlie to disguise himself as a lady in order to be near Edna, his newfound sweetheart, after her father has forbidden her to see him.

THE BANK (1915)

Charlie the janitor loves Edna, the pretty bank secretary, but her sweetheart is another Charles, the cashier. One of the best of the Chaplin Essanay comedies, the film's plot is a reworking of his Keystone film *The New Janitor*, incorporating a dream sequence inspired by Fred Karno's *Jimmy the Fearless*. Just as in the Karno sketch—in which Chaplin starred as Jimmy, a downtrodden young man who becomes a hero in his dreams—in *The Bank* Charlie dreams he saves Edna in an attempted bank robbery, only to wake up and discover it was a dream. The film's equivocal ending was new to film comedy. Such endings became a signature of the Chaplin films. The memorable close-up of Chaplin in *The Bank*, when his note and gift of a few flowers to Edna are rejected, anticipates the ending of *City Lights*.

A NIGHT IN THE SHOW (1915)

This exceptional comedy was adapted from Fred Karno's sketch *Mumming Birds*. Chaplin plays dual roles in the film: his old stage success Mr. Pest and Mr. Rowdy, a dissipated working man, both of whom are attending a vaudeville performance. Mr. Pest manages to cause as much disorder in the orchestra stall as does Mr. Rowdy in the gallery.

Opposite top: Charlie is throttled by two gentlemen (Billy Armstrong and Charles Insley), while the girl (Edna Purviance) and her mother (Marta Golden) helplessly clasp their hands with concern, in A WOMAN (1915).

Opposite bottom: Charlie dons female attire in A WOMAN, Chaplin's third and final female impersonation of his career. (Frame enlargement from 35mm motion-picture film)

Above: Charlie the bank janitor, distracted by two pretty young women, carelessly leans on a woman's bustle in THE BANK (1915).

Right: Charlie is heartbroken when the simple flowers and note he has given Edna, the secretary, are rejected in THE BANK. Chaplin's use of the close-up anticipates the famous close-up that concludes CITY LIGHTS. (Frame enlargement from 35mm motion-picture film)

Right: Chaplin as Mr. Pest scowls his disapproval at the conductor of the pit band (John Rand) in one of his dual roles in A NIGHT IN THE SHOW *(1915).*

Below: Mr. Pest is entertained by Tootsy Frutti, the snake charmer, in A NIGHT IN THE SHOW.

Opposite top: Chaplin as Darn Hosiery in BURLESQUE ON "CARMEN" *(1916), his effort in a type of parody popular at the time*

Opposite bottom: Charlie receives a silver dollar as he bids farewell to the compassionate young woman (Edna Purviance), who spared him from being arrested for attempting to burgle her home, in POLICE *(1916).*

HIS REGENERATION (1915)

Chaplin made a guest appearance in this one-reel G. M. "Broncho Billy" Anderson drama, as the Tramp in the film's dance-hall sequence. That the main title states that Anderson was "slightly assisted by Charles Chaplin" suggests that Chaplin may have had a hand in the construction and direction of the film as well. The plot of the drama bears a close resemblance to the story used in Chaplin's *Police*.

BURLESQUE ON "CARMEN" (1916)

Chaplin's burlesque of Cecil B. De Mille's popular film version of *Carmen* (1915), starring the great opera diva Geraldine Farrar, as well as a rival version of *Carmen* (1915), starring Theda Bara, was originally intended as a two-reel comedy. In Chaplin's version, Don José becomes Darn Hosiery (Chaplin), with Edna Purviance as the seductress Carmen. However, after Chaplin left Essanay, the company inserted discarded material and created new scenes, extending the film to four reels when it was given a general release in April 1916. The altered version of the film sent Chaplin to bed for two days. He later put forward an unprecedented claim of the moral rights of artists, suing Essanay on the grounds that the expanded version would damage his reputation with the public. Although Chaplin lost the court battle, he later wrote that Essanay's dishonest act "rendered a service, for thereafter I had it stipulated in every contract that there should be no mutilating, extending or interfering with my finished work."[3]

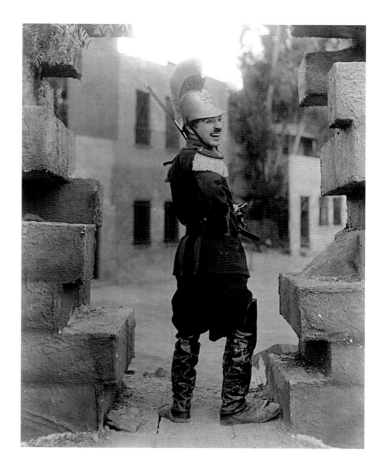

POLICE (1916)

Police uses comedy to make pointed—if glancing—social statements, a method that over the years became central to Chaplin's work. The film is arguably the most mature in the series and anticipates later films such as *Modern Times* (1936). The Tramp, released from prison, is "once again in the cruel, cruel world" where he meets a former cellmate and sets about to rob the home of a young woman. *Police* was altered by Essanay after Chaplin had edited the film, removing an extended doss-house sequence that reappeared two years later in *Triple Trouble*.

TRIPLE TROUBLE (1918)

This film, which Essanay claimed was a "new" Chaplin comedy, was released nearly three years after the conclusion of Chaplin's contract with the company. The film was assembled from the discarded portions of *Police*, the ending of *Work*, and an abandoned feature-length production entitled *Life*, along with some new footage directed by Leo White in 1918. The plot has Charlie working in the home of an eccentric inventor from whom some German spies are attempting to obtain a formula. *Triple Trouble*, however, is best seen as an opportunity to view portions of the abandoned *Life*, Chaplin's first attempt to direct himself in a feature-length film, and the doss-house sequence intended for *Police*.

Mutual-Chaplin Specials

By 1916, just two years after appearing in his first motion picture, Chaplin had become the most famous entertainer in the world. Buoyed by his enormously successful comedies for Keystone and Essanay, he was offered the largest salary ever extended to a motion-picture star—$670,000 for a single year's work—to make twelve two-reel comedies for the Mutual Film Corporation. As a group, these films remain the finest two-reel comedies of the silent era.

Few artists seminal to a medium leave a detailed history that charts the early evolution of their craft. Although the initial Mutuals have the feel and structure of Chaplin's earlier, less sophisticated films, the progression of the series to the final four Mutuals is truly remarkable. Viewing the Mutual-Chaplin Specials is comparable to turning a camera on Thomas A. Edison in Menlo Park and capturing unhindered the inventor's moments of pure inspiration. The thrill in watching nearly all of the Mutuals comes in the Promethean moment when Chaplin's inventiveness intersects with his genius and produces cinematic comedy sequences unlike any before. The Mutuals are Chaplin's laboratory, offering an unprecedented glimpse into the inner workings of the mind of a great cinema pioneer.

Charlie saves the girl (Edna Purviance) trapped by fire in her third-floor room in THE FIREMAN *(1916).*

Chaplin signs a contract with John R. Freuler of the Lone Star Corporation (a newly formed subsidiary of the Mutual Film Corporation), New York City, February 26, 1916. Between the signatories is Chaplin's brother and business manager, Sydney, who negotiated the agreement. The contract called for twelve two-reel comedies in twelve months for which Chaplin was to be paid the unprecedented amount of $10,000 a week plus a $150,000 signing bonus. The $670,000 deal made Chaplin the highest-paid entertainer in history up to that time.

The Mutual Film Corporation created a subsidiary called The Lone Star Corporation solely to make the Chaplin films. Lone Star paid Chaplin $10,000 a week plus a $150,000 signing bonus for the twelve two-reel comedies. The unprecedented sum would set the standard for the salaries of motion-picture stars. Indeed, Mary Pickford, known as "America's Sweetheart," did not allow Chaplin's record-breaking salary to go unchallenged. The company provided Chaplin his own studio, named the Lone Star Studio. The facility was formerly the Climax Studios, located at 1025 Lillian Way in Hollywood, and later would be used by Buster Keaton to make all his independently produced silent two-reel and feature-length films. For Mutual, Chaplin produced what many film historians believe to be his best works. He made approximately one film a month but several required more time, and the series ultimately took eighteen months to complete. Although this may appear to be remarkably swift work, it was a leisurely pace compared to the speed he had been required to maintain at Keystone and Essanay.

The press and public were amazed at the amount of Chaplin's earnings. A Mutual publicist wrote, "Next to the war in Europe Chaplin is the most expensive item in contemporaneous history."[1] Chaplin was sanguine. "It means that I am left free to be just as funny as I dare," announced Chaplin, "to do the best work that is in me. . . . There is inspiration in it. I am like an author with a big publisher to give him circulation."[2] Mutual provided Chaplin the freedom to explore all his comic ideas and to discard anything he believed failed to work on film.

Henry P. Caulfield (succeeded by John Jasper in June 1917) produced the Mutual series. Chaplin chose William C. Foster as the first cameraman and Rollie Totheroh as his second (two negatives were made of each shot). Foster left the Lone Star Studio after four films, leaving Totheroh as head cameraman and George C. Zalibra as the second. Totheroh trained at Essanay, where he first met Chaplin. (He had played several seasons of minor-league baseball prior to working in films.) From the Mutual period onward, Totheroh had a lasting professional association with Chaplin. He was cinematographer for every Chaplin film through *Modern Times* and remained on Chaplin's payroll until 1954. Totheroh's tolerance of Chaplin's infamous volatility contributed to their long working relationship. He was also an elemental film technician who provided the director exactly what he wanted.

Totheroh's cinematography has been criticized as unimaginative and static. Except for an occasional tracking shot in *The Vagabond, The Count, Easy Street,* and *The Cure,* the camera remained stationary to match Chaplin's style of direction, which was similar to filming a scene as if the action were set on a theatrical stage. Chaplin refined and altered his performance over several takes but he almost never changed camera position on a set-up. As innovative as he was with his screen comedy, he was relatively unimaginative with the camera prior to *A Woman of Paris.*

"Placement of camera is cinematic inflection," Chaplin wrote in his autobiography. "There is no set rule that a close-up gives more emphasis than a long shot. A close-up is a question of feeling; in some instances a long shot can effect greater emphasis." Chaplin cited *The Rink,* his eighth film for Mutual, as an example of his methodology with respect to camera placement:

> The tramp enters the rink and skates with one foot up, gliding and twirling, tripping and bumping into people and getting into all sorts of mischief, eventually leaving everyone piled up on their backs in the foreground of the camera while he skates to the rear of the rink, becoming a very small figure in the background, and sits amongst the spectators innocently reviewing the havoc he has just created. Yet the small figure of the tramp in the distance was funnier than he would have been in a close-up.[3]

Indeed, he once remarked, "Life is a tragedy when seen in close-up, but a comedy in long-shot."[4]

Chaplin ordered Totheroh to film the action at an eye-level, full-figure distance or, for a medium shot, at a waist-high-figure distance, depending on what the scene demanded. Close-ups were seldom filmed. Similarly, Chaplin's lighting was also basic, without any tricks or attempt at mood. His rudimentary approach to camera placement and lighting was a conscious decision to remain focused on the actors and to leave the performance area accessible for improvisation at all times. Moreover, complicated camera set-ups required time. When the mercurial Chaplin was ready to act, he did not want to be waiting on technicians. From his first film to his last, Chaplin remained a man of the theater, and his primary concern was to convey to the audience the action and the emotion of a scene through the performances of his actors, not through innovative or elaborate photography, lighting, or editing.

Chaplin's method of filmmaking departed from that of most other silent-era directors. First of all, he disliked filming on location and avoided it whenever he could, preferring the controlled conditions of his studio, which allowed him to do insert scenes days or weeks later and have them match the master scenes. Moreover, Chaplin took too long to film anything substantial on location. In the silent era, just as today, every shot was given a separate number. Silent filmmakers did not utilize a clapperboard, which is useful for synchronizing action and sound, but a simple slate board to mark the scenes. Chaplin's unorthodox system was to mark each take in chronological order, rather than to assign a number to each scene. Eschewing formal scripts, Chaplin devised ideas for scenes in advance and had them typed up as notes. Often, however, inspiration would strike him on a set and there would be no time to have the notes typed.

By any standard, Chaplin's directing style, perfected during the filming of the Mutuals and employed throughout the rest of his career, was extraordinary and unique in the cinema. He simply acted out the parts of all the actors as he wished them to be played, down to the slightest gesture of the hand or movement

Chaplin poses with a clay figure at the Lone Star Studio, c. 1917.

of the eyebrow. Chaplin and his cast would be in full costume and makeup while he rehearsed scenes and refined ideas over and over again on film. This directorial style was considered eccentric even in 1916, and the time he lavished on his films was the envy of every filmmaker. Yet for Chaplin, a laserlike concentration on performance and perfection to the exclusion of all else was his unyielding obsession, even until the end of his career.

Chaplin neither wrote about nor discussed his filmmaking methods at length. He felt, "if people know how it's done, all the magic goes."[5] However, despite Chaplin's later orders to have the outtakes destroyed, an extensive amount of outtakes—primarily from the Mutual period—survives as a detailed record of his creative process. They reveal that Chaplin was willing to film a scene over and over again, even if he had an idea only partially worked out, until he was completely satisfied with the result.[6] Totheroh later recalled:

> He didn't have a script at the time, didn't have a script girl or anything like that, and he never checked whether the scene was in its right place or that continuity was followed. The script would develop as it went along. A lot of times after we saw the dailies the next morning, if it didn't warrant what he thought the expectation was, he'd put in some other sort of a sequence and work on that instead of going through with what he started out to do. We never had a continuity. He'd have an idea and he'd build up. He had sort of a synopsis laid out in his mind but nothing on paper. He'd talk it over and come in and do a sequence. In a lot of his old pictures, he'd make that separation by using titles about the time: "next day" or "the following day" or "that night"—these would cover the script gaps in between.
>
> Charlie would rehearse them. He'd rehearse everybody, and even in silents we had dialogue. It came to a little woman's part, and he'd get out there and he'd play it. He'd change his voice and he'd be the character that he wanted the little old woman to play. He'd build their lines up and rehearse them, even before he rehearsed himself in it. He rehearsed so many darn different ways with them that when he came in there, it'd be changed all around with what he put down. You had to be on the alert for him.
>
> I never got away from the camera, looking through that lens. And all those rehearsals, I sat right there, watching every move he made. Then if he came along and something spontaneous hit him, you had to be ready there to take it and get it.
>
> As a director, Mr. Chaplin didn't have anything to say as far as exposures, things like that. Otherwise, I used to say, "Take a look through here." The idea of that was that if he was directing, he'd have to know the field that I was taking in. Of course, in the early days, the role of the cameraman was much bigger than it is now. It was up to the cameraman to decide what angle to shoot for lighting; or outside, which is the best angle on a building or whatever it is. Then you figure what time of the day it would be better to shoot that shot, whether you want backlight or cross-light or whatever on your set. I had to keep the set pretty well lit. You couldn't under-light and get some nice shadows. No, Charlie wanted to look like a clown. He wanted that pretty near white-face. And you had to watch out; you couldn't

have shadow over here or back of you because you never knew where he was going to work. You had to watch out and keep your eye out all the time.

On a typical day, we'd shoot from around eight or nine in the morning right straight through till lunch. Of course, this was before unions. And a lot of times he'd want to shoot two hours after dinner. After we'd break for lunch or for dinner, we'd start up again. I could always tell my set-ups because I was smoking Bull Durham and I used so many matches. You could see all these matches all over the floor.[7]

Although Chaplin created his own comedic sequences, he was assisted on the Mutuals by a capable scenario staff. Vincent Bryan, a writer of vaudeville sketches and songs who had worked with Chaplin at Essanay, was chief scenario editor. Maverick Terrell was also engaged to assist Chaplin develop his ideas. As Terry Ramsaye wrote, "He surrounds himself with these interesting and gifted persons, not to have them do his work for him, but to supply gravel for his mental gizzard."[8] Albert Austin also contributed comedy ideas, as did Chaplin's elder brother, Sydney. Evidence from outtakes of films such as *The Pawnshop* shows that Chaplin also trusted Sydney to assist him in direction. Chaplin, who suffered from insomnia during this period of his life, began to use a phonographic dictating machine by his bedside to record any comedy idea that occurred to him, a practice that would remain with him for many years.

Although Chaplin directed his actors as if he were playing every part, he wanted an excellent ensemble of performers. He engaged Edna Purviance, his leading lady from Essanay, for effective underplaying to complement his own performances. The English actor Eric Campbell, who stood six feet four inches and weighed nearly 300 pounds, was engaged to be the "heavy" (Chaplin, by comparison, stood five feet six and one-half inches and weighed 125 pounds during this period). Campbell had worked for Karno, where he first met Chaplin, and was playing on Broadway in *Pom Pom* at the Cohan Theatre when Sydney Chaplin saw him during his visit to New York in 1916 to negotiate his brother's contract with Mutual. Shortly thereafter, Chaplin asked Campbell to sign an agreement with Lone Star. A shy, gentle man in real life, the hulking Campbell was the perfect Goliath for Chaplin's David. Yet the association between the two men, although immortal in film comedy, was short-lived. The last film in the Mutual series, *The Adventurer*, was Campbell's last screen appearance. Campbell was killed instantly in a car accident on December 20, 1917, in Los Angeles at the age of thirty-seven.

Others in the Chaplin company were Karno alumni Albert Austin and John Rand as well as character actors Leo White and Henry Bergman. Chaplin also hired Charlotte Mineau to portray mature and female "heavy" roles and Lloyd Bacon to play young men (Bacon later became a successful film director). Of course, Chaplin's excellent ensemble was merely support for his own protagonist in each film.

Chaplin and Eric Campbell at tee for THE GOLF LINKS, *the intended twelfth and last film for Mutual that was abandoned, 1917. Chaplin returned to the idea of a comedy featuring golf four years later with* THE IDLE CLASS.

Chaplin was considered a somewhat solitary figure in Hollywood during the Mutual period. Instead of reveling in the pleasures of early Hollywood, he remained engrossed in his work and focused on expanding his career. Purviance was his constant companion, and he spent most evenings dining with her at the Los Angeles Athletic Club, where Chaplin was then living. She was a placid, calming force during his most turbulent moods and provided him unconditional love and stability in his otherwise chaotic, nonstop working life and through the strain of his stupendous worldwide celebrity. He gave her his affection, a career, and intellectual stimulation. Chaplin remembered that the two "were serious about each other, and at the back of my mind I had an idea that some day we might marry, but I had reservations about Edna. I was uncertain of her, and for that matter uncertain of myself."[9]

During this period, Chaplin improved his standard of living for the first time in any significant way since he began in films. He purchased his first car, a Locomobile, and engaged a valet, Tom Harrington, and a chauffeur, Kono Toraichi. His social activities were confined to people within his profession. His only routine pleasures were watching Jack Doyle's Friday night boxing matches in Vernon, attending an evening of vaudeville at the Orpheum Theater or the Morosco Theater's stock-company productions, or taking in an occasional symphony at Clune's Philharmonic Auditorium. Chaplin recalled, "But writing, acting and directing fifty-two weeks in the year was strenuous, requiring an exorbitant expenditure of nervous energy. At the completion of a picture I would be left depressed and exhausted, so that I would have to rest in bed for a day."[10]

Chaplin amazingly departs from the famous Tramp costume in several of the Mutuals. He portrays a firefighter in *The Fireman*,

The Fireman, like The Floorwalker, shares the knockabout comedy style of the Essanay films. Chaplin had produced a film carefully tailored to what he felt was the public expectation. He then received a letter from an admirer who had seen The Fireman at a large Midwestern cinema and conveyed his disappointment. It was perhaps one of the most important letters he received in his career:

> I have noticed in your last picture a lack of spontaneity. Although the picture was unfailing as a laugh-getter, the laughter was not so round as at some of your earlier work. I am afraid you are becoming a slave to your public, whereas in most of your pictures the audiences were a slave to you. The public, Charlie, likes to be slaves.[17]

It was a great lesson to Chaplin. For the rest of his career, he trusted and adhered to his own ideas and likes rather than attempting to speculate on the perceived preferences of the public.

THE VAGABOND (1916)

The Vagabond, Chaplin's third Mutual film, was an important step in Chaplin's career, in which he interweaves pathos as an integral part of the comedy. Indeed, The Vagabond is the prototype of The Kid (1921) and The Circus (1928). The film opens with a shot of the Tramp's famous feet shuffling forward under the swinging door of a saloon. He is a street musician whose violin solo is overwhelmed by a German band. Charlie passes the hat, which everyone presumes is for the band. When the German band members discover he is collecting the money that should be coming to them, they chase him out of the bar. The Tramp saves and then falls in love with a gypsy drudge (Edna Purviance), forced into slavery by a cruel gypsy chief (Eric Campbell) and his caravan. But a handsome young artist (Lloyd Bacon) encounters the girl and they fall in love. Before the film's happy conclusion, there is a scene in which the artist and the girl's long-lost mother

(Charlotte Mineau) take the girl away from the Tramp, leaving the little fellow alone. Chaplin employs the same romantic triangle seen in The Tramp that he would revisit in Sunnyside (1919) and The Circus. He imposed an unlikely happy ending on The Vagabond, in which the gypsy drudge demands that the car she is being taken away in be turned around so she can bring Charlie along with her.

Legend has it that Chaplin originally intended the film to end with a scene in which Charlie attempts a watery suicide, is saved by an ugly farm woman, and plunges in again after one look at his rescuer.[18] However, the few surviving outtakes from the film do not substantiate this claim.[19]

The Vagabond relies less on outright comedy than did Chaplin's earlier work. His direction of the film shows sensitivity and restraint in the treatment of melodramatic material, such as the dramatic device of the lost child finally identified by her unique birthmark. Chaplin's performance reveals great warmth and depth.

Strains of *The Vagabond* appear in many of Chaplin's later films. The film's ambiguous ending regarding Charlie's future with the girl and his care of her foreshadows Charlie's relationship with Jackie Coogan in *The Kid*. The cruel gypsy chief is the precursor to the cruel stepfather of *The Circus*. The scenes in the film of Charlie as the violinist (particularly Charlie, in a musical frenzy, falling into a tub of water) anticipate *Limelight*. *The Vagabond* clearly shows the development of film elements that Chaplin would use throughout his career, particularly the subtle blending of comedy and drama.

ONE A.M. (1916)

One A.M., Chaplin's fourth Mutual, is an impressive piece of virtuosity, a solo performance except for a brief appearance by Albert Austin as a taxi driver. The film is a tour de force of Chaplin's superb pantomime and comic creativity performed in a restricted space, a brilliant experiment that he never repeated. Chaplin reportedly remarked, "One more film like that and it will

be goodbye Charlie."[20] The film's simple situation revolves around a drunken gentleman as he arrives home early one morning and tries to get upstairs into bed. In his inebriated state, every inanimate object seems to conspire against him: a coatrack, a tiger-skin rug, a revolving table, and taxidermy terrors are among the malevolent props placed in his path. Once Charlie negotiates the double staircase, he is knocked down by the wide-swinging pendulum of a giant wall clock. Finally upstairs, he must fight with a folding Murphy bed, which twirls him around, pins him to the floor, bounces him, swallows him up into the wall, and pulls itself from underneath him. The classic bed sequence anticipates Buster Keaton's use of such props—the yacht of *The Boat* (1921), the steamship in *The Navigator* (1924), and the train engine in *The General* (1926)—and Chaplin's own treatise of humanity trapped in a world of machines, *Modern Times*. Defeated by the folding bed, Charlie takes refuge in the bathtub. Art director Scotty Cleethorpe designed the splendidly surreal set, and technical director Ed Brewer created the folding bed that Chaplin turned into a memorable foil.

The film is not only a remarkable experiment but also an invaluable record of Chaplin's famous drunken character, which began in the Karno sketch *Mumming Birds*. He described what he thought made this type of drunk humorous in an article entitled "What People Laugh At," published in *American Magazine* in 1918:

> Even funnier than the man who has been made ridiculous . . . is the man who, having had something funny happen to him, refuses to admit that anything out of the way has happened, and attempts to maintain his dignity. Perhaps the best example is the intoxicated man who, though his tongue and walk will give him away, attempts in a dignified manner to convince you that he is quite sober.
>
> He is much funnier than the man who, wildly hilarious, is frankly drunk and doesn't care a whoop who knows it. Intoxicated characters on the stage are almost always "slightly tipsy" with an attempt at dignity, because theatrical managers have learned that this attempt at dignity is funny.[21]

THE COUNT (1916)

In the fifth film in the Mutual series, Charlie is an assistant to a tailor (Eric Campbell) who discharges him for incompetence. The tailor, masquerading as Count Broko at a fancy-dress dance party given in the opulent home of Miss Moneybags (Edna Purviance), encounters his former assistant, who is visiting the servant's quarters and romancing the cook (Eva Thatcher). Charlie confronts his former employer and pushes himself in front of him when introductions are made. He poses as the count and introduces the tailor as his secretary. The two men fight for the attention of the beautiful Miss Moneybags. The film reaches its climax when the genuine Count Broko (Leo White) arrives unexpectedly and a chase ensues; the tailor ultimately is led away by police while Charlie escapes down a street.

The Count further develops the situations of Caught in a Cabaret and A Jitney Elopement and anticipates the future Chaplin films The Rink, The Idle Class, and City Lights, films in which Charlie impersonates a man of means in order to underscore the contrast between rich and poor—one of his favorite themes. The film was Chaplin's largest production up to that time, with three substantial sets (the tailor's shop, the kitchen, and Miss Moneybags's home). For the film's dance sequence, Chaplin hired a small orchestra. The slippery floor facilitates some memorable eccentric dancing from Charlie, including splits and elevations done by hooking his cane on the chandelier above him.

THE PAWNSHOP (1916)

In the sixth Mutual film, Charlie is a pawnbroker's assistant in a pawnshop that evokes the London of Chaplin's childhood, and he is constantly involved in altercations with another assistant (John Rand). When he is discharged by the pawnbroker (Henry Bergman), Charlie pleads in pantomime that he has six dependents of various sizes that he must support and he is reinstated, enabling him to continue to work near the pawnbroker's charming—if culinarily challenged—daughter (Edna Purviance). His

Opposite:
An intoxicated Charlie overcomes his inability to open the front door by climbing in through the window in ONE A.M. (1916).

In his drunken condition, Charlie finds all the inanimate objects inside the house appear to have a life of their own.

Charlie calmly smokes a cigarette in ONE A.M., a film that demonstrates Chaplin's virtuosity in comic performance.

This page:
The tailor (Eric Campbell) and Charlie, his assistant, in THE COUNT (1916).

Charlie rides up the dumbwaiter to make a quick escape in THE COUNT. When he peers between the curtains he finds the tailor about to embark on a masquerade.

Charlie, partnered with Miss Moneybags (Edna Purviance), duels with the tailor (Eric Campbell, dancing with Charlotte Mineau) on the dance floor in THE COUNT.

Above: Charlie exerts himself holding a plate of doughnuts baked by the pawnbroker's culinarily impaired daughter (Edna Purviance) in THE PAWNSHOP *(1916).*

Right: Charlie, an assistant to the pawnbroker, carefully attends to the shop's ornamental fixture in THE PAWNSHOP.

Opposite: Charlie contemplates putting an alarm clock to the acid test in THE PAWNSHOP. *Chaplin's dismantling of the clock is one of his most celebrated comedy sequences.*

service of some strange customers angers the pawnbroker, but all is forgiven when Charlie thwarts a robbery and knocks out the crook (Eric Campbell) with a rolling pin.

The film is rich in comic transposition, a key element to Chaplin's genius. The apex of such work in the Mutuals is the celebrated scene in *The Pawnshop* in which Charlie examines an alarm clock brought in by a customer (Albert Austin). Playwright Harvey O'Higgins cited the sequence as an ideal illustration of "Charlie Chaplin's Art" in the February 3, 1917, issue of *The New Republic*:

> [H]e is a clerk in a pawnshop, and a man brings in an alarm clock to pledge it. Chaplin has to decide how much it is worth. He sees it first as a patient to be examined diagnostically. He taps it, percusses it, puts his ear to its chest, listens to its heartbeat with a stethoscope, and, while he listens, fixes a thoughtful medical eye on space, looking inscrutably wise and professionally self-confident. He begins to operate on it—with a can-opener. And immediately the round tin clock becomes a round tin can whose contents are under suspicion. He cuts around the circular top of the can, bends back the flap of tin with a kitchen thumb gingerly, scrutinizes the contents gingerly, and then, gingerly approaching his nose to it, sniffs with the melancholy expression of the packing houses. The imagination is accurate. The acting is restrained and naturalistic. The result is a scream. And do not believe that such acting is a matter of crude and simple means. It is as subtle in its naturalness as the shades of intonation in a really tragic speech.[22]

The sequence with the alarm clock in some ways prefigures Chaplin's most celebrated use of comic transposition, the famous scene in *The Gold Rush* (1925) in which Charlie treats his old boiled shoe in every detail as if it were a delicious Thanksgiving feast.

The pawnbroker was played by Henry Bergman in his first film for Chaplin. Bergman became an indispensable member of Chaplin's team, appearing in every subsequent film up to *Modern Times* and remaining on the Chaplin Studios payroll until his death in 1946.

BEHIND THE SCREEN (1916)

A refinement of his earlier comedies set in a film studio (*A Film Johnnie* and *The Masquerader* for Keystone and *His New Job* for Essanay), *Behind the Screen,* Chaplin's seventh film for Mutual, lampoons the unmotivated slapstick of the kind Chaplin disliked when he worked for Mack Sennett. Chaplin made the film as a parody of the knockabout, pie-throwing comedy of the Keystone films.

David (Chaplin), the energetic and playful assistant of stagehand Goliath (Eric Campbell), does all the work at the motion-picture studio while the lazy and bullying Goliath takes all the credit. David earnestly throws eleven bentwood chairs around his arm; with the chair legs in the air he looks like a wooden porcupine. He tops the gag by picking up an upright piano with his free hand. Applying the finishing touches to a film set, he becomes a barber to a bearskin rug, applying hair tonic, massaging the scalp, carefully combing the hair, and applying hot towels to the bear's face. At lunchtime, David only has slices of bread to eat, which he augments by clandestinely stealing bites off a meat bone belonging to a fellow worker seated next to him (Albert Austin), clamping the meat between his own bread.

An aspiring actress (Edna Purviance), desperate for work, disguises herself as a boy and is hired at the studio as a stagehand when the regular crew strikes (the strikers and their plans to blow up the studio are reminiscent of *Dough* and *Dynamite*). David, discovering that the new stagehand is in fact a girl, gently kisses her just as Goliath enters. "Oh you naughty boys!" Goliath remarks in an intertitle, as he teasingly pinches their cheeks and dances about in an effeminate manner before offering his backside to David, which David promptly kicks. This curious scene representing a homosexual situation is highly unusual in American commercial cinema for its time.

David is recruited to act in the comedy department's "new idea"—a pie fight, a not-so-subtle reference to the unsophisticated comedy Chaplin had left behind. Goliath is also asked to take part. Chaos quickly unfolds as David ignores the director's instructions and throws pies at his boss. The film ends with the terrific explosion of the strikers' bomb, with David and the lovely Edna unscathed, giving the audience a wink as the film fades out.

Opposite: Charlie laughs at his discovery that the property "boy" (Edna Purviance) is actually an attractive young woman in BEHIND THE SCREEN *(1916).*

Left: Charlie and the property "boy" (Edna Purviance) are attentive but unhelpful to the plight of Goliath the stagehand (Eric Campbell), caught in a trap door, in BEHIND THE SCREEN.

Below: Chaplin holds a scenario conference with cast and crew during production of BEHIND THE SCREEN *at the Lone Star Studio. From left to right: unidentified man (sitting on floor), unidentified man, Eric Campbell, Henry Bergman (just visible), Frank J. Coleman, Loyal Underwood, James T. Kelly, Albert Austin (slightly obscured, wearing boater hat), Chaplin, unidentified man, and Rollie Totheroh*

THE RINK (1916)

Chaplin's eighth film for Mutual, *The Rink,* is one of his most popular comedies. Charlie is an inept waiter who prepares the bill of Mr. Stout (Eric Campbell) by examining the soup, spaghetti, melon stains, and other remnants on the sloppy eater's shirt front, tie, and ear. Charlie employs an unorthodox approach to his work. He shakes an unusual cocktail: his whole body does a shimmy while the cocktail shaker remains immobile in his hands. He carelessly places a broiler cover over a live cat that he serves to a startled diner. Yet, inept as Charlie is as a waiter, he is incredibly graceful on roller skates, which is how he spends his lunch break. At the rink, he shields Edna (Edna Purviance) from the advances of Mr. Stout. An angry Mr. Stout and Charlie bounce off each other, but Mr. Stout is no match for Charlie, who twirls him around the rink with his cane, launching him into an adjacent room.

Charlie later poses as Sir Cecil Seltzer, C.O.D., and a grateful Edna invites him to her skating party that evening. Mr. Stout and his wife (Henry Bergman in the first of several female impersonations he would do for Chaplin) also attend the party. The skating begins, and Charlie topples both of the Stouts. He is soon pursued by a line of angry skaters and eventually the police, but he eludes them in a grand chase in which he makes his escape by hooking his cane to a moving automobile that tows him away from his pursuers.

Chaplin developed his skating skills while employed by Fred Karno in the British music halls, and the film was superficially inspired by the Karno sketch *Skating* (which had been partly written by Sydney Chaplin). Chaplin did all of the skating himself. He was aided by wires for only those shots that required him to appear as if he were about to fall backward while on skates, causing pandemonium in the rink. His agility and grace make *The Rink* one of his most memorable early comedies.

Charlie the waiter in THE RINK *(1916)*

Left: Charlie protects Edna (Edna Purviance) from the advances of Mr. Stout (Eric Campbell) in THE RINK.

Below: Charlie causes chaos in THE RINK, *in which Chaplin displays his phenomenal roller-skating skills. Also on the floor of the rink are Edna Purviance, Eric Campbell (with Charlie's roller skate under his chin), and Albert Austin.*

Above: When the bully (Eric Campbell) bends down the lamp-post in a display of strength, Charlie leaps on the bully's back, fits the lamp over the bully's head, and turns on the gas to asphyxiate him in EASY STREET *(1917). It is one of the most famous images in motion-picture comedy. (Frame enlargement from 35mm motion-picture film)*

Bottom: The great Russian ballet dancer and choreographer Vaslav Nijinsky (with his arm around Chaplin at right) and his company visit Chaplin and members of his production (including Eric Campbell behind and to the left of Nijinsky, Edna Purviance standing at center, and John Rand at extreme left) on the set of EASY STREET. *Others pictured include Pierre Monteux, Lydia Lopokova, Olga Spessivtseva, and Richard Herndon (to whom this photograph was inscribed by Chaplin). Nijinsky greatly admired Chaplin's movements and thought him a natural dancer. This idea was echoed sometime later—with more jealousy than admiration—by comedian W. C. Fields, who, after watching* EASY STREET *in a 1930s revival, remarked, "The son of a bitch is a ballet dancer. He's the best ballet dancer that ever lived and if I get a good chance I'll kill him with my bare hands."*

Opposite: After rendering the bully (Eric Campbell) unconscious, Charlie is now feared by all the toughs on his beat in EASY STREET. *The T-shaped street set was based on Chaplin's childhood memories of the streets and alleys of South London.*

EASY STREET (1917)

Chaplin's last four Mutual-Chaplin Specials are among his finest works. While each of the preceding Mutual comedies took approximately one month to make, Chaplin took more time with the last four (ten months in total), which extended his twelve-month contract period to approximately eighteen months. For *Easy Street*, his ninth Mutual film and the most famous of the twelve, Chaplin ordered the first of the T-shaped street sets that he would consistently use to provide a perfect backdrop to his comedy. The look and feel of *Easy Street* evoke the South London of his childhood (the name "Easy Street" suggests "East Street," the street of Chaplin's birthplace). Poverty, starvation, drug addiction, and urban violence—subjects that foreshadow the social concerns in his later films—are interwoven in "an exquisite short comedy," wrote Walter Kerr, "humor encapsulated in the regular rhythms of light verse."[23]

In *Easy Street*, Charlie is a derelict who is reformed in the Hope Mission by a minister (Albert Austin) and a beautiful mission worker (Edna Purviance). He makes a fresh start when he becomes a police officer, but his beat is Easy Street, the toughest section of the city. A giant bully (Eric Campbell) terrorizes the lawless Easy Street, and all attempts by the police to subdue him have failed. After their encounters with the bully and his gang, police officers are carried away on stretchers. Charlie's defeat of the bully is one of Chaplin's most memorable sequences. Charlie pounds the bully on the head with his truncheon, but the bully is unharmed. In a display of strength, the bully bends a lamppost. Charlie quickly climbs on the bully's back, fits the lamp over the bully's head, and turns on the gas, rendering the bully uncon-

Chaplin was justifiably pleased with the film's opening gag, which contained the element of surprise. He wrote in 1918:

> Figuring out what the audience expects, and then doing something different, is great fun to me. In one of my pictures, *The Immigrant,* the opening scene showed me leaning far over the side of a ship. Only my back could be seen and from the convulsive shudders of my shoulders it looked as though I was seasick. If I had been, it would have been a terrible mistake to show it in the picture. What I was doing was deliberately misleading the audience. Because, when I straighted up, I pulled a fish on the end of a line into view, and the audience saw that, instead of being seasick, I had been leaning over the side to catch the fish. It came as a total surprise and got a roar of laughter.[27]

The gag foreshadows a similar gag in the most celebrated moment in *The Idle Class,* in which Chaplin, with his back to the camera, appears to be sobbing, yet when he turns around, he is actually mixing himself a drink with a cocktail shaker.

Undertones of social criticism are suggested in *The Immigrant,* the first of many Chaplin films to contain such themes, which were seldom found in comedy films of this period. For instance, when the immigrants first see the Statue of Liberty the immigration officials rope all the foreigners together like cattle, causing Charlie to cast a quizzical second look at the land of the free. When an officer turns away from Charlie, Charlie kicks him in the backside. Carlyle Robinson, Chaplin's publicity director, joined the Lone Star Studio on the day the dailies of this sequence were screened. Chaplin asked his new employee what he thought of them.

"Very funny and very realistic," Robinson replied.
"Do you find anything shocking in it?"
"Not that I can recall."

Apparently, the social-criticism issue had been raised by one of Chaplin's associates, and Robinson's answer satisfied Chaplin. As Robinson affirmed, "The scene was kept in the final version of the film and there was never the least complaint."[28] Indeed, the critics were not put off by the traces of social commentary in the film. Julian Johnson wrote in *Photoplay,* "In its roughness and apparent simplicity it is as much a jewel as a story by O. Henry, and no full-time farce seen on our stages in years has been more adroitly, more perfectly worked out."[29]

The Immigrant also is significant in Chaplin's evolution as a filmmaker because it is the first film in which his character embarks upon a full-fledged romantic relationship. To help evoke a romantic mood on the set, Chaplin—like many filmmakers of the silent era—employed mood musicians to play music off-camera while scenes were being filmed. Chaplin wrote in his autobiography, "Even in those early comedies I strove for mood; usually music created it. An old song called 'Mrs. Grundy' created the mood for *The Immigrant.* The tune had a wistful tenderness that suggested two lonely derelicts getting married on a doleful, rainy day."[30]

Chaplin retained a special place in his memory for the film. He wrote in *My Life in Pictures,* "*The Immigrant* touched me more than any other film I made. I thought the end had quite a poetic feeling."[31]

Chaplin and his brother Sydney went to San Francisco for a vacation after completing *The Immigrant.* Chaplin was growing tired by the hectic pace of the series; four months passed before the last film, *The Adventurer,* was released—the longest interval between films for Chaplin in his career up to that time.

The most popular of the Mutuals, *The Adventurer* begins and ends with a chase. It is the fastest-paced film of the series, and although it has more slapstick than *Easy Street* and *The Immigrant,* it is redeemed by its construction, its characterization, and Chaplin's balletic grace.

In *The Adventurer,* Charlie is an escaped convict who lives up to his nickname, "The Eel," a slippery character who eludes the police by burrowing into the sand. He scales the side of a cliff at breakneck speed (an effect achieved by undercranking the camera and staging the action in reverse), throwing rocks, kicking, and slipping under the legs of prison guards. In a stolen bathing suit he rescues two women from drowning—a beautiful young woman (Edna Purviance) and her mother (Marta Golden). They bring him home as their guest, and he poses as "Commodore Slick" to conceal the fact that he is an escaped convict. To Judge Brown (Henry Bergman), Charlie looks familiar; and a rival for Edna's affections (Eric Campbell) sees an account of Charlie's escape, published with his photograph, in the newspaper. The rival alerts the police; the prison guards arrive, and Charlie is chased around the house and eventually makes his escape.

A famous moment in the film has Charlie spilling ice cream down the front of his oversize trousers. Chaplin wrote a detailed analysis of the scene in his article "What People Laugh At":

> [A]ll my pictures are built around the idea of getting me into trouble and so giving me the chance to be desperately serious in my attempt to appear as a normal little gentleman. That is why, no matter how desperate the predicament is, I am always very much in earnest about clutching my cane, straightening my derby hat, and fixing my tie, even though I have just landed on my head.
>
> I am so sure of this point that I not only try to get myself into embarrassing situations, but I also incriminate the other characters in the picture. When I do this, I always aim for economy of means. By this I mean that when one incident can get two big, separate laughs, it is much better than two individual incidents. In *The Adventurer* I accomplish this by first placing myself on a balcony, eating ice cream with a girl. On the floor directly underneath the balcony I put a stout, dignified, well-dressed woman at a table. Then, while eating the ice cream, I let a piece drop off my spoon, slip through my baggy trousers, and drop from the balcony onto this woman's neck.
>
> The first laugh came at my embarrassment over my own predicament. The second, and the much greater one, came when the ice cream landed on the woman's neck and she shrieked and started to dance around. Only one incident had been used, but it had got two people into trouble, and had also got two big laughs.

Simple as this trick seems there were two real points of human nature involved in it. One was the delight the average person takes in seeing wealth and luxury in trouble. The other was the tendency of the human being to experience within himself the emotions he sees on the stage or screen.

One of the things most quickly learned in theatrical work is that people as a whole get satisfaction from seeing the rich get the worst of things. The reason for this, of course, lies in the fact that nine tenths of the people in the world are poor, and secretly resent the wealth of the other tenth.

Above: Charlie, an escaped convict known as "the Eel," hides from a prison guard (Frank. J. Coleman) in THE ADVENTURER *(1917).*

Opposite: Chaplin, clad in his prisoner's costume, poses on top of a rock on location for THE ADVENTURER, *with Santa Monica Bay in the background. At five feet six and a half inches in height, Chaplin maintained that had he stood any taller, he would have found it more challenging to be a sympathetic screen character.*

Judge Brown (Henry Bergman), his wife (Marta Golden), and his daughter (Edna Purviance) watch as a suitor for Judge Brown's daughter (Eric Campbell) studies Charlie's face, suspecting he is the escaped convict "the Eel" and not "Commodore Slick" as he pretends, in THE ADVENTURER.

If I had dropped the ice cream, for example, on a scrubwoman's neck, instead of getting laughs, sympathy would have been aroused for the woman. Also, because a scrubwoman has no dignity to lose, the point would not have been funny. Dropping ice cream down a rich woman's neck, however, is, in the minds of the audience, just giving the rich what they deserve.

By saying that human beings experience the same emotions as the people in the incidents they witness, I mean that—taking ice cream as an example—when the rich woman shivered the audience shivered with her. A thing that puts a person in an embarrassing predicament must always be perfectly familiar to an audience, or else the people will miss the point entirely. Knowing that the ice cream is cold, the audience shivers. If something was used that the audience did not recognize at once, it would not be able to appreciate the point as well. On this same fact was based the throwing of custard pies in the early pictures. Everyone knew that custard pie is squashy, and so was able to appreciate how the actor felt when one landed on him.[32]

Other highlights from the film include Charlie donning a lampshade and freezing in position as the guards run past him and a chase in which he dodges a prison guard and the rival by using sliding double doors. Charlie catches the rival's head between the doors.

It is ironic that in his last film of the demanding Mutual series Charlie escapes from prison. In contrast with Essanay, Chaplin's relationship with the Mutual Film Corporation ended amicably. Indeed, Mutual offered him a million dollars for eight more films, but Chaplin sought even greater independence. He later wrote, "Fulfilling the Mutual contract, I suppose, was the happiest period of my career. I was light and unencumbered, twenty-seven years old, with fabulous prospects and a friendly, glamorous world before me."[33]

The Mutual-Chaplin Specials were frequently revived theatrically, nontheatrically, and in prints sold to libraries and for home use. Chaplin's son Sydney remembered watching some of the Mutual comedies with Jerry Epstein at the Silent Movie Theatre in Hollywood in the late 1940s. They enjoyed the films, but not nearly as much as the man several rows behind them, who was manically and uncontrollably laughing. When the show ended and the two turned to investigate, they discovered the laughter was from Chaplin himself. "It was my father who was laughing the loudest! Tears were rolling down his cheeks from laughing so hard and he had to wipe his eyes with his handkerchief. He was sitting with Oona. He had brought her to the Silent Movie because she had not seen any of them before."[34]

Perhaps Chaplin had such a fondness for the Mutuals because, in many ways, the films served as a foundation for all that would follow in Chaplin's remarkable career. Chaplin's prior films, although wonderful in their time, failed to ignite the cinematic alchemy that would come to be called *Chaplinesque*—the blending of comedy, pathos, and social commentary into a single narrative whole, as seen in *The Vagabond, Easy Street,* and *The Immigrant,* and in all of Chaplin's best films thereafter. No other filmmaker had consistently injected this combination of elements with such an exquisite level of skill into a comedy film. The Mutual films are extraordinary because they represent the only period in Chaplin's career during which he allowed himself to revel in rather than to revile the creative process, to tinker in his comedic laboratory, resulting in some of the finest work of his career. A testament to the enduring quality of the Mutuals is not only that others appropriated sequences from the films (including Chaplin's contemporaries Harold Lloyd and Buster Keaton, and later comedians such as the Marx Brothers), but that Chaplin himself often borrowed liberally from them in his later, more sophisticated films. Perhaps he had great fondness for the Mutuals simply for the same reason that generations of audiences have as well—because of the sheer joy, comic inventiveness, and hilarity of this remarkable series of films.

Above left: Chaplin and Mary Pickford, costumed for REBECCA OF SUNNYBROOK FARM *(1917), on the shoulders of Douglas Fairbanks at the beginning of the trio's friendship, Hollywood, 1917*

Above right: Chaplin, Edna Purviance, and Chaplin's friend and press representative Rob Wagner arrive in Hawaii for a five-week vacation upon the completion of THE ADVENTURER *in August 1917. Chaplin's intimate relationship with Purviance was waning by this time, although they continued to work together until 1923.*

First National and First Marriage

If the films Chaplin made for Mutual served as his early comedic laboratory, the best of the films he created for the First National Exhibitors' Circuit reveal a filmmaker growing into his full artistic power. The First Nationals contain some of Chaplin's best constructed and most-loved films (*Shoulder Arms* and *The Kid*) as well as two failures (*Sunnyside* and *A Day's Pleasure*). In the First National films, Chaplin explored new ideas and approaches, such as emphasizing character and realism rather than the slapstick and sometimes exaggerated performances that had largely characterized his early films. His screen character becomes gentler, the supporting roles are less caricatured and more textured, and the plots and settings are more realistic. Charlie is just as graceful as he was in the Mutuals, but far less frenetic. Most important, he develops his artistic soul during this period, particularly with *The Kid*. The First National films are longer than the Mutuals, which allowed greater character development and content. They may evoke less laughter, but in these films Chaplin courageously eschewed easy laughs in his bold strides toward cinematic maturity.

Above: Chaplin's shoes and footprints in the pavement at Chaplin Studios, anticipating the famous forecourt of Sid Grauman's Chinese Theatre in Hollywood, January 1918

Opposite: Chaplin poses in riding clothes outside the gates of the Chaplin Studios, 1919.

Right: Left to right: Chaplin, unidentified man, Henry Bergman (in costume), unidentified man, Eric Campbell, Albert Austin (in Hindu costume), and Sydney Chaplin at the groundbreaking of the Chaplin Studios, October 1917. Chaplin filmed sequences during the construction for an abandoned film he titled HOW MOVING PICTURES ARE MADE.

Middle right: The Chaplin Studios, c. 1918, which were to serve as Chaplin's filmmaking base for the rest of his career in America. To appease the nearby residents, who were suspicious about the respectability of the motion-picture industry, the exterior was configured as a row of cottages in an English village. The structures have survived into the twenty-first century, having been declared a historical-cultural monument by the Los Angeles Cultural Heritage Board in 1969.

Lower left: Chaplin breaks ground for the Chaplin Studios at the corner of La Brea and De Longpre Avenues, Hollywood, with an informal ceremony witnessed by his permanent crew, October 1917.

Lower right: Chaplin with one his most supportive associates, Henry Bergman, c. 1918. Bergman's devotion to Chaplin was legendary at the Chaplin Studios. Chaplin once joked of Bergman, "He'd kiss me if I'd let him."

Opposite: Charlie is an American soldier who includes in his carrying kit a mousetrap, a kettle, an eggbeater, and a grater (which serves as a back scratcher when the vermin become troublesome).

Left: Charlie sadly sits in a World War I dugout with his fellow doughboys (Park Jones at left and Sydney Chaplin at right) in SHOULDER ARMS. *Chaplin daringly made the real-life horrors of the Western Front—such as the isolation of trench warfare, snipers, and chemical weapons— into a great comedy film.*

Chaplin originally planned *Shoulder Arms* as a feature-length film in three acts. He remembered:

> *Shoulder Arms* was originally planned to be five reels. The beginning was to be "home life," the middle "the war," and the end "the banqueting," showing all the crowned heads of Europe celebrating my heroic act of capturing the Kaiser. And, of course, in the end I wake up.
>
> The sequences before and after the war were discarded. The banquet was never photographed, but the beginning was. The comedy was by suggestion, showing Charlot walking home with his family of four children. He leaves them for a moment, then comes back wiping his mouth and belching. He enters the house and immediately a frying pan comes into the picture and hits him on the head. His wife is never seen, but an enormous chemise is hanging on the kitchen line, suggesting her size.
>
> In the next sequence Charlot is examined for induction and made to strip down to the altogether. On a bevelled glass office-door he sees the name "Dr. Francis [Maud]." A shadow appears to open the door, and, thinking it is a woman, he escapes through another door and finds himself in a maze of glass-partitioned offices where lady clerks are engrossed in their work. As one lady looks up he dodges behind a desk, only to expose himself to another, eventually escaping through another door into more glass-partitioned offices, getting further and further away from his base, until he finds himself out on a balcony, nude, over-looking a busy thoroughfare below. This sequence, although photographed, was never used. I thought it better to keep Charlot a nondescript with no background and to discover him already in the army.[8]

The domestic-life prologue and physical examination scene that Chaplin discarded represented the first month's work on the film. In an era when a month was considered a possible schedule to film a high-quality feature, Chaplin's decision to scrap these marvelous scenes was a staggering display of self-censorship. However, Chaplin assumed all the production costs beyond the $140,000 First National advanced to him and was willing to sacrifice his own money in the pursuit of his artistic vision. When Chaplin resumed filming, he proceeded with a clearer sense of the structure and continued unabated, without the usual breaks to work on the story.

In *Shoulder Arms*, Charlie is a member of "The Awkward Squad" and incapable of the regimentation commands—to stand at attention, to march, to turn, to shoulder arms, and, of course, to keep his feet turned in. "Over There" Charlie arrives in the mis-

Right: True Boardman Jr. (far left), Marion Feducha, and Frankie Lee play Chaplin's sons in the deleted prologue of SHOULDER ARMS. *"All three of us kids found Charlie kind but exacting," remembered Boardman in 2002. "He knew what he wanted in a scene and he'd keep doing takes until he got it. At eight years old, I didn't know what being a perfectionist was, but we were certainly working for one. One day during the lunch break we three children were in the patio area in the center of the then-new Chaplin Studios at Sunset and La Brea. There, on a table, were Charlie's derby hat and cane. Being an enterprising eight year old, I decided to demonstrate my skill at 'being' Charlie Chaplin. I put on the hat, picked up the cane, then proceeded to prove to my fellow 'sons of Charlie' how I could do his famous walk, complete with the revolving cane.*

But then I heard a voice behind me saying, 'True, boy, if you are going to try to imitate someone, you should at least learn to do it correctly.' He then took the hat and cane and proceeded to demonstrate his technique. He then handed them back to me and said, 'Now show us,' which I did. Charlie said, 'Better, my boy. Infinitely better,' and walked off. That was eighty-four years ago. And I can still do it—though still probably not up to Charlie's incomparable and exacting standards."

Below: Chaplin, in part of his tree costume, on location for SHOULDER ARMS. *He recalled in* MY AUTOBIOGRAPHY, *"*SHOULDER ARMS *was made in the middle of a sizzling heat wave. Working inside a camouflaged tree (as I did in one of the sequences) was anything but comfortable."*

Far left: Studio visitor Marie Dressler improvises with Chaplin (out of costume save his helmet and coat) in the trench set during production of SHOULDER ARMS, July 11, 1918.

Left: A pretty young French-woman (Edna Purviance) tends to the wound on Charlie's hand in SHOULDER ARMS.

Below: Charlie (looking similar to the future Adolf Hitler and strik-ing a pose characteristic of Hynkel in THE GREAT DICTATOR) disguis-es himself as a German officer to rescue the Frenchwoman (Edna Purviance) and his pal (Sydney Chaplin) in SHOULDER ARMS.

erable trenches and fantasizes about being back home and comforting things such as a cocktail at a bar. Aside from the comedy, the film contains touching pathos, most memorably the scene in which Charlie is the only soldier who does not receive a letter or package during the distribution of the mail. He stands over another doughboy's shoulder and vicariously reads his letter from home with him, echoing all the reactions that are expressed on the soldier's face—a smile, a look of concern, a sigh of relief. Finally, Charlie is given an unwanted package that contains hard biscuits and Limburger cheese. The cheese stinks so badly that Charlie dons his gas mask to eat it. He ultimately hurls the cheese over his trench and it lands on a diminutive German officer in an enemy trench. Later Charlie's dugout is flooded, and his bunk is submerged under water. He nevertheless settles down into bed, using a gramophone horn as a snorkel.

One intertitle became an often-quoted phrase of the time. Charlie is ordered over the top and captures the entire German trench. Asked how he managed to capture thirteen German soldiers singlehandedly, Charlie simply replies, "I surrounded them."

The trench scenes depicting Charlie and his fellow soldiers coping with the wretched conditions—bad food, floods, vermin, and the constant threat from snipers, shells, and chemical weapons—required four weeks of filming to complete. The scenes were a vivid evocation of the reality of the Western Front. When Chaplin reissued *Shoulder Arms* as part of the compilation *The Chaplin Revue,* he preceded the film with footage of World War I from the archives of the Imperial War Museum in London to demonstrate the veracity of his production.

Clad in a heavy costume, Chaplin spent four days on location in still-rural Hollywood during a blistering summer heat wave to achieve one of his most memorable sequences. Charlie, sent on a spying mission, is disguised as a tree trunk within enemy territory. His legs are encased in barklike sheathing, his arms extended as branches with twigs at the ends, his face cautiously peering through a knothole. He waddles in no-man's-land, freezing into position as a rooted tree when a German patrol arrives to set up camp. A large German soldier with an axe approaches, determined to chop him for firewood, but Charlie cleverly defuses the situation and saves his pal (Sydney Chaplin) from the firing squad before Charlie the tree scurries into a densely wooded forest to seek refuge.

Charlie meets a charming young Frenchwoman (Edna Purviance), but German soldiers soon arrive, and Charlie must make his escape. The French girl is arrested for aiding the Allies, and Charlie climbs into the building where she is being held. Pursued by the enemy, he changes into a German officer's uniform and manages to free the girl as well as his pal, who has again been captured. While the Kaiser plans his campaign, Charlie and his pal overpower the Kaiser's chauffeurs and steal their uniforms. The Kaiser and his entourage enter the car, and while his pal telegraphs Allied command, Charlie and the French

girl, disguised in the uniforms, drive the Kaiser back to Allied lines. Charlie captures the Kaiser, the Crown Prince, and Von Hindenberg. An intertitle reads, "Peace on earth—good will to all mankind." Charlie is feted as a hero until, alas, he is awakened; he is still a new recruit of the awkward squad, and his adventures were just a dream.

Chaplin became tired from the film's long production (seventy-one days shooting and thirty days of preproduction and postproduction for a total of 101 days) and became dissatisfied and discouraged with the film. He claimed in his autobiography to have considered scrapping the film in its entirety until he showed it to Douglas Fairbanks in Chaplin's projection room. "From the beginning Fairbanks went into roars of laughter, stopping only for coughing spells," remembered Chaplin, "Sweet Douglas, he was my greatest audience."[9]

Chaplin was heartened by Fairbanks's reaction and began to understand a truism that he would return to throughout his career: often the best way for the human spirit to cope with unspeakable hardship and tragedy is through humor. The film was released on October 20, 1918, three weeks prior to the Armistice.

Shoulder Arms, released as a three-reel comedy, was one of Chaplin's greatest commercial successes and among the most popular films of the World War I period. For many years, critics and the public used the film as the standard to measure the quality of all comedy films.

THE BOND (1918)

Beyond selling war bonds, Chaplin agreed to donate a propaganda short film to the United States government for the fourth Liberty Loan bond drive. In order to deliver the short on time, he stopped production on *Shoulder Arms* and on August 15, 1918, began *The Bond* (also known as *Charlie Chaplin in a Liberty Loan Appeal*), a one-reel film completed in just six working days. The charming film has four episodes, each introduced by an intertitle and illustrating the various types of bonds: "The bond of friendship" begins a sequence with Charlie having a chance encounter with a friend (Albert Austin) who detains him from an appointment—despite Charlie's attempts to excuse himself—only to ask Charlie to lend him money. "The bond of love" finds Charlie meeting a flirtatious woman (Edna Purviance) who catches his attention by lifting her skirt. Charlie hangs his cane on the stylized crescent moon in the background; Cupid (Dorothy Rosher),

Chaplin and Edna Purviance in a scene from THE BOND *(1918), a one-reel film Chaplin made for the fourth Liberty Loan campaign during World War I. The expressionistic style of the set design was a result of Chaplin's desire to produce the film quickly and economically.*

appears behind the moon and shoots Charlie with an arrow of love. He responds to the puncture with a dance before he and Edna are bonded together by Cupid with a ribbon. "The marriage bond" has Charlie and Edna at the altar, with his friend enthusiastically throwing rice and knocking the bridegroom senseless with a hurled shoe. "And most important of all the Liberty Bond" demonstrates how money given to Liberty Bonds arms the military forces and protects Lady Liberty (Edna Purviance) from Kaiser Wilhelm (Sydney Chaplin). The film concludes with Charlie knocking out the Kaiser with a large mallet representing Liberty Bonds. Charlie assumes the pose of a big-game hunter by placing one foot on the supine Kaiser and encourages the viewer to buy war bonds. As he cheers and smiles at the camera, the scene fades.

The use of simple, suggestive white properties set against a black backdrop was born out of economy but nevertheless gave *The Bond* an appealing, stylized look. A fine blend of comedy and patriotic propaganda, *The Bond* was distributed free to American cinemas in September 1918.

Opposite top: Chaplin during the third Liberty Loan bond drive in Philadelphia, April 1918. Following immediately after a grueling effort to complete A DOG'S LIFE, the strain of the drive left Chaplin ill with exhaustion but not before he sold millions of dollars' worth of bonds.

Opposite bottom: Chaplin with five-year-old Dorothy Rosher during production of THE BOND. Outtakes from the film survive showing Chaplin playing with Dorothy, the daughter of Mary Pickford's eminent cinematographer Charles Rosher, to relax her for the cameras. In her role as Cupid, Dorothy worked two days (August 17 and 19, 1919) at a rate of $10 per day.

Left: The Tramp knocks out the Kaiser (Sydney Chaplin) with a large mallet representing Liberty Bonds at the climax of THE BOND.

Below: Chaplin, Sydney Chaplin (costumed as Kaiser Wilhelm), and Henry Bergman (costumed as John Bull) share a newspaper during production of THE BOND. Alf Reeves, general manager of the Chaplin Studios, is seated in the background.

Chaplin met Mildred Harris, who became his first wife, in the latter part of 1917 at a party held at Samuel Goldwyn's beach house. The blonde-haired, blue-eyed Harris was sixteen years old and had been on screen since 1910. She was at that time appearing in films directed by Lois Weber at Universal. She was captivated by Chaplin, who was Hollywood's most eligible bachelor. Novelist Theodore Dreiser, a friend of Chaplin's, described her in 1920 as "very babydollish."[10] She was also ambitious. She and her mother manipulated Chaplin into marriage. Initially, she flirtatiously asked to be driven home. Later she called him, and he invited her to dinner. "There were dinners, dances, moonlit nights and ocean drives, and the inevitable happened—Mildred began to worry," remembered Chaplin in his autobiography.[11]

Harris informed Chaplin that she was pregnant just as he had completed *Shoulder Arms.* To avoid scandal and possible prosecution for sexual involvement with a minor, he was coerced to marry her. Chaplin and Harris were wed in a simple ceremony on September 23, 1918, and had a weeklong honeymoon on Santa Catalina Island, off the coast of Los Angeles. They first took up residence at a rented house located at 2000 DeMille Drive in the Laughlin Park section of Los Angeles and later moved (along with Mildred's mother) to 674 South Oxford Drive in Beverly Hills. Chaplin was bored with his child-wife from the very beginning. As he confided to Douglas Fairbanks, she was "no mental heavyweight."[12] Mildred was frustrated by his lack of attention to domestic life and his concentration on his work to the exclusion of everything else. Further exacerbating the problems of the marriage was Chaplin's discovery that the pregnancy had been a concocted false alarm. There was a brief reconciliation between the two when Mildred in fact did become pregnant; yet the forced domesticity and incompatibility of the couple negatively affected Chaplin's work.

Mildred gave birth to a malformed son, named Norman Spencer Chaplin, on July 7, 1919. The child lived only three days and was buried in Inglewood Cemetery in a grave marked, "The Little Mouse July 7–July 10, 1919." "The Little Mouse" had been

Mildred's pet name for her pitiful child. Chaplin later told a friend that the undertaker had manipulated a smile on the infant's face, although the baby had never smiled in his short life.[13]

Chaplin later recalled, "Although I had grown fond of Mildred, we were irreconcilably mismated. Her character was not mean, but exasperatingly feline. I could not reach her mind. It was cluttered with pink-ribboned foolishness. She seemed in a dither, looking always for other horizons."[14] Chaplin and Mildred separated during the production of *The Kid,* and Chaplin moved back to the Los Angeles Athletic Club while Mildred stayed at the Beverly Hills house. At first the separation was amicable, but later the press published interviews quoting the attention-needy Mildred that became increasingly less favorable toward Chaplin. Chaplin, in turn, became more irritated with her.

Yet, it was Mildred who ultimately filed for divorce, necessitating the halting of the filming of *The Kid* on March 15, 1920. Initially Mildred accused Chaplin of desertion, but by March 22, 1920, her attorneys changed the grounds to cruelty, perhaps to force Chaplin's hand and obtain a larger divorce settlement. Harris also attempted to attach to her claim future profits from the uncompleted *The Kid.* First National, in dispute with Chaplin over the distribution of the film, assisted her in this effort. By August the divorce suit began, but Chaplin's attorneys indicated that they would not contest it provided that Mildred's lawyers withdrew an order restraining him from selling *The Kid.* The divorce was granted on November 19, 1920, and Mildred was awarded $100,000 and a share of community property.

Mildred Harris's career prospered for a short time as a result of the publicity from her marriage and being billed in films as Mildred Harris Chaplin under contract to Louis B. Mayer. However, her career quickly declined after the divorce, though she did find some minor film roles and later worked as an extra. Harris filed for bankruptcy in 1922 and in the following year married real estate broker Edward T. (Terry) MacGovern, with whom she had a son in 1925. That marriage also ended in divorce. In 1936 she married vaudeville producer William P. Fleckenstein and subsequently worked in vaudeville and nightclubs. She died of pneumonia following surgery in 1944.

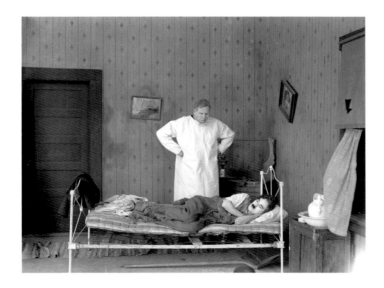

SUNNYSIDE (1919)

Although *Sunnyside*, Chaplin's third film for First National, is an interesting experiment combining the seemingly disparate elements of whimsy in a pastoral setting, routine slapstick, and serious romance, it (along with Chaplin's next, *A Day's Pleasure*) is the least successful of the films he made under his First National contract. Yet, *Sunnyside* is important because it reveals that Chaplin was pushing his Tramp character toward a gentler persona. This transition will come to completion in *The Kid*, a comedy film with true dramatic sequences, in which the Tramp—and Chaplin's films—reach a new level of emotional development.

Chaplin commenced production on *Sunnyside*, which had the working title *Jack of All Trades*, on November 4, 1918, but from the start he did not have a clear concept beyond the rural setting and therefore accomplished very little on the film. What little Chaplin filmed he spent his time editing, becoming so discouraged by the unevenness of his work that he stayed away from the studio for six weeks. It was a creative block unlike any he had ever experienced. Chaplin returned January 29, 1919, still with-

out any inspiration. Finally, in March 1919, after 150 days of production, during two-thirds of which no filming occurred, he had a creative surge that lasted three weeks: he shot 1,000 feet (more than fifteen minutes of film) on many of these days. Chaplin completed production on April 15, 1919, and the film had its premiere exactly two months later.

The film is set in the village of Sunnyside, and Charlie is the entire staff of a rural hotel and farm. His boss (Tom Wilson) is a stern man, yet Charlie submits frequently to kicks in the rear from his employer without retaliation. While the villagers attend church services, Charlie is herding cattle. "His church, the sky—his altar, the landscape" reads an intertitle. Preoccupied with his hymnal, Charlie inadvertently allows his charges to wander off on their own. When he goes off to search for the stray bovines, he discovers one has entered the church and is wreaking havoc upon the service. Charlie attempts to ride the uncontrollable bull into the street but is thrown into a ditch and knocked unconscious. He dreams he is awakened by four nymphs who lead him in a pastoral dance. When Charlie falls onto a cactus patch, his eccentric dancing escalates to an even more erratic and furious pace as he removes the painful needles. The dance, the highlight of the film, was Chaplin's homage to Nijinsky's legendary

Upper left: Charlie's boss (Tom Wilson) looks upon his slumbering farmhand with disapproval in SUNNYSIDE (1919).

Above: Blinded with shaving cream, a villager (Albert Austin) endures Charlie's dubious skills as a barber in a sequence Chaplin filmed and edited together but ultimately deleted from the final cut of SUNNYSIDE. Chaplin returned to this comedy situation twenty years later for one of the

best-known scenes of THE GREAT DICTATOR. As several of Chaplin's associates have noted, Chaplin had a mind like an attic, in which discarded ideas were never forgotten. Frequently, old ideas were referenced in later films.

Left: Chaplin by the studio swimming pool, as Rollie Totheroh films Edna Purviance and three other bathing beauties in the background, for HOW MOVING PICTURES ARE MADE, 1918

Top: Chaplin entertains some local children while on location for SUNNYSIDE.

Bottom: Chaplin demonstrates to Tom Wilson how to throttle Loyal Underwood, as Henry Bergman, Edna Purviance, and cameraman Jack Wilson watch carefully during a staged "rehearsal" during production of SUNNYSIDE, 1919. *The rehearsal footage was intended for the abandoned* HOW MOVING PICTURES ARE MADE. *Although the two-reel comedy documentary was never completed, part of the material filmed for the project was later used by Chaplin to introduce his reissue of three First National films as a compilation titled* THE CHAPLIN REVUE *and later still in Richard Patterson's authorized documentary,* THE GENTLEMAN TRAMP. *In 1982, Kevin Brownlow and David Gill edited the* HOW MOVING PICTURES ARE MADE *material, selectively working from a surviving intertitle list found in the Chaplin Archives for continuity. Some of Chaplin's intertitles they chose to retain, others they did not. Furthermore, they modified the order of some of the sequences and included sequences Chaplin did not specify, calling their film* HOW TO MAKE MOVIES *(Chaplin had provisionally titled the film* HOW MOVING PICTURES ARE MADE *and also* HOW PICTURES ARE MADE*).* HOW TO MAKE MOVIES *was first shown at the twenty-sixth London Film Festival in 1982.*

performance in *L'après-midi d'un faune*, which Chaplin had seen and admired. The scene also displays Chaplin's balletic talents, which had been justifiably praised by critics.

Charlie's angry boss awakens him from his fantasy, and Charlie soon finds that a guest at the hotel is a rival for the affections of the girl (Edna Purviance). The intertitle "His last hope" introduces Charlie in a feeble attempt to imitate his adversary, the city chap, supplementing his best clothes with stockings over his boots to look like the city chap's spats and modifying his bamboo walking stick to suggest the city chap's cane with its built-in lighter for his cigarettes. His rivalry proves to be just a dream, and the city chap gives Charlie a generous tip before he departs, as Charlie and the girl embrace.

In *Sunnyside*, Charlie suffers true romantic despair and loss; and audiences saw, for the first time, more serious sequences of rejection than Chaplin had attempted before. The Tramp in *Sunnyside* is a pathetic little character who at times appears to feel even a little sorry for himself. Although the film ultimately

fails because the comedy seems routine and forced, *Sunnyside* is Chaplin's experiment with combining the elements that will later characterize his greatest films, beginning with *The Kid:* comedy, sentiment, fantasy, and romance. Yet, after *A Dog's Life* and *Shoulder Arms*, the critics and the public were disappointed with *Sunnyside*, regarding it as one of his least successful films. Chaplin blamed the failure of *Sunnyside*, in part, on his belief that his marriage to Mildred Harris was having a negative impact on his work. According to Chaplin, *Sunnyside* was "like pulling teeth. Without question marriage was having an effect on my creative faculties."[15]

In February 1974 Chaplin composed a score for *Sunnyside* with Eric James as his musical associate. The music was all original save for the song "When Other Lips" from *The Bohemian Girl*, which Chaplin was keen on using in the film. He instructed that a few cuts be made from the film as well. The music was recorded in two days in April and May 1974 at the Anvil Studios in Denham, England.

Opposite: Charlie as Pan twirls his hair into two horns and transforms a daisy into a pipe in the first dream sequence of SUNNYSIDE. During this period, Chaplin was fascinated by Nijinsky. Charlie's Arcadian dance with the nymphs (Helen Kohn, Olive Burton, Willie Mae Carson, and Olive Alcorn) is an homage to Nijinsky's legendary performance of L'APRÈS-MIDI D'UN FAUNE.

Left: Charlie is crestfallen after he peers into the window of Edna's home and finds her being courted by the city chap in SUNNYSIDE.

Below: Chaplin, holding a teacup, amuses the young women cast as the nymphs during a break in location filming for SUNNYSIDE.

Right: Chaplin with English sculptor, painter, and writer Clare Sheridan, November 1921

Middle right: Helen Keller, who learned to circumvent her blindness, deafness, and muteness, visits Chaplin at the studio during production of SUNNYSIDE. Keller was able to lip-read by placing her fingers on the lips and throat of those who talked with her. Her indomitable spirit and espousal of socialism impressed Chaplin.

Below: Chaplin signs his name to the main title of SUNNYSIDE. First National prominently used Chaplin's signature on all posters as well as on the main titles of the films themselves in an effort to avoid confusion with the many Chaplin reissues released under new titles and advertised as the latest Chaplin comedy.

Opposite: Charlie prepares to use a pin on the backside of a fellow passenger (Tom Wilson) to secure more seating space for himself and his family in A DAY'S PLEASURE (1919). Edna Purviance plays his wife, and Jackie Coogan (right), in his first film with Chaplin, plays the younger of Charlie's two children.

else, the Tramp reluctantly adopts the little boy. He soon becomes a loving and caring father, cutting diapers out of old cloth with a pair of scissors, stringing an ancient kettle with a nipple at the end of the spout near the baby's improvised hammock, and preparing a cane chair with a hole in its seat to be placed over a pail for toilet training.

Five years pass, and Jackie Coogan is now the ragamuffin child. The Tramp and the Kid are happily living as father and son but also as business partners. The Kid breaks windows, and the Tramp conveniently appears on the scene to fix glass as an itinerant glazier. Jackie inadvertently exposes their operation when, in front of a suspicious police officer, he runs to his "father," who pretends not to know him and kicks him away. Later, a doctor tending to an ill Jackie discovers that Charlie is not Jackie's real father. The doctor informs the county orphan asylum, whose officials attempt to take Jackie away from Charlie, but the two make their escape. Meanwhile the mother has become a star of great prominence; she has discovered that Jackie is her own child and wants him back. The Tramp and the Kid take refuge from the orphanage officials in a doss-house but are betrayed by the shelter attendant seeking the reward money for the child. Charlie, exhausted and defeated, sits on a stoop and dreams a comic pantomime version of heaven.

The dream sequence has been criticized as being incongruous with the rest of the film. Chaplin recalled being disappointed when playwright and novelist James Barrie, the king of whimsy and sentimental fantasy, thought the sequence was entirely unnecessary, to which Chaplin frankly responded that Barrie's own *A Kiss for Cinderella* influenced him.[21] Francis Hackett in *The New Republic* observed:

> The dream of Heaven I thought highly amusing. What amused me was its limitedness, its meagerness. It was like a simple man's version of the Big Change, made up from the few properties with which a simple man would be likely to be acquainted. The lack of inventiveness seemed to be its best point. Others tell me that it was a failure of inventiveness. Mayhap. But after suffering the success of movie-inventiveness so many times, with the whole apparatus of the factory employed to turn out some sort of slick statement or other, I rejoice over this bit of thin and faltering fantasy. And I venture to believe that it represents exactly what Chaplin intended. It was the simplified Heaven of the antic sprite whom Chaplin has created and whose inner whimsicality is here so amusingly indulged.[22]

Another fascinating aspect of the sequence was the casting of twelve-year-old Lillita MacMurray as the flirting angel. Chaplin again engaged her three years later, this time as the leading lady for his film, *The Gold Rush*. It was Chaplin who then gave her the professional name Lita Grey. Early in the production of *The Gold Rush*, Lita dropped out of the film to play the more coveted role of Mrs. Charles Chaplin in a marriage that brought him more unhappiness than his union with Mildred Harris.

The whole of December and the first week of January 1920 were spent on the most celebrated scene of the film, where Jackie is taken away from Charlie. Charlie and Jackie wage a heroic struggle against the orphanage officials, yet they are vanquished. Jackie is forced into the back of a truck and pleads to be returned to his father. A careful viewer can read his quivering lips begging, "I want my Daddy!" and "Oh, please!" as he clasps his hands in prayer and looks to heaven for divine intervention. It is a powerful, raw performance from a young child that has lost none of its emotion with time. Jackie is driven away as if he were another unfortunate stray plucked from the dirty streets. Chased by a police officer, Charlie performs an innovative and desperate race to the rescue as he fervently trips across the rooftops in a frantic attempt to free Jackie from the authorities. The climax of

Above: Charlie and Jackie are reunited in THE KID. *"We were both crying real tears," remembered Jackie Coogan in a 1977 interview with Kevin Brownlow, noting also that the film's original audience was moved and startled to see the mischievous Tramp they had always known shedding tears of joy and relief.*

Opposite: Charlie and Jackie hand in hand in THE KID

Right: Chaplin and Jackie Coogan at the studio during production of THE KID. Chaplin at turns adopted a parental role toward Coogan and extended the childlike aspect of his (and the Tramp's) character through his working relationship with Coogan.

Below: Chaplin plays the violin for Jackie Coogan at the studio.

Top: Chaplin as the eccentric Professor Bosco, the Dickensian proprietor of a flea circus, who has a flea jump from his one hand through a hoop formed by his other hand in the unreleased film THE PROFESSOR. The bulk of the two-reeler—of which only one cut scene and outtakes of another sequence survive—was filmed in three days, from September 30 to October 2, 1919, during a halt in production of THE KID. Much of the film was to be assembled utilizing unused scenes from previous productions. The genesis of the flea-circus routine began in the Essanay one-reeler BY THE SEA. Chaplin later attempted to introduce such a routine in THE CIRCUS and THE GREAT DICTATOR without success before eventually creating it in a simplified form in LIMELIGHT. Chaplin recalled in a 1957 interview with Margaret Hixman, "There's one joke that I've always wanted to use. I thought of it as long ago as THE KID, but I couldn't find a spot for it in that film. It's a man with a flea circus. He goes into a doss-house . . . [a]nd the fleas get loose. He runs around searching for the fleas, calling them by name. Everyone is scratching furiously. Finally, he manages to round up all the fleas but one. There's a big man with a great straggling beard. He spots a flea in the beard, picks it out, studies it intently, then says 'Sorry, wrong one' and puts it back. And the pay-off is when a scrawny old dog starts scratching itself. The flea trainer sees it, makes a grab for the dog; and it races off down the street with the little man, calling his lost fleas, chasing after. I used a little of that in LIMELIGHT, but I've never been able to fit the whole episode in anywhere."

Middle: Chaplin rehearses flying for the dream sequence in THE KID.

Bottom: Chaplin with twelve-year-old Lillita MacMurray (Lita Grey), as the flirting angel, during production of THE KID.

the scene, second only in emotional impact to the final moments of *City Lights*, finds the Tramp fiercely beating back the officials and reclaiming his child. As the Tramp kisses his trembling boy on the lips, tears of joy, relief, and exhaustion stream down their faces. It is quite simply one of cinema's most sublime moments.

As the filming of *The Kid* progressed, Chaplin quickly developed a close friendship with Jackie Coogan that clearly assumed paternal overtones. In many ways, Jackie replaced the child Chaplin had recently lost. Pairing the Tramp with a child also gave Chaplin an opportunity to explore and extend the childlike innocence of his own character. As Chaplin explained fifty years later, Jackie was the perfect actor for him because "He was so malleable."[23]

The late-Victorian setting of *The Kid* reflects the London of Chaplin's youth, particularly the attic room at 3 Pownall Terrace. In *My Life in Pictures,* Chaplin wrote of the garret the Tramp and the Kid shared: "A set means so much to me. I think myself into a thing and whatever comes out has been influenced a great deal by environment. This room was based to a large extent on the places in Lambeth and Kennington where Sydney and I had lived

with our mother when we were children. Perhaps that's why the film had some truth."[24]

Like little, abandoned Jackie in the film, Chaplin was virtually orphaned when his mother was remanded to the Cane Hill insane asylum. The most compelling scene of *The Kid*, when the authorities attempt to take Jackie away from the Tramp, becomes infinitely more poignant when one realizes it is a page out of Chaplin's own autobiography. The absolute terror of the prospect of the little boy being taken into care and put into an orphanage was a searing, emotional scar forever etched in Chaplin's psyche. Through this scene, he was probably reliving his own experience as a child losing his mother. The tears the Tramp cries at this moment in the film are Chaplin's tears, and this was the first time his audience had ever seen him cry in a dramatic context.

Jackie Coogan later recounted Chaplin's direction to him in the film:

> And I can remember him explaining to me what he wanted me to do. Then he also explained *why* he wanted me to do that. He said, "because, Jackie, it's this little boy; he's being torn from his friend." And as he started to dramatize it, I saw it in my mind's eye. He was a marvelous storyteller, narrator. And he put it on an intensely personal basis, so that when he said "Camera" and then "Action," and the welfare worker threw me into this truck, that's when the dam broke. Of course, I was really gone. I was torn up: "I want my daddy," and I was hysterical. And if you are going to portray yourself as being hysterical, you better get yourself hysterical or, brother, it's as phony as a three dollar bill.[25]

In fact, Chaplin actually directed Coogan by crying and playing all the drama off camera as Jackie imitated him.

Walter Kerr offered these observations about Chaplin's direction of Coogan in the film:

> It is not so much a matter of Jackie imitating Charlie as it is of transplanted identities, a give-and-take of personality. Chaplin

is able, through an alter ego and at this central stage in his career, to stand back and study what he is and what he does. It may have been this detachment—this opportunity of seeing himself—that enabled him to resolve the esthetic problem he had posed for himself when he set out to make seriousness funny.[26]

What is most intriguing about *The Kid*, however, is not that Chaplin sets the film in the London of his youth, but that he uses this setting to stage a revision of his own history. Scholars have suggested that an important element of Chaplin's psychological makeup reflects an unresolved relationship with his absent father. If this is the case, *The Kid* is a catharsis—Chaplin working out his frustration by creating the Tramp as the attentive, loving father that he never had. Psychiatrist Stephen M. Weissman has also noted that Chaplin is what psychologists call an "invulnerable"—a superachiever who responds to childhood adversity by

being "smart, resourceful, streetwise," behavior that is mirrored in the Kid.[27] To round out the fantasy, Chaplin even provides the child with a successful mother who, near the end of the film, welcomes the boy with tears and open arms. It is not coincidental that the Kid's mother finds her success as a vocal star. Chaplin's own mother longed to be a successful singer, but was impaired by illness and a voice that frequently failed her.

In early August 1920, when production of *The Kid* was completed, Chaplin—like his character in the film—was forced to flee to safety out of California with his negative of *The Kid* in an effort to thwart Mildred Harris's attempts to attach the film in her divorce settlement. In the early morning hours Chaplin ordered Totheroh and Jack Wilson to pack the 400,000 feet of uncut negative (Totheroh later recalled that the negative, mounted on 200-foot rolls, was packed in coffee tins that were crated).[28] The

Opposite top: Filming a scene, later abandoned, in which an unidentified actor in the role of the bully (ultimately played by Chuck Riesner) fires a pistol at Charlie.

Opposite middle: Charlie is restrained as a police officer (Tom Wilson) and a welfare official (Frank Campeau) attempt to take Jackie away from him in THE KID.

Opposite bottom: Chaplin hands over the negative of THE KID *to First National executives at the Chaplin Studios, December 30, 1920. Sol Lesser (second from left) accepts the film from Chaplin. Alf Reeves (center) displays the check. Sydney Chaplin is on the far right.*

Left: Chaplin examines the dailies of THE KID *in his editing room at the studio, 1920.*

twelve crates traveled by train with Totheroh, Wilson, and Chaplin to Salt Lake City, Utah, where California community property laws did not apply. They improvised an editing room in a hotel room and made a rough cut of the film, reducing 400,000 feet to 5,300 feet, and previewed it in Salt Lake City to great enthusiasm from the audience. Confident that the film was his finest work to date, Chaplin asked for better terms from First National. They feigned indifference and offered to pay him as if it were three two-reelers. Chaplin then spirited the film to New York and rented a vacant studio in Bayonne, New Jersey, to complete the editing and laboratory work. Throughout the adventure, Chaplin traveled incognito for fear he might be served a subpoena from Mildred's lawyers. After an acrimonious dispute, Chaplin asked for and eventually received from First National an advance of $1,500,000 and fifty percent of the net profits after the company recouped the advance. Chaplin recalled in his autobiography that by this time First National's "ruthless attitude had so embittered me that it impeded the progress of my work."[29]

The Kid had its world premiere on January 21, 1921, at Carnegie Hall in New York City, as a benefit for the Children's Fund of the National Board of Review of Motion Pictures, followed by its regular Broadway engagement at the Strand Theater on February 6. It was one of the great triumphs of Chaplin's career. All the reviews were ecstatic. Chaplin later recalled, "The reviews of my pictures have always been mixed. The one *every-body* praised was *The Kid*—and then they went too far, talked about Shakespeare. Well, it wasn't *that!*"[30] Perhaps not

Shakespeare, but comparisons to Dickens were appropriate. *The New Statesman* declared, Chaplin "is in *The Kid* a man of Dickensian genius,"[31] and prominent English drama critic James Agate thought the film "sublime," adding, "There is, at least to me, more emotion in a single tear of *The Kid* than all the bucketfuls of "Vesti la giubba" . . . I do not laugh at Charlie til I cry. I laugh *lest* I cry, which is a very different matter."[32]

The film made Jackie Coogan the most famous and successful child star of his time. One reason he had such an impact on audiences was that he symbolized all the orphans recently created as a result of World War I. Coogan went on to make several feature films for First National, most notably *Peck's Bad Boy* (1921) and *Oliver Twist* (1922), and later worked at the Metro Pictures and Metro-Goldwyn-Mayer studios. However, by the late 1920s his career had waned. Coogan was led to believe by his parents that the money he had earned from his own production company, Jackie Coogan Productions (an estimated four million dollars), would be his when he reached the age of twenty-one. In May 1935, nearly five months before his twenty-first birthday, his father and two other passengers were killed when the car he was driving crashed. His father's estate was left to his mother, who denied the existence of a trust fund for Jackie. In 1938 Coogan sued his mother and Arthur L. Bernstein, his former business manager, whom his mother had married. A settlement was reached in 1939, although by that time most of the money had dwindled away. Coogan's misfortune led to the passage in 1939 of California's Child Actors Bill, which was popularly known as the Coogan Law, legislation designed to protect the assets of minors working in the motion-picture industry under long-term contracts. Coogan reconciled with his mother, served in World War II, married four times (among his turbulent marriages was his first, to Betty Grable), and later became a journeyman actor. His most celebrated role in later years was as Uncle Fester in the television series *The Addams Family* (1964–66).

In 1971 Chaplin removed scenes from *The Kid* that he thought might appear too sentimental fifty years later and composed and recorded a musical score for the film for theatrical reissue, which premiered at Philharmonic Hall, New York City, for the Film Society of Lincoln Center's gala tribute to Chaplin on April 4, 1972, with Chaplin himself in attendance. It was also in 1972 that Chaplin and Coogan met for the last time, in Beverly Hills, at the Governor's Ball following the Academy Awards ceremony, at which Chaplin received an honorary Oscar. There are two conflicting stories of the meeting. One version is that Chaplin greeted Coogan warmly, and, as the brief meeting ended, Chaplin emphatically told Coogan's wife, "You must never forget that your husband is a genius."[33] The other account, told by Carol Matthau, wife of actor Walter Matthau and a close friend of Oona Chaplin, was that at first Chaplin feigned not to recognize Coogan. After the encounter, Chaplin indicated to his wife, Oona, that he was afraid Coogan wanted to ask him for residuals.[34] A bittersweet ending to an extraordinary friendship.

The Kid remains an important contribution to the art of film, not only because of its innovative use of dramatic sequences within a feature-length comedy but also because of the revelations it provides about its creator. Undoubtedly, when Chaplin penned the preface to *The Kid*, "A picture with a smile—and perhaps, a tear," he had his own artistic credo—and life—in mind.

THE IDLE CLASS (1921)

The two-reel film *The Idle Class*, Chaplin's sixth film for First National, is one of his funniest short comedies. Production on the film began on January 22, 1921, with the working title of *Vanity Fair*. Ultimately, Chaplin favored a more equivocal title—*The Idle Class*—for it is purposely not clear in the film which is the idle class: the idle rich or the idle poor. Chaplin plays both. The film took five months to complete, an amazingly long time for a two-reel comedy. As a point of comparison, the great silent feature-length drama *Tol'able David* (1921) was completed in seven weeks.

In *The Idle Class*, Chaplin plays dual roles as the alcoholic (euphemistically described as "Absent-Minded") Husband and the Tramp, his double. The Tramp travels south under the trains instead of inside them to indulge his pleasure—golf. He plays with balls he finds on the golf course and inadvertently takes another golfer's clubs. Soon Charlie has caused havoc on the links. Charlie's double, the Absent-Minded Husband, leaves his hotel room unaware that he has forgotten to put on his trousers. In the lobby he realizes his missing clothes, swipes a newspaper, and then poses as a midget, crouching behind the opened newspaper to cover himself as he hurries back to his suite.

Chaplin had devised the idea of a golf comedy while at Mutual and intended it to be his last film of the Mutual series before he

Opposite top: Chaplin with the great Russian ballerina Anna Pavlova at the Chaplin Studios, c. 1922

Opposite bottom: Chaplin with Max Linder at the Chaplin Studios, 1920. Linder was the one great cinema comedian before Chaplin, and Chaplin acknowledged his debt to Linder. Of Chaplin, Linder wrote in 1919, "He calls me his teacher, but I have been the happy one, to take lessons in his school."

Right: Charlie's neighbor on the park bench has his pocket picked by the man behind them. Charlie, however, is blamed for the theft and is soon chased by the police officer (Allan Garcia) in THE IDLE CLASS *(1921). In the background is the Beverly Hills Hotel. Photograph by Stern*

Right: Charlie the golf-loving Tramp prepares to tee off in THE IDLE CLASS. *Photograph by Stern*

Below: Charlie gladly takes a cigarette offered to him by a fellow golfer (John Rand) and stealthily appropriates the cigarette case as well while sharing a laugh in THE IDLE CLASS. *Photograph by Stern*

Opposite top: Chaplin on location in Griffith Park during production of THE IDLE CLASS. *Also seated are Mack Swain (center left, with cigar in mouth) and Allan Garcia (right). Photograph by Stern*

Opposite bottom: Charlie as the Absent-Minded (and inebriated) Husband carefully gauges the mood of Edna (Edna Purviance) as she arrives at their hotel suite accompanied by her two French maids in THE IDLE CLASS. *Lillita MacMurray (Lita Grey) and her mother, Lillian Parker, Chaplin's future wife and mother-in-law, played Edna's maids. Photograph by Stern*

Right: The Tramp is mistaken for the Absent-Minded Husband by his wife (Edna Purviance) and her kilt-wearing father (Mack Swain) at a costume party in THE IDLE CLASS. Photograph by Stern

Below: Chaplin and Mack Swain in the abandoned film THE PLUMBERS, August 1921. Chaplin recalled in MY AUTOBIOGRAPHY, "At the completion of THE IDLE CLASS I intended starting another two-reeler and toyed with the idea of a burlesque on the prosperous occupation of plumbers. The first scene was to show their arrival in a chauffeured limousine with Mack Swain and me stepping out of it. We are lavishly entertained by a beautiful mistress of the house, Edna Purviance, and after she wines and dines us we are shown the bathroom, where I immediately go to work with a stethoscope, placing it on the floor, listening to the pipes, and tapping them as a doctor would a patient. This is as far as I got." After filming just 348 feet of film, he stopped production and decided to take a vacation in Europe.

Opposite: Local children who dressed as the Tramp were given free admission to a screening of THE IDLE CLASS at the Liberty Theater in Bellingham, Washington, 1921. Charlie Chaplin look-alike contests were popular with children and adults in the 1910s and 1920s. A legend began that Chaplin himself anonymously entered one such contest and came in third place. Chaplin stated emphatically in 1966 that the legend was not true and had no basis in fact. "In the first place," Chaplin explained, "I'm working hard all day. I certainly don't want to do that."

abandoned the concept to make *The Adventurer*. Privately, Chaplin loathed the game of golf.[35]

While playing golf, the Tramp watches Edna, a lonely wife (Edna Purviance), riding on horseback. He is instantly love struck and wistfully fantasizes that he is a gallant gentleman who rescues her from a runaway horse, marries her, and they start a family together. (As in *His Prehistoric Past, The Bank, Shoulder Arms, Sunnyside,* and *The Kid,* the film has a romantic dream sequence.) When she departs on her horse so does his dream, and he realizes that he is just a lonely tramp. Charlie is mistaken for a pickpocket and eludes the police by stepping through a parked limousine from which guests are emerging for a costume party (Chaplin returned to this device to establish the Tramp being mistaken as a millionaire in *City Lights* nearly ten years later). Edna mistakes Charlie for her husband costumed as a tramp, and Charlie mistakes her attention as his dream come true. The husband appears locked in a suit of armor, furious at seeing his wife and the Tramp in a compromising situation. A fight ensues between Charlie and the armor-encased husband. Charlie opens the visor with a can opener and hammer to reveal the husband inside it (a double). The mistaken-identity confusion is quickly resolved and Charlie is soon on his way again.

The Idle Class comprised 131 work days with fifty-three days of actual filming and seventy-eight days of preproduction and postproduction. Although it was completed on June 25, 1921, it was not released until three months later.

It is perhaps ironic that the story of *The Idle Class* centers on an unhappy marriage between an absent-minded husband and a lonely wife. This state of affairs could easily describe the principal characters of the tragicomedy that was Chaplin's own mar-

riage. In the film Chaplin manages to dramatize the two sides of his own personality: the self-reliant, sympathetic tramp and the rich and neglectful husband, absorbed in his own interests and indifferent to others. The latter was certainly how Mildred Harris regarded Chaplin.

In the film's most celebrated sequence, the husband receives a note from his wife, "I will occupy other rooms until you stop drinking." He turns his back, looks at his wife's portrait, and appears to sob uncontrollably. When he turns around he reveals he is calmly shaking a cocktail shaker.

In the summer of 1971 Chaplin composed a score for *The Idle Class* with Eric James. It was recorded over three October days at the Anvil Studios in Denham. Chaplin stretch-printed the film for reissue, a process of copying the original film so that every second frame is reproduced twice, with the alternate frames reproduced only once. This has the effect of achieving an apparent projection speed of sixteen frames per second despite the projector actually operating at the modern sound speed of twenty-four frames per second. Unfortunately, the Chaplin First National films were intended to be projected at nineteen to twenty-one frames per second, so the stretch-printed version is as much too slow as uncorrected prints at sound speed would have been too fast. Further, very rapid actions acquire a visual "pulse" or "picketing" effect when stretch-printed. Although modern technology allows slowing the film to the correct frame rate, stretch-printing was the only method available to Chaplin when he reissued *The Idle Class* and his other First National reissues that employed stretch-printing, *The Chaplin Revue* (1959). Chaplin's heirs have elected to perpetuate this version of *The Idle Class:* the filmmaker's own last revision to his work.

Below: Chaplin's London home-coming, September 9, 1921, drew crowds unparalleled in Great Britain in the twentieth century apart from those at a few national or royal events. From Waterloo Station to the Ritz Hotel, the streets were filled with people waiting for a chance to glimpse their idol in the flesh. Encountering crowds of this magnitude everywhere he went prompted Chaplin to remark on more than one occasion, "I am better known than Jesus Christ." Photograph by L.N.A. Photo

Opposite: Chaplin in his prime, c. 1921. Photograph by Baron de Meyer

CHAPLIN'S TRIP ABROAD

Upon completion of *The Idle Class*, Chaplin started a film with the working title *Come Seven*, featuring himself and Mack Swain as a pair of wealthy plumbers, but abruptly stopped production and decided to travel to Europe. His unhappy marriage and divorce from Mildred Harris, the demands he placed on himself and his work, his nostalgia for London, and the knowledge that *The Kid* was about to open in London and Paris—he had never attended a European premiere of one of his own films—all contributed to Chaplin's decision. Tired after seven years and seventy-one films, he wanted a break to enjoy his success.

Chaplin left New York on the *Olympic* on September 3, 1921, and arrived in Southampton six days later. He stepped on his native soil for the first time since he had left England in 1912. His London homecoming was strikingly different from his departure in steerage class eight years earlier. In London he was mobbed by crowds and entertained by notable figures of the time. Chaplin reveled in the crowds that greeted him. He revisited the places associated with his youth, experiencing the powerful pull of the past that never left him and, in fact, became stronger as he grew older. He was deeply saddened to discover that Hetty Kelly, his early love interest whom he was anxious to meet again, had died three years earlier in the Spanish influenza epidemic that had killed hundreds of thousands at the end of the war.

Charlie as the escaped convict "Lefty Lombard," a.k.a. "Slippery Elm," in THE PILGRIM *(1923)*

Opposite: The series of portraits taken by photographer James Abbe during production of THE PILGRIM *are unusual among the thousands of Chaplin publicity photos because of their superb lighting and composition. The images were widely published before and after the release of the film. Abbe later recalled, "A creature of moods, Charlie had probably been in a new mood the night he got into his off-beat clerical Pilgrim garb and makeup, he left every pose up to me. He responded so rapidly I used up the twenty-four 8x10 films of my twenty-four-film holder within forty-five minutes. A record for me on an important job and a record, Charlie told me later, in his posing for stills." Photograph by James Abbe*

to find it full of cold water. Even that moment of peace is short-lived, however, as his wife drives him from the house.

The outstanding scenes in *Pay Day* are those in which Charlie, perched on a two-story scaffold, expertly catches bricks tossed up to him by two coworkers below and stacks them in neat piles. As the foreman orders him to work faster, he catches the bricks with superhuman speed and in unusual ways: with both hands, between his legs and knees, on his toe, beneath his chin, and under his arms. The illusion was achieved by carefully choreographing the variations in reverse and then utilizing reverse photography and undercranking the camera.

Pay Day is filled with small but notable technical flourishes. Some subtle backlighting is used in the interior shots, which was uncommon in Chaplin's films. He usually gave his films very flat lighting. Some night exteriors (such as the rain scene in which Charlie waits for a streetcar) were filmed at the studio and matched with exteriors filmed on location (such as the scenes using the streetcar) with skillful use of artificial lights. The scene in which Charlie tries to board impossibly overcrowded streetcars was inspired by his trip to New York City while en route to Europe in 1921 and influenced Harold Lloyd's similar treatment of this situation in his *Safety Last!* (1923).

Monta Bell, having completed his work on *My Trip Abroad*, was brought on as a general assistant and bit player. Bell's contribution to *Pay Day* and Chaplin's next film, *The Pilgrim*, was assisting Chaplin in developing the scenario and gag material on paper prior to production. This made it possible for Chaplin to film *Pay Day* out of sequence, which was not his usual practice; he preferred to film in order. The second half of the film, in which Charlie returns home to his wife, was filmed first, during the end of November 1921 and much of December. The first half was filmed in four work weeks. A total of thirty-one filming days were needed to complete the film by February 23, 1922. However, the film had a protracted 164 days of preproduction and postproduction, interrupted by his trip abroad. *Pay Day* was released April 3, 1922.

After its initial release, *Pay Day* was unseen for decades except in unauthorized prints. In 1972 Chaplin composed a score for *Pay Day* with Eric James for theatrical reissue. The music was all original save "The Gentle Maiden," a tune his mother used to sing to him when he was young, which Chaplin was intent on using in his own arrangement, and which replaced the film's direct cue of "Sweet Adeline." He altered the film slightly (removing the "End" title, which featured his shivering legs) but otherwise kept the film intact. The music was recorded in two days in November 1972 at the Anvil Studios in Denham.

THE PILGRIM (1923)

The Pilgrim is one of Chaplin's richest—and most neglected—films. Released in 1923, it concluded Chaplin's contract with First National. Like *The Adventurer*, his last film for Mutual, *The Pilgrim* is about an escaped convict. Chaplin's films often reflected his life, and these films perhaps alluded to his escape from

confining film contracts. *The Pilgrim* is also the last film in which Chaplin appears with longtime leading lady Edna Purviance and the last to have the light spirit of the Chaplin short comedies.

Planned as a two-reel short, *The Pilgrim* "took on the proportions of a feature-length film," according to Chaplin, and was released as a four-reel feature.[37] It was filmed in forty-two working days and was by far the most economically made of Chaplin's silent feature films. When filming began on April 10, 1922, the film's narrative continuity had largely been prepared on paper. Unlike *The Kid,* there were few days during the filming of *The Pilgrim* when work was halted owing to "work on story," to quote the production reports. Indeed, with Monta Bell's help, Chaplin was attempting to move away from his earlier method of creating and improving on the set and on film toward a greater degree of advance planning.

As the surviving scenario and gag notes indicate, the film was originally intended as a Wild West comedy, with a first working title of *Western.* It was to be a morality tale of sorts, in which Charlie, as an escaped convict, steals the clothes from a minister only to be mistaken for the new parson sent to rescue the Western town of Hell's Hinges. The convict introduces ragtime in place of hymns and dice games in place of the passing of the collection plate. His "improvements" are an immediate success; the saloons empty and the church fills up. The film was to end with Charlie being discovered for his true identity and arrested by the sheriff. The congregation demands Charlie's release and threatens the sheriff, but Charlie bids them to take a nonviolent course and stick with the church. The congregation shouts his praises as he goes up the church aisle and out with the sheriff into the fade-out. From this scenario, Chaplin developed a film that had the working title *The Tail End,* a humorous reference to the end of his First National contract.

Chaplin began preparing the story and scouted locations while sets were being built the week ending April 1, 1922. Although he generally disliked location shooting, he made extensive use of locations for *The Pilgrim,* such as the Saugus railway station, Culver City, South Pasadena, Eagle Rock, Sawtelle, Roscoe, Newhall, and the Western street set at Universal Studios. Scenes not on location were filmed on the recently roofed-over stage at the Chaplin Studios.

Director Lewis Milestone was the first to note that one of the film's outstanding qualities is its economy of action, most evident in the subtlety of Chaplin's pantomime and his direction.[38] In just five shots, Chaplin establishes the film's complex exposition and sets the stage for its dominant theme—mistaken identity. Shot one: a prison guard posts a notice offering a $1,000 reward for the capture of an escaped convict. Shot two: Charlie's picture is seen on the notice. Shot three: a man who had been swimming in a lake discovers that his clothes are missing. Shot four: in their place is a black-and-white-striped prison uniform. Shot five: waddling toward the camera is Charlie, dressed as a minister. He later is mistaken for, then poses as, the new minister of the small, aptly named Texas town of Devil's Gulch. This economy continues throughout the film, a feature with a running time of less than one hour. Chaplin gives the viewer only the essentials; nothing is superfluous.

As contemporary as *The Pilgrim* is in many ways, its roots can be found in classic theater. Molière's masterpiece *Tartuffe,* one of theater's greatest comedies, concerns an escaped convict who worms his way into a respectable household by posing as a religious man. Shades of Molière's *Tartuffe*—a role that every classically trained comic actor aspires to play—are evident in Chaplin's *Pilgrim.*

The traditions of the British music hall can also be seen in the film. The much-celebrated David and Goliath sermon Chaplin performs is the sort of music-hall turn many variety entertainers had in their repertoires. As marvelous as the sequence remains, it is no more impressive than the small moments of pantomime and comic transposition that permeate the film. Most notable among these is the transformation Charlie makes from minister to riverboat gambler—with the slightest alteration of his clerical costume—in order to retrieve the money stolen from the Brown family. It is the type of quick change that the Amazing Monsieur Trewey and others performed in the music halls, but Chaplin's alteration of expression and gait makes his metamorphosis complete. It is one of Chaplin's most extraordinary tours de force.

Although *The Pilgrim* is not quite pure satire it does contain many satirical elements that make it more than just a comedy.

The sharp edge is quite evident in the church scenes. Charlie quickly adopts the deacon's pious gestures, suggesting the hypocrisy of the deacon (who keeps a bottle of whiskey in his back pocket) and of the sanctimonious churchgoers in general. With his flamboyant sermon, the escaped convict-turned-minister converts church attendance into a glorified theatrical event, complete with an admission fee. The collection sequence, in which Charlie the minister makes certain everyone contributes and compares the day's take in the two collection boxes (complimenting the more generous half of the congregation), is Chaplin's comment on the mercenary nature of organized religion.

The afternoon tea scene, in which a brat kid (Dean Riesner) torments not only the minister but his own mother (Mai Wells) and father (Sydney Chaplin), raises the question, how could such upstanding moral people have raised such a horrible child? (Chaplin himself noted that this character was "the antithesis of Jackie Coogan in *The Kid*.")[39] The scene escalates with great balance and rhythm, as the child first accosts the adults with slaps, then pelts them with water from a nearby fishbowl, pokes them with a knitting needle, and plasters flypaper on his father's

Opposite: Charlie, having purloined a minister's frock coat and round hat, uneasily pours himself a drink of water at the train station, as a police officer (Monta Bell) watches, in THE PILGRIM. *Bell worked for two years at the Chaplin Studios, primarily as a scenario assistant. He later became a talented director and producer.*

Above: Charlie enacts the story of David and Goliath (one of Chaplin's favorite parallels to his own screen character) as his sermon in THE PILGRIM. *Charlie, like David, is the little man who must confront and overcome all sorts of Goliaths. This pantomime at the pulpit—complete with a theatrical flourish and curtain calls at the end—is one of Chaplin's most celebrated sequences.*

*Above: Chaplin directs Sydney
Chaplin in the afternoon tea
scene in* THE PILGRIM *with Mai
Wells, Mack Swain, and Loyal
Underwood. The set of the Brown
family home was built on the interior stage of the Chaplin Studios
and utilized artificial light.*

*Opposite: The American stage
comedienne Elsie Janis takes hold
of one of Chaplin's curls while
visiting the set of* THE PILGRIM.

face. The satisfying conclusion has Charlie giving the boy a well-earned kick when everyone else has fled the room. However, that does not stop the brat's reign of terror. The child places his father's derby hat over a pudding in the kitchen, and Charlie unwittingly decorates it with chocolate sauce and white frosting. At afternoon tea, Charlie attempts to cut into it, and soon the assembled company discovers they are eating a hat.

Dean Riesner, who portrayed the brat kid, remembered:

> I managed to do all the things that Charlie asked but when the time came to shoot the big finale of my scene, problems. Someone told me that I was to haul off and slap Charlie and there I drew the line. Water? Fine. Derby hats? Fine. But slapping? No way. I told them I had no intention of slapping Uncle Charlie. So Charlie and Sydney had a talk with me. I remember they were sitting on a couch and Charlie said, "If there's one thing in the world I really *love* it's being slapped in the face." Then to his brother Sydney he said, "Don't you love it, Sydney?" And Sydney said, "Love it? I *adore* it!" with which Charlie and his brother began slapping themselves in the face harder and harder as they laughed and chortled and chuckled and seemed to be having the grandest time. Soon I became convinced that they really did enjoy it just before the Chaplin brothers managed to inflict permanent damage on themselves. The out-takes show how convinced I was because after seven or eight takes I really got into the swing of it."[40]

The brat kid sequence reveals that Charlie is a pilgrim in a not-so-holy land. When a former cellmate (Chuck Riesner) robs the Brown family of their mortgage money, Charlie selflessly recovers it and returns it to Mrs. Brown's daughter. The town sheriff, however, has discovered Charlie's true identity. Appreciating his gallantry in returning the stolen money, he arrests Charlie but sets him free at the Texas-Mexico border.

The ending of *The Pilgrim* is one of Chaplin's best. Torn between law on the American side and anarchy on the Mexican side, the Pilgrim indecisively straddles the international line. One interpretation of this ending is that it reflects Chaplin's growing belief in himself as a "citizen of the world" without patriotic loyalty to any one country. Foreshadowing his political troubles to come, it seems fitting that the only place he can walk at the end of the film is the international line.

The Pilgrim was an unqualified success. Although not as well known as *Shoulder Arms* and *The Kid*, for many it is one of the outstanding Chaplin comedies. One reason *The Pilgrim* has been underrated over the years is that it was long unavailable for reappraisal. Even after Chaplin rereleased it as part of his compilation film *The Chaplin Revue,* it did not receive wide distribution in the United States, where Chaplin's reputation had suffered because of his alleged communist sympathies.

Ironically, even the original release of *The Pilgrim* was restricted. Several state censors, church organizations, and even the Ku Klux Klan demanded either elimination of scenes satirizing organized religion or total withdrawal of the film. Robert

Sherwood's review in *The Best Moving Pictures 1922–23* noted that Chaplin had apparently struck a nerve: "Perhaps the most hilariously humorous aspect of *The Pilgrim* was provided by the Pennsylvania censors, who barred the picture from that sacrosanct State because, said they, it made the ministry look ridiculous. A number of interested observers have been waiting, since then, to hear that the Pennsylvania censors have suppressed several thousand clergyman on the same charge."[41]

With the completion of *The Pilgrim*, Chaplin ended his contractual obligations to First National so that he could join Mary Pickford, Douglas Fairbanks, and D. W. Griffith in releasing films through United Artists Corporation, the company they formed in 1919. Chaplin's relationship with First National had not been a happy one. He believed the company to be "inconsiderate, unsympathetic, and short-sighted, and I wanted to be rid of them. Moreover, ideas for feature films were nagging at me."[42]

After the rights reverted to Chaplin, he licensed several of the First National films to Pathé for reissue. Withdrawn from distribution with the advent of sound films, the films remained unseen for many years except in bootleg prints. Print problems always plagued the First National films; indeed, they were victims of their own popularity. So many prints were made that the two original negatives wore out. Unfortunately, the current circulating versions of Chaplin's First National films are not the original ver-

Above: Charlie transforms himself from parson to riverboat gambler and recovers the mortgage money stolen by Howard Huntington (Chuck Riesner), undeterred by a holdup in progress inside the saloon/gambling house in THE PILGRIM.

Right: Charlie is given his freedom by Sheriff Bryan (Tom Murray), who releases him at the Mexican border, at the conclusion of THE PILGRIM. His enjoyment of a new world is short-lived, as two bandits emerge from the sagebrush and begin shooting at each other, with Charlie caught between them. He retreats toward the border. Straddling one foot in Mexico and the other in the United States, he scuttles off into the distance.

sions. After Chaplin had Rollie Totheroh prepare a new negative of *Shoulder Arms* to accommodate a request for prints from the Armed Forces Institute Film Services, he instructed Totheroh to make a new negative for each of the First National comedies from the best surviving material. Totheroh spent much of 1943 completing this task. Intending to combine the best of each remaining negative to make one good one, Totheroh instead found them to be very worn. He therefore assembled entirely fresh negatives from alternate takes and outtakes—often quite different from the takes Chaplin selected and used in the films as shown in 1918 to 1923—so that the films would once again be clean and intact. Only these versions were preserved by Chaplin and his heirs.

The Chaplin Revue, Chaplin's compilation feature of three First National films (*A Dog's Life*, *Shoulder Arms*, and *The Pilgrim*), was distributed theatrically by United Artists in 1959–60. Chaplin had all of *A Dog's Life* and sequences of the other films stretch-printed in an effort to slow down the action, since he felt sound-speed projection distorted their comic pace. He experimented with more stretch-printing for later reissues and disliked the results so much they were scrapped (with the exception of *The Idle Class*, as noted previously). However, despite the reissue of *The Chaplin Revue* and his creating scores for his other First National films, they remained generally unseen until the advent of home video in the late 1970s.

Chaplin with four-year-old "Dinky" Dean Riesner, the brat kid in THE PILGRIM, *in a publicity photograph taken on the lawn of Chaplin's Summit Drive home in Beverly Hills, 1923. It is somewhat ironic that Riesner—the gentlest of children until Chaplin taught him to enjoy hitting people for his role—later became the screenwriter of several of Clint Eastwood's most violent films, including* COOGAN'S BLUFF *(1968),* PLAY MISTY FOR ME *(1971),* DIRTY HARRY *(1971), and* THE ENFORCER *(1976).*

United Artists

In 1919 Hollywood's greatest motion-picture artists, Chaplin, Mary Pickford, Douglas Fairbanks, and D. W. Griffith, embarked on a revolutionary arrangement in which they became their own distributors. The impetus was their discovery that an impending merger between Paramount Pictures/Famous Players-Lasky (the world's largest film producer and distributor) and the First National Exhibitors' Circuit (Chaplin's own distributor, which was originally created to combat Famous Players-Lasky by financing and distributing productions) was imminent. The merger was conceived as a means to halt the astronomical salaries commanded by the major motion-picture stars. Chaplin and his associates responded by forming their own distribution company, United Artists Corporation, for their independently produced films. The announcement, which was made January 15, 1919, created much surprise and skepticism. Disgruntled Metro Pictures president Richard A. Rowland remarked, "The lunatics have taken charge of the asylum."[1]

United Artists Corporation was officially formed on April 17, 1919, to distribute the productions of the owners and those of other independent, high-quality producers who wished to join them. United Artists was neither to produce nor to have any ownership interest in the films themselves or share in the profits of the productions. Rather, the corporation served as a distribution and marketing service for a commission.

Chaplin signs the certificate of incorporation of the United Artists Corporation, flanked by (from left to right) D. W. Griffith, Mary Pickford, Albert Banzhaf (Griffith's attorney and one of the board of directors), Dennis O'Brien (counsel for Pickford and Fairbanks and vice president of the corporation), and Douglas Fairbanks, Hollywood, February 5, 1919.

The "Big Four" of United Artists: Douglas Fairbanks, Mary Pickford, Chaplin, and D. W. Griffith, Hollywood, February 5, 1919

The details of the incorporation were devised and drawn up by President Woodrow Wilson's secretary of the treasury, William Gibbs McAdoo, whose services were subsequently retained as general counsel. Oscar Price, who had been press representative for the treasury department in the Liberty Loan campaigns, was elected as the first president of the corporation. McAdoo, Price, and the four owners had first met during their productive association with the third Liberty Loan drive.

In the 1920s, United Artists became synonymous with motion pictures of the highest quality. The organization was never a company for profit; it was designed to service producers at actual cost of distribution, allowing them to enjoy as production profit what otherwise would have been a distributor's profit. To finance the company's operations, each of the founder-partners purchased $100,000 of preferred stock, and each agreed to deliver a specified number of films to the company. However, three and a half years elapsed before Chaplin completed his contractual obligations to First National and finally became an active partner with his first United Artists release, *A Woman of Paris* in 1923.

Originally, United Artists sold their films on the basis of a flat fee paid by the exhibitor. In 1920 this policy was changed to selling on a percentage basis. Chaplin—like the other owners—originally distributed his films, receiving the huge percentage of the 80/20-percent split of the domestic gross and the 70/30-percent split of the foreign gross profit (for *Limelight,* Chaplin's last American film, the split was 75/25 percent for both the domestic and foreign gross save the United Kingdom, which was 80/20 percent). Unlike Fairbanks and Pickford, Chaplin was unwilling to allow United Artists to share in the lucrative premiere engagements to his films, which strained his relationship with members of the company. He wanted United Artists to handle only the general release that he could not manage himself.

In an effort to increase the amount of United Artists' product, producer Joseph M. Schenck was allowed to buy into the company, becoming an owner-partner in 1924, and was elected chairman of the United Artists board of directors to replace McAdoo and Price, who had by then departed. Given the authority to reorganize the company, Schenck brought to United Artists the productions of Samuel Goldwyn, Gloria Swanson, and his own productions starring Norma Talmadge, Constance Talmadge, and Buster Keaton. Schenck also formed the United Artists Theatre Circuit in order to secure suitable outlets for United Artists films.

Samuel Goldwyn became the second new member-owner of United Artists in 1927. As the 1920s ended, D. W. Griffith was no longer producing independently (he sold back his United Artists shares in 1933), and Douglas Fairbanks was producing only to honor his commitments as a partner in the organization. In the 1930s an effort was made to bring new talent to the organization, the most notable of whom were Walt Disney, who released his celebrated Mickey Mouse and Silly Symphonies animated short subjects through the company between 1932 and 1936, producer

Alexander Korda (the next producer to be elected to ownership in 1935), and producer David O. Selznick (who became an owner-partner in 1941).

As part-owner of United Artists, Chaplin vehemently opposed any discussion of the corporation providing financing to producers as being antithetical to the history of the organization and its original purpose. He frequently tried the patience of his partners with his unwillingness to allow the company to function in any way that differed from precisely how he wanted the company to operate, which he succinctly described to historian Tino Balio in 1971: "I never thought of United Artists as a money-making scheme. . . . It was a way of distributing my films."[2]

By the 1940s, only Chaplin and Pickford remained of the original founders and the two controlled the corporation. They were invariably at odds with each other. Chaplin resisted any sort of change to or expansion of United Artists. Pickford held a maternal pride in the company and wanted to see it expand and grow. They quarreled bitterly and demonstrated an inability to agree on anything (or, if they did agree, usually at the very last moment one of them would refuse to sign or vote as agreed). Their constant impasses resulted in a succession of company stewardships that ultimately placed the firm on the verge of bankruptcy.

By the late 1940s, Goldwyn, Korda, and Selznick had parted company with United Artists. As United Artists did not finance or produce films, difficulties arose in finding suitable product for the company to distribute. After World War II, with cinema attendance low, production limited by a paucity of bank financing, and a less profitable foreign market as a result of import quotas, high taxes, and other restrictions, United Artists began to decline rapidly. A succession of managing executives failed to alleviate the downward spiral. Finally, in 1951 a new management team led by motion-picture industry law partners Arthur B. Krim and Robert S. Benjamin took control of the company for a three-year period. Pickford wrote about the occasion in her autobiography:

> At length, after years of continual wrangling, in February 1951 we finally sat down in a conference room one day and signed over the company to six young men who then had the power to put United Artists back on its feet. And that was the last time I saw the obstinate, suspicious, egocentric, maddening, and loveable genius of a problem child, Charlie Chaplin.[3]

After the voting trust agreement was signed, Chaplin and Pickford no longer were involved with or beholden to the company. In February 1955 Chaplin sold his quarter interest in United Artists (which consisted of 4,000 shares of stock) for $1.1 million (Pickford sold her quarter interest one year later for $3 million) and ended his thirty-six-year association with the company he helped to create. However, he continued to use United Artists as his distributor for his last American film, *Limelight,* and for various reissues of his earlier films. The last Chaplin film to be reissued through United Artists was *The Circus,* which went into general release throughout the world in 1970.

A Woman of Paris

Chaplin celebrated his independence as a filmmaker with *A Woman of Paris*, "A Drama of Fate" featuring Edna Purviance, in which Chaplin does not appear except in a brief, heavily disguised walk-on role. The film, his first United Artists release, established Chaplin's reputation as one of the finest directors of the silent-film era and an artist beyond his talents as an actor. *A Woman of Paris* was an innovative film in its ingenious narrative style, character portrayal, and subtle performances. So influential was the film that its techniques were widely and quickly assimilated by other filmmakers.

Chaplin was committed to fulfilling his promise to Edna Purviance to launch her film career in an independent, starring vehicle. Chaplin recalled in his autobiography that although he and Purviance were "emotionally estranged,"[1] he nevertheless wanted to help her career as a dramatic actress, as she was growing matronly and unsuitable for his future comedies. He contemplated an adaptation of *The Trojan Women*, and also Purviance in the role of Josephine Beauharnais to his Napoleon Bonaparte.

The inspiration for *A Woman of Paris* came from the recollections of Peggy Hopkins Joyce, which she had shared with Chaplin during their "bizarre, though brief, relationship"[2] in the summer of 1922. Joyce—for whom the term *gold digger*

Chaplin and Peggy Hopkins Joyce relax aboard a yacht off Santa Catalina Island in the summer of 1922. For two weeks Chaplin and Joyce were inseparable. Her stories of her Parisian love life inspired A WOMAN OF PARIS *(1923).*

was later coined—had already married and divorced five millionaires before arriving in Hollywood in 1922 seeking a career in films. For a couple of weeks after she was introduced to Chaplin she regaled him with anecdotes of her affair with the wealthy Parisian publisher Henri Letellier (who was the inspiration for the film's character Pierre Revel) and of a young man who so desperately loved her that he had committed suicide. Joyce also insisted that she was just a simple woman who really wanted to marry and have a family.[3] Intrigued by Joyce's apparent confusion about her own identity, Chaplin developed several of her Parisian exploits together with his own impressions of the Latin Quarter in Paris and of European high society from his recent 1921 trip. He conjured the story of a young woman who becomes the mistress of a wealthy man-about-town but is torn between the life of luxury he represents and the emotional bond she shares with a struggling young artist.

Although the film's inspiration came from Joyce, aspects of the central characters are intriguingly like Purviance and

Chaplin. Purviance, like the character Marie St. Clair, was rural born, relocated to a big city as a young woman, and became involved with a prominent man. A defining moment for both women is when each learns from a published account that her lover has married or will marry someone else (Purviance had learned of Chaplin's marriage to Mildred Harris in the newspaper). The obvious parallels between fact and fiction end there; Marie St. Clair eventually breaks free of Pierre Revel to find happiness elsewhere. Purviance was not as fortunate; she lived the rest of her life on Chaplin's payroll, his way of providing her with a pension out of a sense of personal obligation. The male characters Chaplin created, Jean Millet and Pierre Revel, mirror aspects of Chaplin's own personality. Jean Millet is, like Chaplin, a sensitive artist who loves Marie (Purviance) and considers her a muse. Neither Jean nor Chaplin can reconcile Marie/Purviance as she is in the present with what she was when they first knew her. (In the film, Jean Millet depicts Marie in his portrait in the plain clothes she used to wear rather than the expensive silver dress in which she poses.) Just as Marie commissions the portrait, Purviance, in a sense, commissioned the film; Chaplin made it out of his obligation to her. The character of Pierre Revel, like Chaplin, is the cynical, celebrated, self-indulgent womanizer who is content to keep the woman as his mistress.

Another influence on the film was Chaplin's relationship with the exotic European film star Pola Negri, whom he had first met in 1921 when he visited Berlin. Negri arrived in America in September 1922 to pursue her screen career in Hollywood under a new contract with Paramount following her success in Ernst Lubitsch's *Madame Dubarry* (*Passion*, 1919). A month after her arrival they became inseparable, and for the next nine months news of their romance and the announcement, retraction, and announcement again of their engagement made headlines. The affair had run its course by the end of June 1923. However, his

Above: Chaplin and Pola Negri at the press conference to announce their engagement, January 28, 1923

Right: Chaplin plays the part of a drunken Latin Quarter party guest groping the voluptuous Malvina Polo, in the role of demi-mondaine Paulette, during a rehearsal for A WOMAN OF PARIS.

Opposite: The wild bohemian life of the Latin Quarter is depicted in a party scene in A WOMAN OF PARIS. In an elaborate striptease, a "master of revels" serves as a human spool as he unwinds a woman (Bess Flowers), swathed only in a bolt of cloth, standing on a revolving pedestal. Chaplin imbues the scene with eroticism without revealing any more than her bare feet and shoulders. Flowers recalled in 1981 that she was in fact naked under the cloth.

association with Negri inspired some of the continental sophistication of *A Woman of Paris*.

In a small French village, Marie St. Clair (Edna Purviance) and her boyfriend Jean Millet (Carl Miller) decide to elope to Paris despite the objections of their fathers. The sudden death of his father (Charles French) prevents Jean from arriving for the rendezvous at the train station at the appointed time. Marie interprets his failure to appear at the station (and their interrupted telephone conversation) as his rejection of her and decides to journey to Paris alone. A year later she is the elegant mistress of wealthy Parisian bachelor Pierre Revel (Adolphe Menjou). She has a chance encounter with Jean, who has moved to Paris with his widowed mother (Lydia Knott) to establish himself as an artist. Marie commissions him to paint her portrait, and the two rekindle their love for each other. She resolves to leave Pierre when Jean proposes marriage to her. Later, Marie overhears Jean reassuring his disapproving mother that he will not marry her and that his proposal was made in a moment of weakness. Marie returns to Pierre,

and Jean, filled with remorse and despair, shoots himself. Jean's mother blames Marie for her son's death and seeks vengeance against her. However, the two women are reconciled when the mother discovers the disconsolate Marie beside Jean's body.

Time passes, and the film concludes with Marie and Jean's mother finding solace by raising orphan children in the country. As Marie rides with one of the children on the back of a horse-drawn farmer's cart down an open country road, a luxurious car races by in the other direction with Pierre Revel and his secretary. Neither party recognizes the other, and the secretary inquires of Pierre, "By the way, whatever happened to Marie St. Clair?" Pierre answers with a shrug as the two contrasting vehicles transport the characters to their respective destinies.

Chaplin engaged four assistants who contributed much to the success of *A Woman of Paris*. Monta Bell worked closely with Chaplin on the scenario of the film, helping to develop the characters and narrative. A. Edward (Eddie) Sutherland was hired as an assistant director. Primarily, Sutherland ran the set and direct-

Chaplin plays the role of "master of revels" during a rehearsal of the Latin Quarter party scene.

weeks and rewrite and perfect it and rehearse it and rarefy it. Charlie had the patience of Job. Nothing is too much trouble. A real perfectionist.

With this basis of working, it took us about a year to shoot the picture, because Charlie had another theory that he really believed. He said, "I shoot a sequence, and, if I'm not happy with it, I shoot it over the next day. That only puts me one day behind schedule." Well, he didn't figure it put him one day behind schedule every day. That's the way he worked and that's the way he did good pictures, because he could afford to and he was a great perfectionist.[4]

ed the extras, leaving Chaplin free to think of the images and work with the actors. Two Frenchmen, Comte Jean de Limur and Henri d'Abbadie (Harry) d'Arrast, were employed as research assistants to ensure an authentic French atmosphere.

Peggy Hopkins Joyce had pointed out actor Adolphe Menjou to Chaplin in a Hollywood restaurant as having a similar style to Henri Letellier, the inspiration for Chaplin's character Pierre Revel. Menjou had established himself as a character actor in Douglas Fairbanks's *The Three Musketeers* (1921) and *The Sheik* (1921), starring Rudolph Valentino; he also knew Bell and Sutherland. Their support prompted Chaplin to interview Menjou for the role, something Chaplin hardly ever did personally as he was loath to turn an actor down if an interview went poorly. However, Chaplin was pleased with Menjou and cast him as Pierre Revel at $500 per week, an unheard-of salary for an actor at the Chaplin Studios. Edna Purviance's salary was $250 per week.

A Woman of Paris had the original working title *Destiny*, which later changed to *Public Opinion*. As with his comedies, Chaplin began filming without a formal script. The scenario had been so formed in his mind over months of story conferences and notes that he felt he did not need a script. This was highly unusual for a dramatic production. Eddie Sutherland remembered:

We had a basic idea of the story, then we would do the incident every day. We'd shoot for three or four days, then lay off for two

The film's continuity reports indicate that once on the set, Chaplin was precise and knew exactly what he wanted (the exception was that he remained unclear on how to end the film as late as the beginning of June 1923, eventually favoring the film's ironic ending). Indeed, only three minor sequences were filmed that were not used in the final cut. Filming began on November 27, 1922. Despite his firm knowledge of the film's scenario, Chaplin kept to his practice of filming in narrative order, a method as unusual in 1922 as it is in the twenty-first century. The final scene (apart from a couple of days of exteriors and close-ups) was filmed on June 25, 1923. He had filmed a total of 3,862 takes, amounting to 130,115 feet of film (on one camera), which were edited to the length of the finished film, 8,432 feet. The production cost a total of $351,853. Postproduction was completed on September 29. Although filming was finished in ten months, with preproduction and postproduction work included the film took one year, one month, and fourteen days to complete.

Chaplin's commitment to the film was total, and his attention to detail was absolute. Menjou remembered that Chaplin "insisted on our learning dialogue and saying it exactly as it was written, something that none of us had ever done before in pictures. This was because he felt that certain words registered on the face and could be easily grasped by the audience."[5] British film producer and director Victor Saville visited the set for a day and observed Chaplin instruct Jack Wilson, who was operating the second camera, to follow his timing in fade-outs, something that Chaplin maintained was crucial.[6] Chaplin's moods during production were notorious; his assistants believed his mood could be predicted by the color of the suit he was wearing and would telephone his valet inquiring what clothes Chaplin had put on that morning. His green suit signified he was in a bad mood. "Every time he wore it all hell broke loose," remembered Sutherland.[7] The blue suit with pinstripes brought a happy, productive day. The gray suit meant an in-between mood, with the cast and crew gingerly feeling their way until Chaplin's definite mood developed.[8]

Although the plot of *A Woman of Paris* reads like a Victorian melodrama, the sophistication and subtlety in the telling of the story made the film innovative. Chaplin remembered:

> Some critics declared that psychology could not be expressed on the silent screen, that obvious action, such as heroes bending ladies over tree-trunks and breathing fervently down into their tonsils, or chair-swinging, knock-out rough stuff, was its only means of expression. *A Woman of Paris* was a challenge. I intended to convey psychology by subtle action.[9]

One of the film's most celebrated moments occurs when Marie St. Clair stands alone at the train station as the fateful train for Paris arrives. In shooting the scene, Chaplin was not intentionally attempting to be artistic but rather he was creatively solving the problem of how to establish a train station without having to go to the expense of re-creating a train for two shots. Totheroh remembered, "We made some real effective shots, like the one

Chaplin in a moment of concentration on the set of A WOMAN OF PARIS.

down by the railroad station. Charlie had this wind machine that blew up dust like a train coming by. I cut out a piece of cardboard about ten feet long and cut slits in it like the windows on a train. I put a couple of spots behind it and we dragged the cardboard across. And of course, you didn't see the train."[10] The light cast upon her face looked like the reflected light of a moving train. The effect was breathtaking to audiences in 1923.

Chaplin's other innovations were more deliberate. The most notable is how he reveals the nature of the relationship between Marie and Pierre. Menjou recalled in his autobiography:

> Because of the censorship boards in various states (there was no Hays Office of censorship at the time) Chaplin had to indicate this relationship [between Pierre Revel and Marie St. Clair] in a way that would not be obvious or offensive. He accomplished it in a manner that was, at that time, amazingly subtle.
>
> This is the way the scene was developed: Revel came to the girl's luxurious apartment and was admitted by a maid. The audience had no idea who or what this man was in her life. Apparently he was just an admirer calling to take her out to dinner. Chaplin wanted to find some casual piece of business that would suddenly reveal that Revel was a frequent and privileged caller. A good many devices were discussed. . . .
>
> Finally Chaplin thought of the handkerchief businesses, which solved the problem. I went to a liquor cabinet, took out a bottle of sherry and poured a drink, then sipped it. But when I started to take a handkerchief from my pocket, I discovered that I had none, so I turned casually and walked into the bedroom. Edna was at her dressing table, fully dressed but still fussing with her coiffure. I didn't look at her and she paid no attention to me as I crossed to a chiffonier. There I opened a top drawer and took out a large gentleman's handkerchief, put it in my pocket, and walked out. Immediately the relationship was established: we were living together and had been for some time.
>
> It happened that when Chaplin thought of this piece of business, the property man had not dressed the drawers of the chiffonier because he didn't know they would be used. So I went to my dressing room and brought back several handkerchiefs and some of my dress collars and other accessories to fill the drawer. Later, when I rehearsed the scene, my sleeve caught on one of the collars and it fell out of the drawer. This gave Charlie an idea for a later scene in which the maid accidentally dropped a collar and thus disclosed to the girl's [Marie's] former sweetheart that she was living with Revel. Little touches like this gave the picture a flavor that was new to picture making.[11]

Chaplin's observant details that intimated the thoughts and situations of his characters were in many respects just good theater sense. He reflected in his autobiography:

> To me theatricalism means dramatic embellishment: the art of the aposiopesis; the abrupt closing of a book; the lighting of a cigarette; effects off-stage, a pistol shot, a cry, a fall, a crash: an effective entrance, an effective exit—all of which may seem cheap and obvious, but if treated sensitively and with discretion, they are the poetry of the theatre.[12]

Most examinations of *A Woman of Paris* select a key scene, such as Marie on the train platform or Pierre removing a handkerchief from Marie's dresser drawer, or the natural and simple approach to performance as the basis for the film's critical laurels, while overlooking Chaplin's overall construction of the visual narrative. However, the film's greatness is not limited to a few isolated scenes. Chaplin's directorial skill and the film's power are demonstrated in the careful and direct way that Chaplin tells a simple story. Chaplin achieved his purpose of conveying "psychology by subtle action" throughout the visual narrative by imbuing the decor with symbolism, by using objects for their metaphoric and metonymic value, and by parallel storytelling and editing.

Chaplin worked closely with the film's art director, Arthur Stibolt, on the design and décor of the film. Since most of the narrative unfolds in interior settings, the decor takes on meaning in the film and operates as part of the action. The contrast of life in the simple, pure country to that in the sophisticated, decadent

city appealed to Chaplin (he would return to it in *Monsieur Verdoux*) as did the dark, moody lighting of the current German films he had seen.[13] The interiors of the homes of Marie's stepfather and Jean's parents in the rural French village are small, dark, and oppressive. These elements help to define the characters' situations, independent of their actions, creating a sense of the cheerless confinement that forms the emotional backdrop against which the first act of fate occurs to Marie.

Chaplin immediately contrasts this decor with that of Marie's first scene in Paris. An intertitle conveys the difference: "from the drabness of the village to the gayety of Paris." Marie is in a large restaurant filled with people, and the room has high ceilings and chandeliers. In tone and scale, the restaurant matches the interior of Marie's Parisian apartment, in which much of the film's action occurs. The decor reflects the changes taking place in Marie's character. Its narrative weight is forcefully demonstrated in a nightclub scene with Marie and Pierre. Two seemingly inanimate figures holding balloons appear high above the ground near the ceiling. Chaplin reveals they are not statuary but women, tied with ropes, who swoop down into the large room and shower the crowd with balloons—a moment that deliberately calls the viewer's attention to the decor and its function as a character in the story.

Marie accidentally meets Jean on her way to a party in the Latin Quarter. His apartment is

A final important aspect of Chaplin's overall narrative style is the abundance of parallel events in the film. Consider the entrances of Marie's father and Jean's father. They are both seen first in expressionistic shadows that distort their bodily forms. Chaplin introduced these two key figures in a parallel manner to express the affinity between them in a terse, evocative way—on a basic level, it is the interference of these two men that ultimately leads Marie to Paris. Another parallel within the visual narrative draws a meaningful connection between two scenes. There is a scene in Marie's apartment in which she is in bed and showered with flowers. This precedes a similar scene with Pierre Revel in a bed strewn with ticker tape. These objects illustrate the difference between the two characters: flowers are symbols of romance and love; the ticker tape suggests money and wealth. By using these motifs in a parallel fashion, Chaplin offers meaning with visually economical means.

Having shown in *The Kid* that comedy and drama could be successfully combined in a feature-length film, Chaplin demonstrated in *A Woman of Paris* that a feature-length "drama of fate" could contain high comedy. Although Chaplin prefaced the film with a title indicating he did not appear, he made a brief appearance disguised as a porter at the railroad station who recklessly drops a large trunk, inaugurating the film's comic touches. Other comic highlights include the encounter between the epicurean Pierre and the chef in a restaurant kitchen, the wild Latin Quarter

reminiscent of the home they left behind in the village. Chaplin uses the decor of Jean's apartment to match Marie's inner psychological state. There is a hearth, a symbol of home, and a kitchen in plain view, further extending the metaphor of domesticity. Neither a hearth nor a kitchen is visible in Marie's apartment.

Another important aspect of the film's visual construction is Chaplin's use of objects for their metaphoric and metonymic value, which increases the mental engagement of the audience. For example, a close-up of a smoldering pipe stands in for the death of Jean's father, and in the next shot the audience recognizes that Jean's father is dead, not sleeping. Similarly, a particularly potent metonymic connection is established between a man's shirt collar and the audience's knowledge of Marie and Pierre's relationship.

Metaphoric meaning is also conveyed through objects. For example, Pierre's saxophone surfaces in a few scenes to symbolize his flippant attitude toward Marie. In the scene of Marie at Jean's bier, objects from previous scenes are presented in a different context: Marie's silver dress, the portrait of Marie painted by Jean, Jean's gun, and Jean's note to Marie. Visually, this climactic scene is full of ironic content. The portrait of Marie is prominently displayed above the bier, while Marie, in her silver dress, is at the foot of the bier. The painting is a metaphor for how Jean saw Marie: the girl from the village he had known.

party, and a delightful scene in which the pampered Marie claims she has nothing and proudly throws the pearl necklace Pierre has given her out the window into the street. She quickly notices a tramp picking up the pearls off the street and immediately changes her mind—much to Pierre's amusement—and tears after the startled tramp to retrieve them. As an afterthought, she dashes back to give the tramp a monetary reward as she hobbles to her room, having broken the heel of one of her elegant shoes in the process, which Chaplin recalled in *My Life in Pictures* as "a final touch of absurdity to her insincere heroic gesture."[14]

A Woman of Paris is notable in its portrayal of the complexity of human character and relationships. The heroine is a kept woman who wants both happiness and luxury; the weak-willed hero was emotionally scarred by an overbearing father and lives with his possessive mother; and the villain is charming and magnanimous. Simplicity and restraint are employed in favor of moralizing and emotionalism. For example, when Pierre finds Jean visiting Marie in the next room, instead of becoming enraged Pierre simply sug-

gests to Marie's maid that Jean should be offered some of Marie's box of chocolates. Chaplin's attitude toward his characters is best expressed in a draft he wrote as a possible foreword to the film, of which only an abbreviated version was eventually used: "Humanity is composed not of heroes and villains, but of men and women, and all their passions, both good and bad, have been given them by God. They sin only in blindness, and the ignorant condemn their mistakes, but the wise pity them."[15]

Original reviews, accounts by critics and filmmakers, and comparison with other films of the time reveal how truly startling *A Woman of Paris* appeared to audiences in 1923. *Motion Picture Magazine* declared Chaplin "dared to discard all the old stereotyped ideas."[16] Several critics commented upon the strained relations between Jean and his mother. *Motion Picture Classic* wrote of Chaplin being "exceptionally daring in having the boy abuse his mother"[17] and of the scenes depicting his anger at her.[18]

A Woman of Paris was also innovative in its subtle approach to acting. "It was remarkable how much Chaplin made us tell with just a look, a gesture, a lifted eyebrow,"[19] Menjou reflected in his autobiography. He recalled:

> Not until we started shooting did I begin to realize that we were making a novel and exciting picture. It was Chaplin's genius that transformed the very ordinary story. Aside from his own great talent as an actor he had the ability to inspire other actors to perform their best. Within a few days I realized that I was going to learn more about acting from Chaplin than I had ever learned from any director. He had one wonderful, unforgettable line that he kept repeating over and over throughout the picture. "Don't sell it!" he would say. "Remember, they're peeking at you."
>
> It was a colorful and concise way to sum up the difference between the legitimate stage and the movies—a reminder that in pictures, when one has an important emotion or thought to express, the camera moves up to his face and there he is on the screen with a head that measures six feet from brow to chin. The audience is peeking at him under a microscope, so he can't start playing to the gallery 200 feet away, because there is no gallery in a movie theater; the audience is sitting in his lap.
>
> From my early days in movies I had been schooled in the exaggerated gestures and reactions that were thought necessary to tell a story in pantomime. But when I, or any other actor, would give out one of those big takes, Chaplin would just shake his head and say, "They're peeking at you." That did it. I knew that I had just cut myself a large slice of ham and had tossed the scene out the window.
>
> Since then I have never played a scene before a camera without thinking to myself, "They're peeking at you; don't sock it."
>
> Another pet line of Chaplin's was, "Think the scene! I don't care what you do with your hands or your feet. If you think the scene, it will get over."

> And we had to keep shooting every scene until we *were* thinking it—until we believed it and were playing it with our brains and not just with our hands or our feet or our eyebrows. . . . Chaplin was satisfied with nothing less than perfection, or as close to it as we could come.[20]

Chaplin's relentless pursuit of subtlety and restraint was such that it required two days and more than ninety takes to film a short scene in which Marie throws down her cigarette and declares that she will not go out that evening. That attention to detail makes the performances of Menjou and Purviance appear valid and modern to twenty-first-century audiences.

For older actors like Lydia Knott who were set in their ways, Chaplin's approach was difficult. Instead of broad, uncontrolled anguish, Chaplin wanted an underplayed, restrained performance when the mother learns of her son's death. Eddie Sutherland recalled:

> Lydia Knott played the mother, and Charlie wanted her to give a reaction of complete shock. As the Sureté asked her all the usual questions—"What's his name, how old was he?"—he asked her for a totally dead nonreaction. He wanted the audience to supply the emotion, not the actress. I can't tell you how many times we shot it. She kept playing it as sweet, smiling, courageous old lady. She was a very fine person, and very determined, so it was tough going. . . . Finally, the old lady got so angry that she swore at us. "All right," she snapped. "If that's the way you want it. But it's not the way I am." And she went through the scene in such a temper that we got it. . . . Lydia Knott was the only player I ever knew to argue with Chaplin.[21]

Opposite: The disapproving masseuse (Nellie Bly Baker) absorbs every word of salacious gossip spoken by Marie's demi-mondaine friend Fifi (Betty Morrisey), as she massages Marie (Edna Purviance), in A WOMAN OF PARIS. *Baker was not an actress but a secretary at the Chaplin Studios. Her performance was so memorable that it prompted her to leave her position at the studio and pursue work as a character actress in films throughout the 1920s.*

Left: Chaplin with Carl Miller during production. Not much is generally known about Miller's life. Born Charlton Miller in 1893, he had previously worked with Chaplin in THE KID *playing the role of the artist. He had an indifferent career in silent films and early talkies (his later work was mostly in westerns) and died in Hawaii in 1979.*

The scene with Knott necessitated thirty-nine takes on Friday May 4, 1922, and an additional forty-one takes on the following day, before Chaplin was able to get the reaction of numbed despair he wanted from her. However, more than fifty years later, Chaplin still shuddered at certain moments of Knott's perform-ance that he felt were overacted.[22]

A Woman of Paris premiered on September 26, 1923, as the first attraction of the Criterion Theatre (formerly the Kinema Theatre) in Los Angeles. Chaplin even devised a live prologue for the engagement, which he titled *Nocturne*. However, he was not in attendance for the world premiere of his film because he and Purviance were en route to New York City for the premiere at the Lyric Theatre on October 1, 1923. The unanimous rave reviews the film garnered were some of the best of his career. *A Woman of Paris* was universally praised as a screen masterpiece. Influential critic Robert Sherwood wrote in *The New York Herald*, "There is more real genius in Charles Chaplin's *A Woman of Paris* than in any picture I have ever seen."[23]

The reviewer of *Exceptional Photoplays* best explained the film's appeal:

> Mr. Chaplin . . . has not done anything radical or anything eso-
> teric. He has merely used his intelligence in the highest degree,
> an act which has ceased to be expected of motion picture peo-
> ple for many years. He has written and directed a story in which
> all the characters act upon motives which the spectator immedi-
> ately recognizes as natural and sincere, and therefore *A Woman
> of Paris* breathes an atmosphere of reality, and thereby holds the
> attention of any perceptive audience in thrall. . . . *A Woman of
> Paris* has the one quality almost every other motion picture that
> has been made to date lacks—restraint. The acting is moving
> without ever being fierce, the story is simple and realistic with-
> out ever being inane, the settings are pleasing and adequate
> without ever being colossally stupid. The result is a picture of
> dignity and intelligence and the effect is startling because it is
> so unusual.[24]

However, the public was less enthusiastic about Chaplin's drama. It was far removed from what audiences expected from him. Despite the quality of the film and the unanimous critical response, *A Woman of Paris* was not a financial success. The New York City engagement ended after only four weeks with a net loss, and both the seven-week Los Angeles and four-week London runs barely covered their guarantees. The film grossed $634,000 domestically, equivalent to the other least successful United Artists films produced by the founder-partners. After patiently waiting four years for Chaplin to fulfill his contractual obligations to First National, his partners at United Artists were frustrated and concerned over his decision that his first film was to be a drama in which he would not star. Their reservations were now justified. United Artists had lost money in its first three years of operation (1920–22), and the hope was that Chaplin's film would give the struggling company much-needed revenue. This proved to be an intense disappointment to Chaplin, who had never experienced commercial failure with a film.

A Woman of Paris failed to achieve its intended goal of build-ing a new screen career for Edna Purviance. It was, in fact, her last Hollywood film to be released. According to Rollie Totheroh, Purviance had "got to drinking pretty heavily. One day we were looking at rushes and Charlie could see it. 'Course Edna took the marriage to Harris pretty hard and never quite got over it."[25] After *A Woman of Paris,* Purviance starred in the unreleased *A Woman of the Sea,* directed by Josef von Sternberg and produced by Chaplin, and one film in France, *L'Education du Prince* (1927), directed by Henri Diamant-Berger. She then retired from the screen. She later married John Patrick Squire and remained on Chaplin's payroll until her death from cancer in 1958. *A Woman of Paris* had the opposite result for Adolphe Menjou. After years of playing character roles and second leads, Menjou emerged a motion-picture star, specializing in roles requiring suave, cynical, continental sophistication.

Despite its commercial failure, *A Woman of Paris* was closely examined and discussed among those in the film industry and the intelligentsia. Chaplin wrote in his autobiography, "the film was a great success with discriminating audiences. It was the first of the silent pictures to articulate irony and psychology. Other films of the same nature followed, including Ernst Lubitsch's *The Marriage Circle,* with Menjou playing almost the same character again."[26]

Lubitsch and Chaplin were friends, and Chaplin had shown him a rough cut of *A Woman of Paris.* Unquestionably, the film influenced Lubitsch to abandon directing the large historical dra-mas that had made his reputation and return to the type of films he had been making in Germany years before. Chaplin's film was the primary inspiration for his American comedies. Lubitsch him-self told an interviewer in 1923, "*A Woman of Paris* is a great step forward . . . a picture that, as you Americans say, left something to the imagination."[27] Fresh from Mary Pickford's elaborate produc-tion of *Rosita* (1923), Lubitsch must have found it liberating to adopt Chaplin's minimalist style and direct a well-made film that discarded all but the essentials.

studio, eventually directing *The Red Shoes* (1948) and *Peeping Tom* (1960). He reflected on *A Woman of Paris* in 1980, "I reckoned that if the film was capable of this sort of subtlety, it was the medium for me."[31]

Film director Martin Scorsese also holds the film in high regard:

> *A Woman of Paris* is beautifully directed and the acting is subtle for its time. The sets are sumptuous—like something out of an Erich von Stroheim or Rex Ingram picture. It's one of the great silent films. . . . The reason it isn't well known is because back then—and the same holds true today—audiences didn't necessarily want to see a Charlie Chaplin film without Charlie Chaplin in it. Given the level of careful craftsmanship he gave the picture, that must have been devastating to Chaplin as a director.[32]

After *A Woman of Paris* was withdrawn from distribution at the end of the silent era, the film developed a legendary status based on its reviews, its place in books on early film history, and the memories of those who had seen it, recalling it as one of the great film masterpieces. Film historian Herman G. Weinberg championed Chaplin's film as a major influence upon the "Lubitsch touch" and the progenitor of sophisticated film comedy, an opinion that was widely believed in the absence of the film itself for reappraisal.[33] Chaplin chose not to reissue the film for

Film critic Edwin Schallert wrote in 1925, "*A Woman of Paris* turned out to be much more of an influence than at first anticipated, and Lubitsch has carried on in much the same vein, although he is in every sense original, and really antedates Chaplin, when one considers his European films, in the employment of flashing 'tricks of business' that depend on visualization rather than on mere subtitled words."[28]

As the silent era was drawing to a close, two of the medium's greatest directors—Rex Ingram and Sergei Eisenstein—recorded their high esteem for *A Woman of Paris* and its importance. Ingram wrote in 1928: "As things stand today, the first two milestones in studio production during, say, the last ten years, are *Intolerance* and *A Woman of Paris*. Each is important for an entirely different reason. Both were pioneer efforts."[29] Eisenstein boldly wrote in 1929 that *A Woman of Paris* is "perhaps the most remarkable cinematographic production of the past epoch of cinematography."[30]

Chaplin's four assistants, Monta Bell, Eddie Sutherland, Jean de Limur, and Harry d'Arrast, were all suddenly in demand to direct films as a result of the critical success of *A Woman of Paris*, and their own work was clearly influenced by it. *A Woman of Paris* also inspired future directors. A young office worker in England named Michael Powell quit his job after seeing *A Woman of Paris* and went looking for work at a motion-picture

Opposite top: Chaplin appears outside the Lyric Theatre in New York City to promote the New York premiere of A WOMAN OF PARIS, *September 1923. Photograph by Kadel & Herbert*

Opposite bottom: Chaplin assumes a Napoleonic pose as he wades through congratulatory telegrams in his suite at the Ritz Hotel, New York City, following the premiere of A WOMAN OF PARIS, *October 2, 1923.*

Left: Chaplin participates in his first radio broadcast, at L. Bamberger's WOR studio in Newark, New Jersey, to promote A WOMAN OF PARIS *in New York City, October 1923.*

more than fifty years, and the myth about the film grew. Finally, Chaplin looked at *A Woman of Paris* in February 1975 with the idea of creating a musical score for it; he had not seen the film in more than two decades. He was not very enthusiastic about the project; in fact, it was it only completed through the efforts of his wife, Oona, who sustained Chaplin's enthusiasm for work despite his failing health. He and Oona prepared a list of cuts to the film—873 feet (approximately eight minutes) in all—to tighten the action and out of deference to changing tastes. Eric James, Chaplin's musical associate, utilized music that he and Chaplin had previously created but never used, along with other Chaplin music that could be reworked for the film to augment the score he created under Chaplin's direction. According to James:

> When I arrived at Chaplin's home in April 1975 his first words to me were, "Eric I haven't an idea in my head for the music of this picture." I jokingly replied, "Never mind, I'll play some ideas to you and you can throw them out or accept them as you see fit." Knowing his style of composition as intimately as I did after so many years working with him, I was able to suggest melodies and ideas that were agreeable to him. I worked with him for two weeks and later returned to the Manoir in October 1975 for about another two weeks of work to complete the score. He was eighty-six at the time, very frail, and found even talking quite an effort."[34]

The music was recorded in five days in February 1976 at the Anvil Studios, Denham.

Fortuitously, film critic and historian Leonard Maltin, who was serving as guest director of the Museum of Modern Art's "Bicentennial Salute to American Film Comedy," wrote Chaplin in 1976 requesting that *A Woman of Paris* be made available for the event. Chaplin agreed, and the film was warmly received at the Museum's screening of the world premiere of the film with the new musical score on December 23, 1976. Inevitably, the film could not live up to the legend that had built up around it, and the film's innovations—which had been absorbed so quickly into the grammar of filmmaking upon its release—were not readily apparent to those who looked at the film without sympathy or imagination. Following the Museum of Modern Art screenings, *A Woman of Paris* was reissued and, just as in 1923, the reviews in the United States and Great Britain were ecstatic, but audiences stayed away from the film. Jack Kroll wrote for *Newsweek* in 1977 that *A Woman of Paris* is "an elegant glittering tale, perversely both chaste and libidinous, of passion, money and art—the trinity of forces that ruled Chaplin's sensibilities."[35]

A Woman of Paris unquestionably shows Chaplin at the height of his directorial powers and is a testament to his ability to be an innovative film director when he was not absorbed with his own screen image. Reaching in its simplicity and suggestion a high degree of art, it remains an important landmark in the history of film and a major work in Chaplin's career.

The Gold Rush

After *A Woman of Paris,* Chaplin was anxious to begin work on his first comedy feature film to be distributed by United Artists. He was determined to top the phenomenal success of *The Kid.* He kept saying to himself, "this next film must be an epic! The greatest!"[1] *The Gold Rush* is arguably his greatest and most ambitious silent film; it was the longest and most expensive comedy produced up to that time. The film contains many of Chaplin's most celebrated comedy sequences, including the boiling and eating of his shoe, the dance of the rolls, and the teetering cabin. However, the greatness of *The Gold Rush* does not rest solely on its comedy sequences but on the fact that they are integrated so fully into a character-driven narrative. Chaplin had no reservations about the finished product. Indeed, in the contemporary publicity for the film, he is quoted, "This is the picture that I want to be remembered by."[2]

The Gold Rush has an epic quality. The film presents adventures on a grand, heroic scale that are organically united through the central character of the Tramp. The hero-clown endures the cruelty of nature and the villainy of humanity through his luck, pluck, and enterprise. Chaplin's theme for the film is the quest for basic human needs—food, money, shelter,

Above: In one of the most famous scenes in THE GOLD RUSH *(1925), Charlie is so desperate with hunger that he is reduced to boiling and eating one of his shoes.*

Opposite: Charlie is a lone figure known to no one in the dance hall.

A small-scale model of the cabin, operated with wires, was
used for several shots. A miniature exterior set was built to scale
with the model, and a miniature mechanical doll of Chaplin
approximately five inches tall was used in the scenes in which the
Tramp swings outside the cabin door.[9]

Other visual effects involve the Tramp leaping from the cabin
just as it slips off the edge. This was accomplished by double
exposure, requiring the same type of careful camera work used
with the dissolve for the chicken shots. First the cameramen
filmed the miniature cabin on the cliff. Then they rewound the
exposed film to the exact frame they had just shot and photographed Chaplin leaping in front of a plain white backdrop on
the same strip of film. This double-exposure work proved so
effective that it was used again for the visual effect of the spectacular death of Black Larsen by avalanche, the last scene shot for
The Gold Rush, on May 14–15, 1925.[10] The visual effects in *The
Gold Rush* are deceptively simple and work well in the context of
the film as a whole. More important, they appear effortless on
screen, just as Chaplin intended.

The Gold Rush concludes with the Tramp and Big Jim now
millionaires, thanks to Big Jim's lucky strike. The little fellow discovers Georgia on board the ship returning home. (These final
scenes were filmed in April 1925 aboard an actual boat, *The Lark*,
on its regular route between San Diego, Los Angeles, and San
Francisco.) Georgia reveals her kindness and genuine love for the
Tramp when she protects him from the ship's captain, who
believes him to be a stowaway. The film marks Chaplin's first
major attempt to portray the Tramp in a true romantic relation-

but cut it by an additional reel after the premiere to the film's final length of 8,555 feet.

Chaplin traveled to New York to attend the premiere in that city at the Mark Strand Theatre, held at midnight on August 16. At the end of the film, United Artists president Hiram Abrams predicted the film would gross at least $6 million—which it ultimately did. *The Gold Rush* was the most successful film comedy of the 1920s, and second only to King Vidor's World War I drama *The Big Parade* (1925) in popularity in 1925. Following the premiere, Chaplin spent an eventful two months in New York, where he not only suffered a nervous collapse but also had an affair with eighteen-year-old Ziegfeld Follies dancer (and future silent-film actress) Louise Brooks.

At its premiere engagements at the Tivoli Theatre in London (where the BBC broadcast on radio ten minutes of laughter recorded during a showing of the film), the Salle Marivaux in Paris, and elsewhere throughout the world, *The Gold Rush* proved to be one of Chaplin's greatest critical and commercial successes. At the Berlin premiere, the audience gave the dance of the rolls scene such a thunderous ovation that the management instructed the projectionist to rewind the scene and present an immediate encore. Similar incidents were reported elsewhere.

Despite its success, a few critics raised concerns that Chaplin was becoming too serious; they wanted even more comedy and less pathos, a complaint he would face again with *City Lights* and nearly all his subsequent films upon first release. However, the film was much praised by the most influential critics for its mixture of comedy, pathos, and drama and was celebrated as the highest example of screen comedy. Indeed, Chaplin demonstrated with *The Gold Rush* that a great comedy could also be a great

ship. It ends happily with Charlie getting the girl in the last scene. Chaplin seems to have anticipated that critics would question the appropriateness of the Tramp finding love at the end. As Charlie and Georgia are posing for a still photographer, the little fellow spoils the photograph by kissing the girl. The film's last intertitle, the photographer exclaiming, "Oh, you've spoilt the picture!" has been interpreted as Chaplin's conscious comment that he has possibly compromised his film. He removed this scene completely when he reissued *The Gold Rush* in 1942, preferring a more ambivalent ending.

The Gold Rush was seventeen months in the making with 170 days of actual filming. The entire production cost $923,886, making it the most expensive comedy of the entire silent-film era. More than 230,000 feet of film were exposed (on one camera). As was his practice, Chaplin had already edited certain key sequences during the course of production. Chaplin spent nine weeks—from April 20, 1924, to the premiere on June 26—editing the balance of the film. Following a preview at the Forum Theatre on May 28, *The Gold Rush* had its world premiere at Grauman's Egyptian Theatre in Hollywood, where cinema exhibitor Sid Grauman staged his most lavish event to date. (Grauman had gone to Truckee with the Chaplin company and, having participated in a gold rush himself, acted as an unofficial adviser on the film.) Chaplin worked with composer Carli Elinor to compile and arrange a musical score for the Egyptian Theatre engagement. He premiered the film at an approximate length of 10,000 feet

motion picture. He defined the comedy genre to such an extent that other comedians would be compared to him. Starting with *The Gold Rush,* the time between each new Chaplin release grew longer, to the point where his films were perceived as illustrious cinematic events.

Chaplin reissued *The Gold Rush* in 1942, giving the film a soundtrack of his own musical score, sound effects, and spoken commentary replacing the original intertitles. He also edited the film and inserted a few extra shots to help continuity; he rearranged some sequences and discarded several scenes, reshaping his 1925 original in an effort to "modernize" the film and shorten its length so that it could be shown in the double-bill cinema programs of the period. The most significant alterations were scenes that develop the relationship of the dance-hall girl and her caddish lover Jack Cameron (Malcolm Waite) and the last scene of the Tramp and Georgia posing for a photographer aboard ship. The reduction of Georgia Hale's role, however, negatively impacts the gradual development of her love for the Tramp, and film historians argue that these cuts compromise the film's psychological subtlety.

At a time when silent films were considered antiquated, Chaplin saw the adding of narration as a means of making *The Gold Rush* commercially viable to a new generation of film audiences. Few silent films had been reissued since the transition to talkies; Chaplin's lavish reissue of *The Gold Rush* was daring for its time.

Chaplin's score for *The Gold Rush* suggests the kind of accompaniment that was heard in late-nineteenth-century melodrama, establishing the various moods and heightening the comic and dramatic moments. Chaplin's narration was partly inspired by poet Robert W. Service's frontier ballad, "The Shooting of Dan McGrew," giving the humorous action a melodramatic and seri-

ous tone. Chaplin refers to his character throughout the reissue as "the little fellow," a moniker that became interchangeable with the Tramp. The 1942 reissue was dedicated to writer and critic Alexander Woolcott, who wrote of Chaplin's screen persona, "it must be said of Charles Chaplin that he has created only one character, but that one, in his matchless courtesy, in his unfailing gallantry—his preposterous innocent gallantry in a world of gross Goliaths—is the finest gentleman of our time."[11]

Left: Chaplin gives evidence in court against imitator Charles Amador in February 1925. Chaplin was plagued by Hollywood imitators who shamelessly copied his costume and comedy ideas. As early as November 1917 he sought and was granted a permanent injunction against several film companies and individuals that imitated him. Billy West is generally acknowledged as having been the best Chaplin imitator in films. Chaplin was particularly irritated by Amador, who billed himself as "Charlie Aplin."

Above: Charlie is reunited with Georgia (Georgia Hale) at the conclusion of THE GOLD RUSH. Hale made her last film in 1931 and later worked as a dance teacher. She died in 1985.

Opposite: Chaplin, c. 1929. This formal portrait is unique in being the only photograph of himself that Chaplin displayed in one of his films; it hangs over Calvero's mantlepiece in LIMELIGHT. Photograph by Homer Peyton

Marriage to Lita Grey

Chaplin's relationship with Lita Grey was perhaps the most destructive he ever had with a woman. Their marriage, the result of an unwanted pregnancy, ended in a bitter and expensive divorce that scandalized Hollywood in the 1920s. It was the first of the many sensationalized Hollywood divorces that followed. The perverse attraction of the mature Chaplin to the young actress jeopardized his feature-length production *The Circus*, his studio, and his corporation, and it even seriously threatened his health.

Lillita MacMurray was born in 1908, a ninth-generation Californian and scion of an illustrious Spanish family.[1] Lita Grey was the screen name Chaplin created for MacMurray, believing that it was better suited for cinema marquees than her given name. She had been introduced to Chaplin by his assistant director, Chuck Riesner, a neighbor of Lita's mother and grandparents. Chaplin was intrigued by the prettiness of the tall, big-boned young girl with large, expressive eyes when he cast her in *The Kid*, signing her to a one-year contract.

Lita believed Chaplin's attraction to her was immediate and complex. She later speculated, "He [Chaplin] was so creative that he even liked to create people. He liked to see the girl come alive. He was fascinated by the awakening of a girl . . . and he had a fetish for virgins."[2]

Upon the signing of her first contract in 1920 for *The Kid*, Chaplin had twelve-year-old Lillita sit for a photograph in the pose of Sir Joshua Reynolds's famous portrait of an angelic little girl, *The Age of Innocence*. He created the role of the flirting angel in *The Kid* for Lita and constructed the elaborate dream sequence to accommodate her character. Lita's performance was both portentous of the difficult days to come and illustrative of Chaplin's fascination with awakening sexuality. The intertitles throughout the sequence are steeped in irony and metaphor: "The trouble begins." "Vamp him." "Innocence." "Getting flighty." Rollie Totheroh remembered Lita as a decidedly immature girl for whom Chaplin developed an immediate attraction. He recalled watching dailies with Chaplin of a sequence that does not appear in the finished film:

> There was a big close-up [in *The Kid*] where she [Lita] ties this villain up, supposed to be—Chuck [Riesner]—up there in heaven. Boy, he'd [Chaplin] run that back and forth and look at it; Jesus, his mouth would drool, and I said, "Oh, Jeez," I said to Jack [Wilson, second cameraman on *The Kid*],

"What the hell? That god-damn kid, a little bony-legged thing and that—what does he see in that?"[3]

Lita and her mother, Lillian, appeared briefly as French maids (and as extras in the costume-party sequence) in *The Idle Class*. Chaplin chose not to renew the option upon the expiration of Lita's one-year contract. However, a few years later, when Chaplin was auditioning for a new leading lady for *The Gold Rush*, fifteen-year-old Lita presented herself at the Chaplin Studios. Chaplin met with Lita and arranged for a screen test that day.

Apparently, Chaplin thought Lita was talented; after running her screen test several times—and despite the reservations of some of his associates—he signed her for the role of the dance-hall girl. The studio publicity department reported her age as nineteen in its press releases. Despite Lita's tenure as the film's leading lady for more than six months,

Lillita MacMurray (Lita Grey) in a 1920 photograph, posed, under Chaplin's instructions, like the figure in Sir Joshua Reynolds's painting THE AGE OF INNOCENCE. *Photographed at the Chaplin Studios by Roland H. Totheroh*

Chaplin filmed only one important scene with her, three weeks after signing her. The studio continuity reports from March 24, 1924, reveal Chaplin's preoccupation with his sexual attraction to Lita and the depth to which it was influencing his work. The scene evokes his own fantasies of her as his "forbidden fruit":

> Scene 14: Close-up. Dissolve. C. asleep in kitchen on couch. Lita standing over him with cake—wakens him—he sits up— she sits down beside him—smiles—takes berry—gives it to him—he turns forward—eats it—smiles—she takes another berry—starts to give it to him. She says: Close your eyes and open your mouth. He does so and she throws whole cake in his face and laughs. C. takes cake off—face all smeared with cream—Fade out and fade into close-up in cabin with C. asleep in cot—blanket over body but not on head—snow on neck and face—snow drops down from roof five times—he wakes up then sits up—and looks around room—brushes snow off—gets up— comes forward left of camera. O.K.[4]

The dance-hall girl does not appear until nearly one-third of the way through *The Gold Rush*. This odd structure perhaps reveals Chaplin's difficulty in constructing scenes that he felt the immature Lita was capable of playing. Indeed, most extant photographs of Lita from the production show her sitting idle or are merely costume tests, and the production records indicate that

Chaplin filmed few scenes with her. All but one of these scenes were shot on location at Truckee, the exception being the "forbidden fruit" dream sequence, which was filmed at the Chaplin Studios. During this period, Chaplin and Lita began a sexual relationship. He managed to rid them of Lita's mother as chaperone by using his friendship with Thelma Morgan Converse as a diversion. According to Lita:

> Charlie's chaperone subterfuge was working well, and the three of us regularly enjoyed evenings at the Montmartre Café or the Ambassador Hotel. . . . No matter where we went, the evening would always conclude with our dropping Thelma off early at her home, and then the two of us would spend some time alone at his Beverly Hills house. . . . We would invariably end the evenings in his bedroom; he always wanted to make love to me. Contraceptives were never used; Charlie believed that there was no danger of my becoming pregnant. I was young and totally inexperienced—I had never even been on a date before— and I had such complete hero worship for Charlie Chaplin that I trusted him implicitly. As I look back on those evenings, it astounds me that Charlie was never troubled by the possibility of my becoming pregnant. I can only attribute this to the child-like nature of the man.[5]

In September 1924, during the production of *The Gold Rush*, Lita became pregnant with their first child, Charles Chaplin Jr., and Chaplin ceased production on the film for more than three months. Initially, Chaplin asked Lita to have an abortion, which she refused. He next offered her $20,000 to marry someone else. That was also rejected by Lita's family. Lita's uncle, San Francisco attorney Edwin T. McMurray, informed Chaplin that California law viewed having sexual relations with a minor as statutory rape, with penalties of up to thirty years in prison. To quell looming legal threats and scandal, Chaplin married the sixteen-year-old Lita Grey in a clandestine ceremony held in Empalme, Mexico, on November 25, 1924, although the relationship had lost all passion for him. With the growing child distorting her thin

for forcing him into a marriage he did not want and his bitterness regarding their shameless attempt to ruin his reputation in order to obtain a large settlement was quite justified. Also in Chaplin's defense, by fifteen years of age, the well-developed Lita must have recognized her sexual charms and their effect on Chaplin. Flirtatious, self-absorbed, and naughty, Lita surely could not have been as innocent and unaware as she always maintained. Both of them were responsible for their own actions. But Chaplin, thirty-five years old at the time of the marriage and veteran of a previous unwanted teenage pregnancy and marriage to Mildred Harris, should have known better.

Some of Chaplin's bitterness toward Lita diminished as he became older, but he was still loath to discuss her. On the rare occasion when Lita came up in conversation, Chaplin reiterated, "I loved all the women in my life, except her."[14]

The continued fascination with Lita may in part be owing to Chaplin's own public silence about her. Indeed, Chaplin makes scant reference to Lita in his two autobiographical volumes, *My Autobiography* and *My Life in Pictures*. In *My Autobiography*, he writes only:

> During the filming of *The Gold Rush* I married for the second time. Because we have two grown sons of whom I am very fond, I will not go into any details. For two years we were married and tried to make a go of it, but it was hopeless and ended in a great deal of bitterness.[15]

Similarly, in *My Life in Pictures*, Chaplin avoids revealing any details of the marriage:

> My second marriage was even more disastrous than the first. The one good thing that came from it was the birth of two sons—Charles Jr. and Sydney. Lita Grey had played a small part in *The Kid* before I engaged her for *The Gold Rush*. We were married in 1924 and only remained together two years. The divorce was surrounded by an atmosphere of bitterness and squalor. This period in my life was a time of great professional prosperity but also of private grief. In addition to the unpleasantness of my relations with Lita Grey, I had the deep sorrow of my mother's death.[16]

Much of Lita's divorce settlement was paid to her legal team. Her excessive spending, poor money management, and the stock-market crash eliminated much of her remaining fortune. She also suffered later emotional trauma as a result of her abusive relationship with Chaplin. In 1928 she began what was to be nearly a decade of work singing on the Radio-Keith-Orpheum vaudeville circuit. Their two children, Charles Jr. and Sydney, continued to aggravate the lingering hostility between the former husband and wife. Chaplin and Lita were back in court in 1932 when he filed a petition objecting to their sons appearing in a film for Fox, for which she had signed a contract. The ruling was in Chaplin's favor. The following year, Chaplin's attorneys summoned Lita to court questioning her administration of the boys'

trust funds. The only agreement between the two during this period was to enroll the children in Black-Foxe Military Institute in Hollywood. Thus, the parents could arrange to have the children with them on various weekends with little contact between the two hostile parties. By 1936, Lita was an alcoholic and suffered the first of two nervous breakdowns from which she was to fully recover. Despite four subsequent marriages and divorces after her divorce from Chaplin, she always retained the name Lita Grey Chaplin. After the death of Charles Jr. in 1968 as a result of alcoholism, she began work as a sales clerk at Robinson's department store in Beverly Hills, a position she kept for fourteen years until her retirement at the age of seventy-seven.

By the time of Lita's death in 1995, she was Chaplin's last-surviving wife and the only one of his wives to leave an account of life with him. She had come to terms with her bitter divorce and her feelings of anger. She wrote two volumes of autobiography: *Wife of the Life of the Party*, completed at the end of her life, resulted from her conviction that she should correct the inaccuracies contained in her first "autobiography," *My Life with Chaplin: An Intimate Memoir*, which emphasized the more scandalous aspects of their relationship.

Lita often remarked that she saw Chaplin as two people, the man and the artist. She explained, "Charles Chaplin the man was very serious. The artist, when he was in costume, was a humorous man. I love Chaplin the artist. I believe him to be a multifaceted genius. But I also knew the man—in every conceivable mood— and Charlie's real love was his work. Anything that threatened that would bring out the worst in the man."[17] Although young Lita Grey had fallen in love with Chaplin the artist, it was the man she married. It was this dichotomy that proved the couple's undoing.

The Circus

After the critical and commercial success of *The Gold Rush,*
Chaplin was at a loss. He considered the film to be the summit
of his art and believed that surpassing (or even equaling) its success was a nearly impossible task. He first thought of producing
an idea he called *The Suicide Club* for his next project.[1] This
idea was quickly aborted in favor of a comedy production tentatively titled *The Dandy,* as it was reported in the *New York Times*
on November 29, 1925. However, when production had commenced on November 2, the third Chaplin film for United Artists
had the working title *The Traveler* and was planned as a five-
reel comedy, a less ambitious project than the nine-reel *The
Gold Rush.* By December 3, Chaplin had a circus tent under
construction and was rehearsing on a tightrope, which was to be
used in the film's climactic sequence. Henry Bergman remembered the genesis of *The Circus* in an interview:

> Before he had made *The Circus* he said to me one night,
> "Henry, I have an idea I would like to do: a gag placing me in
> a position I can't get away from for some reason. I'm on a high
> place troubled by something else, monkeys or things that
> come to me and I can't get away from them." He was mulling
> around in his head a vaudeville story. I said to him, "Charlie,
> you can't do anything like that on a stage. The audience would

Charlie is given a tryout as a clown in THE CIRCUS *(1928).*

be uncomfortable craning their necks to watch a vaudeville actor. It would be unnatural. Why not develop your idea in a circus tent on a tightrope. I'll teach you to walk a rope."[2]

The Suicide Club, The Dandy, and a film about Napoleon Bonaparte were discarded in favor of a comedy in which the Tramp unwittingly becomes the star attraction of a traveling circus. He falls in love with the equestrienne Merna, the ringmaster's stepdaughter, and loses her to Rex, the tightrope walker (Harry Crocker). The film concludes with the Tramp, having arranged the marriage of Merna and Rex, shuffling off alone into the distance, ready to begin life anew.

As indicated by the use of her name in the daily production reports and extant story notes from *The Circus,* Chaplin had originally intended the role of the equestrienne to go to Georgia Hale, the dance-hall girl in *The Gold Rush.* Hale's contract expired on December 31, 1925, however, and was not renewed. No primary source adequately explains the reason for her severance, but Hale probably was anxious to expedite her career. The production of *The Circus* would move along too slowly, so she had decided to move on herself. In Hale's place, Chaplin signed Merna Kennedy as his leading lady.

According to Lita Grey Chaplin:

> Merna Kennedy and I had been friends ever since dancing school together when we were small children. When Mr. Chaplin made it known that he was planning a film on the circus, it occurred to me that my friend Merna would be ideal for the leading lady and I asked him if he would consider testing her. He did not like me, or for that matter his crew even, to make suggestions about these matters, but he finally, after my pestering him, agreed to make a test of her. . . . Mr. Chaplin was very pleased with the test and paid me a compliment for suggesting that he consider her.[3]

Kennedy, along with her brother Merle, had toured in vaudeville in a dancing act. She had not only a pretty face but also the developed legs of a trapeze artist/equestrienne. Her contract commenced on January 2, 1926.

David Robinson wrote that *The Circus* "was to be a production dogged by persistent misfortune. The most surprising aspect of the film is not that it is as good as it is, but that it was ever completed at all."[4] Indeed, the film faced many potentially life-threatening pitfalls, four major disasters in all, suggesting a Chaplinesque version of *The Four Horseman of the Apocalypse.*

When Chaplin began filming, his first order of business was to shoot the seminal tightrope sequence. To photograph the climactic scene first was not in keeping with Chaplin's usual method of shooting films in chronological order. However, since he had been training to walk the tightrope and this sequence was fully worked out in his head, he decided to begin production with the difficult scenes.

On December 6, 1925, an incident occurred that foreshadowed the disasters that were to plague the production. On that afternoon, a violent storm tore apart the nearly completed circus tent on the studio back lot, destroying the film's largest set. Although the tent was reconstructed, a more tempestuous storm was brewing in the Chaplin Studios laboratory. The first of the film's four major disasters struck when the studio's film-processing laboratory discovered that the dailies of the tightrope scenes, filmed during the first month of production, were marred with scratches. There is no record of what exactly occurred, but an incensed Chaplin fired his entire laboratory staff. He then placed his studio laboratory under the supervision of William E. Hinckley. Chaplin must have been pleased with Hinckley's work, for he granted him an unusual screen credit in the completed film. Nevertheless, Chaplin was forced to shoot the difficult tightrope sequences all over again after weeks of arduous training and filming. For Chaplin, however, the ordeal of filming *The Circus* was only beginning.

On September 28, 1926, the second major disaster, a fire, swept through the studio. Before the fire was brought under control, the interior stage, props, electrical equipment, and thousands of glass panes in the walls and roof were destroyed by fire and water.

Hanging around the circus side shows hungry and broke, the Tramp ingratiates himself with a small child looking over his father's shoulder. The baby extends his hot dog to the Tramp, who takes a bite. The Tramp has no qualms about taking candy—or a frankfurter—from a baby in THE CIRCUS.

While the damaged sets and props were being rebuilt, the undaunted Chaplin began filming two sequences taking place en route to and inside a café, involving himself, Kennedy, Crocker, and Doc Stone (in a dual role as prizefighter Twin Spud and his twin brother), on October 3. The sequences were finished in eleven days; however, Chaplin did not see fit to include them in the final film. The mammoth 21,000 feet of unedited footage exist in the Chaplin Archives, and the sequences were assembled by Kevin Brownlow and David Gill and played in their entirety in the final episode of the three-part documentary *Unknown Chaplin* (1983), where they can be seen as delightful, perfectly constructed comedy pieces.

The cut café sequences were not the only film shot during the production of *The Circus* destined never to be shown in the cinema. While working on *The Circus*, Chaplin produced for the only time a film by another director. Josef von Sternberg, who had caught Chaplin's eye directing Georgia Hale in *The Salvation Hunters*, was writer and director of *A Woman of the Sea*, an Edna Purviance vehicle. *A Woman of Paris* had failed to meet Chaplin's expectations in establishing Purviance as a dramatic actress; he hoped Sternberg could utilize his early directorial promise by making *A Woman of the Sea*—and Purviance—a success.

Filming the Noah's ark funhouse sequence, on location in Venice, California

With the working title *Sea Gulls*, preproduction of *A Woman of the Sea* commenced on January 16, 1926, almost simultaneously with *The Circus*. Although Chaplin had no hand in the film, members of the *The Circus* crew also worked on the Sternberg film, such as cameraman Mark Marlatt and art director Danny Hall. *A Woman of the Sea* told the story of two daughters of a fisherman on the California coast. Purviance portrayed the good sister, Joan, and Eve Southern was cast to play Magdalen, Joan's manipulative sibling. The story was nothing more than a simple melodrama. The bad sister, Magdalen, leaves her fisherman fiancé, Peter (Raymond Bloomer), to seek the hedonism of the big city with a playboy novelist (Gayne Whiteman). Following Magdalen's departure, Joan marries Peter and begins a modest, yet happy, life with him. Soon Magdalen

returns and attempts, with some initial success, to tear Peter away from her sister. Magdalen's efforts are ultimately dashed, however, as Joan and Peter reconcile to resume their life together at the film's close.

The filming of *A Woman of the Sea* began on March 8 and was completed on June 3, 1926, but the film was never released. Upon seeing the finished version, Chaplin deemed it a failure. His ownership gave Chaplin the authority to shelve the film indefinitely, which he promptly did. Ultimately, the negative of *A Woman of the Sea* was destroyed by fire for tax purposes in 1933.[5] Chaplin's second attempt at making Purviance a star had failed. The anxiety of creating one film while making the executive decisions regarding another had placed a tremendous strain upon the

Above: Chaplin considered this
scene of Charlie being trapped
in the lion's cage as the only true
gag sequence in the film.

Opposite: Chaplin is distraught
over the damage caused by a
fire at the Chaplin Studios during
production of THE CIRCUS,
September 28, 1926.

increasingly harried Chaplin, during an increasingly difficult period of his professional career.

The divorce from Lita Grey was the third and most devastating disaster to strike the production of *The Circus*. All of Chaplin's marital and separate property (allegedly totaling $16 million) was placed into receivership pending the outcome of divorce litigation. In short, through the magic of the legal rules of civil enjoinder and attachment, Lita and her attorneys had embroiled all of Chaplin's net worth. Desperate to save his studio and his film, on December 3, 1926, Chaplin had nine reels of cut positive and thirteen reels of uncut negative of *The Circus* packed for removal to safety in New York. Remembering his previous difficult divorce (from Mildred Harris during the filming of *The Kid*), Chaplin had the foresight to protect his work before lawyers and court orders could seize it.

The divorce was but one of Chaplin's legal problems in January 1927. Just three days before Lita filed for divorce, Chaplin filed a complaint in federal court against *Pictorial Review*, a magazine that had just published the first installment of a four-part biography purporting to be the "*Real* Life Story" of Charlie Chaplin. The articles had been written by Jim Tully, an employee during the production of *The Gold Rush* who was known professionally as the "hobo author." Fearful that the Tully biography would generate negative publicity that might affect the impending divorce, Chaplin sued *Pictorial Review* on the grounds that the biography was unauthorized. Chaplin's attorney, Nathan Burkan, sought $500,000 in damages for the first published article and an injunction to prevent the release of the remaining installments. Chaplin's request was denied by the court, which allowed the remaining installments to be published on schedule. Even with his wealth of legal resources, and in no position to endure further public humiliation, the Tramp had been bested by the "hobo author."[6]

Adding to Chaplin's already woeful legal problems (and marking the fourth major disaster to beset *The Circus*), the Internal Revenue Service declared that Chaplin and the Charles Chaplin Film Corporation owed more than $1,670,000 in back taxes[7] and promptly put a lien on Chaplin's assets (the second lien to be placed on his property in January). The Chaplin Studios, however, had suspended operations on December 5, 1926. The corporation's daily production report from the following day states: "Studio operations suspended temporarily. Staff of employees cut down throughout studio, including actors, with exception of those remaining on list." The chosen few on that list were the film's principal players: Chaplin, Henry Bergman, Harry Crocker, Merna Kennedy, and Allan Garcia.

On January 16, 1927, the *New York Times* reported that the strain of these crushing legal and financial blows had finally taken its toll on Chaplin. While visiting his attorney Nathan Burkan in New York, Chaplin suffered a nervous breakdown. He did not work on *The Circus* again for eight months.

367

It is a testament to Chaplin as a man and as an artist that he was able to overcome these difficulties. His determination to continue making *The Circus* and the public's affection for him and his art would prevail. Throughout the eight-month hiatus, Chaplin sought refuge in New York City. The influential press of that city supported him, its society embraced and entertained him, and its citizenry delighted him with mountains of fan mail. Chaplin would later reward his loyal New York City admirers by holding the world premiere of *The Circus* in Manhattan on January 6, 1928, at the Mark Strand Theatre.

Chaplin finally resumed production of *The Circus* on September 6, 1927. The film was virtually complete at the time of the suspension; the material shot in the weeks after work resumed was to fill out and refine what had already been photographed. Upon his return, Chaplin edited and titled the picture. Ever the perfectionist, he shot 211,104 feet of film (on one camera), which were reduced to the finished length of approximately 6,500 feet. In these final weeks there was to be, however, one last trial to challenge the production unit. The circus wagons, which were to be used in the final scene of the picture, went missing. The police determined that they had been taken by some students to be used for a bonfire. An entire freshman class was arrested, but Chaplin declined to prosecute. The wagons were subsequently returned. The incident was but a final salvo to barrage the most difficult production of Chaplin's professional life.

The nightmarish incidents that besieged Chaplin during the production of *The Circus* later sullied his recollections of this period of his life. No doubt the film's enervating production history explains why Chaplin failed to devote one word to *The Circus* in his autobiography and why he chose not to revive the film for so many years after its initial release.

The Circus is a reflection of its time, a creation of the late 1920s. Like the decade of indulgence that spawned it, the film lavishly eschews any notions of economy in film production. Indeed, one of its outstanding qualities is its high production value. The one-ring circus created by Danny Hall, the film's designer, is superb. The exemplary design was further embellished by the animals and the numerous extras engaged to create an authentic circus atmosphere. (Starting with *Modern Times*, Chaplin's attention to such authenticity lessened, as he opted in later years to use rear-screen projection rather than constructing altogether authentic environs.) He was certainly not the only filmmaker engaging in elaborate film production. One need only look at the films of Chaplin's friend and United Artists partner, Douglas Fairbanks, whose *Douglas Fairbanks in Robin Hood* (1922) and *The Thief of Bagdad* (1924) were the apex of costly, larger-than-life cinema. In a time when Americans indulged themselves in bathtub gin, Babe Ruth, and the Charleston, American-made films had to compete for popular attention by providing comparable spectacle and excitement.

The Circus is one of several films to exploit a genre that thrived in the 1920s as a result of E. A. Dupont's influential film *Varieté*

Above: Charlie and the bareback rider (Merna Kennedy) in THE CIRCUS. Kennedy had a short and indifferent film career. She married choreographer-designer Busby Berkeley in 1934 and divorced two years later. Shortly after her second marriage in 1944, she died of a heart attack.

Opposite: Filming the Tramp, having fled the lion cage, atop a tent pole. Merna Kennedy is standing at center with Jack Wilson, Harry Crocker, Kono Toraichi, and Henry Bergman behind the camera. Seated in the chair is continuity secretary Della Steele.

(*Variety*, 1925), which explored the world of the variety stage and inspired many filmmakers to create pictures about theater, music-hall, or circus life. The trappings of a circus gave Chaplin the opportunity to make comic use of a wide selection of props. Indeed, Chaplin had originally decided to make a film about the circus expressly for that purpose, knowing that comic situations would develop from the location, not unlike a routine of the *commedia dell'arte*. According to a *New York Times* article, Chaplin had studied the early traditions of clowning as traced in M. Willson Disher's book *Clowns and Pantomimes,* in preparation for filming *The Circus*.[8] Chaplin's link to clowns of the past was not a novel conception. As a result of the tremendous success of *The Gold Rush,* the intellectual critics had begun to crown Chaplin a counterpart to great clowns such as Grimaldi and Grock. Disher suggests *The Circus* when he writes, "Charlie Chaplin begins as a half-wit, grows into an artful dodger and threatens to develop the theme of a clown's unrequited love in a serious cinema tragedy."[9] *The Circus* embodies the traditions of both popular cinema and classic clowning.

Perhaps the greatest influence on Chaplin's psyche, however, as he began to piece together the comic routines, situations, and circumstances that would become *The Circus,* was the arrival of talking pictures. In 1927, talkies were still a novelty, but the specter of sound film was not lost on Chaplin. Nowhere is this conflict more evident than in the final sequence of *The Circus*. As the Tramp sits alone in what once was the center ring of the circus, a parallel to Chaplin's situation is apparent. Not unlike Chaplin, the Tramp arrived at the circus and revolutionized the slapstick comedy, but that no longer pleased the audience. The Tramp had been wildly popular for a time under the big top, but now that time has passed. The show is moving on, leaving the Tramp alone in the very spot where he had enjoyed his great success. Chaplin must have felt the same profound isolation, fearing that talking pictures might soon leave him and his subtle artistry behind.

He began shooting the film's final sequence on October 10, 1927, four days after the premiere of *The Jazz Singer* (1927), the film that ushered in talking motion pictures. When Chaplin and Arthur Kay compiled a score for the premiere engagement of *The Circus,* Chaplin underscored the film's final sequence with one of the songs that had made *The Jazz Singer* a popular success—Irving Berlin's "Blue Skies." He rejected Al Jolson's exuberant rendition of the Berlin standard, opting instead to have it played slowly and sorrowfully. It is the final ironic comment in *The Circus,* one of the finest films of the 1920s and the last Chaplin film made in the silent era.

One of the most memorable sequences in the film involves the Tramp in the lion's cage. Indeed, it is as perfectly conceived, choreographed, and executed as any sequence in all of Chaplin's work. A possible influence for this sequence was Max Linder, who in his feature *Seven Years Bad Luck* (1921) enters a lion's cage to elude the police.[10] Prior to filming the scene, Chaplin had rehearsed a sequence with snakes, and would later film a sequence that included several tigers, but both scenes were later discarded. Shooting of the lion sequence began on August 4, 1926. Chaplin continued to refine the scene over the next two weeks of shooting, as indicated by the bit of business involving the bulldog, which was incorporated into the sequence on August 7. He tentatively finished the scene on August 13, after nine days' work, edited the scene, and shot retakes on August 17. The daily

production report of August 20 indicates that Chaplin was finished with the lion segment and was "cutting and working on balance of story." August 25 found Chaplin, ever the perfectionist, again shooting the lion sequence for the last time.

The fact that Chaplin's encounter with the lion lasts only three minutes (at twenty-four frames per second) but took three weeks and more than two hundred takes to film is a measure of the care and precision Chaplin devoted to this important scene. In the completed film, a tiger only briefly appears when Charlie opens a small hatch in the lion cage, revealing a snarling tiger in an adjacent wagon.

L'Estrange Fawcett, the British film critic for the *London Morning Post*, recorded his impressions of watching Chaplin film the lion's-cage sequence, corroborating that it was special for Chaplin, who considered it the only true "gag" in the picture. Chaplin told Fawcett:

> In this film we have a continuous working story and this scene
> with the cage is the only bit that can really be called a gag. In other
> words, we are interrupting the story momentarily to put this scene
> in. Hence, it must be exactly right, otherwise we shall spoil the
> general sense and upset the audience. You are only entitled to
> switch from the main theme if the switching is worthwhile.[11]

Opposite top: Chaplin, out of costume and makeup, rehearses a sequence of the Tramp preparing a snake sandwich that was abandoned from THE CIRCUS.

Opposite bottom: Spanish actress and chanteuse Raquel Meller visits Chaplin at the studio during production of THE CIRCUS, *June 16, 1926. Her singing of José Padilla's "La Violetera" ("Who'll Buy My Violets") made a great impression on Chaplin. He later used the song as the principal theme for the blind flower girl in his musical score to* CITY LIGHTS.

Above: The cast and crew of A WOMAN OF THE SEA *on location in Carmel, California, 1926. Edna Purviance is seated on the rock (center), with director Josef von Sternberg to the left and Gayne Whiteman to the right of her. Behind Whiteman is Eve Southern; to the right of her are Raymond Bloomer and Charles French. Cinematographer Mark Marlatt is next to the camera.*

Right: The Tramp, on the tightrope, is beset by three escaped monkeys in the climax of THE CIRCUS. *Photograph by Stern*

Below: Chaplin performed the close-ups of the tightrope sequence while standing on a wooden platform.

Opposite: In order to get the monkeys to perform the desired actions in the tightrope sequence, they were attached to fine strings that were manipulated off-camera by trainers.

183

would rob his screen character of its universality. What language would he speak and with what accent? He was concerned that, as the biggest name in the world market of motion pictures, he might lose a considerable amount of his audience if he made an English-language sound film.

Chaplin's unwillingness to discard the universality of the Tramp, compounded by the technical failures of the first talkies and the clumsy, stilted, and inartistic use of the new medium in its early stages, led him to begin his next film as a silent. As Chaplin wrote in My Autobiography, "I did not wish to be the only adherent of the art of silent pictures. . . . Nevertheless, City Lights was an ideal silent picture, and nothing could deter me from making it."[1] His only concession to the new medium would be a musical score of his own creation and sound effects that would be recorded for the film soundtrack.

Thus, City Lights, arguably the biggest gamble of Chaplin's career, became one of his greatest triumphs, a lyrical and sublime comedy of timeless humor and beauty. The film contains some of Chaplin's greatest sequences, including the film's opening scene in which a stone statue is unveiled to reveal the Tramp asleep in its lap; later scenes in which the Tramp accidentally swallows a whistle; his fighting in a boxing match; and the celebrated finale in which the once-blind flower girl recognizes the Tramp as her benefactor.

The financial demands of his divorce from Lita Grey and his personal and corporate income-tax troubles forced Chaplin to begin story work on the film before the Hollywood premiere of The Circus. Chaplin's first scenario idea was another circus story: a clown, who has lost his sight in an accident at the circus, conceals the fact from his nervous and unwell little daughter until she is strong enough to understand because the shock might be too great for her. Chaplin ultimately rejected the idea as too sentimental. However, the idea of blindness captured his imagination, and from the story of the clown evolved the story of the Tramp and his affection for a blind flower girl, a subject similar to Harry Langdon's finest comedy, The Strong Man (1926).

Chaplin worked on the story for more than a year, inventing, refining, and rejecting ideas; voluminous working notes of discarded plot devices and gags survive in the Chaplin Archives. He finally developed two definite ideas: the character of the blind girl and the final recognition scene between the girl and the Tramp. To start filming City Lights with a clear plan for the film's final scene was unusual for Chaplin. Normally, he would have several scenarios in mind and would work them through on the set and see where they led him. But Chaplin's thoroughness in preparation shows that he was looking for a simple, linear tale in which to set the Tramp character. He also intended from the start for the Tramp to be more self-consciously romantic than in his previous films (the film would be labeled "A Comedy Romance in Pantomime" in the main titles).

The genius of City Lights lies in its simplicity. The film tells the story of the Tramp's love for a blind flower girl who mistakes him

for a rich man. The Tramp's devotion to the girl forces him to undertake a slew of menial jobs to earn the money to play the part of a gentleman. He also befriends an eccentric millionaire whom he saves from suicide in a moment of drunken depression. An alcoholic, the millionaire is expansive and treats the Tramp lavishly when intoxicated but forgets knowing him when he becomes sober.

The Tramp learns that the girl's sight might be restored if she travels to Vienna for an operation. He unsuccessfully works as a street cleaner and as an amateur boxer to earn the money for her trip. Once again he encounters the inebriated millionaire, who gives him the money. A burglary of the millionaire's home coincides with the gift; the event sobers up the millionaire, and the Tramp is suspected of the theft. He goes to prison, but not before he has given the money to the blind girl.

The Tramp is eventually released from prison in a dejected and tattered state. The flower girl, however, is now cured of her affliction and manages her own flower shop. She longs to meet her benefactor— whom she imagines to be handsome and rich. When the Tramp wanders in front of her prosperous shop, he gazes upon her with delight. She takes pity on him by offering him a flower and a coin. As he attempts to shuffle away, she presses the coin into his hand, which she

gradually recognizes by the touch. "You?" she asks him in an intertitle, realizing that he is the man who was her benefactor. He nods and says, "You can see now?" "Yes, I can see now," she responds. This moment of recognition, which concludes the film, is perhaps the most sublime and celebrated sequence in all of silent cinema.

Chaplin began preproduction on *City Lights* on May 5, 1928. It was during this period of preparation that Chaplin's mother, Hannah, died at the Glendale Hospital, on August 28. She had been taken to the hospital about a week before her death, suffering from an inflammation of the gall bladder. Chaplin had often found it too anguishing to visit his mother during the seven-year period she lived in a small, rented home in present-day Studio City under the care of a married couple. His visits with her made him very depressed and unable to work for days. Both Chaplin's grandmother and mother had been clinically insane, and he was worried that the infirmity was hereditary. However, he suppressed his fears and visited her at the hospital every day, forcing himself to laugh with her as she endured severe abdominal pain. The stated cause of death was cholecystitis, and she was buried at Hollywood Memorial Park Cemetery. Chaplin was devastated by the loss of his mother, and it is perhaps no coincidence that in his new film his character rescued a disabled woman and caused her to be cured of her affliction.

Throughout much of the work on *City Lights,* Chaplin was in an unusually nervous state over the risks of making an anachronistic silent film. Adding to his anxiety was Chaplin's desire to create for the first time a fully developed and believable romance

Above: Chaplin rehearses Virginia Cherrill for the first meeting of the Tramp and the blind flower girl in CITY LIGHTS, with Rollie Totheroh behind the camera. In the finished film, the meeting of two characters appears as natural as "water running over a pebble," in the words of Alistair Cooke. However, this scene gave Chaplin more difficulty than any other, taking weeks of work. Chaplin later recalled, "We took this day after day after day. She'd be doing something which wasn't right. Lines. A line. A contour hurts me if it's not right. She'd say, 'Flower, sir?' I'd say, 'Look at that! Nobody says flower like that.' She was an amateur." The scene holds the Guinness World Record for the highest number of retakes.

Below: Charlie meets the blind flower girl (Virginia Cherrill) and buys a flower. Cherrill was briefly married to actor Cary Grant. She retired from film work to become the second wife of the ninth earl of Jersey and an international socialite. Her final marriage was to Florian Martini, with whom she moved to Montecito, California, where she became a figure in the local community and was admired for her charity work. She died in 1996.

Opposite: Chaplin demonstrates how Virginia Cherrill is to play her part as the blind flower girl. Cameraman Rollie Totheroh is in the background. "He would act out every part and show you exactly—every nuance, every glance, and every movement— how he wanted it played," remembered Virginia Cherrill. "He completely took on the different characters. You found yourself feeling that he was you . . . and that he was that person."

for the Tramp. It is with typical Chaplinesque irony that he would achieve his most satisfying cinematic romance with the one leading lady to whom he felt the least romantically attached.

Chaplin had auditioned many young actresses before he noticed twenty-year-old Virginia Cherrill when they both sat ringside at a boxing match at the Hollywood Legion Stadium. Although a beautiful blonde, it was the manner in which she coped with her nearsightedness that earned her the role. "Being young and wanting the attention of men, I did not wear glasses,"[2] remembered Cherrill. Her myopia could help her successfully convey the appearance of being blind without compromising her striking beauty. She was, according to Chaplin, the only actress he tested who "could look blind without being offensive."[3] The Illinois native was visiting California, where she had been recovering from a difficult divorce from Chicago attorney Irving Adler. She had no previous acting experience. Nevertheless, on November 1, 1928, Chaplin put her under contract.

With his leading lady in place, on December 31 Chaplin began filming *City Lights*. He had been working for almost a year on the story, yet it was far from its final structure. However, he was anxious to film the first meeting of the Tramp and the blind flower girl.

Chaplin devoted much time and energy to Cherrill, spending days choreographing and filming the first meeting sequence. He would not hesitate to retake a scene if he felt she was holding a flower improperly, if the timing of her movement was off, if she was not completely concentrating on the scene, or even if she spoke the line of dialogue, "flower, sir?"—which no one would hear in the finished film—incorrectly. Another problem that plagued Chaplin was his inability to craft a plausible reason why she should assume the Tramp to be a rich man. Cherrill was convinced that if Chaplin did not know what he was going to do next, he would simply retake the same sequence over and over again until he was inspired. His unrelenting direction of Cherrill in his quest for perfection was such that the scene in which they first

premiere took place at the George M. Cohan Theatre, where it ran twelve weeks, setting records and grossing more than $400,000 (at admission prices of fifty cents and one dollar). The theater circuits were eager to play *City Lights* after the record-breaking opening run, and United Artists had no problems getting Chaplin's desired percentage of the gross for rentals of the film. Chaplin's negative cost for *City Lights* was $1,607,351. The film eventually earned him a worldwide profit of $5 million ($2 million domestically and $3 million in foreign distribution), an enormous sum of money for the time.

After the triumphant premieres in Los Angeles and New York City, Chaplin traveled to London for the British premiere at the Dominion Theatre and the start of a world tour that was to last a year and four months. He chose to savor his success and was not eager to return to Los Angeles and contemplate his future film work in the era of talking films. Moreover, the Depression had hit the motion-picture industry, and, despite income from *City Lights,* Chaplin gave the directive to Alf Reeves at the Chaplin Studios to terminate the employment of the staff. From Great Britain, Chaplin traveled on to Germany, Austria, Italy, France, Algeria, and Spain; he went back to Paris and England before visiting Singapore, Bali, and Japan, finally returning to Los Angeles in June 1932.

While on this extended trip he was hosted by many luminaries of the period—Winston Churchill, George Bernard Shaw, H. G. Wells, Albert Einstein, the Prince of Wales, and Mahatma Gandhi among them. He also embarked on a succession of romantic adventures, the most notable of which was with May Reeves, a multilingual Austrian or Austro-Hungarian woman who was initially hired to translate mail written in languages that Chaplin's publicist Carlyle Robinson could not read. Reeves chronicled the affair in her 1935 book *Charlie Chaplin Intime,* in collaboration with Claire Goll. Chaplin also read a great deal and spent some of his time while traveling writing a new economic plan that he believed might solve the current worldwide depression.

For the most part, *City Lights* was enthusiastically received by the press and public all over the world.[15] In the final analysis, Chaplin had done what many thought impossible. He had produced a critically and commercially successful silent film three years after the demise of American silent cinema. (Conversely, Buster Keaton and Harold Lloyd were both anxious to make talking films as soon as they could, which contributed to their artistic eclipses in the early 1930s.) More astonishing was the *City Lights* reissue in 1950, when it was praised by *Life* magazine as "the best movie of 1950,"[16] which firmly established the film's place as one of the finest motion pictures ever created. *City Lights* also holds the special distinction of being Chaplin's own favorite of all his films. Indeed, the film is his most perfect blend of comedy and pathos. It has the same lovely humanity of *The Kid* and *The Gold Rush,* and it remains one of his best-loved and most critically acclaimed films.

The depth of musical layering and color of the orchestrations of Chaplin's music were not fully appreciated until 1988, when the score was reconstructed by Carl Davis for a rerecording of the original music track and performed the following year as live orchestral accompaniment to the film at performances commemorating the centenary of Chaplin's birth.

After a preview on January 19, 1931, at the Tower Theatre in Los Angeles, Chaplin edited the film slightly based on the audience reaction (reediting, which had been a common practice in silent films, was not as inexpensive or simple with sound film). In the intervening three years since the advent of talking pictures, silent film had become a curiosity. Yet Chaplin turned the novelty of the film's non-talking status to his advantage as a daring artistic choice. On January 30, the world premiere of *City Lights* was held at the new Los Angeles Theater, the last and most lavish of the great movie palaces built on Broadway in that city. It was said to be one of the greatest premieres in Hollywood history up to that time, with a crowd of almost 25,000 nearly causing a riot. Chaplin's personal guests were Professor and Mrs. Albert Einstein.

For the New York City opening, Chaplin decided to exhibit *City Lights* independently, as United Artists hesitated to accept Chaplin's wish that the distributor charge fifty percent of the gross in all the first-run theaters, an unprecedented price. The

Opposite: Chaplin appears justifiably worried by the thousands of admirers gathered to greet him upon his arrival at Paddington Station in London, February 19, 1931.

Above: Chaplin and George Bernard Shaw in the dress circle of the Dominion Theatre for the London premiere of CITY LIGHTS, February 27, 1931. Shaw proclaimed Chaplin to be "the only genius developed in motion pictures." In 1947 Shaw modified his proclamation, "Nobody is the ONLY genius. Mr. Chaplin, no longer Charlie, is probably one of the best half-dozen."

Left: Chaplin meets Mahatma Gandhi at the modest home of an Indian physician living in the East End of London, September 22, 1931. Gandhi's ideas regarding machinery influenced the assembly-line sequences Chaplin later created for MODERN TIMES.

Modern Times

The genesis of *Modern Times* is rooted in Chaplin's sixteen-month world tour following the premiere of *City Lights* in 1931. As he traveled, he saw firsthand the economic and political consequences of the Depression and met some of the most influential thinkers of the era, such as Churchill, Shaw, Einstein, and Gandhi. This journey provided the context for *Modern Times*. Chaplin wrote a five-part series of articles about his trip titled "A Comedian Sees the World," originally published in *Woman's Home Companion* in 1933 and 1934, which demonstrates his desire to address social and political issues. Upon his return to the United States, Chaplin was struck with the idea for the film after learning about healthy young men who had been lured away from their farms to work in factories in Detroit but, after several years on the assembly line, succumbed to nervous breakdowns.[1] *Modern Times* evolved into a comedy that embraces difficult subjects such as strikes, riots, unemployment, poverty, and the tyranny of automation. Like *The Great Dictator* that would follow, the film is steeped in the political and social realities of its time.

Modern Times is also Chaplin's self-conscious valedictory to the pantomime of silent film he had pioneered and nurtured

Charlie the factory worker is a nineteenth-century cavalier trying to survive the alienating, materialistic, and technologically driven twentieth century in MODERN TIMES (1936).

Opposite: Chaplin had been intrigued with Napoleon Bonaparte since early childhood, when his mother told him that his father resembled the emperor. In 1922, while searching for a dramatic vehicle for Edna Purviance, Chaplin first entertained the idea of a film about Napoleon and Josephine Beauharnais. He first wore this costume at a fancy-dress party in 1925; shown here is a c. 1930 test photograph he made in costume for the role. Chaplin completed two motion-picture scripts on the subject before abandoning his efforts to bring the Little Corporal to the screen.

Top: Chaplin liked this photograph of himself (a detail of a larger photo of Chaplin flanked by members of the Yiddish Theater in Los Angeles in 1934) and arranged for it to become his official United Artists portrait, which was used in numerous company publications into the early 1950s.

Middle: Chaplin aboard his boat, the PANACEA, c. 1934. "All boats should be called PANACEA, for nothing is more recuperative than a sea-voyage," Chaplin wrote in his autobiography. "Your worries are adjourned, the boat adopts you, and cures you and, when finally she enters port, reluctantly gives you back again to the humdrum world."

Bottom: Chaplin, out of costume and makeup, rehearses the feeding-machine scene in MODERN TIMES, October 1934, with assistant director Carter De Haven at left. Chaplin manipulated the revolving table and mouth wiper with levers concealed underneath the table.

Charlie goes beserk on the assembly line, assuming the pose of Pan. Stanley J. "Tiny" Sandford, Heinie Conklin, and Walter James are the workers in the background.

into one of the great art forms of the twentieth century. Although technically a sound film, very little of the soundtrack to *Modern Times* contains dialogue. With the exception of the mechanical salesman scene, there are only ten lines of dialogue in the eighty-nine-minute film. The soundtrack is primarily Chaplin's own score and sound effects as well as a performance of a song by the Tramp, in gibberish. Chaplin remembered:

> Since the innovation of sound in movies, I could not determine my future plans. Although *City Lights* was a great triumph and had made more money than any talking picture at that time, I felt that to make another silent film would be giving myself a handicap—also I was obsessed by a depressing fear of being old-fashioned. Although a good silent film was more artistic, I had to admit that sound made characters more present.

> Occasionally I mused over the possibility of making a sound film, but the thought sickened me, for I realised I could never achieve the excellence of my silent pictures. It would mean giving up my tramp character entirely. Some people suggested that the Tramp might talk. This was unthinkable, for the first word he uttered would transform him into another person. Besides, the matrix out of which he was born was as mute as the rags he wore.[2]

The opening title to the film reads, "Modern Times: a story of industry, of individual enterprise, humanity crusading in the pursuit of happiness." The first shots of the film are of sheep intercut with factory-bound workers crowding out of a subway. At the Electro Steel Corporation, the firm's president (Allan Garcia) occupies himself by working on a jigsaw puzzle and reading a comic strip when not broadcasting his stern face over the closed-circuit video screen. The Tramp is a worker on a factory conveyor belt. The little fellow's early misadventures at the factory include being volunteered for a feeding machine, a time-saving device employed so that workers may continue working during their lunch breaks. Ultimately, the Tramp has a nervous breakdown and throws himself down a chute into the belly of the factory. Released from the hospital, he quickly lands in prison as a communist leader when he innocently picks up a red flag that has fallen from a truck and finds himself inadvertently leading a workers' parade. After the Tramp prevents a jail break, life in prison becomes so pleasant (he is better fed, clothed, and sheltered in the safe and secure prison than in the chaos of society during the Depression) that he is saddened to be pardoned.

At first the Tramp is determined to return to jail, yet decides to remain in the world when he meets the Gamine (Paulette Goddard), an adolescent orphaned when her father is killed in a labor dispute, who is being pursued by juvenile-care authorities. Both the Tramp and the Gamine yearn for the American Dream of domestic life, imagining themselves in a simple home in a suburban development. Inspired by the Gamine to get a job instead of returning to prison, the Tramp is hired as a night watchman in a department store. He lands in jail again when the department store is robbed by some of his former factory-worker compatriots. When released from prison again, the Tramp finds that the Gamine has acquired them a "home," in a dilapidated shanty shack, a comic version of the Hoovervilles of the period. Having found work at the Jetson Mill, the Tramp promptly loses the job in

Charlie's dance of dynamo rebellion in MODERN TIMES

a labor walkout. Meanwhile, the Gamine has found work dancing in a café and persuades the proprietor (Henry Bergman) to
hire the Tramp as a singing waiter. The Tramp's complete lack of
skill tending to tables in the café is compensated for by his great
success as a singing waiter. However, the juvenile-care authorities pursue the Gamine, forcing them to flee their new jobs and
take to the open road. Discouraged, the Gamine asks the Tramp,
"What's the use of trying?" Summoning his trademark optimism,
the Tramp responds, "Buck up! We'll get along!" Heartened, the
Gamine replies, "You betcha! Let's go!" Arm in arm, they walk off
toward the horizon, off to pursue a better life. It is the Tramp's
very last shuffle down the open road. This time, however, he has
a companion by his side.

Paulette Goddard had been Chaplin's real-life companion as
well since July 1932, and on September 4, 1934, he put her under
contract and cast her as the "Gamin," as he called the character
in the film (although he would later correct this to *gamine* in his
autobiography). Chaplin wrote:

> Paulette struck me as being somewhat of a *gamine*. This would
> be a wonderful quality for me to get on the screen. I could imag-
> ine us meeting in a crowded patrol wagon, the tramp and this
> gamine, and the tramp being very gallant and offering her his
> seat. This was the basis on which I could build plot and sundry
> gags. . . . From then on, the theme is about two nondescripts try-
> ing to get along in modern times. They are involved in the
> Depression, strikes, riots and unemployment. Paulette was
> dressed in rags. She almost wept when I put smudges on her
> face to make her look dirty. "Those smudges are beauty spots,"
> I insisted.[3]

The Gamine is first seen stealing bananas from a boat on the
waterfront. She is a free spirit with an almost Fairbanksian joie de
vivre. Her adventures provide an independent, parallel narrative

to the Tramp's own pursuits, and Chaplin's pairing of the two is a
departure from his screen relationships with past leading ladies.
The Gamine is the Tramp's partner, like Jackie Coogan in *The
Kid,* and not a romantic interest, which had been the pattern. The
impecunious Gamine is almost a female reflection of the Tramp.
The pair's chaste relationship is confirmed at their Hooverville
shack, where the Tramp sleeps in a doghouse. The ending of the
film reinforces the notion of their true companionship and insep-
arability as they walk together, hand in hand, side by side, down
the lonely, open road.

Paulette Goddard is superb in the film. With *Modern Times,*
Chaplin established Goddard's acting career and star quality,
succeeding where he had failed in his attempts to boost his longtime leading lady, Edna Purviance. "That was my best film
work," recalled Goddard late in her life, "and it's still my favorite
movie. Charlie could be difficult at times, but it was an education
and a marvelous experience."[4]

Chaplin began preproduction on *Modern Times* in March
1933 and filming began on October 11, 1934, at his Hollywood
studio and nearby locations. Art directors Danny Hall and Russell
Spencer supervised the construction of the impressive factory
interiors in the studio, although their large scale was partially an
effect: Rollie Totheroh used a hanging miniature to achieve the
illusion of a vast factory. (The hanging miniature is a visual effect
created by hanging a small-scale set in front of the camera in perfect alignment and perspective with an existing full-size set in the
distance to achieve the desired background.) Similarly, rear-
screen projection—a technique incorporated by Chaplin for the
first time in this film—was employed for the factory's monitoring
system as well as the scene in which a boat is accidentally
launched (a full-scale boat and miniature boat were used to complete the scene). Other elements of illusion integrated into the
film include the Tramp's brilliant roller-skating routine in the

5-P-178

The impecunious Gamine (Paulette Goddard) delights in stealing bananas and feeding the hungry. This photograph conveys some of Goddard's considerable sexual charm.

empty department store where he is engaged as the night watch-man. The "thrill" comedy of the Tramp skating perilously close to the edge of a balcony without a balustrade was achieved with a glass shot to create the illusion of height. (A glass shot involves a painted scene on a pane of glass that is placed in front of the cam-era and precisely aligned with the existing set to achieve the desired effect.) However, no illusion is involved with Chaplin's considerable skating skills, first demonstrated in *The Rink* nearly twenty years earlier. He devoted eight days to filming the roller-skating routine.

Chaplin tended to work longer days on *Modern Times* than on his previous films. In the last stage of filming, which was com-pleted on August 30, 1935, Chaplin's concentration was so focused that he in fact lived at the studio. Actual production took 147 days, and 263 days were spent on preproduction and post-production work. Totaling 410 days (approximately thirteen-and-a-half months), actual filming of *Modern Times* was in fact the shortest of any Chaplin film since *A Woman of Paris*. (As a point of comparison, a typical A feature film of the period would have taken forty to fifty production days to complete while B films were often finished in five to seven production days.) Chaplin filmed 213,961 feet of film (on one camera) to achieve the final length of 8,126 feet.

Because of the high esteem in which the film is held, it is easy to forget that Chaplin took a great risk in making an essentially speechless film so many years removed from the end of the silent era. He had actually tested some scenes of dialogue between the Tramp and the Gamine at the end of November 1934 but ulti-mately discarded them. A dialogue script prepared for all the scenes up to and including the department-store scene survives in the Chaplin Archives. For the scene where the Tramp and the Gamine sit on a curb and introduce themselves before contem-plating their dream home (called "the road scene" in the script), Chaplin prepared the following exchange, which indicates the quick, silly, and simple dialogue he was considering for the Tramp:

> Girl: What's your name?
> Tramp: Me? Oh, mine's a silly name. You wouldn't like it. It
>   begins with an "X."
> Girl: Begins with an "X"?
> Tramp: See if you can guess.
> Girl: Not eczema?
> Tramp: Oh, worse than that—just call me Charlie.
> Girl: Charlie! There's no "X" in that!
> Tramp: No—oh, well, where d'ya live?
> Girl: No place—here—there—anywhere.
> Tramp: Anywhere? That's near where I live.

Despite all of Chaplin's preparation for talking sequences, he ultimately filmed only one dialogue scene. While in the jail war-den's office, the Tramp, in his confusion, reduces the surname of the minister and his wife—Stumbleglutz—to "Rumblegutz." This faux pas frames the stomach-rumbling sequence, in which the

Tramp encounters the minister's wife and must endure her stony silence during the embarrassment of a duet of their empty, gur-gling stomachs. Totheroh recalled that Chaplin was his own sound-effects artist for many of these sounds; he created the sound of rumbling stomachs by blowing bubbles into a large pail only partially filled with water with a sheet covering the top of it.[5] Although the dialogue for the scene was ultimately abandoned, the sound effects remain in the film.

For a speechless film, *Modern Times* is remarkably full of sound. It is brimming with various sound effects—including pieces of dialogue—making the use of sound vastly more com-plex than in *City Lights*. The spoken parts in the film, which are transmitted primarily through machines in a cold and impersonal manner (closed-circuit television, the portable phonograph recording of the mechanical salesman for the demonstration of the feeding machine, and radio bulletins and commercials), emphasize Chaplin's theme of the deterioration of human rela-tionships and the dehumanizing effects of mechanization.

The most famous sound sequence in the film is the one in which the Tramp is called upon to sing in the café but cannot remember the words, so the Gamine writes them on his cuff. When he loses his cuffs while making an energetic entrance just prior to singing, he resorts to making up the words. Chaplin is ingeniously "silent" by speaking only gibberish but is inventive with his use of the spoken word and sound. The song itself is sung in a comic language with hints of French, Italian, and German to the tune of "Je cherche après Titine" (a popular song of the time by Leo Daniderff that was called "Titina" in America). Chaplin's intonation, expression, and pantomime as he sings make the gib-berish perfectly understandable.

This remarkable performance marks the first time audiences ever heard Chaplin's voice on screen and the only time the Tramp ever spoke. Chaplin resisted talking pictures in part because the Tramp's silence made him understood around the world. However, with the gibberish song, Chaplin ingeniously answers his critics by implying that talking in any one language is mean-ingless in all others, while at the same time allowing the Tramp to "speak" in a way that is universally understood. The song was filmed live with an off-camera orchestra and not dubbed in post-production. Conductor Alfred Newman and fifty players were brought to the studio in the evening to avoid the noise of the day-time traffic of nearby La Brea Avenue. Curiously, Chaplin later cut the last verse of the song from the film for his 1954 reissue.

Modern Times boasts possibly Chaplin's finest film score. Work on the music commenced in August 1935, with Newman as conductor (a role he had performed on *City Lights*) and Edward Powell as orchestrator. Powell had engaged David Raksin to assist in the orchestrations and work directly with Chaplin for his musical input. Chaplin had some initial misgivings about Raksin's age and relative inexperience. After only a week and a half he fired Raksin. However, ultimately the two men reestablished pro-fessional and musical harmony, which resulted in four-and-a-half

5-P-246

Above: Filming Chaplin in front of the rear-screen projection that simulates the inadvertent boat launch in MODERN TIMES, *at the Chaplin Studios*

Opposite: Chaplin and Goddard on location on West Bluffside Drive, Studio City, California, in April 1935. Continuity secretary Della Steele is seated on the right. Photograph by Max Munn Autrey

months of fruitful collaboration neither had thought possible at the onset of their relationship. Despite the high quality of the score, Chaplin had a disagreement with Newman during a grueling recording session on December 4, 1935, which ended with Newman storming out of the session enraged, never to return. Powell took over the remaining work as conductor.

Chaplin's most recognizable and commercially viable song, "Smile," emerged from a melody used by him in *Modern Times*. It was created to promote the reissue of *Modern Times* in 1954. United Artists engaged Geoffrey Parsons and John Turner to refine and provide lyrics to the Chaplin melody and landed recording star Nat King Cole to sing it. "Smile" is still considered a popular standard today.

Modern Times is perhaps best known for its factory sequences. Each of the gags in the factory plays on the film's theme of the loss of humanity in a mechanized world. Chaplin places the Tramp into a variety of automated nightmares, including the feeding

machine gone haywire and ultimately, in a profound statement of humanity's subordinate role to automation, the cogs of the factory machinery itself. In the hilarious sequence in which the Tramp is chosen to try the experimental "Billows Feeding Machine," he confronts a turntable with arms that push food directly into his mouth, followed by a sterilized mouth wiper. A malfunction (the "mesh transmission" becomes out of sync with the "double shaft knee action") causes the feeding machine to spill soup on his face, grind a whirling ear of corn into his mouth, and smash cake in his face, after which he is repeatedly slapped in the face faster and faster by the mouth wiper.

In another scene early in the film, the Tramp, driven mad by the monotonous task of tightening nuts on the assembly line, dances a joyful revolt against automation. He gleefully squirts the workers on the line with his oil can, as if to chide them for shedding their humanity and acting like mere gears in the system. But the most famous factory sequence—and one of the most celebrat-

ed moments from all Chaplin's films—follows the Tramp's nervous breakdown: he is literally swallowed whole by the massive machines at the factory when he hurls himself down a chute at the end of a conveyor belt in a desperate attempt to tighten a nut. The Tramp is pushed along the gears of the machine as if he were another cog, stripped of all his humanity. The image of man eaten by machine was formed in Chaplin's mind when, as a boy, he worked three weeks at Straker's, a printing and stationery shop, operating a Wharfdale printing machine. The first day he was a nervous wreck for he felt the enormous machine, over twenty feet long, was going to devour him.[6] This fear never left him, and he incorporated it in *Modern Times* to superb effect.

With *Modern Times* Chaplin proves to be quite a prescient futurist. More than ten years before George Orwell's *1984* and at a time when practical television was little more than a laboratory demonstration, Chaplin utilizes in *Modern Times* a prototype of Big Brother's invasive monitoring system.

Chaplin in his director's chair during production of MODERN TIMES. *Assistant director Carter De Haven is seated with his legs crossed beyond Chaplin. Behind the camera are Ira Morgan and Rollie Totheroh. Seated behind Chaplin is continuity secretary Della Steele. Standing at far right is Paulette Goddard.*

Above left: Chaplin directing Paulette Goddard on location in Los Angeles during production of MODERN TIMES. Photograph by Max Munn Autrey

Above right: Jackie Coogan visits Chaplin at the studio during production of MODERN TIMES and poses as the Kid grown up, 1935. Coogan had recently lost his father in a car crash and was experiencing financial difficulties. He appealed to Chaplin for assistance, who readily gave him $1,000 that day.

Right: English novelist H. G. Wells, former heavyweight boxing champion Gene Tunney, and Chaplin (with his arm in a sling from an injury that occurred during production of MODERN TIMES) at the Vendome Café, where Chaplin arranged an informal party for Wells during his visit to Hollywood, December 2, 1935

Above: Charlie feeds lunch to the walrus-mustached mechanic (Chester Conklin), who has been caught up in the wheels of a gigantic machine, in MODERN TIMES. Conklin, a veteran of Chaplin's Keystone comedies, worked for three weeks to complete his sequence in the film.

Right: The Tramp performs his gibberish song as a singing waiter. (Frame enlargement from 35mm motion-picture film)

Opposite: The Tramp and the Gamine travel down the open road at the end of MODERN TIMES, ready to face together whatever the future might bring. Photograph by Max Munn Autrey

Although Chaplin's inventiveness is rife throughout the film, a well-known claim was made by the Franco-German company Films Tobis Sonores requesting 1.2 million francs in damages for alleged plagiarism of the assembly-line sequence in René Clair's *À Nous la liberté* (1931). The case never went to trial, and in 1947 the company dropped its claim in consideration of $5,000 in America and 2.5 million francs (about $25,000 in 1947 dollars) in France. Clair was quoted in *Le Soir* on October 28, 1936, "Chaplin is too great a man and I admire him too much to admit that his creative genius should be contested in any way. I, myself, owe him very much. And besides, if he has borrowed a few ideas from me, he has done me a great honor."[7] Chaplin believed that the obstinacy of the claim was an effort by the Nazi-influenced German firm Tobis to humiliate him after he announced that he was making *The Great Dictator*. Although Chaplin maintained he did not intentionally borrow from *À Nous la liberté*—his concept for the feeding machine and other ideas about the dehumanization of technology went as far back as 1916—one scene in the film is unmistakably influenced by Clair. The Tramp, an inept waiter

in the café, attempts to carry a roast-duck dinner on a tray across a crowded dance floor and must contend with a few inebriated collegians who pick up the duck and start tossing it around like a football. The Tramp finally intercepts a pass and runs his touchdown. The roast-duck football/rugby skirmish is nearly identical to a scene with a folded jacket in Clair's *Le Million* (1931).

Chaplin previewed *Modern Times* at the United Artists Theatre in San Francisco in December 1935 and later at the Alexander Theatre, Glendale, in January 1936. The world premiere took place at the Rivoli Theatre in New York City on February 5. After the premiere, Chaplin, Goddard, and her mother went on an extended vacation to Hawaii and then throughout Asia.

Before the opening of *Modern Times*, a few columnists wrote that they had heard rumors the picture employed communist themes. These views were based on reports of the proletarian ideas demonstrated in the factory scenes and in the scene where the Tramp picks up a red flag and unwittingly leads a communist march. The film originally had the working title *Commonwealth* and later *The Masses*, which led some to draw conclusions about

This page and opposite:
An alternate ending for MODERN TIMES, in which Paulette Goddard's character of the Gamine becomes a nun, was filmed in May and early June 1935. Chaplin was experimenting for a way to match the ending of CITY LIGHTS in its pathos. A screening of the assembled material at the studio in July quickly convinced him of the error of this mawkish finale. The sequence began with the Tramp, recovered from another nervous breakdown brought on by factory work, being visited by the Gamine (who became a nun during his convalescence) and her Mother Superior in the hospital reception room on the day he is discharged (right). The Tramp is bewildered by the Gamine's transformation; a barrier has risen between the two friends. Charlie is unable to speak and becomes embarrassed as she holds his hand (below). The Tramp and the Gamine bid their final goodbyes at the entrance of the hospital (opposite top) before Charlie slowly walks away (opposite bottom). According to Chaplin's scenario, as the little fellow walks away the Gamine, standing as though lost in a dream, watches after him and "her spirit goes with him, for out of herself the ghost of the Gamin [sic] appears and runs rampant down the hospital steps, dancing and bounding after him, calling and beckoning as she runs toward him. Along that lonely road she catches up with him, dancing and circling around him, but he does not see her, he walks alone."

superhuman power the Tramp acquires when accidentally drugged, which allows him to thwart the criminal element, is reminiscent of *Easy Street*. Perhaps he recognized that *Modern Times* was the swan song for the Tramp and deliberately included many gags and sequences as a loving farewell to the character and an homage to the visual comedy tradition. However, the spine that holds the story together is the journey of survival taken by the Tramp and the Gamine. The final shot of the film, as the Tramp walks down a road into the unknown, is more than a reprise of Chaplin's signature finale. This time, the Tramp is not alone. And this time, the Tramp carries the legacy of silent film down the road with him. *Modern Times*, as Hollywood's last silent film, represents the end of an era.

Unlike Buster Keaton's and particularly Harold Lloyd's screen personae, Chaplin's Tramp, who had first appeared before World War I, was very relevant in the 1930s as one of the millions coping with poverty and unemployment. French critic Roland Barthes, in his analysis of the film in his 1957 book *Mythologies*, wrote:

> Chaplin has always seen the proletarian under the guise of the poor man: hence the broadly human force of his representations but also their political ambiguity. This is quite evident in this admirable film, *Modern Times*, in which he repeatedly approaches the proletarian theme, but never endorses it politically. What he presents us with is the proletarian still blind and mystified, defined by the immediate character of his needs, and

a potential communist-leaning political bent to Chaplin's new film. *Modern Times* was banned in Germany and Italy because of its supposed communist tendencies. Nazi Germany had already banned reissues of Chaplin's films because of speculation of Chaplin's Jewish ancestry, and it was believed that the similarity of the Tramp's mustache to Hitler's might make the dictator appear absurd.

The press reaction to *Modern Times* was decidedly mixed. Some were disappointed that the film begins as a satire of mass production that ultimately is not fulfilled. Graham Greene, then film critic of *The Spectator*, wrote that *Modern Times* had no real political point of view: "Mr. Chaplin, whatever his political convictions may be, is an artist and not a propagandist. He doesn't try to explain, but presents with vivid fantasy what seems to him a crazy comic tragic world without a plan. . . . He presents, he doesn't offer political solutions."[8] The film does not have the integrated structure of Chaplin's previous feature films, particularly his best-constructed film, *The Gold Rush*. Otis Ferguson, writing for *The New Republic*, noted that the film could be divided into a collection of one- or two-reel shorts, with the proposed titles being *The Shop, The Jailbird, The Watchman*, and *The Singing Waiter*.[9] Chaplin does borrow from several of his older routines in the film: the inspired ballet on roller skates first appeared in *The Rink*; the escalator in the department store recalls *The Floorwalker*; and the

his total alienation at the hands of his masters (the employers and the police). For Chaplin, the proletarian is still the man who is hungry; the representations of hunger are always epic with him: excessive size of the sandwiches, rivers of milk, fruit which one tosses aside hardly touched. Ironically, the food-dispensing machine (which is part of the employers' world) delivers only fragmented and obviously flavorless nutriment.[10]

Modern Times brought in $1.4 million in domestic gross receipts, more than half a million less than *City Lights,* released at the height of the Depression. Nevertheless, it was one of the most popular and discussed films of 1936. The film was successfully reissued by United Artists in 1954; by its subsequent 1972 reissue, the film's political connotations had faded, and the film was seen as a hilarious comedy of the Tramp's struggle in an increasingly technological and impersonal world. Since then, the continuing appeal of *Modern Times* has been demonstrated by its lofty designation in 1995 by the Vatican's Pontifical Council for Social Communications, which singled out the film (along with forty-four other films in world cinema) as having special artistic merit. In 2003, *Modern Times* enjoyed the prestigious position of closing the Cannes Film Festival.

Modern Times is perhaps more meaningful now than at any time since its first release. The twentieth-century theme of the film, farsighted for its time—the struggle to eschew alienation and preserve humanity in a modern, mechanized world—profoundly reflects issues confronting the twenty-first century. The Tramp's travails in *Modern Times* and the comedic mayhem that ensues should provide strength and comfort to all who feel like helpless cogs in a world beyond control. Through its universal themes and comic inventiveness, the film remains one of Chaplin's greatest and most enduring works. Perhaps more important, it is the Tramp's finale, a tribute to Chaplin's most beloved character and the silent-film era he commanded for a generation.

Paulette Goddard

Chaplin enjoyed an eight-year professional and private relationship with actress Paulette Goddard, his leading lady in *Modern Times* and *The Great Dictator* and wife in a common-law marriage. Chaplin later reflected, "The bond between Paulette and me was loneliness. . . . It was a case of Robinson Crusoe discovering Friday for both of us."[1]

Paulette Goddard was born Marion Goddard Levy in New York in 1910. As a child she was called Pauline. Like Chaplin, she came from a broken home and supported herself at an early age; she was modeling clothing before she was a teenager. At the age of fifteen she was employed as a Florenz Ziegfeld showgirl, had bleached her naturally chestnut-colored hair platinum blonde, and gave herself a new name—Paulette Goddard. At seventeen she married a man twice her age, Edgar James, president of the Southern States Lumber Company of North Carolina, whom she divorced in 1929; she then went to Hollywood with her $375,000 divorce settlement. At the time she met Chaplin, Goddard had appeared as an extra and in bit parts in films such as the Laurel and Hardy two-reel comedy *Berth Marks* (1929) and the Eddie Cantor vehicle *The Kid from Spain* (1932) and was under contract to Hal Roach Studios.

Paulette Goddard in a glamorous portrait taken on the MODERN TIMES factory set. Photograph by Max Munn Autrey

Chaplin escorts a platinum blond Paulette Goddard to a Hollywood premiere, October 15, 1932.

Chaplin met the twenty-two-year-old starlet and divorcee on Joseph Schenck's yacht one weekend in July 1932. Goddard's ravishing beauty—as well as her charm and intelligence—instantly captivated him. She was considering investing $50,000 in a dubious film project and sought Chaplin's advice. He dissuaded her from making such an uncertain investment and immediately took charge of her. Soon he encouraged her to return her hair to its natural color, bought up her contract to Roach, signed her to the Chaplin Studios, and instilled a discipline in her with his coaching. He also invited her to live with him.

Chaplin liked to control young women—he invariably needed to be in command and in power in his intimate relationships. His first two wives and many of his lovers were subservient young women he was able to dominate, Pola Negri being one exception to this general pattern. Usually, he became bored at some point: the sexual conquest was no longer exciting; the woman became pregnant; or she grew wise to or wary of his ways. Goddard, however, did not fit the usual mold. She understood him from the start, and he treated her as an equal and as his companion. Her independence, intelligence, and talent made her unique among Chaplin's women. She was also a very shrewd woman who knew

exactly what she wanted and was ambitious enough to vigorously pursue her goals.

After *City Lights* Chaplin was reluctant to begin work on either another silent film or a talking film. His time with Goddard during this period was filled with diversions. "With Paulette I did all the witless things: attended race meetings, night spots, and all the public functions—anything to kill time,"[2] Chaplin recalled in his autobiography. At her urging, Chaplin purchased a boat he named the *Panacea*, a thirty-eight-foot motor cruiser that slept four and accommodated up to twenty passengers. It had a one-man crew, Andy Anderson, a former Keystone Kop, who navigated their frequent trips to Santa Catalina Island.

Chaplin was inspired by his own private relationship with Goddard to create for her the role of the Gamine in *Modern Times*. That character was more of a partner than the usual woman-on-a-pedestal typical of Chaplin's previous films. Under his direction, Goddard's winning performance in *Modern Times* transformed her into a movie star.

Public curiosity arose regarding the nature of Chaplin's relationship with Goddard. She was anxious to succeed on her own rather than as "Mrs. Charlie Chaplin." For his part, he did not care to pander to the popular press. They therefore jointly refused to announce their marital status to satisfy public curiosity. They managed the situation so deftly that it excited an interest in their relationship without igniting public contempt.

Following the premiere of *Modern Times*, Chaplin and Goddard impetuously decided to turn a vacation to Hawaii into an extended trip to the Far East in February 1936. In Shanghai Chaplin had a new idea for a film he tentatively entitled *Stowaway* about a White Russian countess who works as a prostitute in a Shanghai dance hall and stows away in the cabin of an American millionaire. He worked on this as a vehicle for Goddard until the end of October 1937, planned to direct it, but later shelved the project (it was later revised and became Chaplin's last film, *A Countess from Hong Kong*).

Upon their return to Los Angeles in June 1936, Goddard became anxious to build upon her success in *Modern Times* with other films. Chaplin, however, was slow to develop his next film project. A rift began, as the ambitious Goddard was held back by her agreement with Chaplin, who would not release her for other projects (she was being paid $2,500 a week by contract whether she worked or not). He eventually consented to her signing a five-year contract with producer David O. Selznick, which stated that Chaplin could reclaim Goddard's services by giving Selznick sixty days' notice. Goddard was vying (along with virtually every other top Hollywood actress) for the role of Scarlett O'Hara in *Gone with the Wind* (1939), a film produced by Selznick. She was actually one of the four finalists for the part, but her inability to produce a certificate of marriage to Chaplin cost her the role, as Selznick feared negative publicity from civic and church groups.

Goddard did not care for Toraichi Kono, who had faithfully

served Chaplin as chauffeur and later private secretary and major-domo for eighteen years, and she usurped him as the one who ran the Chaplin household. She was also responsible for Chaplin's seeing more of his sons, Charles Jr. and Sydney, whom she made certain were regularly invited to join them on weekends and during summer vacations from school. Both children adored their stepmother and remembered their time with her with only the fondest of memories.[3] In early 1937 Chaplin and Goddard began drifting apart, and Goddard had romances with composer George Gershwin and later painter Diego Rivera. Chaplin spent much of 1938 in Pebble Beach working intermittently on the script of *The Great Dictator.*

When production on *The Great Dictator* began in September 1939, Chaplin was even a more painstaking taskmaster with Goddard in her role as Hannah than he had been with her on *Modern Times.* She remembered that Chaplin's relentless perfectionism frequently had her in tears.[4] As it was Chaplin's first dialogue film, he was particularly anxious and believed that more would be expected by the public of both him as a filmmaker and her as an actress. They continued to live together in Chaplin's Summit Drive home in Beverly Hills. As Chaplin explained in his autobiography, "Although we were somewhat estranged we were friends and still married."[5]

Chaplin and Goddard both attended the world premiere of *The Great Dictator* in New York City on October 15, 1940, but they did not arrive there together; Goddard traveled from Mexico, where she had visited Diego Rivera for the second time in six months. Chaplin introduced Goddard at *The Great Dictator* premiere as "my wife."[6] The long-awaited clarification made headlines. Despite this avowal of unity, Goddard promptly

returned to Beverly Hills following the premiere and by December had moved into a beach house lent to her by Myron Selznick, her agent. Chaplin stayed on in New York until February 1941.

Goddard supposedly obtained a divorce on June 4, 1942, in Juarez, Mexico, on the grounds of incompatibility and separation for more than one year.[7] This action received little press coverage, unlike Chaplin's divorce from Lita Grey. Both Chaplin and Goddard publicly maintained that they were married in Canton, China, in 1936. However, Chaplin—in private—did not exert this claim, and, in fact, there is no evidence to suggest that their union was anything more than a common-law marriage.[8] Goddard's monetary settlement was rumored to be anywhere from a quarter of a million to a million dollars and included ownership of their yacht, the *Panacea.* Chaplin later wrote, "The wrench naturally hurt, for it was hard cleaving eight years' association from one's life."[9]

Many years later, Goddard reflected, "He was *enchanting, captivating, fascinating.* And sweet. I mean you couldn't know anyone who was so perfectly charming in every sense of the word. Difficult, but charming."[10]

Goddard was a Paramount star for most of the 1940s. Her most notable films include *The Women* (1939), *So Proudly We Hail* (1943), *Kitty* (1946), and *The Diary of a Chambermaid* (1946). She later married actor Burgess Meredith in 1944 (they divorced in 1949) and novelist Erich Maria Remarque, to whom she remained married until his death in 1970.

Although Chaplin and Goddard both resided in Switzerland in later years, they never met there by design. "We live on different mountains"[11] was Goddard's explanation. She did seek him out at the Film Society of Lincoln Center's gala tribute to Chaplin in New York City on April 3, 1972, where Goddard approached Chaplin at a reception with their old favorite greeting for each other, "Hello, baby." Chaplin, his eyes filled with tears, replied "Oh, oh! My little baby." "Yes," Goddard responded. "Your only little baby."[12] It was their last meeting. She died in 1990 of complications from emphysema, and bequeathed the bulk of Remarque's literary estate and $20 million to New York University.

The Great Dictator

It is perhaps ironic that one of the most beloved men in history was born within four days of the most despised—and that the demon, Adolf Hitler, so strongly resembled the clown, Charles Chaplin. Some claimed that Hitler deliberately chose his mustache to resemble Chaplin's, who had enjoyed the love and respect of audiences around the world. Contemporary journalists and cartoonists delighted in pointing out the similarity in appearance between the two men. A song about Hitler, published in England in 1938, asked the question, "Who is this Man? (Who Looks like Charlie Chaplin)."

In many ways, the creation of *The Great Dictator* was virtually inevitable. How could Chaplin, who had reached the zenith of his popularity and influence, avoid the role that fate seemingly had thrust upon him? Thus, more than a decade after the motion-picture industry had accepted talking pictures as the status quo, the greatest star of the silent-film era set out to make his first full-dialogue film. His subject was Adolf Hitler and his theme, the dangerous rise of European fascism.

The genesis of Chaplin's decision to make a film satirizing fascism was undoubtedly his world tour in 1931–32, following the premiere of *City Lights* in London. His travels took him from

Chaplin in a test portrait as Hynkel. Photograph by William Wallace

began to observe odd behavior that revealed her less-than-stable mental state. Chaplin later admitted to even noticing it in his early meetings with Barry: "there was something queer and not quite normal about them."[2] However, Chaplin—caught in the thrill of creativity—thought he had made a discovery in Joan Barry. He put her under contract at a salary of $250 per week to play in a screen adaptation of Paul Vincent Carroll's play *Shadow and Substance*, which ultimately was never produced.

Soon Barry's strange behavior intensified into outright madness, and almost overnight Chaplin's existence became a nightmare. Frequently, and always late at night, Barry would appear at Chaplin's home, drunk, belligerent, and incoherent. On one occasion she crashed her car in his driveway, on another she smashed his windows when he refused to come to the door. In an attempt to rid himself of Barry for good, Chaplin arranged for the termination of her contract, paid off $500 of her debts, and bought her and her mother cross-country train tickets to return to New York in October 1942.

Less than a month later, Barry was back in Hollywood and began to call Chaplin's home incessantly. Not hearing from him, she broke into his house waving a gun and threatening to kill herself. Chaplin claimed that, to protect himself and his teenage sons, he locked the doors leading to the room where Barry continued to rant. Barry's version was that, after she calmed down, they engaged in the sexual encounter that would produce the child at issue in the subsequent paternity suits. It is undeniable that Barry was mentally unstable; yet, perhaps in some way this made her more sympathetic and even attractive to Chaplin, whose mother and grandmother had both been clinically insane. When Barry returned about a week later, Chaplin finally had her arrested; she was quickly given a ninety-day suspended sentence and ordered to leave Los Angeles immediately.

In May 1943, after several months of relative quiet, Barry again invaded Chaplin's life. As he dined at home with his new love, Oona O'Neill, and some friends, she called Chaplin's home and told the butler that she was pregnant with Chaplin's child. One month later, apparently with the help of gossip columnist Hedda Hopper, she leaked her pregnancy and her accusation of Chaplin's paternity to the press.[3] The story was nothing short of a blockbuster. It would take Chaplin two years to rid himself of

Above: Chaplin is fingerprinted by George Rossini of the U.S. Marshal's office, while his attorney Jerry Giesler watches, after a federal grand jury indictment charged Chaplin with violation of the Mann Act and conspiracy to defraud Joan Barry of her civil rights, February 14, 1944.

Opposite: Chaplin in court during his Mann Act trial in Los Angeles, April 3, 1944. According to Chaplin's attorney, Jerry Giesler, Chaplin was "the best witness I've ever seen in a law court." Even when he was merely sitting at the counsel table, Giesler remembered in his autobiography, "He looked helpless, friendless and wistful, as he sat there with the weight of the whole United States Government against him."

Barry, yet he would never quite accomplish clearing his name. The scandal would ultimately become a contributing factor in the United States government's pursuit of him, feeding speculation that Chaplin was not only a communist sympathizer but morally unfit as well.

Despite Chaplin's repeated claims that he was not the father of Barry's unborn child, Barry's mother, Gertrude, filed a paternity suit on behalf of her granddaughter, demanding $10,000 for pre-natal care and $2,500 per month in child support. Chaplin refused to settle and vowed to prove that he was not the father. Because California law gave the benefit of the doubt to the mother, he was forced to pay for Barry's support and later child support while the case progressed. However, Barry agreed to a blood test after the child was born to determine conclusively whether or not Chaplin was the father.

On October 2, 1943, Joan Barry gave birth to a daughter, whom she named Carol Ann Barry. Despite the pending civil paternity case, the federal government, ever eager to exploit a chance to go after Chaplin and fueled by a persistent negative press, indicted Chaplin on February 10, 1944, on charges that he had violated the Mann Act, a 1910 law making it illegal to trans-port a woman across a state line for immoral purposes. FBI files reveal that agency director J. Edgar Hoover took a personal inter-est in the Barry case and ordered that the claim against Chaplin be pursued vigorously.[4] The government asserted that Chaplin had purchased the ticket for Barry on October 5, 1942, not to get rid of her but to take her from Los Angeles to New York in order to have sexual relations with her. Chaplin's celebrated attorney, Jerry Giesler, brilliantly argued that it was absurd to conclude that Chaplin would have gone through the trouble of transporting Barry across the country to have sex with her when she would have willingly submitted herself to him at any time and in any place. After Chaplin took the stand in his own defense, his case was sent to the jury. It took them three hours and several ballots to arrive at an acquittal. But Chaplin's nightmare was far from over. He now had to face paternity proceedings.

Chaplin's attorney in the paternity suit, Charles A. Millikan, had struck a deal with Barry's attorney, Joseph Scott, that if the blood tests came back negative, Barry would drop the case. Chaplin's blood was type O, and Barry's was type A. The baby's was type B. According to the Landsteiner blood table, Chaplin was conclusively excluded from being the child's father. However, Gertrude Barry did not drop the case. Guardianship of Carol Ann was assigned to the court of Los Angeles, which pressed on with the claim while Chaplin maintained his inno-cence. Rumors swirled in the press that Chaplin had fixed the blood test. Another rumor claimed that tycoon J. Paul Getty, who may have had an affair with Barry, was the father of the child.

Despite the conclusive blood tests, Superior Court Judge Stanley Mosk denied Chaplin attorney Loyd Wright's motion to dismiss, stating, "the ends of justice will best be served by a full and fair trial of the issues."[5] Chaplin believed that remarks such as these were intended to influence the jury against his case. The strong scientific evidence determining Chaplin's innocence apparently proved no match for Scott's oratorical and advocacy skills, and Scott held sway with several members of the jury, who were unable to reach a verdict (however, a majority did appar-ently favor Chaplin).

Before the ordeal was over, Chaplin was forced to endure two paternity trials—a trial and a retrial—both conducted before Los Angeles juries. Chaplin, who had held up well during cross-examination in the Mann Act trial and whose testimony, in some accounts, was credited for his acquittal, was shredded by the el-derly Joseph Scott, the histrionic lawyer for the prosecution. He called Chaplin "a lecherous hound," "a gray-headed old buz-zard," "a little runt of a Svengali," and "a cheap Cockney cad," much to the delight of the reporters who had assembled to feast on every morsel that emerged from the trial of the famous filmmaker.

Refusing to settle and committed to clearing his name out-right, Chaplin chose to subject himself to yet another trial. Remarkably, he was found to be the legal father of a child that could not possibly have been his. In the face of Scott's bombastic delivery and inflammatory charges, and in the wake of Chaplin's growing unpopularity, the judge and jury simply chose to ignore the obvious scientific facts. Judge Clarence L. Kincaid ordered him to pay $75 a week (with increases to $100 as the child's needs grew) in child support until Carol Ann Barry reached the age of maturity, at the time twenty-one years of age. Chaplin's motion for a new trial was denied on June 6, 1945, after being considered for four weeks.

By 1953, the child's mother and Chaplin's albatross, Joan Barry, was committed for eleven years to Patton State Medical Hospital in San Bernardino, California, diagnosed as schizo-phrenic. Carol Ann was sent away to be raised by relatives. In that same year, the California State Legislature, to avoid unjust results such as in the Chaplin case, passed a measure to prevent paternity cases when a blood test has proven conclusive. Many

legal scholars believe the case of Berry v. Chaplin, 169 P.2d 442 (1946), helped to popularize the common use of blood tests to determine paternity. When the case was filed only ten states, not including California, allowed blood tests as evidence to disprove paternity.

After two grueling years the Barry case was finally behind him, yet Chaplin would never quite recover from the damage the matter had wrought on his reputation. Coupled with the government's suspicions that Chaplin was a communist, the Barry case—which was fueled by the FBI feeding stories to Hollywood gossip columnists—dealt a serious blow to his standing with the public. However, in an ironic plot twist that can only be called Chaplinesque, Chaplin's steep descent in popularity was matched only by the rise in his personal happiness, brought by the peace and serenity of his marriage to his last wife, Oona O'Neill, and his glorious life with her and their growing family.

Opposite: Chaplin, in a moment of anger on the witness stand, being questioned by prosecuting attorney Joseph Scott during the paternity trial in Los Angeles, 1944

Above: Chaplin stands with Joan Barry (holding her child, Carol Ann) before the jury box during the paternity trial in Los Angeles, December 26, 1944. The American judicial system that had exonerated Chaplin in the Mann Act trial failed him in the Barry paternity trial, despite the blood-test evidence that proved his innocence.

Marriage to Oona O'Neill

In the midst of his troubled times with Joan Barry, fifty-three-year-old Chaplin met seventeen-year-old Oona O'Neill, who brought him the unconditional love and companionship he had been seeking. Despite their considerable difference in age, their marriage withstood the paternity suit and the accusations of communist subversion, as well as exile and Chaplin's decline in his final years. "A light came into Charlie's eyes which had never existed before he met Oona," Chaplin's second cousin Betty Chaplin Tetrick remembered. "The love they shared for each other was real and lasting."[1]

Oona O'Neill was born in Bermuda in 1925, the daughter of the great playwright and Nobel laureate Eugene O'Neill and his second wife, Agnes Bolton. Her parents divorced when Oona was four years old, and she had little contact with her father. She attended the Brearley School in New York City and developed a reputation as a party girl. In 1942 she was voted Debutante Number One of the year, receiving considerable media attention. Her very public social life and her lack of interest in attending Vassar College infuriated and devastated her father, who refused all future contact with her. Oona was beautiful, charming, intelligent, sheltered, and capricious. Her romances had already included J. D. Salinger and Orson Welles before the teenager met Chaplin in late 1942.

Chaplin with Oona and the first two of their eight children, Geraldine (right) and Michael (left), on the lawn of their Beverly Hills home, 1948. Photograph by John Engstead

Above: Chaplin and Oona enjoy
the Pacific Southwest Tennis
Championships in Hollywood,
September 18, 1944. "Oona had
beautiful long hair," remembered
Chaplin's second cousin Betty
Chaplin Tetrick. "After Geraldine
[the couple's first child] was born
she couldn't decide whether or not
to cut it. She was young, and like
young girls she made a big thing
of it. Charlie got the scissors and
made the decision for her. He
loved to cut hair. He started cutting but he couldn't get it even,
so he kept cutting. The poor
thing ended up with this short
and jagged haircut."

Right: Chaplin places the wedding
ring on Oona's finger as Justice
of the Peace Clinton P. Moore
officiates at their marriage. The
simple ceremony took place in
Carpinteria, California, and was
attended by Chaplin's secretary,
Catherine Hunter, and his publicist, Harry Crocker, June 16, 1943.

Opposite: Chaplin and his new
bride make their first public
appearance since their marriage,
at the Mocambo, a Hollywood
nightclub, July 3, 1943.
Photograph by Phillip Gendreau

Oona had moved to Los Angeles intent on pursuing an acting career. Her agent, Minna Wallace, knew Chaplin was searching for a young woman to play Brigid, an Irish girl who has visions of her namesake, St. Brigid, in his proposed screen adaptation of Paul Vincent Carroll's 1937 play *Shadow and Substance*. She mentioned O'Neill to Chaplin and later arranged for them to meet at a dinner party. Chaplin was captivated by her "luminous beauty, with a sequestered charm and a gentleness that was most appealing. . . . As I got to know Oona I was constantly surprised by her sense of humour and tolerance; she could always see the other person's point of view. This and multitudinous other reasons were why I fell in love with her."[2]

Although instantly enchanted by Oona herself, her youth and inexperience made him uncertain whether she was capable of portraying the role of Brigid. However, when Minna Wallace informed Chaplin that Twentieth Century-Fox was interested in offering O'Neill a contract, he promptly signed her. By the end of the year, Chaplin had shelved *Shadow and Substance* and was dating O'Neill, with whom he had grown totally smitten. He per-

ceived her as different from any of the women with whom he had previously been involved. Although O'Neill herself denied she was seeking a father substitute, she was emotionally scarred by her absent father's indifference. Clearly she found in Chaplin, whom she often called "Pops," the father figure she had been deprived of by Eugene O'Neill. When Oona became ill with a serious upper respiratory infection, Chaplin moved her into his home and was convinced she was suffering from tuberculosis. Under his care, she fully recovered and stayed on at his home. After her eighteenth birthday they decided to marry. They married in a simple ceremony on June 16, 1943, in Carpinteria, near Santa Barbara, California, and spent nearly six weeks in Santa Barbara as a honeymoon.

Oona Chaplin's close friend Carol Matthau recalled:

> They clung to each other through all that went against them in the outside world. It did not put a strain on their love because they had fallen so deeply in love they had already exiled themselves in an odd way. . . . She woke up every morning to spend the whole day and night with him. He did the same, with the

exception of his work. He wanted to be with her all the time. . . . With her mind, she could have done anything, but part of her always had to be a little girl. Charlie's little girl. He always had to be The One. He had had that from the public for a long time, but then the public turned on him. He still had to get that, all of it, but from one person, Oona. He was not easy to live with; she didn't expect him to be.[3]

As soon as they were married, Oona Chaplin decided she no longer wished to pursue a career in films but instead wanted to devote herself to being Chaplin's wife and the mother of their children. They had four children during the time they lived in Beverly Hills: Geraldine Leigh in 1944, Michael John in 1946, Josephine Hannah in 1949, and Victoria Agnes in 1951 (their brood eventually numbered eight).

Chaplin's energetic and exacting personality, which constantly demanded attention and approbation, found a perfect counterpart in Oona's intelligent, unassuming, and selfless manner. In a rare 1960 interview, she reflected:

> There certainly is no father fixation about my feelings for him. He has made me more mature and I keep him young. . . . My security and stability with Charlie stem much more from the difference in years between us. Other young women who have married mature men will understand what I mean. . . . Our happiness is not governed by the children. The gang have their place, of course. A mighty large place at that. But for me, Charlie comes first.[4]

"I never have seen two people so much in love as Charlie and Oona," Sophia Loren remarked of the Chaplin marriage, a sentiment echoed by many friends of the couple.[5] Chaplin, for his part, recorded his love for Oona in *My Autobiography*:

> Schopenhauer said happiness is a negative state—but I disagree. For the last twenty years I have known what happiness means. I have the good fortune to be married to a wonderful wife. I wish I could write more about this, but it involves love, and perfect love is the most beautiful of all frustrations because it is more than one can express. As I live with Oona, the depth and beauty of her character are a continual revelation to me. Even as she walks ahead of me along the narrow sidewalks of Vevey with simple dignity, her neat little figure straight, her dark hair smoothed back showing a few silver threads, a sudden wave of love and admiration comes over me for all that she is—and a lump comes into my throat.[6]

In his last years, Oona frequently told friends, "Charlie looked after me when I was young and needed looking after. It is now my turn to look after him."[7] She was a loyal and devoted wife and completely devastated by his death in 1977.

At first she tried to develop a new life for herself, purchasing an apartment in Manhattan and embarking on love affairs with Ryan O'Neal and David Bowie and later serious relationships with screenwriter Walter Bernstein and psychiatrist Christ L. Zois. As a favor to producer Bert Schneider, she appeared as the alcoholic mother in the film *Broken English* (1981). However, she soon retreated to the home she and Chaplin shared in Switzerland and withdrew more into herself, becoming a reclusive alcoholic. She died of pancreatic cancer in 1991 at the age of sixty-six. A gifted writer, the journals she wrote of her private thoughts and marriage to Chaplin survive, although her wishes were that they be read only by her children after her death and then destroyed. Claire Bloom, Chaplin's leading lady in *Limelight* and a friend of the Chaplin family, wrote in her 1996 memoir, *Leaving a Doll's House*:

> In later years Oona had everything in life except Charlie, and nothing would ever make up to her for the loss; neither the love of her children or grandchildren nor the devotion of her friends. Oona had lived through and for Charlie, and although she survived him by several years, her life meant little to her without him.[8]

Oona Chaplin, 1948. Photograph by John Engstead

Monsieur Verdoux

Monsieur Verdoux, subtitled "A Comedy of Murders," is Chaplin's darkest and most intricate film, released during a tumultuous period in his career and public life. The "glorious future" Chaplin had envisioned at the end of *The Great Dictator* seemed remote after the actual horrors of the concentration camps, the atomic bomb, and the death of millions during World War II. Having been embroiled in a fraudulent paternity suit and attacked for his politics, Chaplin lashed out at his many accusers in the subversive and perverse *Monsieur Verdoux,* a scathing social critique of capitalist society where murder is simply business as usual. The eponymous protagonist marries then kills women for their money in a story played as a comedy. *Monsieur Verdoux* is a film that aspires to be brilliant, yet it engages political and philosophical concepts it does not fully explore and contains internal contradictions it cannot resolve. The film shows that Chaplin's genius was always more emotional and intuitive than intellectual.

Chaplin began work on *Monsieur Verdoux* in November 1942, at the height of the war. He envisioned Verdoux as a character

Chaplin as Henri Verdoux, the title character of MONSIEUR VERDOUX (1947). In an interview before the film was released, Chaplin stated, "The picture has moral value, I believe. [German military strategist Karl] von Clausewitz said that war is the logical extension of diplomacy; M. Verdoux feels that murder is the logical extension of business. He should express the feeling of the times we live in—out of catastrophe come people like him. He typifies the psychological disease of depression. He is frustrated, bitter, and at the end, pessimistic. But he is never morbid; and the picture is by no means morbid in treatment . . . Under the proper circumstances murder can be comic."

quite different from the Tramp, a darker persona unlike anything Chaplin's audience was accustomed to seeing him portray. His fans had accepted him as the dictator Hynkel, his first villain, but only because he was lampooning a despised madman. However, even Chaplin loyalists would be jarred by Verdoux, a complex and deeply flawed man whose compromised morality allows him to kill for money. Ultimately, the public would not accept Chaplin in the role of a villain, particularly at a time when his own morals and loyalties were being called into question. It is unfortunate that the sophisticated artistic content of the film would be subverted by this unavoidable tension.

At its heart, *Monsieur Verdoux* is a film that espouses leftist political thought, released into a Cold War environment that was hostile to such views. In the 1940s, Chaplin's burgeoning anti-fascist political and social views were shaped by his interaction with a group of German intellectuals in exile in Hollywood, including Bertolt Brecht, Thomas Mann, and Hanns Eisler, among others.[1] This group—several of whom were German-Jewish refugees—along with American radicals Clifford Odets and Donald Ogden Stewart was made up primarily of artists, and their politics emphasized a leftist and anti-fascist agenda. Influenced by this salon of progressive friends, Chaplin began to focus his humor through a more cynical and political lens, as can be seen throughout *Monsieur Verdoux*. For example, the film's main character, Henri Verdoux, not only equates business with murder but, when on trial, defends himself by expressing a thin-

Above: Chaplin with Lou Costello (of the comedy team Abbott and Costello) at a party held at Chaplin's Beverly Hills home, May 1942. Costello was a great admirer of Chaplin. He claimed to have seen SHOULDER ARMS *thirty times and* THE GOLD RUSH *sixteen times, and attempted to buy the screen rights to* THE KID *from Chaplin.*

Right: Chaplin twirls an imaginary mustache for reporters in a preview of his forthcoming film project, based on serial killer Henri Landru, which ultimately became MONSIEUR VERDOUX *(1947), October 1942. Chaplin spent weeks cultivating a genuine mustache for his role as Henri Verdoux. Photograph by John Albert*

Opposite: Filming MONSIEUR VERDOUX *at the Chaplin Studios in 1946. Among the technicians are associate director Robert Florey (tall man standing without a hat) and Rollie Totheroh, seated behind Florey.*

ly veiled assault on America's use of the atomic bomb (although the film is ostensibly set in France between the two world wars).

The suggestion of a film about Henri-Désiré Landru, France's infamous "Bluebeard" serial killer, was made to Chaplin by Orson Welles. Welles had wanted to direct a documentary-style film, with Chaplin sharing screenplay credit as well as playing the role of Landru. Chaplin, however, wanted to develop a comedy loosely based on the Landru character and bought the idea and the title, "The Lady Killer," from Welles for $5,000; hence the screen credit: "Based on an idea by Orson Welles."[2] Chaplin's Verdoux is merely inspired by Landru, although he shares many of Landru's attributes: he is a family man leading a double life, a lover of roses, and a dealer in secondhand articles. Like Landru, Verdoux entices widows with the prospect of matrimony, strips them of their assets, kills them, and then burns their bodies in a stove. Early-nineteenth-century forger and murderer Thomas Wainwright was also a model for the film's title character.

Yet *Monsieur Verdoux* is a flawed film, in part because of Chaplin's propensity to impose himself upon the character he portrays. At times the film appears at war with itself as it is pulled in three different directions: toward the historical Landru, toward the provocative ideas suggested by Welles that Chaplin retained for his own script,[3] and toward Chaplin's own vision of the story and character. Ultimately, Chaplin is not true to his subject matter, and the tension between the film's subversive, dark, and cutting-edge elements (based on the Landru story and Welles's ideas) and the sanctimonious pontifications of business as murder (injected by Chaplin) wrenches the film apart.

Chaplin worked diligently on the controversial script—despite the interruptions and distractions caused by the war, the Joan Barry scandal, his marriage to Oona, and his war speeches—from November 1942 until the start of production in April 1946. He devoted a dozen pages of his autobiography to his negotiations with the censors at the Motion Picture Association of America, presided over by the director of production-code administration, Joseph Breen. Dark and ironic, the script is unlike that of any other Chaplin film and later proved to be influential among many filmmakers. The film's opening, with an image of a tombstone marked "Henri Verdoux 1880–1937" and the dead man laconically introducing his story in a voice-over narration, was reworked in later films, most notably Billy Wilder's *Sunset Boulevard* (1950). The ironic comedy style of the film shared similarities with the work of several filmmakers, such as Monta Bell, Harry d'Arrast, and Eddie Sutherland, who had once worked for Chaplin and had gone on to direct comedies inspired by *A Woman of Paris*.

Monsieur Verdoux is set in France in the 1930s, from the onset of the Depression through the outbreak of the Spanish Civil War. Chaplin plays Henri Verdoux, a faithful bank clerk for thirty years until he loses his job. To support his legitimate wife Mona (a name recalling Oona, Chaplin's own wife), who is an invalid, and their young son, Peter, Verdoux is "forced" into the business of marrying rich spinsters and murdering them. He becomes a Bluebeard, using his considerable charm to marry and murder at least fourteen women.

Assuming many aliases in order to remain undetected, Verdoux's guise is that of an antique furniture dealer. His business enterprise is located in Paris, while his home is a pastoral cottage outside the city. Chaplin sets up a stark dichotomy with these two locations—the city, teeming with the decadence of capitalism, set against the countryside, devoid of such sinister influences. The cottage where Verdoux's wife and child reside reflects the proletarian utopia that Chaplin previously depicted in a dream sequence in *Modern Times* (in which the Tramp envisions himself a noble worker in pristine surroundings, where fresh fruit is taken directly from the vine and fresh milk is delivered by an obedient cow). Verdoux tells Mona, "When the world looks dark and grim, then I think of another world, you and Peter, all that I love on this earth." This dual structure of the film reveals the notion, inherent in communist thought, that a worker's utopia—an enclave removed from the horrors of the brutish bourgeois marketplace, a refuge from the "jungle fight" of business—is an ideal that must be achieved at all costs.

The character of Verdoux is, in Chaplin's own words, "a paradox of virtue and vice."[4] He adores and provides for his invalid wife, yet has murdered fourteen women and plans to kill more. He is a kind man, a vegetarian, and a gentleman who takes pity on cats. (In one domestic scene he reproaches his son: "Peter, don't pull the cat's tail. You have a cruel streak in you, I don't know where you get it. Remember, violence begets violence.") Because Henri Verdoux is a man of compassion and kindness, Chaplin suggests it is society that has made him a killer. Verdoux does not kill out of passion or blood lust or greed or even madness. He kills because the world around him has devolved into such insanity that he, quite simply, is left with no other choice.

Of all Chaplin's characters, Verdoux comes closest to the amoral side of his creator. Norman Lloyd, a friend of Chaplin's since the late 1940s, reflected:

> Charlie had some of the characteristics of Verdoux. He had an extreme temperament. The scene where Verdoux avoids stepping on a caterpillar, while one of his wives burns in an incinerator behind him, reminds me of Charlie. I believe that Charlie, if he wanted to, could have killed a man—but not a butterfly. I'll explain. We went to play tennis one day and he saw this injured butterfly on the court. He became upset and asked that I take it and put it on the grass, which I did. He didn't want to hurt that butterfly. Yet I also remember one weekend with him on his yacht off Catalina Island. Oona was in the water swimming when a motorboat came dangerously close to her and just kept going. Charlie was furious! He couldn't get his boat started fast enough to try and chase after the motorboat. If he had chased that motorboat, he could have killed the man driving it. And I mean *kill* that man. His anger was *limitless*.[5]

The comedic high points of the film center on Verdoux's failed attempts to eliminate an old wife, the indestructible Annabella Bonheur, portrayed with hilarious zest by comedienne Martha Raye. In one attempt, Verdoux has an untraceable new poison he wishes to use on Annabella. He pours the poison in a bottle of peroxide for safekeeping, places the bottle in the medicine cabinet of the lavatory, and proceeds to help Annabella prepare their intimate dinner. When Annette, Annabella's off-duty maid, decides to dye her hair, she unwittingly uses Verdoux's poison and then breaks the bottle, which she replaces with a new and genuine bottle of peroxide. Verdoux later pours the "poison" into the bottle of wine Annabella is to drink and sits in dismay as she drinks glass after glass with no ill effects. All the while Annette becomes hysterical, as her bleached hair begins to fall out. Verdoux's last attempt to kill Annabella, in a rowboat out on a secluded lake, plays like a parody of the climactic murder scene in Theodore Dreiser's novel *An American Tragedy*. Raye's vulgar and obnoxious Annabella is a perfect counterpoint to Chaplin's gallant and witty Verdoux. The physically unattractive Annabella, who lavishes extravagances on herself yet is stingy with Annette, represents Chaplin's belief that the rich dwell in an ugly society that allows them to thrive while millions throughout the world are starving and unemployed.

Martha Raye had idolized Chaplin since childhood. "I learned more from Chaplin than from anyone else I've ever worked with," she recalled more than forty years after making the film. "For me, working with him was like working with God."[6] Initially in awe of him, the only way she could overcome her reticence was to start calling Chaplin "Chuck." He in turn called her "Maggie" (her real name was Margaret Reed). They developed a wonderful comic rapport. "They were like two peas in a pod," remembered Marilyn Nash, who plays the young prostitute in the film. "They enjoyed making the other laugh and it was actually hard for the two of them to get much accomplished when they had to do a scene together, they had so much fun."[7]

Above: Verdoux (assuming his alias as Monsieur Floray) listens to a conch shell as a distraction from the drone of Madame Floray.

Top left: Chaplin in his director's chair during production of MONSIEUR VERDOUX. Associate director Robert Florey found the experience of working with Chaplin (whom he had known since 1921) disillusioning. "Charlie . . . has two distinct personalities," Florey later wrote. "There is first Charlie . . . that the whole world adores, the Charlie who wants to please, to amuse, to seduce. And the tyrannical, wounding, authoritarian, mean, despotic man, imbued with himself. One could attribute to him, by masculinizing it, the verse of Corneille, in the tragedy of MEDEA, 'Me, me alone, and that's enough.'" Florey also maintained that Chaplin "is the irreconcilable enemy of all that is photographic composition, daring camera shots. All that is not immobile in long shot, showing him from head to feet, is for him 'Hollywood chi-chi.'" Indeed, it was during this period of his career that Chaplin was quoted as saying, "I am the unusual and do not need camera angles." Photograph by Robert Florey

Bottom left: Verdoux contemplates the horrors of modern life with the invalid wife (Mady Correll) he loves and supports at their country home.

Above: Chaplin with Martha Raye during production. Cinematographer Curt Courant is in the background. Raye made only a few films after MONSIEUR VERDOUX but remained active on stage, radio, and television. She married seven times and died in 1994.

Upper right: Chaplin's sons Sydney (left) and Charles Jr., recently demobilized from the army, visit their father at the Chaplin Studios during production of MONSIEUR VERDOUX.

Lower right: Robert Florey and Chaplin examine a volume dedicated to French film pioneer Georges Méliès during production of MONSIEUR VERDOUX.

Opposite: Verdoux (assuming his alias Captain Bonheur) with the wife he tries repeatedly without success to kill, the lucky Annabella Bonheur (Martha Raye)

Chaplin hired Robert Florey, a Paris-born film director who had been a friend and admirer of Chaplin's for more than twenty years, as an associate director on the film. Although an accomplished director, he readily accepted a subordinate role to work with Chaplin, who was especially interested in Florey's technical advice on French settings. Florey, whose most important films include *The Cocoanuts* (1929), *Murders in the Rue Morgue* (1932), and *The Beast with Five Fingers* (1946), had directed Martha Raye in *Mountain Music* (1937) and had suggested her to Chaplin for the part of Annabella Bonheur. Although Chaplin served as director on all scenes in which he appeared, Florey directed some scenes in *Monsieur Verdoux* in which Chaplin was not present. Originally a French press representative, Florey had written his first book on Chaplin in 1927. He retained his journalistic instincts and later chronicled his time with Chaplin.[8]

Florey found that his idol was a difficult man whose tantrums were so severe that he often felt he could not work with Chaplin again the following day. Yet, when Chaplin would arrive the next morning and begin acting amusing pantomime routines between setups and telling stories to the cast and crew, he was so charming that Florey repeatedly forgave him. According to Marilyn Nash:

> Robert Florey was very unhappy—you could tell that—but he never said a word. And when Charlie would say, "That's not the right kind of set. I want something different," Florey would say, "Charlie, what would you like?" That's the way it went. There wasn't any tension between the two men, and yet I understand that Florey was very unhappy afterward. Florey didn't have any real involvement in direction, blocking, camera set-ups, nothing. And he was far more technically advanced than Charlie, but Charlie didn't want his advice, he wanted to do it his way.

So Florey was absolutely blocked out. He thought he was going to be a real associate director on the film—he was not. He was more of a "runner."[9]

Marilyn Nash was Chaplin's discovery for the role of the prostitute. Although beautiful, poised, and intelligent, Nash had no previous acting experience or natural acting talent. Chaplin spent a lot of time patiently rehearsing her for her small but important role. Despite Nash's limitations as an actress, her character provides a hopeful counterpoint to the morally ruined Verdoux, espousing a philosophical viewpoint not unlike the Tramp's. In one scene the prostitute muses, "I was beginning to lose faith in everything. Then this [Verdoux's kindness toward her] happens and you want to believe all over again. . . . It's a blundering world, and a very sad one . . . yet a little kindness can make it beautiful." Verdoux ends the conversation, "You'd better go before your philosophy corrupts me." With this line Chaplin conveys to his audience that this film is a darker offering that will not allow the Tramp's sentiments to overtake the cynical, ironic posture of its complex themes.

Chaplin's loyal cameraman Rollie Totheroh assumed cinematography responsibilities jointly with Curt Courant, known for his technical expertise. Beyond Totheroh, very little of the old Chaplin company was left. Henry Bergman was too ill to work

Above: Verdoux is quietly disturbed by the robust constitution and table manners of his indestructible wife Annabella (Martha Raye). The vulgarity of Annabella and most of Verdoux's victims is misogynistically contrasted with his own elegance and refinement.

Above right: Verdoux brings to his home a friendless young woman working as a prostitute (Marilyn Nash) to try out a new untraceable poison but spares her when he discovers that she, like himself, not only loves cats but once loved an invalid so much she could have killed for him.

Opposite: Chaplin and Martha Raye during the filming of MONSIEUR VERDOUX on location in Lake Arrowhead, California, May 1946

and rarely came to the studio; he died shortly after production began. Alfred Reeves, Chaplin's longtime general manager, had been ailing and died in April 1946, just prior to production on *Monsieur Verdoux*. He was replaced by John McFadden, who introduced several efficiencies to the Chaplin Studios, most notably a shooting schedule—which had never been used before—that resulted in the film falling only seventeen days behind schedule. However, Chaplin disliked McFadden, who left the Chaplin Studios just prior to the end of postproduction in March 1947.

Chaplin at one point decided that the role of Madame Grosnay might suit Edna Purviance. For the first time in more than twenty years, Edna returned to the studio on March 18, 1946, and had an emotional reunion with Chaplin and Totheroh. Although she spent a month at the studio testing and rehearsing in the role, it was decided that she was not suited for the part, a decision mutually agreeable to both Chaplin and Purviance. The part went to Isobel Elsom, an English actress who enjoyed a distinguished stage and film career.

The minimum staffing requirements and salaries demanded by the postwar Hollywood unions were even more daunting to Chaplin than those he had endured on *The Great Dictator*. Indeed, the rising costs had necessitated that the Chaplin Studios rent out its studio space when Chaplin was not in production. As a result of escalating costs and McFadden's efficiencies, *Monsieur Verdoux* was made much more quickly than previous Chaplin films. Production began on May 21, 1946, and finished September 5, 1946; the remainder of the year was spent on the editing and composition of the music. The relatively quick production and tight budget show in the film's anachronistic look (the primitive camera placements and awkward blocking of the film's opening scene of the Couvais family is particularly unfortunate), the obvious rear-screen projection to simulate exterior backgrounds, and the substandard editing, which was something critics had noticed since *Modern Times,* became even more apparent without the Tramp providing a focal point. However, French director Jean Renoir, in his contemporary defense of Chaplin and *Monsieur Verdoux,* praised these flaws as part of Chaplin's artisan spirit:

> One feels it in a certain decent way he has of going into a scene, in the almost peasant-like thriftiness of his sets, in his wariness of technique for technique's sake, in his respect for the personalities of actors, and in that internal richness which makes us feel that each character has just too much to say.[10]

Given Chaplin's notoriety for his leftist politics and poor treatment of women, including the explosive Joan Barry scandal, a new film in which Chaplin's character justifies killing his wives for their money because the capitalist system has failed him provided his critics with an easy target. Chaplin maintained that he did not attempt to make Verdoux a sympathetic character, but there are several places in the film in which he clearly draws sympathy for him, both early in the film (a former bank colleague states, "Poor old Verdoux. You know he got a pretty raw deal") and later (Verdoux explains to the prostitute that his murderous activity was a terrible nightmare and he has only just awakened, never realizing what he was actually doing).[11] In fact, some critics have suggested that Chaplin's affection for the despicable Verdoux actually subverts the black comedy of the film. His affinity for the character and the similarity between Verdoux's disturbing actions and Chaplin's own reputed behavior and thoughts certainly did nothing to help him win back the once enthusiastic audience he was beginning to lose. Indeed, Chaplin and Verdoux also share a keen awareness of what is wrong in society while being devoid of the self-awareness to understand the flaws in themselves.

At the conclusion of the film, Verdoux finally surrenders to the police and is put on trial. During his trial he shows mild surprise

rather than remorse. In his view, the course of his life merely reflects the logical extreme to which capitalist society has driven him. Verdoux states:

> However remiss the prosecutor has been in complimenting me, he at least admits that I have brains. Thank you Monsieur, I have. And for thirty-five years I used them honestly. After that, nobody wanted them. So I was forced to go into business for myself. As for being a mass killer, does not the world encourage it? Is it not building weapons of destruction for the sole purpose of mass killing? Has it not blown unsuspecting women and little children to pieces, and done it very scientifically? Ha! As a mass killer I am an amateur by comparison.

Verdoux's last words to the judge and jury indict a society that is in the process of destroying itself: "I shall see you all very soon, very soon." Later, awaiting execution, Verdoux answers a reporter who protests that other people do not conduct their business in Verdoux's way: "That's the history of many a big business. Wars, conflict, it's all business. One murder makes a villain, millions a hero. Numbers sanctify, my good fellow."[12]

The film ends with Verdoux's execution. Offered a glass of rum to ease his exit from this life, Verdoux first refuses but then changes his mind, remarking, "I've never tasted rum." His hands are bound as the door to his cell is opened. He takes a last deep breath, then shuffles slowly away from the camera on his way to the guillotine. Chaplin created the walk down the lonely road in *The Tramp,* and refined it memorably in *The Circus* and *Modern Times.* In *Monsieur Verdoux* it becomes the ultimate, ironic walk down the road to where, in Chaplin's way of thinking, capitalism claims another corrupted soul.

The premiere of *Monsieur Verdoux* was held at the Broadway Theatre in New York City on April 11, 1947. A faction of the audience supported the film, while another group came to demonstrate their hostility toward Chaplin as a result of the Barry scandal and his leftist politics. "A certain contingent in the audience hissed and some actually booed at the screen," remembered Robert Lewis, who played Bottello in the film and was there that evening. "Chaplin was devastated. The audience that was for him that night didn't appreciate the film's irony. The audience that was against him made their displeasure clear."[13] After a while, Chaplin could no longer endure the audience's negative response and waited in the lobby until the film had ended. The postpremiere reception for 150 people at the "21" Club "was far from festive," remembered Lewis. "Chaplin tried to entertain everyone with some of his best pantomime routines, but it was futile. He downed a few drinks—unusual for him—and became drunk. Donald Ogden Stewart and I had to help him to his hotel suite."[14]

Three days later, Chaplin endured a disastrous press conference in the Grand Ballroom of the Gotham Hotel, where he was grilled more on his politics than on the new film he was there to promote. One defender present was the great critic James Agee, who later devoted three columns to the film in *The Nation.* He praised *Monsieur Verdoux* as a masterpiece, writing in the second column, "Chaplin's performance as Verdoux is the best piece of playing I have ever seen" and "I love and revere the film as deeply as any I have seen, and believe that it is high among the great works of this century." He began his third column by proclaiming that *Monsieur Verdoux* is "permanent if any work done during the past twenty years is permanent."[15] Although the public was largely unconvinced by Agee's apologia for *Monsieur*

Verdoux, he would nevertheless make a great impact two years later in one of his classic writings, "Comedy's Greatest Era," an eloquent appreciation of Chaplin and silent-film comedy that was the cover story of *Life* magazine.[16]

With the exception of Agee, the reviewers expressed opinions that were either mixed or negative. Inexplicably, unlike any of Chaplin's previous United Artists features, *Monsieur Verdoux* had no advance publicity campaign. As a result, the New York run of the film was a disaster. Pressure groups, particularly the Catholic War Veterans and the American Legion, threatened to picket cinemas that booked the film. The Loew's Theater circuit refused to play it. *Monsieur Verdoux* played just five weeks at the Broadway Theatre, owing to a severe drop in receipts. The film was withdrawn from distribution in an effort to devise an advertising campaign for a rescheduled national release.

Compounding the film's difficulties was the fact that Chaplin was called to testify before the House Un-American Activities Committee in its probe of alleged communist infiltration of the motion-picture industry. Following the damaging press conference in April, Chaplin decided to stay out of public view and let the United Artists advertising campaign for the film—with the challenging slogan, "Chaplin Changes! Can You?"—speak for him. Publicist Russell Birdwell, who devised the campaign, believed that the controversial nature of the film and Chaplin should be emphasized. Indeed, Birdwell wanted at one point to exploit Chaplin's personal controversy and plan the film's release around the HUAC hearing. Yet the following telegram, from Chaplin to United Artists president Gradwell Sears dated September 17, 1947, shows Chaplin's behind-the-scenes involvement with the distribution of the film and his growing frustration with both the negative response to its subject matter and the animosity in America toward him:

> Tell Birdwell under no circumstances to quote me personally in the press. This blast of the Un-American Activities Committee at this time will do more harm than good both to me and to the picture. I am not by nature ignorant or one that asks for trouble. I told Birdwell specially not to drag in the Un-American Activities Committee in connection with my picture. It can only antagonize the public. Neither do I want politics of any nature connected with the picture. It is bad showmanship and will create the impression that the picture is dull and not funny. Another item to tell Birdwell is to correct the radio spots. They are spoken too slowly. Under no circumstances release them in present form. They are too arrogant and egotistical. New ones should be made in lighter vein.[17]

The new campaign failed to build an audience for the film. Robert Warshow, in an essay first published in the *Partisan Review*, perhaps best explained why the film failed with American audiences:

> [T]he movie must be approached with a willingness to understand and enjoy it as a shifting pattern of ambiguity and irony, made up of all the complexities and contradictions not only of our society but of Chaplin's own mind and the mind of the spectator. Much of the hostility to the movie seems to come from reluctance to accept its shifting point of view, its remarkable quality of being at once uncompromising and uncommitted. We are used to flat and simple statements, especially in the movies; as a consequence, some who have seen *Monsieur Verdoux* have

Chaplin's longtime collaborator Henry Bergman (center) visits the Chaplin Studios during production of MONSIEUR VERDOUX. *Rollie Totheroh is between Bergman and Chaplin. Robert Florey is on the left of Bergman and Wheeler Dryden is behind Florey. The ailing Bergman, who had no role in the production, died soon after this photograph was taken in 1946.*

Opposite: Chaplin photographed through the camera tripod during production of MONSIEUR VERDOUX. Photograph by Robert Florey

Left: Before being led to the guillotine, Verdoux is visited by a priest (Fritz Leiber) who says, "May the Lord have mercy on your soul." "Why not?" Verdoux replies. "After all, it belongs to him." This exchange as well as other dialogue and situations from MONSIEUR VERDOUX were criticized by Joseph Breen, vice president and director of production-code administration for the Motion Picture Association of America, the Catholic War Veterans, and other professional moralists and patrioteer groups in America.

Below: Preparing to film Verdoux being led to the guillotine at the conclusion of MONSIEUR VERDOUX. Camera operator Wallace Chewning is at the camera. Photograph by Robert Florey

Right: Chaplin lunches with Orson Welles at the Brown Derby restaurant in Hollywood after completing MONSIEUR VERDOUX, March 30, 1947. Welles had wanted Chaplin to act in a script he proposed to write and direct titled THE LADY KILLER, a serious treatment of the French Bluebeard Landru; but Chaplin had wanted to write a comedy script of his own based on Landru. Anxious to avoid any possible plagiarism claims, Chaplin bought the idea from Welles for $5,000 and for a screen credit in MONSIEUR VERDOUX that reads, "Based on an idea by Orson Welles."

Middle: Chaplin escorts Mary Pickford and Oona to the world premiere of MONSIEUR VERDOUX at the Broadway Theatre, New York City, on April 11, 1947. Pickford had been to a cocktail party earlier in the day and was late in joining the Chaplins for dinner at the "21" Club. In the packed theater lobby, she negotiated the crowded room to get to a microphone. While still holding Chaplin's hand, she began, "Two thousand years ago Christ was born, and tonight . . ." but proceeded no further, as she was separated from the microphone by a push from the crowd. Chaplin often wondered how her statement would have continued. Photograph by Morris Lettoft

Bottom: Chaplin and Mack Sennett leaving D. W. Griffith's memorial service held at Masonic Hall, Hollywood Boulevard, July 27, 1948. Photograph by Mike Merritt

Opposite: Chaplin speaks to reporters at a press conference to promote MONSIEUR VERDOUX, held at the Grand Ballroom of the Gotham Hotel, New York City, April 14, 1947. The reporters were more interested in Chaplin's politics than his new film. Despite his explicit statements that he was not a member of the communist party or any other political party, pressure groups intensified their campaign against him.

found it unpleasantly disturbing, and some have simply refused to recognize its complexity at all, condemning Chaplin because they disagree with Verdoux—though Verdoux certainly does not ask for agreement, and, if he did, it would still not be clear what he wanted us to agree to.[18]

United Artists finally withdrew *Monsieur Verdoux* from distribution in the United States and Canada in December 1948. Originally, Chaplin and the debt-laden distributor had hoped the film would gross $12 million worldwide; at the time of its withdrawal, the film had played just 2,922 exhibition contracts and grossed a paltry $325,000 in America. Despite the film's poor reception, Chaplin was nevertheless nominated for an Academy Award for best original screenplay. Although the dark, ironic comedy of *Monsieur Verdoux* was not embraced in America, the film was better received in Great Britain, where it garnered generally favorable reviews, and it was particularly well received in French-speaking countries. However, overall *Monsieur Verdoux* did not even gross $6 million worldwide.

Chaplin wrote in his autobiography, "I believe *Monsieur Verdoux* is the cleverest and most brilliant film I have yet made."[19] He felt differently two years later when he spoke with Richard

Meryman (see page 365) and later confessed to Francis Wyndham, "There was some clever dialogue in *Monsieur Verdoux* but now I think it was too cerebral and should have had more business. If you have a bit of a message it's better to put it over through business than through words—better for me, anyhow."[20]

Unfortunately, *Monsieur Verdoux* did little to bridge the growing gulf between Chaplin and the American public that once adored him, and even exacerbated the circumstances leading to his exile. Chaplin's left-leaning, anti-capitalist message only served to confirm the enmity of his enemies. However, in an irony that Verdoux himself might have appreciated, *Monsieur Verdoux* was reappraised as a masterpiece nearly twenty years ahead of its time when it was revived in New York City in 1964 as part of a yearlong Chaplin retrospective at the Plaza Theatre. With McCarthyism by then discredited, American audiences were sophisticated enough to celebrate and embrace the film for its groundbreaking macabre comedy and courageous social criticism without being distracted by its political overtones. *Monsieur Verdoux* contains flashes of brilliance and easily could have been a masterpiece, ahead of its time in its complexity and ironic gravity, had the film's internal flaws not ultimately overshadowed it.

Limelight

Disenchanted with postwar America, Chaplin decided that his next film would be a nostalgic recollection of the London and the music halls of his youth. Few would fail to see the parallels between the film's protagonist, Calvero, the "Tramp Comedian" and fading music-hall star, and Chaplin himself, the aging cinema legend. Like Calvero, Chaplin was a great artist coming to terms with the loss of his audience and the evolution of his craft beyond him. And like Calvero, Chaplin ultimately was saved by the love and friendship of a young woman. *Limelight* is Chaplin's last great film, and it plays like a self-conscious summing up of his life and career. As a journey back to his beginnings and an often rapier-sharp self-critique, *Limelight* is Chaplin's most deeply personal and introspective film.

Limelight begins with a simple plot description, "A story of a ballerina and a clown . . . " Chaplin portrays Calvero, a once-beloved music-hall clown who has lost his ability to make audiences laugh. He saves a struggling ballerina (Claire Bloom) from suicide in the London boardinghouse where he lives. Taking the girl under his wing, he manages to regain his own lost confidence while encouraging her. As the ballerina, named

Above: Chaplin preparing to become the animal trainer for one of the music-hall routines in LIMELIGHT *(1952). Photograph by W. Eugene Smith*

Opposite: Chaplin dons the Tramp's derby hat and cane while costumed as Calvero on the set of LIMELIGHT. *Although the film is about Calvero the comedian, it is arguably Chaplin's least comic film. Photograph by Hommel*

Right: Chaplin directs the first rehearsal of the dramatized version of W. Somerset Maugham's RAIN *at the Circle Theatre, Hollywood, 1948. Seated in the front row from left to right are William Schallert, June Havoc, Earl Herdan, and Terry Kilburn. Jerry Epstein is to the right of Chaplin, and Sydney Chaplin is at right with head on hand. The Circle Theatre was started in 1946 by a group of UCLA students including Epstein, Sydney Chaplin, and Schallert. Although Chaplin directed several of their productions, he did not promote his involvement because he was concerned that the controversy surrounding him might draw focus away from the accomplishments of the Circle. "Chaplin as a stage director was insightful, endlessly inventive, and the soul of patience," remembered Schallert, who played the Reverend Davidson in the Circle production of* RAIN. *"He completely gave himself as fully as he could. He had a great generosity of spirit toward us young actors, and, of course, we were entirely in awe of his genius as an actor and filmmaker . . . Chaplin's every physical movement was elegant and graceful; his physical language was pure genius. That was, perhaps, his problem as a director. Ninety-nine percent of the time he just showed us what he wanted and we were supposed to imitate him. Our problem as actors was that we were not as graceful as Chaplin. He kept us all night rehearsing; we were staggering and he still had this incredible energy. Oona would have to call to get him to come home. At dawn he climbed behind the wheel of his black Ford—the most unpretentious car imaginable—and drove home to his mansion in Beverly Hills."*

Lower right: Chaplin's children Michael, Josephine, and Geraldine appear as waifs in LIMELIGHT *(1952). Behind them, an inebriated Calvero returns to the boardinghouse where he lives. Photograph by Hommel*

Terry, is cured of her psychosomatic illness (the inability to walk), the clown is strengthened to make a comeback. Terry's gratitude becomes adoration, and she begs Calvero to marry her. But Calvero comprehends her heart better than she and does not permit her to sacrifice her radiant youth to his old age, particularly after he discovers that she is actually in love with a young composer named Neville, portrayed by Chaplin's own son, Sydney. Calvero reclaims his audience in several music-hall routines for a theatrical benefit. In the last of these sketches, Calvero, while appearing in a frenetic musical duet with his comedy partner (Buster Keaton), falls into a bass drum, which induces a heart attack. He dies in the wings of the theater as he watches Terry, now a beautiful prima ballerina, dance on stage. *Limelight* ends reflective of the film's opening title, "The glamour of Limelight, from which age must pass as youth enters," a sentiment that at once closes the film and, in a sense, Chaplin's great career.

The theatrical setting of *Limelight* was perhaps chosen in part as a result of Chaplin's involvement with the Circle Theatre, a small theater group founded in 1946 by Jerry Epstein, which included several young actors, including Chaplin's son Sydney. Chaplin became interested in the group and directed several of their productions. He hired Epstein as an assistant on *Limelight*, and Epstein remained a collaborator and family friend for the rest of Chaplin's life.

Certain ideas surfaced in *Limelight* that Chaplin had worked on as far back as the 1920s. For example, the *New York Times* reported on November 29, 1925, that Chaplin intended to commence production on a film to be called *The Clown*:

> It is called *The Clown*, and in it Chaplin is to be clad as a circus clown except for his big shoes, his little cane and his tiny bowler hat. This story was described as another dramatic comedy, and in its method something after the style of *The Gold Rush*, except that it was to have a tragic ending—the fun-maker impersonated by Chaplin is supposed to die on the tanbark while the spectators are applauding his comic pantomime.[1]

There are enough similarities to suggest that ideas from *The Clown* were incorporated into Chaplin's *Limelight*.

Parallels can also be drawn between *Limelight* and *The Circus*. Both films are set in a theatrical milieu and explore similar themes: age giving way to youth (in each film an older man gallantly relinquishes his love for a younger woman to a younger man), clowns who lose their ability to make people laugh, and what Ira S. Jaffe has termed "the anxious labor of performance."[2] *The Circus* and *Limelight* are more noticeably autobiographical than any of Chaplin's other works (with the exception of *The Kid*).

Chaplin worked on the script for *Limelight* for more than three years, the longest concentrated period of time he ever devoted to a single script. He began dictating story ideas for *Limelight* in early 1948 and was still working on the script in January 1951. *Limelight* had the working title *Footlights* and was set in the period of the British music halls just prior to World War I. As part of

Chaplin in costume at the studio during production of LIMELIGHT. *Photograph by W. Eugene Smith*

his preparation of the script, Chaplin wrote a novel of approximately 100,000 words in which he described the plot of the film as it was finally written in the script and also provided the back stories of Calvero and Terry.[3]

Chaplin wrote in his autobiography that Calvero was based partly on the American stage comic Frank Tinney, who—like Chaplin himself—eventually lost contact with his audience.[4] Chaplin also was inspired by the Spanish mime Marceline and by his own defeated father and broken mother. Like Calvero, Chaplin's father was an alcoholic with marital problems. The fallen ballerina Terry was based on Chaplin's mother, and Chaplin clearly explored part of his own family history in the various interactions between Calvero and the ballerina. He was asked by an interviewer during the film's preproduction in 1950 whether or not his new picture was autobiographical. The reporter recorded Chaplin's response: "'Everything is autobiographical' he says with an eloquent movement of his small hands, 'but don't make too much of that.'"[5]

Ultimately, Chaplin indicated that the character of Calvero was a person who "grew old and introspective and acquired a feeling of dignity, and this divorced him from all intimacy with the audience."[6] Norman Lloyd, who appeared in the film as Bodalink, thought the film expressed much of Chaplin's personality and thinking of the time. "Chaplin was a great nineteenth-century romantic, and I think that is much of what *Limelight* is. It was also Charlie at the point where he felt he could no longer make people laugh."[7]

Chaplin began an anxious search for a leading lady in February 1951. "In casting the girl's part I wanted the impossible: beauty, talent, and a great emotional range. After months of searching and testing with disappointing results I eventually had the good fortune to sign up Claire Bloom, who was recommended by my friend Arthur Laurents,"[8] remembered Chaplin in his autobiography. Playwright Arthur Laurents had seen the twenty-year-old English actress Claire Bloom in the West End production of *Ring Round the Moon* (Christopher Fry's adaptation of *L'Invitation au château* by Jean Anouilh) at the Globe Theatre and suggested her to Chaplin. Bloom initially ignored the Chaplin Studios' request for photographs of her because she thought she had no chance to be cast in his film, but ultimately she received a telegram that read, "WHERE ARE THE PHOTOGRAPHS? CHARLES CHAPLIN."[9] "I sent the photographs," remembered Bloom, "and from that point there was nothing more I wanted in the world than to work for him."[10] Finally, Bloom traveled by air to New York from London at the end of April 1951 to test with Chaplin. She believed she got the part because she bore an extraordinary resemblance to Oona.[11] "He wanted the girl in *Limelight* to be like Oona," confirmed Sydney Chaplin.[12]

However, Chaplin did not make the final decision until August. When he did, he insisted Bloom bring her mother as a publicly visible chaperone because he could not afford any more negative publicity regarding a young actress. Bloom's contract stipulated three months' work for $15,000 plus travel expenses and a weekly allowance for her and her mother.

Bloom later offered the following on how the character of Terry fit into a pattern in Chaplin's films:

> Theresa—she is just one in the line of damaged heroines inspired by the memory of his mother, heroines extending from the blind flower-seller of *City Lights* to the penniless waif of *Modern Times* and the young female ex-con of *Monsieur Verdoux*. I think that what particularly excited Chaplin about the *Limelight* story was that at long last the damaged girl was to develop into a mature woman, strong, independent, completely in command of her powers . . . the example of Oona—of her loving devotion and her quiet strength—was responsible for finally erasing the image of broken womanhood that his mother's suffering had imprinted on his artistic conscience.[13]

Bloom also remembered Chaplin's obsessive attention to every detail with respect to the character:

> Chaplin had already decided upon every last detail of every garment I was to wear. He remembered the way his mother had worn such a dress and the way his first girlfriend had worn such a shawl, and I quickly realized, even then, that some composite young woman, lost to him in the past, was what he wanted me to bring to life.[14] . . . "My mother wore a dress like that, she wore a shawl of that color" [he said]. I realized that it was a composite picture he wanted me to create for him; not only his young mother, lost to him in the past, but also his young wife, Oona, loving and devoted. The two most important female images in his life were to be fused in the one portrait of a young and helpless girl, whom he was now able, in the guise of a film character, to rescue from her fate, and to make whole again.[15]

Chaplin's artistic contributions to the film were so legion that he even sired some of the cast. The romantic lead went to his son Sydney. His eldest son, Charles, plays a police officer in the film's harlequinade ballet and his half-brother, Wheeler Dryden, plays both a doctor and clown in the harlequinade. Chaplin's younger children Geraldine, Michael, and Josephine all appear in the film. Even Oona appears briefly, doubling for Claire Bloom in a couple of pickup shots after Bloom had returned to England in February 1952.

Chaplin's direction was as tireless and exacting as ever, particularly toward members of his family. Sydney Chaplin later offered this critique of his father's directorial style:

My father was a marvelous director. He was a much better stage director than a film director. He shot his films like a stage director. He also had an old-fashioned style toward acting that was excellent in theater. This actually worked to his advantage in *Limelight* with all the theatrical scenes. He had an excellent sense of stage drama and what was effective and what wasn't in the theater. He was generous with other people, but he was tough on me. He'd expect me to get it right away. And there was a lot of pressure from him. With me, it was always, "Come on Syd, what the hell is the matter with you!" Which does not make it easier. We had a strange relationship. It used to blow hot and cold. I don't know why.[16]

Left: Calvero, as a flea-circus trainer, watches his performing fleas Phyllis and Henry cavorting back and forth between his two hands during a music-hall sketch in LIMELIGHT. Photograph by W. Eugene Smith

Below left: Calvero removes his makeup after suffering humiliating failure on stage. Photograph by Hommel

Opposite: Calvero, busking the streets of London, accepts a contribution from Neville (Sydney Chaplin), the young composer recently drafted by the military, whom he meets by chance in a pub. Photograph by Hommel

Despite Chaplin's theatrical tendencies, "He was constantly fighting the actors for less theatrics. He was always pushing Claire to be more relaxed, easier, and simpler," remembered Sydney.[18] Bloom's theatricality would receive a terse admonition from Chaplin, "You're working for Charlie Chaplin now. No Shakespeare, please!"[19] Even an experienced film actor like Norman Lloyd was not immune from Chaplin's criticism. Sydney recalled, "In the scene where he explains the ballet, my old man thought Norman was trying to act it like Hamlet's advice to the players. It was too theatrical. My father really let him have it, 'Jesus Christ, just act like a human being!' he roared at Norman."[20] Despite the fulsome dialogue in *Limelight*, Sydney remembered his father saying around this time that he preferred silent films to talking films. "My father used to explain that dialogue just gets in the way in films."[21]

Bloom may have thrived under Chaplin's exact direction (Norman Lloyd described Bloom as having a "neck of steel"),[17] but Sydney became nervous on the set. His considerable charm and talent as a romantic leading man—which is only seen intermittently in *Limelight*—would be fully revealed in the original Broadway productions of *Bells Are Ringing* in 1956 (for which he won a Tony Award for best featured actor in a musical) and *Funny Girl* in 1964.

As the young leads who fall in love, Claire Bloom and Sydney Chaplin emulated their on-screen characters and struck up a romance during the production of the film. "I had never met an English girl," Sydney recalled. "It was a romance—but not too serious. Claire wanted to save herself until she played the part of Juliet. She was playing Juliet at the Old Vic when *Limelight* was to have its world premiere in London, so I followed her to London."[22]

Perhaps the great love story of the film is what Chaplin expresses about his own relationship with Oona through the characters of Calvero and Terry. Although Calvero ultimately finds such an older man–younger woman union impossible, Chaplin did not. But like Chaplin, Calvero is also a comedian whose own spirit is renewed when he helps restore the health and confidence of a young woman. Oona had been ill with an upper respiratory infection during her courtship with Chaplin, who at one point even thought she was suffering from tuberculosis. He helped nurse her back to health, just as Calvero tends to Terry.[23] Similarly, Chaplin (like Calvero) credits the unconditional love of his young companion with rescuing him during the most difficult period of his life and career. Seemingly deliberate parallels like these between the plot of *Limelight* and Chaplin's own life make *Limelight* the most autobiographical film of Chaplin's career.

After the disappointing American box-office returns of *Monsieur Verdoux*, Chaplin, for the first time in his independent career, considered getting a bank loan to finance his new film rather than risking his own money. "Charlie went to the banks and explored the possibility of getting a loan to finance the costs of *Limelight*," remembered Norman Lloyd. "They were willing, but they wanted to cross-collateralize all of Charlie's old pictures that he owned. He would have none of that."[24] Instead, Chaplin arranged for United Artists to reissue *City Lights*, which opened in New York City on April 8, 1950, and the profits paid the costs of *Limelight*. He also made money by renting out studio space during idle periods to companies such as Cathedral Films (which made religious short films) and Proctor and Gamble (for the production of early television commercials), as well as producer Walter Wanger (to make a screen test of Greta Garbo in May 1949, her last appearance before a motion-picture camera).

Chaplin ultimately spent $900,000 of his own money to finance *Limelight*. It was considered a shoestring budget for such a film. The film was made at the Chaplin Studios, with street exteriors filmed at Paramount's back lot in Hollywood and the theater interiors at the RKO-Pathé studio in Culver City. By all accounts, Chaplin was euphoric while shooting the film.[25]

Lonnie D'Orsa was hired as the film's production manager, overseeing all the physical production, scheduling, hiring the stages, and running the crew. "He was a good production man who kept it going," remembered Norman Lloyd. "Charlie wanted someone, as he said, 'to drive the picture through.'"[26] As an assistant director, Chaplin engaged

Robert Aldrich, who would go on to direct *Kiss Me Deadly* (1955), *Whatever Happened to Baby Jane?* (1962), and *The Dirty Dozen* (1967). Filming was finished in fifty-five days, including four days of retakes. The production adhered to a tight schedule until Chaplin came down with influenza during the filming of the music-hall scenes and had to close down work for a week. Chaplin originally had hoped to complete production in a mere thirty-six days.

One of the ways Chaplin economized and made *Limelight* so quickly was the unusual method of filming he employed. Jerry Epstein recalled:

> Charlie and I planned every camera set-up and lighting change to save time and money. All the long shots in Calvero's flat were filmed together. We didn't move the camera. This was done all out of continuity. Once a shot was finished, Charlie would change costumes and then film all the long shots for another scene. With the long shots finished, we then moved the camera for the medium shots and then the close-ups. Charlie and Claire knew their scenes inside and out with all the weeks of rehearsal so shooting scenes out of continuity was no problem for them.[27]

One scene that gave Chaplin particular concern and was filmed more times than any other was Claire Bloom's big scene in which Terry shakes free of her psychosomatic illness, regains her ability to walk, and begins shouting, "I'm walking!" Bloom remembered that when Chaplin criticized her acting she became so upset she burst into tears:

> We rehearsed the scene in New York originally—he auditioned me with that scene—and we later rehearsed it—with the rest of the film—on the lawn of his home in Beverly Hills. They were meticulous rehearsals. The scene required an enormous emo-

tional depth for a twenty-year-old actress in her first film. I had difficulty crying on demand. Mr. Chaplin summoned me to his dressing room one morning and told me he wanted to review the scene "technically" and not to tire myself emotionally. When I gave him just what he had asked, he became furious and I burst into tears. When I tried to explain that I only was doing what he had told me to do, he became enraged. He said, "There is no such thing as technical acting, only bad acting." I became undone emotionally and he quickly escorted me onto the set where the crew, which he had alerted earlier, waited and shot the scene. . . . He knew just how to manipulate me to get precisely the emotion he had wanted.[28]

As he had done on *The Great Dictator,* Chaplin hired the distinguished cinematographer Karl Struss to be director of photography. Rollie Totheroh was assigned to a token role of "photographic consultant." Chaplin wanted the film to have a beautifully rich black-and-white look. Concerned with being labeled old-fashioned, he wanted the best lighting and photography. As a result, the production is technically more polished than most Chaplin films. Although Struss later said, *"Limelight* was slightly the more interesting of the two films photographically" that he had worked on with Chaplin, he maintained that he did not see the film as particularly advanced in terms of cinematography. This was "because he [Chaplin] had no knowledge of cam-

Right: Chaplin and Claire Bloom, just prior to filming one of the backstage ballet scenes in LIMELIGHT, *at the RKO-Pathé studio in Culver City. Photograph by W. Eugene Smith*

Opposite: Chaplin demonstrates the ending of André Eglevsky's dance solo at the RKO-Pathé studio in Culver City. Photograph by W. Eugene Smith

era direction, his films were completely 'theatre.' It was very routine work with him; you'd just set up the camera and let it go and he and the other actors would play in front of it."[29]

Nevertheless, *Limelight* is the best lit and most artistically photographed of Chaplin's sound films. Struss elevated the simple Chaplin camera setups with some flourishes and refinements, such as in the final scene where Struss pulls back the camera in a tracking shot following Calvero's death to reveal Terry dancing on stage. Struss also carefully lit the audition scene to conceal in shadows the face of dancer Melissa Hayden, who substitutes for Claire Bloom in the dancing scenes. The film also boasts an unusual number of long close-ups of Chaplin, all of which are haunting and effective: Calvero, as the flea-circus trainer in a dream, looks out at the empty theater that dissolves to his own distraught face awakened by the nightmare; Calvero in the Middlesex music-hall dressing room wipes his makeup in the mirror and stares at himself as a failure; Calvero looks onto the darkened stage after watching Terry's audition; and Calvero, his face twitching with tired and sad eyes, dies in the wings.

Limelight reflects Chaplin's personal devotion to and excitement about theater. To achieve the proper atmosphere of the British music halls of his youth, he hired the talented art director Eugene Lourié, who designed superb and convincing ballet and music-hall backdrops. Chaplin was quite conscious of being called old-fashioned and his sets being labeled cheap. Lourié later wrote:

> In writing about Chaplin's early films, some critics have noted that his sets were "shabby" and "unimportant." I personally find that all of Chaplin's early pictures had sets that rightly expressed the style of his comedies. They were "shabby" intentionally. There was a certain power in their impersonality. In remembering Chaplin's comedies, you can hardly disassociate them from their settings. Thinking of Chaplin's pictures in retrospect, I see the vivid images of his sets: a memorable one for *Easy Street* filmed in 1917, the precariously swinging cabin in *The Gold Rush*, and others. In general, insignificance can be an achievement. In fact, the best art direction in films is often that which you are not aware of. As a general rule, if you especially notice the sets or admire them, it means that the art direction has surpassed its functions.[30]

Right: Chaplin directs the extras in the music hall during production of LIMELIGHT. *The man wearing the derby hat behind Chaplin is Harry Crocker, Chaplin's assistant director on* THE CIRCUS *(who also played Rex in the film) and* CITY LIGHTS. *Crocker was engaged to handle publicity for Chaplin on* LIMELIGHT. *Photograph by W. Eugene Smith*

Below: Wearing his animal-trainer costume, Chaplin rests between takes, in an uncharacteristic display of exhaustion. In fact, Chaplin was fighting a viral infection that later suspended production of LIMELIGHT *for a week. Photograph by W. Eugene Smith*

The fine production values of *Limelight,* however, are occasionally marred by obvious rear-screen projections simulating exterior backgrounds. Perhaps the most glaring instance of this sort of economy is a backdrop behind Bodalink, the dance director, to simulate an empty theater interior; it is clearly a painted canvas on which is reflected Norman Lloyd's shadow.

Chaplin hired two leading New York dancers, André Eglevsky and Melissa Hayden, to perform the film's ballet sequences. He was an admirer of Eglevsky and asked him if he would perform a forty-five-second solo and provide choreography (not unlike his famed "Blue Bird Pas de Deux") to Chaplin's music. Chaplin ultimately composed twelve minutes of ballet music to which Eglevsky and Hayden danced. "It was one of the thrilling moments of my film career to see them dance to it. Their interpretation was most flattering and gave the music a classic significance," Chaplin wrote.[31]

Music figured more prominently in *Limelight* than in any of Chaplin's previous works. He began work composing and recording the film's musical score prior to production. Despite the importance of the music, Chaplin curiously settled for a novice, Ray Rasch, a pianist with no previous experience with orchestration and arranging, to help him. Beginning in December 1950, the pair worked five to seven hours a day several days a week on the music until October 1951. Rasch's lack of experience did not faze Chaplin, who told him, "You have got to do it somehow."[32] Perhaps Chaplin wanted an associate with little experience who would merely orchestrate what the director wanted rather than pressing his own ideas. "At first I was sure that I had met up with a madman," remembered Rasch:

> I couldn't believe that this was genius at work. He would bellow for hours at a time and all that I could hear was a senseless jumble. But suddenly he would strike a note or sometimes a whole phrase and would scream at me to play it and jot down the notes. It was a wonderful experience and I learned a good deal I didn't know before about music. . . . When a melody satisfied him, he would go over it and over it. He didn't seem to care that I was just playing on a piano. He would ask for French horns in one spot; then violins and 'cellos and woodwinds. I just kept pounding away until he was satisfied.[33]

Rasch engaged Larry Russell to help with the arrangement of the film's score. A fifty-five-piece orchestra recorded the music for *Limelight* in September 1951. When the film went into general release in 1953 the song "Eternally" (also known as "Terry's Theme"), the main musical theme for the film, became a tremendous international hit, second only to Chaplin's popular song "Smile," first released with the reissue of *Modern Times* in 1954.

The music-hall routines in *Limelight* serve as comic relief, as the film is fundamentally a drama (posters and other advertisements billed the film as "human drama").[34] These sequences, filmed with simple, fixed camera placements in a theater, ideally suit Chaplin's directorial style. The most famous of the music-hall

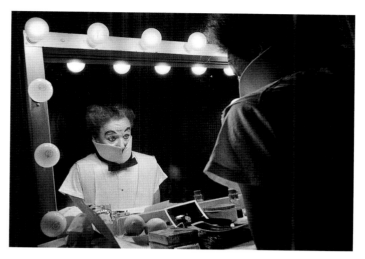

Chaplin experiments with his costume in front of his dressing-table mirror during production of LIMELIGHT. *Photograph by W. Eugene Smith*

scenes, and perhaps the most famous scene in the film, is the historic comic duet that pairs Chaplin and Buster Keaton, the two great geniuses of silent-film comedy. Chaplin and Keaton worked together on their scenes for three weeks, from December 22, 1951, to January 12, 1952. Chaplin determined that he would not use a laugh track for the scene (or for any of the other music-hall scenes), even though it is supposedly performed before an audience, because he felt cinema audiences watching the routine would provide the proper, enthusiastic response. The scene marks the only time the two great silent clowns ever worked together on screen. Keaton's opening line, "I never thought we'd come to this!" is played for deliberate comedic and ironic effect.

In the sketch, the two play slightly crazed musicians: Chaplin, the violinist whose legs keep shrinking up inside his trousers, and Buster, the bespectacled pianist who is constantly fumbling his sheet music. After dismantling a piano and ruining a violin, they perform a duet that ends with Calvero—in a musical frenzy—falling off the stage into the bass drum in the orchestra pit.

Following the opening of *Limelight* a rumor began, perpetuated in books and articles, that Chaplin jealously cut out all of Keaton's best gags from the music-hall routine. Although a friendly rivalry existed between the two to make the crew laugh at their improvised gags, apparently this is where their rivalry ended. According to Jerry Epstein:

> People have written over the years that Charlie cut out the best stuff of Buster Keaton. That's completely untrue, and I should know as I was with Charlie every day in the editing of the picture. He shot enough for ten films from just that sequence. He cut out some of Keaton's stuff but he also cut some of his own best gags. Narrative meant more than anything else, no matter how good any one gag was. He would never sacrifice anyone's performance. He looked for the best of everyone. . . . The sequence was completely improvised. It was Charlie, in the

editing, that kept cutting back to Keaton with the music sheets falling off the piano.[35]

"For Buster Keaton to suddenly be funny was not in the story," maintained Sydney Chaplin. "The story is that Calvero makes a comeback. It would have been inconsistent if Keaton or another actor had overpowered him."[36] Buster Keaton himself believed it was a rumor begun by his business partner, Raymond Rohauer, in an effort to build up Keaton's reputation while at the same time diminishing Chaplin's.[37] Keaton was grateful to be involved in the film. At the time Chaplin offered him the part, he had been working steadily in television but had not enjoyed much recent work in feature films.

The main shooting of *Limelight* was completed on January 25, 1952. Chaplin spent the next three months editing. At the beginning of May he ordered that the sets be rebuilt in order to shoot retakes of certain scenes. After an August 2 preview of *Limelight* to a small group of film-industry friends on the Paramount lot in Hollywood, Chaplin was ready to premiere his film to the public.

He decided the event should take place in his native London, given the London music-hall setting of the film. Chaplin left California on September 6 for New York, and on September 17 he and his family left New York for England on the luxury liner *Queen Elizabeth II*. Although Chaplin did not realize it when he stepped onto the gangplank to board the ship, he would not return to America for nearly twenty years. Unfortunately, he did not even enjoy those last moments in his adopted country because he had begun his trip in haste while attempting to evade a process server over a nuisance lawsuit brought against United Artists by Max Kravitz, an associate of Paul McNutt's former management team. Kravitz tried to argue that his option in the company was still valid and he was entitled to a partnership in United Artists—he lost.

Two days at sea, Chaplin received a cable informing him the United States Attorney General's office had rescinded the reentry permit Chaplin had applied for and received prior to leaving the country. Chaplin would have to reapply for immigration papers and face a hearing if he returned.[38]

Opposite: Calvero and Terry (Claire Bloom) as two orphans of the theater, one at the end and the other at the beginning of a career. A half century after LIMELIGHT, Bloom remained active in films, theater, and television, and published two volumes of autobiography. Photograph by Hommel

Right: Terry (Claire Bloom) holds Calvero's hand and tells him how much she loves him backstage at his music-hall benefit. Photograph by Hommel

Below: Calvero's final and most memorable music-hall comedy sketch finds his legs inconveniently shortening and vanishing into his oversized trousers as he attempts to perform a musical duet with Buster Keaton. The sequence is one of Chaplin's finest, and a fitting tribute and memorial to the visual-comedy tradition. Photograph by W. Eugene Smith

Despite the devastating news from America, Chaplin proceeded with the world premiere of *Limelight* in London. "When *Limelight* was finished I had fewer qualms about its success than any other picture I had ever made,"[39] Chaplin wrote in his autobiography. The premiere was held on October 16, 1952, at the Odeon Theatre in Leicester Square, with proceeds going to aid the Royal London Society for Teaching and Training the Blind. Princess Margaret attended the premiere, representing the royal family. It was the first London film premiere to be covered live on television by the BBC and was by all accounts a spectacular event. Chaplin went to Paris to open the film on October 31. Following the screening, President Vincent Auriol conferred on Chaplin the French government's highest accolade, the Legion of Honor. Chaplin next went to Amsterdam, Stockholm, Brussels, and Rome to open the film; he was greeted like royalty and honors were bestowed upon him.

Unlike Chaplin's three previous films—*Modern Times, The Great Dictator*, and *Monsieur Verdoux*—*Limelight* was not in any way politically or socially controversial and did not contain the elements of bitterness that had alienated his audience. Yet reviews of the film were mixed. Most film critics reacted positively toward Chaplin's noble intentions for the film, emphasizing that Chaplin was a great artist and therefore the film—however flawed—was important. The unabashed sentiment and the old-fashioned nature of the film's melodramatic plot invariably found detractors. Some critics pointed out Chaplin's propensity to talk and his fondness for aphorisms such as: "That's all any of us are— amateurs. We don't live long enough to be anything else," and

Right: Chaplin listens intently as Buster Keaton tells a story during a break in the filming of LIME-LIGHT at the RKO-Pathé studio in Culver City. Keaton later said of Chaplin in his autobiography, "At his best, and Chaplin remained at his best for a long time, he was the greatest comedian that ever lived." Photograph by W. Eugene Smith

Middle right: Chaplin marks a work print with a grease pencil, assisted by the nominal editor, Joseph Engel (right), while Chaplin's assistant, Jerry Epstein, watches in the background during postproduction editing of LIMELIGHT. Photograph by Hommel

Below: Chaplin with conductor Keith Williams and musical arranger Ray Rasch during production of LIMELIGHT. Chaplin and Rasch worked more than nine months on the film's musical score. Photograph by Hommel

Opposite: Sydney Chaplin towers over the family as he joins his father, Oona, and his half-siblings Geraldine, Michael, Josephine, and Victoria at the world premiere of LIMELIGHT at the Odeon Theatre, Leicester Square, London, October 16, 1952.

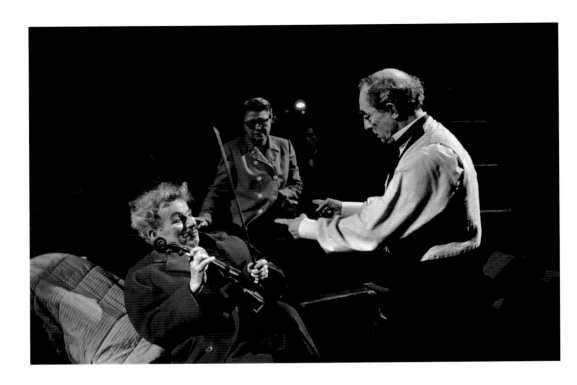

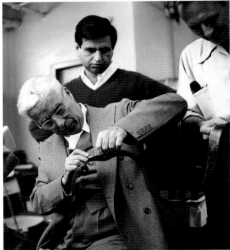

role in *Limelight:* "I realize only now how courageous it was of him to appear in a public place at that time in New York. People dining at other tables continually looked in his direction, some commenting audibly, and far from kindly, about his political opinions."[26]

The American government's relentless pursuit of Chaplin reached its climax in 1952 as he embarked upon the liner *Queen Elizabeth II,* bound for London to attend the world premiere of *Limelight.* Chaplin received word by cable on September 19 that United States Attorney General James P. McGranery, on the basis of Hoover's FBI investigation, had withdrawn Chaplin's permit to reenter the country. McGranery cited the U.S. Code of Laws on Aliens and Citizenship, which granted him the authority to bar aliens from the country on grounds of "morals, health or insanity, or for advocating Communism or associating with Communist or pro-Communist organizations."[27] He further ordered that the INS should prepare for possible deportation hearings if Chaplin were to seek to return. A little more than a month later, McGranery said his action was prompted by "grave moral charges" and that Chaplin would only be allowed back if he "can prove his worth and right to enter the United States."[28] In an instant, Chaplin had been unceremoniously ousted from the country where he had resided for nearly four decades, and where he had made much of his fame and fortune.

However, even in exile, Chaplin did nothing to endear himself to the citizens of his former home. He met with communist Chinese Prime Minister Chou En-lai in 1954, for example, and accepted a World Peace Council Award sponsored by the Soviet Union during the same year.

Chaplin's first film in exile, *A King in New York,* is both auto-biographical and political. The film is the tale of an exiled monarch who comes to America to build support for his plans for a utopian society where nuclear bombs are converted into cheap energy for the masses. This theme reflects contemporary socialist views against the rise of atomic weaponry for national defense. Chaplin frequently spoke out against the proliferation of nuclear weapons. The film's climax finds King Shahdov subpoenaed to testify before a committee investigating communist sympathizers. At the conclusion of a farcical turn of events, the King inadver-

tently douses the committee with a powerful fire hose. Chaplin, it would seem, had exacted his comedic revenge against those who pursued him in America. He shared his political views as they stood in 1957 in an interview with family friend Ella Winter: "As for politics, I'm an anarchist. I hate governments and rules and—fetters. . . . Can't stand caged animals. . . . People must be free."[29] Despite the overt political themes and subject matter in *A King in New York,* Chaplin's political interests waned soon after the film's release, as his focus increasingly centered only on work and family. By 1960, he was quoted as saying, "I remain just one thing, and one thing only—and that is a clown. It places me on a far higher plane than any politician."[30]

In 1962, a decade after his exile from the United States, Chaplin was interviewed by his friend Harold Clurman, the renowned theater critic and director, for *Esquire* magazine. Clurman left the interview characterizing Chaplin as "avowedly apolitical."[31] Indeed, in later life, Chaplin apparently no longer had any use for politics and was able to release any lingering bitterness concerning his exile. He was quoted in a 1971 *Life* magazine interview, "I like America. I always did. I have no ill feelings. That's politics, and when you live as long as I have, all politics look pretty foolish."[32] This is a remarkable statement, given how preoccupied with political thought Chaplin had been for most of his career.

Chaplin did not return to America again until April 1972, when he received the Film Society of Lincoln Center award in New York City and an honorary Academy Award from the Academy of Motion Picture Arts and Sciences, for his lifetime of achievement in film, in Los Angeles. A generation of distance from the unfortunate events surrounding his exile apparently had healed most of the negative sentiment against him. Chaplin was warmly received by the United States upon his return.

Today, Chaplin is better known for his beloved Tramp character than for his controversial political views. However, despite his protestations to the contrary, Chaplin was one of the most political artists of the twentieth century, a distinction that nearly ruined him yet provides a common thread throughout his extraordinary body of work.

Exile

On September 19, 1952, a spokesperson for United States Attorney General James P. McGranery announced publicly that Chaplin's reentry permit had been revoked and that Chaplin would have to answer questions from the INS about his political beliefs and moral behavior before he would be allowed to return to the United States. Soon afterward McGranery himself informed the press that Chaplin "is in my judgment an unsavory character" and charged him with "making statements that would indicate a leering, sneering attitude toward a country whose hospitality has enriched him."[1] The government was pursuing charges of both communism and moral turpitude, although the FBI files indicate they did not have much of a case on either count.[2] However, the charges were moot because Chaplin never again was to live in the United States.

Oona Chaplin returned briefly to America in November 1952 to make the necessary arrangements to remove Chaplin's personal fortune, most of which was contained in a safe-deposit box, to Europe. Chaplin was understandably anxious during the ten days she was away, terrified the American government might discover some way to confiscate his holdings or prevent Oona from again leaving the country. Once she had safely returned and their financial affairs were in order, Chaplin surrendered his reentry permit in April 1953 and began to divest

things were not shared with us. He was a Victorian father—he was a Victorian man! He wanted us to have the security and protection he never had as a child, but it could be restrictive and isolating. It was difficult for us—but I am sure it was also difficult for him to raise a large family when most men his age were grandfathers.[4]

The happiness Chaplin and Oona mutually felt in their marriage was such a complete world of love that the children felt somewhat excluded from them. Moreover, Chaplin did not like sharing his wife's time and kept his own time with the children measured. Michael Chaplin remembered:

My father believed in discipline and structure for his children. We were mostly looked after by our nannies. My father didn't like having dinner with all of his children at once, so we'd take turns having dinner with our parents. I resented the discipline, the nannies, and the control, and I would sometimes introduce topics of conversation that I knew would upset him. I remember asking him at dinner once, "How many wives have you had?" and he answered, "None of your business" and looked at my mother and said, "He's provoking me."[5]

Chaplin wearing the white cotton gloves that covered the eczema on his hands, c. 1956. "He had a terrible problem of eczema," recalled Geraldine Chaplin. "People heard about it from the newspapers and they used to send him homemade potions, baths, and all sorts of cures. He went through several allergy tests and discovered he was allergic to film. Isn't that incredible? Charlie Chaplin allergic to film. He attributed it to all those years he spent editing nitrate film." Photograph by Oona Chaplin

Left: Chaplin with his brother Sydney on the veranda of the Manoir, c. 1956. Sydney, who starred in the successful comedies CHARLEY'S AUNT (1925) and THE BETTER 'OLE (1926), retired from films and returned to Europe in 1929. Although he again lived briefly in the United States during World War II, most of his remaining years were spent living in France. Photograph by Oona Chaplin

Middle left: Chaplin with his eldest daughter, Geraldine, on the veranda of the Manoir, c. 1956. Photograph by Oona Chaplin

Below: Chaplin with his son Michael, c. 1955. Photograph by Oona Chaplin

Left: Chaplin with his daughter Josephine on the veranda of the Manoir, c. 1956. Photograph by Oona Chaplin

Below: Chaplin with his daughter Victoria on the veranda of the Manoir, c. 1954. Photograph by Oona Chaplin

Bottom: Chaplin with his son Eugene (nicknamed "Tadpole") next to the swimming pool at the Manoir, c. 1957. Photograph by Oona Chaplin

In exile, Chaplin's work still took precedence over everyone and everything. Geraldine Chaplin recalled:

> We had to be quiet when Daddy was working, and he seemed to work all the time! There were exceptions, of course, but generally speaking we kept quiet, especially downstairs. He could be driven mad if his concentration was blown by a group of children galloping down the stairs. He made sure we were kept busy. Education was very important to him. He used to tell us, "Education is the only defense." He wanted us to have the education he never had and become professionals: doctors, lawyers, engineers, and architects. . . . I went to a convent school after we moved to Switzerland. I never heard of God or religion before. At first, I thought God was the owner of the school! I was taught religion, God, good and evil, and that if you didn't believe in God you'd go to Hell. I had nightmares my father and mother were going to Hell and I talked to him about it. It was one of the few conversations I had with him about school. I said, "You *must* believe in God. Otherwise, don't you know that when you die, you're going to go to Hell?" And he said, "I am so happy you believe. I would give anything to believe. It makes life so much easier, but I can't. I would love to believe, but I can't."[6]

Chaplin and Oona enjoyed occasional trips to London and Paris, and there were family vacations spent outside Switzerland (the Easter holiday was traditionally spent in Ireland). Chaplin continued to make headlines when he announced new film projects and rereleased his old films, or when the latest child was born. Family trips and even his birthday every April 16 were reported, and photographs circulated widely in the press across the world.

Theodore Huff's 1951 biography *Charlie Chaplin*—for many years the definitive work on Chaplin until David Robinson's *Chaplin: His Life and Art* superseded it in 1985—was the beginning of a proliferation of books published about him in the 1950s. None of these books was authorized. Chaplin's memoir, which he began to write in 1959 after finishing work on his compilation film *The Chaplin Revue*, was one of the most widely anticipated autobiographies of the period. For the two years in which he worked on the book uninterrupted, Chaplin followed a disciplined routine of waking at seven, taking a swim in his outdoor pool, joining Oona for breakfast, and retreating to his library, where he worked on the book until lunch. After the midday meal, he returned to work on the book until five. Chaplin would then play tennis, followed by a steam bath, an aperitif (gin and tonic), and dinner at a quarter to seven in the evening. After dinner he would work in the library until ten. His handwritten pages were then typed, revised, and retyped until he was satisfied, just as was done with his motion-picture scripts.

The Bodley Head, helmed by Max Reinhardt, published Chaplin's *My Autobiography* in September 1964. Chaplin received a $500,000 advance for the British and American rights alone. The first printing was 80,000 copies; within a month the

Top: Chaplin revisits 287 Kennington Road, South London, where he lived briefly with his father in the autumn of 1898, during a nostalgic journey to some of the important places of his youth prior to writing his autobiography, 1959. Photograph by Jerry Epstein

Above: Chaplin at work on the manuscript of MY AUTOBIOGRAPHY *in his library, c. 1960. Photograph by Oona Chaplin*

Opposite: Chaplin's favorite picture of himself in his later years, c. 1956. Photograph by Oona Chaplin

Above: Chaplin in the salon of the Manoir, c. 1960. Photograph by Oona Chaplin

Right: Chaplin with Professor George Ostrogorsky of Belgrade University walking in a procession from Trinity College to Oxford Town Hall, where both men were honored by Oxford University at its summer encaenia degree ceremony with the honorary degree of Doctor of Letters, June 27, 1962

Lower right: Chaplin with his eldest son, Charles Jr., and his granddaughter, Susan, at the Manoir, c. 1960. Susan Maree Chaplin, born May 11, 1959, was Chaplin's first grandchild. Photograph by Oona Chaplin

The Chaplin family poses with some of the different editions of Chaplin's MY AUTOBIOGRAPHY, which was translated into over twenty-five languages. In descending order of age (from right) are Josephine, Victoria, Eugene, Jane, Annette, and Christopher. By this time, the two eldest of Chaplin's children with Oona, Geraldine and Michael, had left home. Photograph by André Favez

book was in its third printing. *My Autobiography* was translated into more than twenty-five languages. Although the book was an immediate best-seller, the reviews were far from being unequivocally enthusiastic. The general consensus of the book, which ran more than five hundred pages, was favorable toward the first eleven chapters pertaining to Chaplin's childhood and stage work prior to his motion-picture career (subsequent research validates his extraordinary memory of these early events in his life). The remaining chapters suffer from Chaplin's unwillingness to discuss his films in great detail (*The Circus* and *A King in New York* are not even mentioned), some curious omissions (his reluctance to mention Lita Grey by name), his failure to acknowledge key collaborators (Rollie Totheroh, Henry Bergman, and Georgia Hale are among those named in passing or not at all), occasional pomposity, and an excessive amount of name-dropping anecdotes. The redundancy of the "my" in the title was also widely noted. Despite its unevenness and flaws, *My Autobiography* remains a carefully crafted and highly readable memoir. The tremendous worldwide attention the book received reinvigorated Chaplin.

A King in New York

As the reality of his expulsion from the United States began to sink in, Chaplin's initial conciliatory posture toward his adopted home of nearly forty years became increasingly more critical. Embittered and under attack, he undertook the formidable task of extricating all of his financial assets from the United States, a feat hampered by his inability to return to American soil to settle his affairs himself. Chaplin's treatment by the government, the cowardice of Hollywood in failing to rush to his defense, and the divisive anti-communist witch hunts of the House and Senate Un-American Activities Committees angered him. *A King in New York*, Chaplin's first film made outside America and his last starring vehicle, was a personal response to his exile: the deposed king of comedy played an overthrown monarch thrust into modern America. The film is unique in cinema as the only contemporary direct attack on the rampant political hysteria of McCarthyism, which persisted for five years after Chaplin had left the United States. Once again, Chaplin found humor in what may have at first appeared a humorless subject and would use his considerable powers of comedy and pathos as a weapon of pointed satire against his enemies.

King Shahdov bungles his way through a bombastic rendition of the famous "To be or not to be" soliloquy from HAMLET *at Mrs. Cromwell's party, unaware that he is part of a live television broadcast, in* A KING IN NEW YORK *(1957). Photograph by Eric Gray*

King Shahdov offers assistance
to Ann Kay (Dawn Addams),
who has feigned an injured ankle
in order to get his attention in
A KING IN NEW YORK. "Chaplin is
like a musical conductor when he
directs," recalled Addams in a
1957 interview with FILMS AND
FILMING, "This is also true literally because he has composed the
musical score himself and has it
in his head as he is directing.
Sometimes he will suddenly
become a saxophone or a violin

to give one the mood of the scene
as the spectator will watch it.
Charlie understands music so
well that he harmonizes a scene
according to a musical criterion.
He watches for the key theme and
then leads it up to a crescendo.
Timing film comedy is so different
from what one is used to on the
stage—and I learned for the first
time the importance of putting in
a bit-of-nonsense after a big laugh
so that dialogue is not lost."
Photograph by Eric Gray

In Switzerland Chaplin had met several deposed monarchs, among them the queen of Spain, and became intrigued with the fascinating and sometimes harrowing stories of how they fled revolutions in their home countries. Visualizing comedy situations with himself as an exiled king, he began working on a script in late 1953. In May 1954 Chaplin announced his forthcoming film, tentatively titled *The Ex-King*. Although it would deal with complex, serious subjects, the film was originally envisioned to be a musical, and several short passages of the songs Chaplin wrote for *A King in New York* remain in the final film.

In the autumn of 1955 Chaplin began preproduction on *A King in New York* with Jerry Epstein assisting him. He established a new production company, Attica Film Company, and decided that, as he had done with his previous films, he would once again finance the film entirely himself. This would ensure his complete artistic control of the project. One significant difference was that he would have to give up the autonomy of his own studio and instead rent studio space and hire an unfamiliar crew who were unaccustomed to his methods.

From the start, Chaplin was determined to keep the budget of the film to a minimum. Because of his low popularity in the United States, he prudently discounted the American market. He was also forced to withhold the release of the film in the United States pending resolution of an Internal Revenue Service claim against him for back taxes (the amount of which Chaplin disputed). All United States profits from the film could be seized by the IRS to pay the debt. Moreover, Chaplin understood that the American release would doubtless prove a box-office failure. Unfortunately, this had the effect of denying the film to the very audience Chaplin wanted its message to reach.

In the film Chaplin portrays King Shahdov, dethroned monarch of the mythical nation of Estrovia, who travels to America for political asylum but instead finds that the country has become an insane asylum. His desires to use his personal fortune to develop peaceful uses for atomic energy and engender a social utopia are dashed when he discovers his prime minister, Dr. Voudel (Jerry Desmonde), has absconded to South America with the funds of the Estrovian treasury and all of His Majesty's per-

King Shahdov, unable to make himself heard above the din of a nearby band, pantomimes to the waiter his order for caviar, as Jaume (Oliver Johnston) looks on. Photograph by Eric Gray

Above: King Shahdov attends a formal dinner party given by Mrs. Cromwell (Joan Ingram) that is being televised live without his knowledge. He is perplexed by the conversational non sequiturs of Ann Kay (Dawn Addams), which are, in fact, commercials to her unseen audience. Photograph by Eric Gray

Opposite top: King Shahdov, appearing in a live commercial for Royal Crown Whiskey, chokes on the product he has unwisely failed to sample prior to promoting it. Photograph by Eric Gray

Opposite bottom: Chaplin demonstrates to Shani Wallis the choreography for her nightclub song during production of A KING IN NEW YORK. Photograph by Eric Gray

sonal securities. Broke in New York City, Shahdov soon finds himself exploited and later persuaded by television advertising specialist Ann Kay (Dawn Addams) to submit himself to appearing in television commercials for profit. Through the eyes of the bewildered Shahdov, Chaplin takes aim at fads of modern American life: rock-and-roll music, wide-screen movies, progressive schools, plastic surgery, and in particular the crass commercialism embodied in television. The king's name also is evocative of Chaplin's sour disposition toward the United States: "Shahdov" sounds very much like the English expletive "sod off."

Shahdov befriends the obstreperous Rupert Macabee (Michael Chaplin), a ten-year-old boy whom he meets on a tour of a progressive school. Rupert's schoolteacher parents, victims of a House Un-American Activities Committee (HUAC) persecution, admit to having once been communists but refuse to inform on their friends. They are cited for contempt and jailed, and later Rupert is taken into custody. Shahdov's contact with Rupert causes him to be summoned to appear before the HUAC, but the hearing is a literal washout when the king arrives with his finger stuck in the nozzle of a fire hose, inadvertently dousing the entire committee with water. Cleared of all charges, Shahdov again meets Rupert, who is spiritually broken after having furnished the names of his parents' friends in order to suspend their prison sentences. Shahdov, disenchanted by the political bigotry and paranoia in the United States, decides to return to Europe. Before he leaves, he optimistically assures the boy that these difficult times will pass.

For the role of Ann Kay, the advertising specialist, comedienne Kay Kendall was first considered but the part eventually went to Dawn Addams. Chaplin had met Addams in Hollywood when she was making *The Moon is Blue* (1953), just prior to his leaving the country. He and Oona had attended Addams's wedding to Prince Don Vittorio Masimo in Italy, and when Chaplin saw her opposite Vittorio De Sica in *Il Letto* (1954), he concluded she had the qualities he wanted for the part of Ann Kay. The relationship between Shahdov and Ann Kay is far from romantic. Rather, the two characters submit to each other to achieve their own desires: she to further her advertising career in television and he for a sexual conquest. Ann Kay in some respects embodies America for Chaplin. Shahdov at one point tells Kay, "You are nothing but a delusion and a snare." He is attracted to her while at the same time has feelings of anger and contempt for her.

The film has several memorable scenes. There is heavy irony in the scene in which Shahdov explains to a reporter how moved he is by the warm friendship and hospitality of the land of liberty while being fingerprinted by immigration officials (harkening back to the humiliation Chaplin himself endured in the course of the Joan Barry scandal). Other notable sequences find the king

attempting to order caviar and turtle soup in pantomime when he is unable to make himself heard above the din of a nearby band; encountering the obnoxious brats at the progressive school (Chaplin's eldest daughter, Geraldine, had attended such an academy in Los Angeles); and trying to recover after a disastrous face-lift that leaves him with an upper lip so abbreviated that he can not say his "*ps*" or his "*ms*" let alone drink through a straw.

Chaplin also expresses his disdain toward the surveillance tactics of the FBI, the INS, and other American government agencies that had relentlessly pursued him throughout his life. Early in the film, Shahdov peers at a bathing Ann Kay through a keyhole in the door between their adjacent hotel rooms. Later, Kay turns the tables on the king as she attempts to coax conversation from him at a dinner party aimed at promoting various products. All the while a hidden camera captures their exchanges for a live television audience while the king remains unaware that he is being watched. Chaplin intended these sequences to relay his suspicion that the American government had become too aggressively voyeuristic in its pursuit of information about those residing within its borders.

It is unfortunate that Chaplin wastes time on several insignificant targets in the film and demonstrates hesitancy toward the big one. The film becomes fully focused only when he meets Rupert, the unfortunate lad who is at the center of a communist probe, played by Michael Chaplin, the eldest son of Chaplin and Oona.

Originally, Chaplin had intended to find a child actor to portray Rupert, and Michael Chaplin was going to take the small role of a boy who enjoys picking his nose while baking Viennese pastries at the progressive school. However, at Oona's urging, and impressed by his son's playful imitation of his performance of Hynkel in *The Great Dictator*, Chaplin decided that Michael could convey the emotion required to carry the role of Rupert. Many critics do not agree with Chaplin's assessment of his son's

acting ability. In several scenes, Michael can be seen mouthing his father's lines to him in anticipation of his own.

The character of Rupert is Chaplin's alter ego just as Jackie Coogan had been in *The Kid*. Rupert is the source of the film's pathos rather than the farcical Shahdov. From Rupert's mouth comes the dialogue that best expresses Chaplin's political ideology. Rupert rails against the greed of capitalism, the tyranny of atomic weapons, and the threat of "too much power" held by the United States to the safety of the world. This philosophy is evident in the following exchange between Shahdov and Rupert:

> Shahdov: Well, if you're not a communist, what are you?
> Rupert: Nothing. I dislike all forms of government.
> Shahdov: But somebody must rule.
> Rupert: And I don't like the word *rule*.
> Shahdov: Well, if we don't like the word *rule,* let's call it leader-
> ship.
> Rupert: Leadership in government is political power, and politi-
> cal power is an official form of antagonizing the people.
> Shahdov: But my dear young man, politics are necessary.

Above: King Shahdov poses for an advertising campaign under the direction of Ann Kay (Dawn Addams). Addams continued to work on stage, film, and television sporadically until the early 1980s. She died in 1985. Photograph by Eric Gray

Opposite: Chaplin behind the still camera used by Dawn Addams's character Ann Kay in A KING IN NEW YORK. *Photograph by Eric Gray*

Rupert: Politics are rules imposed upon the people.

Shahdov: In this country rules are not imposed, they are the wish of all free citizens.

Rupert: Travel around a bit, then you'll see how free they are!

Shahdov: Yes, but you didn't let me finish—

Rupert: They have every man in a straitjacket, and without a passport, he can't move a toe. . . . In a free world they violate the natural rights of every citizen. They have become the weapons of political despots! And if you don't think as they think you are deprived of your passport. To leave a country is like breaking out of jail. And to enter a country is like going through the eye of a needle. . . . It's incongruous that in this atomic age of speed we are shut in and shut out by passports. . . . And free speech, does that exist? And free enterprise? Today, it's all monopoly . . . monopoly is the menace of free enterprise. . . . And the atomic bomb! It's a crime that when the world cries for atomic energy, you [indicates Shahdov] want to make atomic bombs.

Michael Chaplin remembered his work on the film fondly:

I had a wonderful time working with my father on *A King in New York*. I was in a boarding school—which I hated—and I was taken out of it to work in the film. It was the only time, really, that I had a relationship with my father—with him coaching me and acting with him. I was able to become part of his creative world. . . . I recall the advice he gave me on acting was, "What you have to try to achieve is to be as natural as possible." It was a wonderful time.[1]

Michael—like his screen character—became rebellious as a teenager and left home. He briefly experimented with drugs, studied for a short time at the Royal Academy of Dramatic Art, married, and fathered Chaplin and Oona's first grandchild. He caused his parents much embarrassment when he claimed national assistance in 1965 and authored *I Couldn't Smoke the Grass on My Father's Lawn* in 1966, written in conjunction with

two journalists, Charles Hamblett and Tom Merritt, who gave the book an objectionable period vocabulary. Michael regretted lending his name to the book before it was released and unsuccessfully attempted to halt its publication. Chaplin and Michael eventually reconciled their differences in 1974. Michael recalled:

He was a loving father. I always felt loved by him. He was sometimes intolerant, unreasonable, difficult, and angry. Angry especially. I think anger for him began with the humiliations of his childhood. . . . Some of the films—*Modern Times*, *The Great Dictator*, *Monsieur Verdoux*, and *A King in New York*—were born out of an anger he had toward something or someone. I think he used anger to stimulate his creativity. As a young man, I rebelled. I was only able to come to terms with my father—and appreciate him and understand his personality—much later.[2]

Chaplin's main target in the film is his old nemesis: the United States government in general, and the HUAC in particular. Instead of attacking the committee with satirical comedic devices, Chaplin resorts to the comforts of slapstick, as Shahdov inadvertently sprays the panel with water from an unruly fire hose to show, in the vernacular of the period, that the committee is "all wet." It is perhaps unfortunate that Chaplin chooses so blunt a weapon to lampoon the committee when there existed such great opportunities for potent satire.

actor he had directed for half a century, he told Brando how and where to stand, when to turn, how many beats before speaking a line, and every gesture. One day on the set Brando approached Chaplin with a question regarding his character's motive for a scene. Chaplin replied that he did not understand the character's motive either, and even if he did it would not matter. Instead, he told Brando exactly how to play the line, saying it would come off fine if he performed it exactly as Chaplin had instructed him. "He never came to me again," Chaplin recalled.[7] This mismatch of approaches to acting and filmmaking also is ultimately a fatal flaw in the film. Prevented by Chaplin from exploring his role in the way he normally would, Brando often appears completely bored and disengaged. The result is a clunky, uninspired performance that is one of the worst of Brando's career.

If Brando disagreed with and perhaps even resented Chaplin's dictatorial directing style, others in the cast marveled at the elderly filmmaker's energy and agility and delighted in watching him act out the various roles in the film. Since *A Countess from Hong Kong* was financed by Universal, Chaplin agreed to its

Opposite: Chaplin hovers over his actors Marlon Brando and Sophia Loren in an attempt to force some passion into their love scene during a rehearsal.

Above: Chaplin conducts a script conference on the set of A COUNTESS FROM HONG KONG *with Marlon Brando, Sophia Loren, Jerry Epstein, and Sydney Chaplin (back to camera), 1966. Photograph by Hatami*

Right: Chaplin dances with his eldest daughter, Geraldine, during a rehearsal for her brief appearance in A COUNTESS FROM HONG KONG, *March 18, 1966. "I was terrified and he got very nervous directing me," remembered Geraldine Chaplin. "We hadn't a very good relationship. We sort of patched it up after*

seven years of really not speaking to each other—I was a rebellious teenager. We had just made up after I made DR. ZHIVAGO [1965], *and we were infatuated with each other. But, suddenly, when he was directing me, we were both tense again. My father had originally written the part of the society girl for me. She's shimmying and shaking and her bosoms shake on the dance floor with Marlon Brando. It was a funny part. When the time came, he couldn't let me do it. He felt too embarrassed. He was very Victorian and very prudish. He felt embarrassed that his daughter would be shimmying and shaking her boobs. So, the part went to Angela Scoular and I was given this little cameo with one line. I ask Marlon Brando as we dance, 'Do you believe in the immortality of the soul?'"*

request that he allow reporters and other visitors to the set to help promote the film. This arrangement has had the added benefit of providing film historians with a more textured and documented account of Chaplin's directing techniques.[8]

"I wish Charlie would have allowed someone to do a documentary on the making of the film, but he didn't want to be bothered," Tippi Hedren remembered. "That would have been the more interesting film! His way of directing was unlike anything I have ever seen. He acted out every part himself—Marlon's part, then Sophia's part, then Sydney's part—and then he would expect you to imitate it *exactly* the way he did it. And to mimic him was impossible because every movement he made was such perfection and so uniquely him. . . . Sophia and I submitted to Charlie's direction completely and enjoyed the experience. Sydney had worked with his father before and was used to his ways. Marlon hated every single minute of it."[9]

Unlike Brando, Loren revered Chaplin and was responsive to his direction, working hard each day to play her part exactly as Chaplin commanded. "He was a marvelous director," remembered Loren. "I cherish the experience of having worked for him."[10] Loren found working with Brando difficult, especially since the tempestuous star did not conceal his disdain for Chaplin's constraining direction. However, she was encouraged by Chaplin's energy and enthusiasm. "Charlie was always very positive and wouldn't let the problems with Marlon Brando upset him. Charlie was not a man to be intimidated by anyone, and no one but he dictated the mood on the set. Oona was a big help to him and his inspiration. She was on the set every day. Whenever he finished a take, he would look to her for approval."[11]

Chaplin's relationship with Brando, already strained by a clash of personalities and working methods, became untenable after

Above: Chaplin demonstrates to Marlon Brando how he should act his part in a scene with Sophia Loren. Producer Jerry Epstein is just visible holding the script on the left. Photograph by Roddy McDowall

Right: Chaplin and Margaret Rutherford prepare for the filming of her scene. In the film, Rutherford plays the dotty, bedridden passenger Mrs. Gaulswallow, who memorably fusses over smelling salts, a bouquet of flowers, a stuffed panda bear, various assorted ribbons, a box of chocolates, and a thermometer. Rutherford recalled in her autobiography Chaplin's "infinite eye for detail" and that

he "was one of the most helpful people I have worked with. My part was small but I shall always remember it as one of the most enjoyable films that I have ever made. And all because of the genius of Chaplin."

Opposite top: Chaplin amuses Tippi Hedren and his son Sydney.

Opposite bottom: Chaplin on the set of A COUNTESS FROM HONG KONG

Brando observed Chaplin's impatience toward his son Sydney in the role of Harvey Crothers. "Charlie was patient with everyone except Sydney," recalled Epstein. "He directed him just as he had at the Circle and in *Limelight*. But Marlon would watch Charlie direct Sydney and become angry with Charlie. He thought this was some sort of terrible humiliation Charlie was inflicting against his son."[12] Sydney Chaplin reflected, "He and Marlon didn't get along at all. Marlon evidently had a big thing against his father so I think my father must have replaced his father. Especially after he saw how hard my father was with me on the film."[13]

By the end of production, direct communication between Chaplin and Brando was almost nonexistent. Brando's participation had become perfunctory. One behind-the-scenes photograph depicts Brando's dialogue written on a large blackboard erected off-camera, suggesting the star did not always arrive on the set prepared. "Marlon became so angry that he refused to take direction from Charlie," remembered Jerry Epstein. "Whatever Charlie wanted to tell Marlon had to be relayed to him through me."[14]

Brando respectfully chose not to discuss his rift with Chaplin and his true feelings about *A Countess from Hong Kong* until after Chaplin had died. He even remained silent when his own performance (which, of course, he did not regard as his own, but Chaplin's) was assailed by film critics. Later, Brando described Chaplin in his autobiography as "probably the most sadistic man I'd ever met. He was an egotistical tyrant and a penny-pincher." However, he concluded, "I still look up to him as perhaps the greatest genius that the medium has ever produced. I don't think anyone has ever had the talent he did; he made everyone else look Lilliputian. But as a human being he was a mixed bag, just like all of us."[15]

A Countess from Hong Kong proved a family affair for the Chaplins. In addition to Sydney, daughter Geraldine appeared briefly as a young woman who dances with Mears (Brando) in the ship's ballroom; and two of Chaplin's other daughters, Josephine and Victoria, appear briefly as girls clad in tennis clothes entering the lobby of a hotel. Josephine remembered, "My mother believed that we ought to come to the studio and watch our father work. My sister and I watched for three weeks. It wasn't planned, but he arranged for us to appear briefly in the film."[16] Their moment in the film, for which he allows the narrative to stop, must have given Chaplin a particular sense of paternalistic pride. Like his own cameo, their participation has little or no plot justification.

As in *A Woman of Paris*, Chaplin played only a walk-on role, as an old ship's steward suffering from seasickness, a malady that he had injected into his comedy early in his career (*Shanghaied*, *The Immigrant*, *A Day's Pleasure*). Perhaps Chaplin was letting the audience know his real reaction to the film by his exit line: "Oh, just a little sloppy. Nothing serious." He reappears again briefly a few moments later, fending off a comic bout of nausea, playing his final scene in motion pictures in silence. Of course, Chaplin always was much more eloquent in silence, and it is fitting that his last appearance in film was the kind of comic pantomime he perfected, and for which he will always be remembered.

Despite the inevitable friction with Brando, Chaplin enjoyed his work on *A Countess from Hong Kong*. The great pioneer film-maker relished the fact that he was still actively engaged in the art of making movies fifty-two years after starting at Keystone.

Chaplin directed his last scene on May 11, 1966, completing production on schedule and under budget (perhaps owing to the fact that he was liable to pay any budget overages). On October

ble," remembered Sydney Chaplin. "He said it was another dimension that gives a 'candy box' effect to films, whereas black-and-white is much purer and more emotional."[17]

Universal's publicity campaign had generated much excitement and anticipation for the film. However, high expectations made for deep disappointment. A press screening on the day of the world premiere in London was marred by projection problems. "They're ruining my film!" Chaplin reportedly wailed during the screening, as the film at various stages broke and the image became distorted.[18] To the critics, perfect projection would not have salvaged *A Countess from Hong Kong* because the film was ruined already. Chaplin put on a brave front for the premiere, held on the evening of January 5, 1967, as the reviews in the evening editions of the newspapers gave the film the worst notices of his career.

Although *A Countess from Hong Kong* unquestionably suffered from internal flaws, the film also was ill suited to the period in which it was

11, while he was still editing the film, Chaplin was walking with Epstein outside Pinewood Studios when he tripped and fractured his ankle. The fall was a considerable psychological shock to Chaplin, who had never broken a limb. The injury permanently impaired his agility. His family maintained that he also had the first of several mild strokes at this time, which led to his decline in health.

For seven weeks, as he edited, dubbed, and scored the film, Chaplin's leg was in a cast and he walked on crutches. Still, he never missed a day of postproduction at the studio. Assisting Chaplin with the music was Eric James, with whom he had previously collaborated for the music of his compilation film, *The Chaplin Revue*. William (Bill) Lambert Williamson orchestrated the musical themes and conducted at the recording sessions.

Chaplin had very definite ideas for the color grading of his first color motion picture. In the way a painter might adjust a palette to reflect certain moods, Chaplin enhanced the colors for some scenes while intentionally muting the colors in others. He wanted not only what he felt was beautiful and appropriate but also sought to achieve a lightness to his backgrounds, which Chaplin believed was conducive for comedy. However, predictably, Chaplin disliked filming in color. "He always felt color was horri-

released. The film might have been successful had it been made in the 1930s, with Cary Grant and Paulette Goddard in the leading roles, but it seemed out of step with the 1960s, a pivotal decade in which seemingly every moral and historical notion was challenged. The established studio system in America, and the conventional Hollywood films this system generated, had mostly vanished. *A Countess from Hong Kong* was unapologetically of an earlier period. As David Robinson remarked, "In the year *of Bonnie and Clyde, The Dirty Dozen, The Graduate, Weekend,* and *Belle de Jour,* a gentle romantic comedy was an almost incomprehensible anachronism."[19] The critics found fault not only with the material, but also with the execution of the material. Alexander Walker wrote in the *Evening Standard* that the film was "a sad and bitter disappointment." He continued that Chaplin "has always been at his most brilliant when he doesn't depend on words. Here they let him down in scene after scene. His own genius at mime—which we are told he employed liberally in directing his stars—simply hasn't rubbed off on Marlon Brando or Sophia Loren, neither of whom looks at ease or acts with finesse."[20] John Russell Taylor in the *Times* suggested that Chaplin "might be at best a director of very modest competence who just happened to have a rare knack of showing off his own work as a performer to maximum advantage—in contrast to Buster Keaton, for instance, whose film *The General* is one of the most beautifully made films ever," a comment that would reverberate in much film criticism of the late 1960s and 1970s, in which Chaplin was adversely compared to Keaton. Taylor believed *A Countess from Hong Kong* "is likely to be a saddening experience for all lovers of Chaplin's earlier work."[21]

Chaplin was devastated by the unanimously bad reviews of *A Countess from Hong Kong* and defiantly lashed back. "If they don't like it, they're bloody idiots," Chaplin told the press. "A millionaire falling in love with a beautiful prostitute—what better story can they have than that?"[22]

Under Chaplin's direction, the film was cut by approximately six minutes after the London premiere for the Paris premiere, where the film fared much better with critics. Nevertheless, further cuts (approximately another six minutes) were made for the New York City premiere, held at the Sutton Theater on March 15, 1967. Chaplin, however, indicated his preference for the film as shown at the London premiere without the additional editing.

The New York reviewers were even harsher than the London critics had been. Bosley Crowther, the most prominent and vocal critic of the film, wrote in the *New York Times*, "It is so bad that I wondered, at one point, whether Mr. Chaplin, who wrote and directed it, might not be trying to put us on."[23] Crowther followed his vitriolic review with another attack on Chaplin less than ten days later. Jerry Epstein firmly believed that Crowther's venom was inevitable even before he saw the film. The critic apparently was angry that Chaplin was unable to accommodate him with an interview prior to the premiere and also was annoyed that Universal would not arrange an advance press screening.

Opposite: Chaplin, 1966, during production of A COUNTESS FROM HONG KONG

Above: Chaplin originally intended to conclude A COUNTESS FROM HONG KONG *with his character, an old steward, sweeping up the dance floor. However, he cut it out during editing.*

Left: A legendary pioneer of television greets a legendary pioneer of cinema during production of A COUNTESS FROM HONG KONG. *Milton Berle claimed that he had appeared with Chaplin in the part of the newsboy in* TILLIE'S PUNCTURED ROMANCE, *contrary to the fact that the role was played by Gordon Griffith—a child actor in many Keystone comedies—and that there is no evidence that Berle was even on the West Coast in 1914 when the film was made. However, Berle's lifelong veneration of Chaplin is beyond dispute. "As a kid I won a Chaplin lookalike contest," remembered Berle. "That was my first exposure to show business. Chaplin was my idol as a comedian. He was the greatest comic genius who ever lived. No man made more people laugh than he did." Revealed in this photograph are portions of Marlon Brando's dialogue, written in chalk on a blackboard and placed out of camera range. Brando's resistance to Chaplin's method and manner went as far as his reluctance to memorize his lines.*

However, Crowther was not a lone voice. *Time* wrote, "*Countess* is bad enough to make a new generation of moviegoers wonder what the Chaplin cult was all about."[24] These reviews and others unfortunately set an anti-Chaplin critical tone in the United States, and particularly in Great Britain, that marked film criticism and scholarship regarding his work for nearly twenty years.

Even after the New York reviews, Chaplin maintained that *A Countess from Hong Kong* was the best thing he had ever done, particularly the scene where Hudson is both lecherous and coy as he shares the bedroom with Natascha on their "wedding" night. "And I've never done anything as *funny* as the valet Hudson. We took three weeks working out the fight scene in *City Lights*, and it was technically good—but it wasn't so funny as Hudson," Chaplin explained.[25]

After its United States theatrical run was completed, *A Countess from Hong Kong* was ranked sixty-second on the list of 1967 box-office grosses, with $1.1 million in domestic rentals (*The Dirty Dozen* came in first place with $18.2 million).[26] Perhaps Chaplin's only consolation among the many bitter disappointments was that his song from the film, "This Is My Song," was a tremendously popular success around the world.

A Countess from Hong Kong is less interesting than any of Chaplin's previous sound films because it contains neither political nor satirical elements. The film also is not autobiographical, thus it has no subtext or historical significance. The script, a light but by no means empty romantic comedy, is blocked and filmed like a stage play, giving the film a primitive appearance. Like all of Chaplin's films, the story depends primarily on character rather than plot, which in this instance gives the film a weak foundation. Much of the film, therefore, plays like a series of disconnected farcical moments, centering on Mears's unsuccessful efforts to rid himself of the unwanted countess, her clever ruses to stay aboard, and their mutual efforts to prevent her from being seen by those who buzz or knock at the door. For example, the sound of the

Above: Chaplin takes aim at his six-tiered birthday cake during the surprise party at Pinewood Studios to celebrate his seventy-seventh birthday, April 12, 1966. Oona, Melanie Griffith (just visible), and Sophia Loren are the audience to Chaplin's antics.

Right: Chaplin, with Oona at his side, sits with his leg elevated in a screening room at Pinewood Studios just six days after breaking his left ankle in a fall, October 17, 1966. "Once Charlie broke his ankle things became difficult, as you can imagine," Oona wrote Eric James, Chaplin's musical associate, less than two months after the event. "It was no fun being wheeled in and out of the

dubbing room, and it did not improve the nervous tension." However, Chaplin was determined not to let the injury impede his postproduction work on A COUNTESS FROM HONG KONG.

Opposite: Chaplin and members of his family at the premiere of A COUNTESS FROM HONG KONG *at the Carlton Cinema, Haymarket, London, January 5, 1967. From left to right behind him: unknown, Josephine Chaplin, Victoria Chaplin, producer Jerry Epstein, Sydney Chaplin, Noelle Adam (Sydney's then-wife), Patrice Chaplin (Michael's then-wife), Jane Chaplin, and Michael Chaplin*

stateroom's door buzzer initiates a frantic hide-and-seek (with one such moment actually accelerated by the camera in the manner of an early silent-film comedy). Yet, "Charlie was determined that every moment be played completely realistic, despite how ridiculous the situation," remembered Loren of what Chaplin believed was his fresh approach to his material.[27] Cinematographer Arthur Ibbetson adhered to Chaplin's limited camera direction, which Chaplin maintained was not old-fashioned but his own personal style. "Simplicity of approach is always best," Chaplin wrote in My Autobiography:

Personally, I loathe tricky effects, photographing through the fireplace from the viewpoint of a piece of coal, or travelling with an actor through a hotel lobby as though escorting him on a bicycle; to me they are facile and obvious. As long as an audience is familiar with the set, it does not want the tedium of a travelling smear across the screen to see an actor move from one place to another. Such pompous effects slow up action, are boring and unpleasant, and have been mistaken for that tiresome word "art."

My own camera set-up is based on facilitating choreography for the actor's movements. When a camera is placed on the floor or moves about the player's nostrils, it is the camera that is giving the performance and not the actor. The camera should not obtrude.

Time-saving in films is still the basic virtue. Both Eisenstein and Griffith knew it. Quick cutting and dissolving from one scene to another are the dynamics of film technique.

I am surprised that some critics say that my camera technique is old-fashioned, that I have not kept up with the times. What times? My technique is the outcome of thinking for myself, of my own logic and approach; it is not borrowed from what others are doing. If in art one must keep up with the times, then Rembrandt would be a back number compared to Van Gogh.[28]

Chaplin's static, theatrical approach to cinematography—eye-level angles, moving only when actors moved—his lack of concern for editing and narrative continuity, the obvious stock shots of Hong Kong and Hawaii, and rear-screen projection to simulate most exterior backgrounds hindered audience enjoyment of A Countess from Hong Kong.

Another key criticism of the film is Marlon Brando's flat performance as Ogden Mears. Chaplin maintained that the character was meant to be wooden.[29] True to the director's intent,

Brando, perhaps the greatest actor of his generation, is lifeless in the film. His performance is devoid of any comedic or romantic instinct, grace, or charm. Despite this and all the film's other flaws that led to its failure with critics and audiences, A Countess from Hong Kong is occasionally amusing (if not always for the right reasons), with moments of wistfulness and dreamy longing. Chaplin, clearly disenchanted with the present, at times appears to be reaching to create his own reality and ultimately his own conception of beauty. He told Francis Wyndham, "Between you and me and the gatepost, it's a very sad story. This man who leaves his icicle of a wife for a girl who's a whore. I think the end, where they're dancing, is tragic. Perhaps his love for her is just a passing thing, as happens to us all."[30]

Chaplin infuses some of his own comic personality and optimism into Sophia Loren's performance as the dance-hall prostitute, whose character perpetuates Chaplin's lifelong preoccupation with fallen women as heroines. In many ways, Natascha is the proxy for the Tramp in the film, searching for a better life, while always understanding that both happiness and beauty are fleeting. The Tramp's philosophy is expressed by Natascha's dialogue, "Don't be sad. That's too easy. Be like me. At this moment, I'm very happy. . . . That's all we can ask for—this moment." This statement can be applied to the film as well; while it is easy to lament its many failures, particularly because it is Chaplin's last film, it is perhaps best to cherish its wonderful, fleeting comic moments.

Chaplin and Music

Chaplin was not a classically trained musician, a composer, or a songwriter, yet he is credited with the composition of all of his film scores. In fact, several of his songs are still recorded and enjoyed in the twenty-first century. Although he did not compose in the traditional sense (he could neither read nor notate music), the music that accompanies his films is indelibly his own creation. These compositions—like the films themselves—were begot in an unconventional manner.

Chaplin's musical roots are found deep in his memory of a simple melody wafting through Kennington Cross in turn-of-the-century London. He later described the moment in life-altering terms:

> It was here that I first discovered music, or where I first learned its rare beauty, a beauty that has gladdened and haunted me from that moment. It all happened one night while I was there, about midnight. I recall the whole thing so distinctly.
>
> I was just a boy, and its beauty was like some sweet mystery. I did not understand. I only knew I loved it and I became reverent as the sounds carried themselves through my brain *via* my heart.
>
> I suddenly became aware of a harmonica and a clarinet playing a weird, harmonious message. I learned later that it was "The Honeysuckle and the Bee." It was played with such

Chaplin with a cello, c. 1915. Photograph by Ensign Dryer

Above: Chaplin with a violin,
c. 1922. Photograph by Witzel

Opposite: Chaplin with Abe
Lyman and Gus Arnheim during
the recording of their song "Sing
a Song" and Chaplin's "With
You, Dear, in Bombay" for gramo-
phone release, May 25, 1925

feeling that I became conscious for the first time of what melody really was. My first awakening to music.[1]

Chaplin described this as the exact moment that "music first entered my soul."[2] More than a half century later, Chaplin evoked this memory in *Limelight* with a simple melody played by a clarinet and harmonium that lulls Calvero to sleep before the film's first dream sequence, the flea-circus routine.

Chaplin's musical education was not confined to the streets of London. Both of his parents were music-hall entertainers, and he grew up absorbing the popular songs of the day. Their forms and harmonies became his own.

Undoubtedly Chaplin's early connection with music was closely tied to his comedic gifts. His pantomimic performances are conceived in balletic rhythms, consonant with musical composition. Chaplin's early career in the British music halls with Fred Karno was literally underscored by music. In a 1952 BBC radio interview, Chaplin acknowledged this influence:

> They [Karno sketches] had splendid music. For instance, if they
> had squalor surroundings with a lot of comedy tramps working
> in it, then, you see, they would have very beautiful boudoir
> music, something of the eighteenth century, very lush and very
> *grandioso,* just purely as satirical and as a counterpoint; and I
> copied a great deal from Mr. Fred Karno in that direction.[3]

At the age of sixteen, Chaplin started teaching himself to play violin and cello and improvising on piano and organ. He also began taking intermittent lessons from the leader of the orchestra of the music hall in which he was performing or from a musician recommended to him. He played string instruments left-handed and had his violin and cello strung with the bass bar and sounding post reversed. Although he was enthusiastic, Chaplin's gifts as a musician were limited (he liked posing with his cello far more than playing it), and, realizing that he could never achieve excellence with either instrument, he gave them up as a serious pursuit. However, he played piano and organ adequately and spent hours improvising on these instruments.

In 1916 Chaplin's friend Ben Clark, an English comedian, persuaded Chaplin to go into partnership with him in the music-publishing business. Chaplin and Clark rented office space in downtown Los Angeles and, under the banner of the Charlie Chaplin Music Publishing Company, published two songs—"Oh! That Cello" and "There's Always One You Can't Forget"—and the composition "Peace Patrol." Chaplin later dismissed these published works as "very bad."[4]

In 1925 Chaplin published two more songs: "Sing a Song" and "With You, Dear, in Bombay." "Sing a Song" was composed in collaboration with Abe Lyman and Gus Arnheim, with lyrics by Chaplin. The music and lyrics to "With You, Dear, in Bombay" were written entirely by Chaplin. The two compositions—both fox trots—were recorded by Abe Lyman's California Orchestra.

Although Chaplin's silent films were speechless, they were never seen in silence. Silent films were always shown in cinemas with some form of musical accompaniment, at least a piano or an organ or a small ensemble of instruments. Larger theaters employed scores of musicians to accompany the films. From this standpoint, the term *silent film* is a complete misnomer.

In reality, silent-film performances in the large cinemas of the 1920s were extravagant affairs. The cinematographers of the silent era had the achievements of Victorian photography before them and allowed no deficiencies in equipment or film stock, contributing to the impeccable photographic standards of the films. Magnificently lush and varied musical underscoring complemented the action. No one respected the power of musical accompaniment to film more than Chaplin, whose instinct for and exposure to music served him well as he constructed his classic films.

Few silent filmmakers involved themselves with special music for their movies. Independent publishers typically offered music suggestions or "cue sheets"; for some important films, full scores were compiled from existing music, with one or two original themes. Full-length original scores were rare.

Beginning with *A Woman of Paris*, Chaplin worked closely with well-known arrangers to create musical accompaniments that were published and circulated with the initial releases of his films. For *A Woman of Paris*, Chaplin hired Frederick Stahlberg; for *The Gold Rush*, Carli Elinor; and for *The Circus*, Arthur Kay. The scores for these films were compiled largely from published

music in a variety of genres, such as opera, operetta, incidental music, dance band, and popular tunes of the day.

Chaplin was also an aficionado of classical music and both borrowed from and incorporated entire pieces into his film scores. Examples of this practice are Chaplin's reworking of Tchaikovsky's Symphony No. 6 in B minor, the *Pathétique*, for *The Kid*, and his use of Wagner and Brahms in *The Great Dictator* and the 1942 reissue version of *The Gold Rush*.

Chaplin's vintage scores for *A Woman of Paris, The Gold Rush*, and *The Circus* went unperformed for nearly seventy years, until musicologist Gillian Anderson was hired to inventory Chaplin's surviving musical material from the silent-film era in the Chaplin Archives. Anderson uncovered these premiere scores and later performed *The Gold Rush* and particularly *The Circus* to critical acclaim at screenings around the world.

Chaplin's suggested scores, however, were not always the accompaniment actually played to his films when they were shown in the 1920s. Frustrated that he could not control this situation, Chaplin, who resisted the movement to record dialogue, told a reporter in 1926 that he welcomed the recording of music to accompany a film, undoubtedly in an attempt to receive wider distribution of and control over his own scores. Chaplin said:

> Music is extremely important . . . that is why I welcome the efforts being made to provide music by mechanical systems, such as the DeForest and the Vitaphone. Mechanical music

which has the quality of a symphony orchestra is much better as an accompaniment than feeble vamping on a piano or the excruciating efforts of an incompetent or ill-led orchestra.[5]

When Chaplin prepared the reissue versions of *A Woman of Paris*, *The Gold Rush*, and *The Circus*, he dismissed the vintage scores he helped prepare in favor of original music that he composed in association with Max Terr (*The Gold Rush*) and Eric James (*The Circus* and *A Woman of Paris*).

Chaplin's composing style is revealed in his own commentary and interviews and in the writings and interviews of his musical arrangers. Although he relied upon associates to arrange varied and complex instrumentation, the musical imperative is his, and not a note in a Chaplin musical score was placed there without his assent. The experience of each of his arrangers elucidates this subtle distinction.

Chaplin decided to compose an almost entirely original score for *City Lights*, his first film with synchronized sound.[6] He engaged arranger Arthur Johnson to assist with the composition and arrangement, and described the collaboration in this way: "I really didn't write it [the music] down. I la-laed and Arthur Johnson wrote it down, and I wish you would give him credit, because he did a very good job. It is all simple music, you know, in keeping with my character."[7] Despite this rather modest assessment, Chaplin was explicit with Johnson about what he wanted in the *City Lights* score: "I tried to compose elegant and romantic music to frame my comedies. . . . I wanted no competition [between the music and the film], I wanted the music to be a counterpoint of grace and charm."[8]

For the musical accompaniment to *Modern Times*, arguably Chaplin's finest score, Chaplin enlisted the assistance of a twenty-three-year-old musical prodigy named David Raksin, who documented the collaboration. Their working relationship mirrors the complex give-and-take that defined Chaplin's composing style with other arrangers:

> Charlie was generally armed with a couple of musical phrases . . . we would first review the music leading to the sequence at hand and then go on to the new ideas. First, I would write them down; then we would run the footage over and over, discussing the scenes and the music. Sometimes we would use his tune, or we would alter it, or one of us might invent another melody. I should say that I always began by wanting to defer to him; not only was it his picture, but I was working from the common attitude that since I was ostensibly the arranger the musical ideas were his prerogative.[9]
>
> . . . Charlie and I worked hand in hand. Sometimes the initial phrases were several phrases long, and sometimes they consisted of only a few notes, which Charlie would whistle, or hum, or pick out on the piano. . . . I remained in the projection room where Charlie and I worked together to extend and develop the musical ideas to fit what was on the screen. . . . We spent hours, days, months in that projection room, running scenes and bits of action over and over, and we had a marvelous time shaping the music until it was exactly the way we wanted it.[10]

In 1968 Chaplin began writing *The Freak*, a dramatic film about a beautiful girl named Sarapha, the daughter of two retired missionaries who was raised in seclusion among Fuegian Indians. She sprouts wings soon after she is born and has the ability to fly. She is perceived as a freak—half bird and half woman. Orphaned at the age of twelve, she leaves the Fuegian Indians who have adopted her and treat her like a god to live in a cave high up in the mountains "because I'm afraid of everyone and everyone is afraid of me."[2] At the extreme end of Chile, near the South Pole, Professor Latham, a handsome young historian, finds the eighteen-year-old Sarapha wounded on the roof of the house in which he is staying. They are immediately attracted to each other, and he nurses her back to health. She returns the favor when he becomes ill with a fever. Their time together is short-lived, as natives make a pilgrimage to Latham's house believing Sarapha is an angel and can perform faith healings. Two conmen from England abduct, drug, and bring Sarapha to London to exploit her in one of Reverend James Gidson's revival meetings, where her dramatic entrance as an "angel" from Heaven causes screams, hysteria, prayers, and immediate cures.

Sarapha flees from the conmen and the revival meeting and seeks refuge with Margaret, Professor Latham's ex-wife, who lives in London with her husband, Sir Rex Horton. Meanwhile the conmen and the British army, thinking she is an animal they must quarantine for fear she may contaminate people with rabies, search for "the freak." Sarapha kills the drunken Sir Rex in self-defense one evening when he attempts to rape her while his wife attends a costume party in the country. At her trial, Sarapha is exonerated of murder but is nevertheless quarantined for three weeks and kept in a cage. The once-spirited Sarapha is totally defeated by the humiliation of being caged and treated like an

Above: The Chaplin family, 1968. The children from left to right, back row: Josephine, Jane (sitting), Michael, Geraldine, Christopher (sitting in front of Geraldine), Eugene, Victoria, and Annette (sitting in front of Victoria). In front are Chaplin and Oona, who celebrated their twenty-fifth wedding anniversary that year. Photograph by André Favez

Right: Chaplin feeds the birds on Lake Geneva in Vevey, c. 1968. The genesis of the unrealized film THE FREAK *occurred as he watched birds fly across his lawn and became intrigued by the movement of their wings. He soon began to write a tragicomic fantasy about a girl who sprouts wings and can fly. Photograph by Oona Chaplin*

Opposite top: Victoria Chaplin, in a costume test for THE FREAK, *at Shepperton Studios, 1968*

Opposite bottom: Victoria Chaplin wears the wings created for her for THE FREAK *while Chaplin and Jerry Epstein watch in the background, 1974. "One weekend," remembered Victoria Chaplin, "My husband and I were visiting my parents and my father said, 'Let's get out the wings!' The wings were brought out of the basement and we rehearsed the film on the lawn and had a script reading in the library with Jerry Epstein and my sister Josephine. At one point, he left the room and instructed us to shout the lines of the script while attempting to say them as naturally as possible. It was difficult to do that! It was some sort of acting technique he was trying out with us. After a while, he came back in the library and we went on as before." Photograph by Oona Chaplin*

animal. Moreover, she realizes she will always be an outsider and her fleeting happiness with Professor Latham in Chile will never be repeated. On the evening of her release she flies into the pale moonlight and dives into the Atlantic Ocean. Her lifeless form is found floating the next morning. In the conclusion of the script, Latham comments that her life was impossible and that her problems are now over.

Chaplin's script for *The Freak* borrows many themes, ideas, and even phrases from his three previous films but is nevertheless an original story filled with marvelous Chaplin comedy touches, many of which involve Sarapha in her various escapes. He wrote a small role for himself as a London drunk who thinks his eyes are playing tricks on him when he sees Sarapha flying above him. *The Freak,* which Chaplin never filmed, had strong potential for being a very moving—and fitting—swan song.

Chaplin's inspiration for the project came from his sitting on the veranda of his home, watching the crows that pecked at his lawn and observing the movements of their wings. Annoyed with the way the birds repeatedly tore up his lawn, one day Chaplin crept up on the crows like a bird of prey, extended his arms like wings, hissed, and imitated the flapping wings of a large bird. The crows were terrified and flew away.

Chaplin developed the story of *The Freak* in his mind prior to the production of *A Countess from Hong Kong.* The title role was written for his third daughter, Victoria, who Chaplin believed had inherited his comic gift. Indeed, Chaplin said of his daughter in 1969, "She has a much better comedy touch than I have and more charm."[3] The wings that Victoria was to wear in character were created, tests were made, still photographs were taken, storyboards were drawn, and the main musical theme was composed. Chaplin was unsuccessful in negotiating satisfactory financing for the film within the motion-picture industry. Undeterred, he resolved that he would finance the film himself. According to Victoria Chaplin:

> I was dying to do *The Freak,* but I could feel this holding back about the film. I remember my mother telling me at Christmas in 1969, privately in the pantry of the house, "Well, actually, I

don't want him to do it. If he goes through the ordeal, it will kill him." My mother felt that the special effects of the flying scenes, my father's impatience for technical matters on the set, and how easily he tired at that point—he aged enormously after *A Countess from Hong Kong*—would be too much for him. There were also concerns about the financing and whether my father could be insured. I remember my mother said, "I can have him alive or have him die making the film," and I know she believed that.[4]

Earlier in 1969 eighteen-year-old Victoria met and fell in love with French actor Jean-Baptiste Thierrée, who was determined to make a career as a clown by creating his own circus. The day after she was told by her mother that the film was not going to be made, she ran away from the Manoir without telling her father, to live with Thierrée in Paris. Chaplin's fury over the situation was severe and his hurt and disappointment acute; not only was Victoria his special favorite of all his children, but it was also a setback in his plans for *The Freak*. Victoria remembered:

> He was furious with me, and everyone thought my leaving home was the reason why he did not make the film, which was not true. He considered replacing me in the part with a friend of my sister Jane, named Melanie Roe. For over a year he did not mention my name. . . . Growing up, my father and I were very shy toward each other—except when he was mad or when he was enthusiastic about something. I felt close to him—we were a lot alike—and he be could be so sweet. But I never dared talk to him unless he initiated the conversation, so we did not talk much to each other. The few things he said were wonderful. . . . When he became mad at me for leaving home, it took some time for that anger and hurt to leave him. He was terrifying when he got mad. The whole house became *electric* with his anger. Everyone felt it—my mother, my brothers and sisters, Gino [Terni], and the other household staff—so I kept away for some time, but I corresponded with my mother. Yet I have fantastic memories of my father, wonderful family trips. He once told me, "You'll appreciate what I gave you one day," and he was right. In fact, he was always right.[5]

Victoria and Thierrée married in 1971 and created their own traveling minimalist circus, in which Victoria became a performer. Through Rachel Ford's and Oona's efforts, Chaplin grew

Right: Chaplin reenacts the eating of the boiled shoe from THE GOLD RUSH *at the Land of Liberty pub, Denham, England, October 27, 1971, while on a lunch break from a music-recording session for* THE KID *and* THE IDLE CLASS *at nearby Anvil Studios.*

Far right: Chaplin dons a derby hat and improvises a mustache with his index finger as he arrives with Oona for the Film Society of Lincoln Center gala in his honor at Philharmonic Hall, New York City, April 3, 1972.

Bottom: Chaplin with Groucho Marx at an outdoor Sunday lunch party given in Chaplin's honor at the Pacific Palisades home of Carol and Walter Matthau, April 9, 1972. Chaplin's advice to Marx was, "Keep warm, Groucho, you're next." Photograph by Candice Bergen

Opposite: Chaplin receives his honorary Academy Award, at the forty-fourth annual Academy Awards presentation at the Dorothy Chandler Pavilion in Los Angeles, April 10, 1972.

to accept the marriage and Victoria's choice of profession, if not wholly approving of the situation. Meanwhile, Oona and Jerry Epstein, who was to produce *The Freak,* came to a quiet understanding to table the project because Chaplin's physical condition was not commensurate with his creative desire. However, this understanding was not shared with Chaplin, who continued writing and revising the script well into 1974, still hoping to make the film someday.

In his last years, Chaplin began composing new musical scores to his unscored silent films, beginning with *The Circus* in 1968 and followed by *The Kid* and *The Idle Class* in 1971. Unhappy with United Artists' 1970 distribution of *The Circus* with his new musical score, he sought to lease the distribution rights to the films he still controlled, whereby he would receive an advance and a percentage of all revenue, while assigning to others the responsibility of maximizing the value of the films. In 1971 Chaplin entered a distribution deal with Mo Rothman, a former Columbia Pictures worldwide sales manager, whose association with Chaplin began in 1952 when he was continental Europe sales head for United Artists and handled *Limelight.* Rothman and his silent partner Martin Helstern formed the punningly named Red, Inc. (the name was soon changed to Black, Inc., as it became a very profitable organization) to distribute the Chaplin films. The company had worldwide theatrical, television, and home-video rights for an initial fifteen-year period (after which the rights reverted to Chaplin's heirs) for an advance of $4 million against fifty percent of the gross profits, which were to go to Chaplin's Roy Export Company Establishment. Rothman's associate in this venture was Bert Schneider, an independent Columbia producer of films such as *Easy Rider* (1969) and *Five Easy Pieces* (1970). Mo Rothman recalled:

> The essential element that Chaplin loved and adored was money. Once when we were negotiating the agreement, which took a year or so to complete, Chaplin danced for me. He pirouetted around his living room saying, "They're very good pictures, Mo. They're very good pictures." Chaplin was partial to me because we had worked together on *Limelight.* He knew me. I didn't have the money for his advance; I was broke at the time, but he was patient with me. Rachel Ford, his business manager, also liked me. My relationship with Ford was based on toilet paper. During the period of *Limelight,* I had these PX cards [for wartime and postwar rations] and whenever I saw her I gave her a few rolls of toilet paper. So she had a soft spot for me, as it were. Chaplin's reasons for choosing me were strictly emotional. . . . I delivered the goods and made a fortune for both of us with the pictures. He and Oona were delighted. Chaplin called me "Mighty Mo" and "Super Mo." The publicity was phenomenal and the personal appearances added years to his life.[6]

As part of the agreement with Rothman, Chaplin was to take part in promoting the rerelease of the films by making undemanding personal appearances at key venues and celebrations around the world that were arranged to honor him. In 1971, the

twenty-fifth Cannes Film Festival gave Chaplin a special award for his body of work, and at the same time he was invested as Commander of the French Legion of Honor. In September 1972 the Venice Film Festival honored him with a special Golden Lion award. Rothman and Schneider believed the timing was right for an American Chaplin tribute. Rothman remembered, "Chaplin needed to be rehabilitated in America, and we got all sorts of offers. I negotiated the Lincoln Center tribute in New York with Martin Segal and Bert Schneider arranged Chaplin's Academy Award."[7]

Chaplin received invitations to be feted by the Film Society of Lincoln Center in New York City and the Academy of Motion Picture Arts and Sciences with an honorary Academy Award. He was hesitant about returning to the United States, fearful of lingering hostility from certain quarters of the American public. Chaplin and Oona arrived in New York City on April 2, 1972, and the following evening attended the gala tribute at Philharmonic Hall. The 1,500 people in attendance gave him a thundering reception as he entered the hall and cheered *The Kid* and *The Idle Class,* which were first screened publicly with Chaplin's new scores at this event. He was in tears. "This is my renaissance," he said. "I'm being born again. It's easy for you, but it's very difficult for me to speak tonight, because I feel very emotional. However, I'm glad to be among so many friends. Thank you."[8]

Chaplin and Oona traveled from New York to Los Angeles for the forty-forth annual Academy Awards presentation at the Dorothy Chandler Pavilion on April 10, 1972. The presentation of Chaplin's honorary Oscar remains unique in Academy tributes. His was the only honorary award given that year, and it was presented at the end of the evening, after all the competitive awards had been given. Following more than ten minutes of film clips, Chaplin appeared on stage to an emotional standing ovation no one before or since commanded at the Academy Awards. Academy president Daniel Taradash presented the Oscar statuette, the citation on which read: "To Charles Chaplin for his incalculable effect in making motion pictures the art form of this century." Chaplin was again tearful, and all he was able to man-

Above: Chaplin is reunited with Jackie Coogan at the Governor's Ball that immediately followed the Academy Awards, April 10, 1972. Photograph by Sheedy and Long

Below: The Chaplin family, 1972. Back row from left to right: Josephine holding her son Charlie, Jane, Nick Sistovaris (Josephine's then-husband), Eugene, Sydney with his son Stephan in front of him, Noelle Adam (Sydney's then-wife), Victoria holding her daughter Aurelia, Jean-Baptiste Thierrée (Victoria's husband). In front: Annette, Chaplin, Oona, and Christopher. Geraldine and Michael are absent. Photograph by André Favez

Opposite top: Chaplin tips his hat in a pose reminiscent of the Tramp while on holiday in Nairn, Scotland, c. 1973. Photograph by Oona Chaplin

Opposite middle: Chaplin and Oona launch the publication of MY LIFE IN PICTURES, *with a book-signing event and a screening of* THE CIRCUS *along with the newly scored version of* SUNNYSIDE, *at the cinema located inside the Mayfair Hotel, London, October 23, 1974. The volume was realized through the assistance of Oona and writer Francis Wyndham.*

Opposite bottom: Sir Charles and Lady Chaplin pose in their suite at the Savoy Hotel after his investiture at Buckingham Place, March 4, 1975.

age on the occasion was this simple speech: "Thank you so much. This is an emotional moment for me. Words seem so futile, so feeble. I can only say that, thank you for the honor of inviting me here and, oh, you're wonderful, sweet people. Thank you."[9] He then attempted a bit of business with a derby hat handed to him by Jack Lemmon, making it pop up from his head as he had in his silent films. Alistair Cooke observed, "The tears drenched the audiences three thousand miles apart. He was very old and trembly and groping through the thickening fog of memory for a few simple sentences . . . he was now—as the song says—'easy to love,' absolutely safe to adore."[10] Shortly thereafter, Chaplin and Oona, having seen again several old friends and associates (including Jackie Coogan, Georgia Hale, and Martha Raye) and experiencing an emotional drive past the old Chaplin Studios, returned to Switzerland, and Chaplin closed the hitherto unresolved American chapter of his life.

Upon his return to Switzerland, Chaplin accepted a proposal from Max Reinhardt of The Bodley Head to produce an illustrated supplement to *My Autobiography*. *My Life in Pictures*, published in October 1974, was realized in collaboration with Francis Wyndham, who drew on his previous interviews and meetings with Chaplin as well as *My Autobiography* to create the main text. A talented journalist, Wyndham also wrote an excellent appreciation of Chaplin that served as the book's introduction. He later recalled his experience working on the book:

> Charlie was "on the spot," [yet] he would wander and sort of couldn't remember. We brought up batches of photographs from the basement for him to go through and we tried to get him to make comments. There were a great many photos of Paulette Goddard, and he'd point and say, "Who's that girl? I never saw her." And Oona and I got the giggles. It was nice she could laugh. . . . Charlie could talk, but he did repeat himself. He was very sweet and he wanted to please one by remembering, but then he would sort of forget.[11]

Chaplin's speech was growing progressively slower, with long pauses between sentences, and somewhat elliptical in content, filled with non sequiturs. Although his memory of his career had faded, his childhood and early poverty were more vivid than ever. During Chaplin's frequent visits to London, he always stayed in a suite on the fifth floor of the Savoy Hotel with its view of the River Thames. The view as it looked in the present day meant little to Chaplin; its value was in the memories it evoked of South London on the opposite side of the river.[12] During these visits he frequently traveled alone by bus to his childhood haunts. On one such occasion he returned to the Savoy having broken his glasses during the excursion; thereafter his trips to South London were conducted by a hired car.

Despite all the tributes that honored him, Chaplin became more upset over time when he was not recognized. "He became very worried as he grew older that he wouldn't be remembered," recalled Geraldine Chaplin. "You couldn't convince him otherwise."[13] In this respect he was pacified when the company he organized solely to license his image, Bubbles, Inc., entered into agreements with companies such as Brown & Williamson to license the Tramp image for a brand of cigarettes. According to Pamela Paumier:

> When the cigarettes went on trial, we all received a carton of the two different types of cigarettes each week and Charlie loved them. Although Charlie had given up smoking long ago, he had a packet on the table beside him and offered one to all his visitors. He was so proud of all the samples received from our licensees, proof that he was not forgotten.[14]

As if to assure him that his legacy would be properly recorded for posterity, as well as to promote the film package and continue the Chaplin celebration at special events, Chaplin's distributor commissioned a biographical documentary titled *The Gentleman Tramp,* written and directed by Richard Patterson, a young filmmaker who had worked as the editor on the Chaplin clip montage prepared by director Peter Bogdanovich for the Academy Awards tribute. Although Oona Chaplin was initially concerned at how the film clips used in the documentary were chosen to punctuate and relate to Chaplin's life, Chaplin and Oona viewed a rough cut and final edit of the film and gave it their approval.[15] Privately, Chaplin described *The Gentleman Tramp* as "like reading one's own obituary."[16] One of the documentary's most memorable images is the footage of Chaplin and Oona at the Manoir walking arm in arm away from the camera, filmed in the autumn of 1973. Patterson recalled:

Oona thought it best we did not broach the question of filming Charlie until the very last minute. I honestly don't remember how the idea evolved of having him and Oona walk out across the lawn. That was when Oona told him about the camera. If you look at it closely he is obviously into it and trying to swing his cane and walk out into the horizon. He understood what we were trying to do—like him and Paulette Goddard at the end of *Modern Times*—and that's an amazing piece of film. Everything conspired to make it transcendent: the autumn landscape he was walking in, the light, the way Nestor [Alemendros] shot it, the way he pauses and regroups and tries to carry on. That's about as positive an image of death as you are going to get. Some think of it as an image of life—the spunk, he's still carrying on. It's both.[17]

A sympathetic and intelligent tribute to Chaplin, *The Gentleman Tramp* was warmly received upon its release in 1975.

In January 1975 Queen Elizabeth II included Chaplin on her New Year honor list for a knighthood as a KBE (Knight Commander of the Most Excellent Order of the British Empire). Declassified British Foreign Office documents reveal that Chaplin was initially suggested for the honor as early as 1956 but was denied at that time because of the British government's sensitivity to concerns of American political anger toward bestowing the honor, as well as the controversial issues of Chaplin's alleged communist sympathies and his sexual interest in teenage women earlier in his life. The Foreign Office still opposed a knighthood as late as 1969. A

Top: Sir Charles is greeted by Queen Elizabeth II at the official opening of the International Centre, London, the headquarters of the British Academy of Film and Television Arts, where Sir Charles was awarded the Academy Fellowship, March 10, 1976. In the background are Princess Anne (holding the trophy she presented to Chaplin), Sir Richard Attenborough, and Lady Chaplin.

Middle: Chaplin attending the Knie Circus in Vevey, October 1976. The annual ritual of attending the Knie Circus was cherished by the entire Chaplin family, and the excellence and charm of it partly inspired many of the Chaplin children's theatrical ambitions. Photograph by Lawrence Migdale

Bottom: Lady Chaplin pushes Sir Charles in his wheelchair, accompanied by their French poodle, Nicky, on a stroll alongside Lake Geneva in Vevey, October 1977. She told reporter John South, as she wheeled her husband the day this photograph was taken, "I wouldn't have changed a thing. All of the trauma and difficulties and heartbreak with Charlie—it was worth every minute of it. I am as much in love with him now as the day I married him. Charlie's life is my life absolutely. I never leave him alone for a moment. I don't resent that or want to go out and live my own life. He's been the one man in my life. And it's worked." Photograph by Ralph Crane

Opposite: The last formal portrait of Sir Charles Chaplin, taken at home on his birthday, April 16, 1977. The portrait was used on the family Christmas card that year. Photograph by André Favez

more forgiving attitude prevailed in the 1970s. Moreover, according to Jerry Epstein, Prime Minister Harold Wilson was determined that Chaplin should be knighted and sought to rectify the situation in his second term.[18]

His investiture ceremony on March 4, 1975, brought Chaplin and most of his family to London for the occasion, which was treated by both Buckingham Palace and the British press as an occasion to celebrate Chaplin. He had wanted to walk the short distance to the queen for the actual bestowing of the honor, but his legs had by this time become unreliable, and a fall in his bathtub in mid-1972, in which he suffered a hairline fracture to a vertebra, left him timid about walking. Chaplin was therefore wheeled by a palace steward. Afterward, he said he intended to be known as Sir Charles and not Sir Charlie and that the queen had told him "that she had seen many of my films and that they had helped her a great deal." As for Chaplin, he confessed he was "dumbfounded" by the experience and was unable to talk to the queen.[19]

After this grand occasion, despite his failing health, Chaplin returned to London with Oona on a few more occasions over the following year, the most notable of which were to attend the recording and later the dubbing of the musical score to *A Woman of Paris* in the spring of 1976—his last creative work—and to be awarded the British Academy of Film and Television Arts' Academy Fellowship on March 10, 1976, with the queen in attendance. During this period, Oona recalled that she was awakened at four in the morning and heard Chaplin talking aloud in his bedroom about his films: ". . . and they are *beautiful,*" Chaplin said, "and I'll never make them again."[20]

Chaplin suffered a debilitating stroke in 1976, after which he was unable to sustain much enthusiasm for creative work. A television set, long forbidden in the Chaplin home when his children were young, now occupied a focal point in his library. He enjoyed watching news programs—especially those with attractive female announcers—and, even though he did not speak French, appeared to understand them. The stroke also made it difficult for Chaplin to speak. Christopher Chaplin remembered:

> My father became uncommunicative in his last year or so; I was only fifteen when he died. My most vivid memory of him in that last year was that I used to sit across from him at the dinner table and sometimes he would just stare right at me. He had the most piercing blue eyes. I often wondered what he was thinking. My mother sometimes was able to draw him out. She would start singing one of the old music-hall songs and he would sing along in his very frail voice.[21]

Occasionally he and the family watched one of his old films with their 16mm projector on a screen that was erected in the salon. Mostly, Chaplin enjoyed sitting out on the veranda of his home, or in some peaceful spot on the vast property, with Oona at his side. (Oona purchased an electric cart so that Chaplin could still be driven around the grounds.) On October 15, 1977, Chaplin

made his last trip from his home to attend a performance of the Knie Circus in Vevey with Oona, daughter Victoria, her husband Jean-Baptiste, and their two children. Six weeks later, Chaplin, now eighty-eight, required constant care and oxygen, as he had difficulty breathing.

By Christmas Eve, Chaplin was deteriorating quickly. With the exception of Geraldine (who was working on a film in Spain), his entire family had gathered at the Manoir for the holiday. Chaplin, who always hated Christmas for its reminders of the deprivations he suffered as a child, died in his sleep at four A.M. Christmas Day with his family around him. His funeral was held on December 27, 1977, at the Vevey Cemetery. Shortly thereafter, on March 1, 1978, his coffin was stolen from the grave by two mechanics demanding a ransom (their intent was to use this macabre scheme to raise the money needed to establish their own garage). The body was soon recovered in a cornfield just outside nearby Noville, and the clumsy thieves were caught, tried, and sentenced. Chaplin's coffin was reburied under six feet of concrete to ensure no further grave robbing.

The genius of Sir Charles Spencer Chaplin endures in the moving images he created. What Shakespeare is to Elizabethan theater, Dickens to the Victorian novel, and Picasso to modern art, Chaplin is to twentieth-century cinema. He remains arguably the single greatest motion-picture artist who ever lived. His films remain available throughout the world, their discovery a new joy to each succeeding generation.

Chaplin Interviewed by Richard Meryman, 1966

In 1966, Chaplin granted several extensive interviews to journalist Richard Meryman for a *Life* magazine article to promote *A Countess from Hong Kong*. Only a small portion of Meryman's taped interviews was ever published. A copy of the complete transcript, from which this excerpt was taken, is preserved in the Chaplin Archives.

RM: This interview is entirely concerned with your work and your art, and nothing else. I want to give some indication of how you work.

CC: The summation of my character is that I care about my work. I care about everything I do. If I could do something else better, I would do it, but I can't.

RM: Can you talk about the moment you created the Tramp outfit?

CC: It all came about in an emergency. The cameraman said put on some funny makeup, and I hadn't the slightest idea what to do. I went to the dress department and on the way I thought, well, I'll have them make everything in contradiction—baggy trousers, tight coat, large head, small hat—raggedy but at the same time a gentleman. I had a sad, serious face. I wanted to hide that and make it comic, so I found a little mustache. And that mustache was no concept of the characterization—only saying that it was rather silly. It doesn't hide my expression.

RM: When you looked at yourself, what was your first reaction?

CC: It'll do. It didn't ignite anything. Not until I absolutely had to play it in the presence of the camera. Making an entrance, I felt dressed; I had an attitude. I felt good, and the character came to me. The scene [from *Mabel's Strange Predicament*] was in a hotel lobby, and the Tramp was trying to pretend to be one of the guests just so he can get anchored on a soft seat and rest for a while. Everybody looked at him a little suspiciously, and I did all the things that the guests were doing in the hotel, looked at the register, took out a cigarette, lit it, watched the passing parade. And then I stumbled over the cuspidor. That was the first gag I ever did. And the character was born. And I thought, this is a very good character. But not every character I played followed the same format for all the comedy ideas after that. One thing I intended to remain—not so much the dress of the Tramp, but the sore feet. No matter how rambunctious or exuberant he felt, he always had these very tired big feet. I inquired of wardrobe that I wanted two large pairs of old shoes, because I had absurdly small feet, so I wanted these big shoes, and I knew they would give me a comic gait. I'm naturally very graceful, but trying to be graceful in big feet—that's funny.

RM: Much of what the Tramp did was the outrageousness of a child. Did the Tramp appeal to the child in you and the yearning for childlike freedom?

Charlie holds the boutonniere he purchased from the blind flower girl and contemplates romance in CITY LIGHTS.

CC: No, I don't think it comes out of any sense of freedom, and I don't think there's any yearning in a comedian to do childish things. But from the viewpoint of the public, civilization so restricts them, and they have no chance to really kick up, unless a man gets very drunk or something. I think their restricted life becomes a habit, and when they see a clown they enjoy it immensely. It's a release and a great deal of freedom. I don't think it's a yearning. I think we get beyond that.

RM: Do you think the Tramp would work in modern times?

CC: I don't think there's any place for that sort of person now. The world has become a little bit more ordered. I don't think it's happier now, by any means. I've noticed the kids with their short clothes and their long hair, and I think some of them want to be tramps. But there's not the same humility now. They don't know what humility is, so it has become something of an antique. It belongs to another era. That's why I couldn't do anything like that now. And of course, sound—that's another reason. When talk came in I couldn't have my character at all. I wouldn't know what kind of voice he would have. So he had to go.

RM: What do you think was the great appeal of the Tramp?

CC: There is that gentle, quiet poverty. Every soda jerk wants to dress up, wants to be a swell. That's what I enjoy about the character—being very fastidious and very delicate about everything. But I never really thought of the Tramp in terms of appeal. The Tramp was something within myself I had to express. I was motivated by the reaction of the audience, but I never related to an audience. The audience happens when it's finished, and not during the making. I've always related to a sort of a comic spirit, something within me, that said I must express this. This is funny.

RM: How does a gag sequence come to you? Does it come out of nothing, or is there a process?

CC: No, there is no process. The best ideas grow out of the situation. If you get a good comedy situation it goes on and on and has many radiations. Like the skating rink sequence [in *The Rink*]. I found a pair of skates and I went on, with everybody in the audience certain that I was going to fall, and instead I came on and just skated around on one foot gracefully. The audience didn't expect it from the Tramp. Or the lamppost gag [in *Easy Street*]. It came out of a situation where I am a policeman, and am trying to subdue a bully. I hit him on the head with a truncheon, and hit him and hit him. It is like a bad dream. He keeps rolling his sleeves up with no reaction to being hit at all. Then he lifts me up and puts me down. Then I thought, well, he has enormous strength, so he can pull the lamppost down, and while he was doing that I would jump on his back, push his head in the light, and gas him. I did some funny things that were all made off the cuff that got a tremendous laugh. But there was a lot of agony, too. Miserable days of nothing working, and getting more despondent. It was up to me to think of something to make them laugh. And you cannot be funny without a funny situation. You can do something clownish, perhaps stumble, but you must have a funny situation.

RM: Do you see people doing these things, or do they all come out of your imagination?

CC: No, we created a world of our own. Mine was the studio in California. The happiest moments were when I was on the set and I had an idea or just a suggestion of a story, and I felt good, and then things would happen. It was the only surcease that I had. The evening is rather a lonesome place, you know, in California, especially in Hollywood. But it was marvelous, creating a comic world. It was another world, different from the everyday. And it used to be fun. You sit there and you rehearse for half a day, shoot it, and that was it.

Charlie struts triumphantly as the bully-beating police officer in EASY STREET.

RM: So much of your comedy is physical. Was anyone ever hurt while filming?

CC: We've never had an accident in our films. I was the only one that got hurt—in *Easy Street* I had to have three stitches in my nose.

RM: Well, what about the falling?

CC: It was all worked out like a ballet.

RM: You have used the word dance to describe your work.

CC: Everything I do is a dance. I think in terms of a dance. In *City Lights*, with the blind girl, there is a beautiful dance. I call it a dance. Purely pantomime. The girl extends her hand with a flower. And the Tramp doesn't know she's blind. And he says, 'I'll take this one.' 'Which one?' He looks incredulous—what a stupid girl. Then the flower falls to the ground, and she goes to feel for where it is. I pick it up and hold it there for a moment. And then she says, 'Have you found it, sir?' And then he looks, and realizes. He holds it in front of her eyes—just makes a gesture. Not much. That is completely dancing.

RM: Now, you dictate your writing a great deal, don't you?

CC: Yes, I dictate the so-called mechanics of the thing very offhandedly and then go over it carefully, or if I have a scene that's poetic and has emotional content I have to do that alone. And write in pencil.

RM: Do you act it out for yourself?

CC: Oh, yes. I can't sit still much, especially if I get excited, and I act it out. If it's something too personal that I have to do in long hand, it's not very much, maybe a couple hundred words at most.

RM: So you act, and then you go back to the desk and write, and then get up and try it some way, and write again. Do you act for the secretaries sometimes when you're dictating?

CC: It all depends upon the nature of the secretary. Sometimes they are a good audience, sometimes they are a serious worker. It doesn't always come off on paper. Anything very personal, poetic, which I think is emotional, I write myself and then I dictate it, because I'm the only one who can decipher what I've written. I dictate in the very cold language, and that's done.

RM: As far as the technical aspects of your films, do you worry much about lighting or camera placement?

CC: Well, yes. I like the lighting more or less up—I don't like shadows. I don't think it's the most important element in a film. I think if you concentrate on that, you may be neglecting something else. As to the camera, if I have a rule at all, it is the fact that I like to establish orientation—to know where you are. I like to keep the camera way back, then come into a closeup or whatever you want to finish up. You can eliminate time, with discretion, but now they go overboard. I don't mind when they cut away—it's refreshing to me. But I do like to see something smooth. I use the closeup, not in any sense of mechanics, but sort of as an emphasis, as punctuation, like putting in a comma or parentheses. Technique is so much a part of expression through the camera. But I really concentrate more on the performances of the actors.

RM: Do you think cutting is extremely important?

CC: Oh, yes, but simple cutting. Trick cutting doesn't interest me because I'm so much interested in the human equation, and not in photographing a stone or a drop of blood falling on it. I suppose there is merit in the accumulation of what the effect will be, but I don't make pictures that way. I like acting. I'm very fond of acting and human emotion. I like the face, and to concentrate on beauty. Other people might think it's slow. That's my whole approach to motion pictures—to bring out their personality and their acting ability. Cutting is just a juxtaposition of one set or one person to another, you see. I also sometimes sharpen up where I think it might be a little slow. You can do a lot by cutting.

RM: And in the old days when you were cutting the film you could even go back and reshoot.

CC: Yes, although I was always days behind, you see. I would see my action on the screen and I'd say God, I'm like a windmill, throwing my arms all round the place and I'd know what was wrong. Then I'd come the following day and have the thing right. The moment I came out of the room I knew what was wrong.

RM: When you see one of your one- or two-reelers today they're all sped up. Were they sped up in those days?

CC: No, because the projection was slower so that you saw them in natural action. Slightly speeded up because comedy was considered 14 frames per second, and drama was considered 16 frames, which was natural. And now we have 24 frames per second. So that today the comedy would be jerky.

RM: Is realism an integral part of comedy?

CC: Oh, yes, absolutely. I think in make-believe, you have an absurd situation, and you treat it with a complete reality. And the audience knows it, so they're in the spirit. It's so real to them and it's so absurd, it gives them exultation.

RM: Well, part of it is the cruelty—there was a lot of cruelty.

CC: Cruelty is a basic element in comedy. What appears to be sane is really insane, and if you can make that poignant enough they love it. The audience recognizes it as a farce on life, and they laugh at it in order not to die from it, in order not to weep. It's a question of that mysterious thing called candor coming in. An old man slips on a banana and falls slowly and stumbles and we don't laugh. But if it's done with a pompous well-to-do gentleman who has exaggerated pride, then we laugh. All embarrassing situations are funny, especially if they're treated with humor. With clowns you can expect anything outrageous to happen. But if a man goes into a restaurant, and he thinks he's very smart but he's got a big hole in his pants—if that is treated humorously, it's bound to be funny. Especially if it's done with dignity and pride.

RM: But in your films there's a different quality. The story is not necessarily a real story. It's too much coincidence, too much fantasy. It has a truth, yet a fairy-tale aspect in it.

CC: Well, of course I don't think there's anything wrong with coincidence, if you don't overdo it. I think there's a lot of coincidence in life. Those things never bother me, so long as there's a plausible excuse for it. A character is activated in my story. The fairy tale comes in, but I don't strive for that. I strive for comedy and believable comic situations. For instance, *The Circus* is a very funny comedy, and it has lots of invention and little reality. It's so full of adventure. It's a silly story, but, at the same time, you give it a certain treatment, and the audience believes it. It all depends on what the story is. The moment one starts on the basis of a pretty girl interested in the character like the Tramp, then you have to have some convincing situation to bring that about. Sometimes it's very difficult to give the illusion of reality.

RM: Isn't the fairy tale one of the ingredients of romance?

CC: Yes. I think romance is an approach to make life interesting and noble and beautiful. I don't say that in any fitting sense or any moral sense, I say that [without romance] life can be a very horrifying and frightening thing, but if you're going to live it, as people do, they do like it and think it's a wonderful mystery. I mean, romance is the only thing by which to live by. We get away from the so-called realism and enter into it, but, without romance, you may as well be in a prison. It feeds spirituality and your sense of exultation. Something that is romance, is marriage—you look at it from one sense, from the sense of truth and realism, and it can be an irksome, horrible, terrifying thing that is constricting and confining. But if you think of it in terms of romance, the relationship makes life really beautiful. I like romance in comedy. I think the people are more believable.

RM: There must be a lot of romance necessary for a person to be an actor.

CC: Oh yes, absolutely. It is romantic to be someone else, to be placed in such a condensed capsule of situations. The whole attitude toward the theater is romance. People don't go to the theater to seek truth. Truth has a means to an end. To create a believable romance I think you've achieved a great deal in the theater. I suppose when an actor stops feeling romance and starts looking at his profession with a cold eye he can't act anymore.

RM: Your comedy in part is a comedy of incident, too. It's not an intellectual thing, it's things that are happening, that are funny.

CC: I've always thought that incidents related will make a story, like the setting up of a pool game on a billiard table. Each ball is an incident in itself. One touches the other, you see. And the whole makes a triangle. I carry that image a great deal in my work.

RM: You like to keep a terrific pace going and you pack incidents one on top of the other quite a bit. Do you think this is characteristic of you?

CC: Well, I don't know whether it's characteristic of me. I've watched other comedians who seem to relax their pace. I can feel my way much better with pace than I can with being slow. I haven't the confidence to move slow, and I haven't the confidence in what I'm doing. But action is not always the thing. Everything must have growth, otherwise it loses its reality. You have a problem, and then you intensify it. You don't deliberately start with intensifying it. But you say, well, now, where do we go from here? You say, what is the natural outcome of this? Realistically and convincingly, the problem keeps getting more and more complicated. And it must be logical, otherwise you will have some sort of comedy, but you won't have an exciting comedy.

RM: Do you worry about sentimentality or cliché?

CC: No, not in pantomime. You don't worry about it, you just avoid it. And I'm not afraid of a cliché—all life is a cliché. We don't awaken with any sort of originality. We all live and die with three meals a day, fall in and out of love. I think when you have a situation that is justified it's not a cliché. Nothing could be more of a cliché than a love story, and that must go on, so long as it is treated interestingly.

RM: You think the theater is the great training ground for films, don't you?

CC: Oh yes. My experience in the theater has helped me a great deal in films. Even with the settings. That's always been at the back of my mind. I look upon the aperture as a small proscenium. That's why I've never moved my camera much, because I'm influenced by the scene of the theater. And why I haven't liked the closeup too much. I realize that one must come closer for a certain emphasis, which is very important and very valuable. I like the choreography of movement of the theater. I think the entrances, coming on and off, helps one's time. And if you're cognizant of all those things that the theater does present I think it helps in a motion picture.

RM: You've said that you are a better director than an actor. Why do you think that?

CC: Oh, because I think I am. I think every actor has a certain sense of insecurity, whether he can play the part or not. In pretending to be somebody else you're exposing yourself. Acting is reaching out and finding the reality of a scene. Sometimes you get it and sometimes you don't. As a director, sometimes you'll reach out for it and you'll get it. It's like a comedy line in a play. One time it just rings a bell, and they'll laugh, and the next night it doesn't come—it's just lost. For some reason, either in timing, intonation—there are so many aspects. It's difficult to do it. My directing is an emotional process. I don't give a big powwow about the psychology of it. If a person can act, you give them something that's actable, and they can do it.

RM: And you deal in terms of a gesture and the inflection in the voice, or a move here . . . it's external.

CC: No, there's nothing external. I believe everything we touch is the inside, you never do external. But anything that you tell [actors] to do is just as much a part of the spiritual as it is the so-called external, the mechanics. It will bring them into the mood—that's all mechanics are for, to put them in the feeling of it and put them on the track, as it were. Like when we learn lines. It will help to create a mood, and they render a very finished performance. In other words, what differentiates the professional actor, the good actor, from the amateur is the fact that he knows what he is doing—the mechanics every minute. And does it with authority. If you're an authority the audience will listen to you; if you're not, they won't. But the one thing about directing is to know how to act it—to know how to be able to tell, to demonstrate to the actor how to do it and at the same time to feel that you don't interfere with his personality. That's essential. By doing that, it makes the actor comfortable. Directing for an actor is easy. And actors make good directors.

RM: Is there any kind of common fault with actors that you feel over and over again?

CC: I think it's a fault that's partly also a virtue. They're egocentric, of course, and they have to be. Such egocentricity might get in the way of a very good performance, but if it's controlled, I think it's all right. I like actors. Some are very, very humble and realistic and others, of course, are perfectly absurd. And yet, in some way, it doesn't interfere with their giving a magnificent performance.

RM: What is the greatest single quality an actor can have?

CC: I think the love of what they are doing—with restraint. And you have to be in the right key, like striking a sounding fork, or the key can be out of tune with an audience. I think an actor in his first minute or so is tuning himself with his audience and his environment. One of the strange mysteries of a performance, one night it'll come out excellent, and that contact is there, and another time it isn't. No great actor is infallible. And sometimes he gives a great performance and other times he doesn't.

RM: Can you have this experience in film?

CC: It does happen in motion pictures very often. Well, you say, that was good, and I felt it and I know it was right. And then you see it on the screen, and for some reason there's an element lacking. I've had that happen to me. I've come to the conclusion it was the camera. You see only half of one's self that's photographed. There's a shutter that comes in between every frame that's black. And it may catch you between those vibrations. That's my own explanation. It's very fascinating, that you might just be out of sync with that spiritual thing, whatever it is.

RM: Does the opposite happen—something that you thought was fair and it turns out to be marvelous?

CC: I had it once or twice in a broader sense. I had one close-up in *City Lights*, the last scene, and one could have gone overboard. The girl sees through her fingers and realizes, "My God, this is the man." And it was nothing like what she had imagined in her mind. And he just looks curious. I was looking more at her and interested in her, and I detached myself in a way that gives a beautiful sensation. I'm not acting. Sort of standing outside of myself and looking, studying her reactions and being rather slightly embarrassed about it. And it came off. I took several takes before that, but they were all overdone and overfelt. But this one, for some reason, was objective and apologetic. It's a beautiful scene, beautiful; and because it isn't overfelt.

RM: I understand that as the years went on the responsibility multiplied for you—keeping your eye on your own spiral, not being numbed by success and sitting down on the job somehow.

CC: Well, my feeling was, will this thing last? Will I be creative? But it was never with the idea of topping myself. We were simply people out there making a living, and each day was unknown. We didn't know what we were going to do, and so it kept everybody on their toes pretty much. You could never get satisfied—those that did fell by the wayside.

RM: Well, once you were enormously successful, didn't you have to say no to a lot of things that other people said yes to? You never really made personal appearance tours. Do you think it's a danger for someone to start doing that?

CC: Yes. I wouldn't want to commit myself to be exploited, and I knew that it would be very unsatisfactory. I knew that if I once did that it would affect my popularity. I realize I was very rude in many ways. People liked me, and it was too much, and I didn't have any secretaries or anybody to look after that or dictate anything. I couldn't do everything. I hadn't the energy. Douglas Fairbanks used to say, "Charlie has the most instinctive sense of protection." With me, I had to direct, act, write, cut, and produce a film. I did it all, and that's why I was always exhausted.

RM: You gave the idea of *A Woman of the Sea* to Josef von Sternberg, didn't you?

CC: Yes. After *A Woman of Paris*, Edna [Purviance] wanted to

make a picture on her own, and I said fine, as I was getting to where I wanted another character for my films. So von Sternberg used to hang around, and I said, well, I've got an idea. If you can make a picture with Edna it would help me out, and he said he would. I had a sketchy idea. I'd been up to Carmel, Monterey, and Seventeen Mile Drive—very beautiful coastline, rugged, with the waves coming up—and I started to think of all sorts of gags. Edna was getting a little robust and bosomy, and I thought she'd make a wonderful fisherman's wife—fighting against nature to get a big catch, starving, and all that. I can see her with the sheen on her face, pulling in the nets. She's out there and they're going to lose the catch, they almost lose their lives, but they save the catch. So Sternberg said, "Don't tell me any more, that's enough." In those days we didn't have a script, just the story. But he came back with the most puerile, infantile story of a man from the city with a mustache—the heavy—hanging around and peeking through fishermen's nets, looking at Edna. And Edna played this infantile woman just walking around. I said, that's not a fisherman's wife! I wanted to see a woman with a squint and the ocean in her eyes. We lost about $60,000 in cost.

RM: Do you still have the film?

CC: No, I burned it. I didn't want it around. I was completely at a loss about the whole thing, and it depressed me.

RM: How did you feel when you went out to the set each morning?

CC: It was a challenge, and one is resigned to that challenge. You want to get to it like you want to get to the winning post. Each morning, one has to pray for it, like a prizefighter. You must go to bed early, get some good sleep, get up in the morning, and go into the studio. I wouldn't work at night. I would turn off all the worry about what I'm going to do the following day. Sometimes we'd end the day by saying, well, tomorrow we'll set up here and shoot this, and we'll do that. But other times I'd be so tired that I wouldn't know what to do. I knew very well that the following day that I'd be refreshed and enthusiastic. An idea will generate enthusiasm, and then you're off! The enthusiasm only lasts for a little while, and then you wait for another day. It replenishes itself, and you start again. If something is right, and I think it is right, then it will generate enthusiasm. If I get an idea and someone tries to dampen my enthusiasm, then I'm lost. That's what it is. It's the fact that my enthusiasm is the thing that makes me mad and everything else. That's my secret, I think. I'm terrifically enthused, if I like something. I couldn't be an ordinary director. In the first place, I wouldn't have the enthusiasm for other people's ideas. That's where my ego comes in, but I can't help it.

RM: Did you do the eating of the shoe gag [in *The Gold Rush*] many times?

CC: We had about two days of retakes on it. And the poor old actor [Mack Swain] was sick for the last two. The shoes were made of licorice, and he'd eaten so much of it. He said, "I cannot eat any more of those damn shoes!" I got the idea for this gag from the Donner party. They resorted to cannibalism and to eating a moccasin. And I thought, stewed boots? There's something funny there. I had an agonizing time trying to motivate the story, until we got into a simple situation—hunger. The moment you've solved the logic of a situation, its feasibility, reality, and possibility of being able to happen, ideas fly at you. It is one of the best things in the picture.

RM: Did you have any doubts or concerns going into sound?

CC: Yes, oh naturally. In the first place, I had experience, but not academic training, and there's a great difference. But I felt I had talent, I felt I was a natural actor. I knew it was much easier for me to pantomime than it was to talk. I'm an artist, and I knew very well in talking a lot of that would disappear. I'd be no better than anybody else with good diction and a very good voice, which is more than half the battle.

RM: Was it a question of having an extra dimension of reality that might hurt the fantasy of silent film?

CC: Oh, yes. I've always said that the pantomime is far more poetic and it has a universal appeal that everyone would understand if it were well done. The spoken word reduces everybody to a certain glibness. The voice is a beautiful thing, most revealing, and I didn't want to be too revealing in my art because it may show a limitation. There are very few people with voices that can reach or give the illusion of great depth, whereas movement is as near to nature as a bird flying. The expression of the eyes—there's no words. The pure expression of the face that people can't hide—if it's one of disappointment it can be ever so subtle. I had to bear all this in mind when I started talking. I knew very well I lost a lot of eloquence. It can never be as good.

RM: Why did you choose to do *The Great Dictator,* which was really dealing with a very serious theme?

CC: I think it was very obvious. These poor wretched prisoners in the prison camps and the torture that was going on. That was the first knowledge we had of Hitler. And then his attacking of minority people or people that didn't agree with him. If he had won, then the world would have been Nazi for the next thousand years. Those things you can't bear to think of.

RM: Did you study Hitler a great deal for *The Great Dictator?*

CC: No, I don't study much of anything. I didn't have to read a column about Hitler. I did go to the Museum of Modern Art to see a film with him in it. I thought to myself, let me see this ridiculous madman. I thought he was a humorless, horrible man. Naturally a man in his position would be very fretful. I'm sure there were moments when he questioned his own genius, if that is what it was. I'm sure there's a paradox there, where he was so effete and fearful of everything. Everybody going to him and saying, what shall we do, and he, underneath, was just as fearful as the rest.

RM: That speech at the end has been criticized; I wonder whether you regretted it at all.

CC: Oh, no. Not a bit. I saw the picture recently, and the war dates it because it was on a serious note, and that's why I feel slightly embarrassed by the speech. It was a damned good speech and I liked it as far as I was concerned—I was really most sincere. People "think too much and feel too little." I thought this is where one could make a curtain speech. Say, Ladies and Gentlemen, there's a tragedy going on—that's all I wanted to do metaphorically.

RM: But you got pretty high marks for clairvoyance—when you made that film, Hitler was not totally recognized for what he was.

CC: It's true, I did have some foresight. And of course, Oona always kids me about it. I sensed it, it was in his face, this confident ego. This madman, in a way.

RM: Well, up until that point, had your great motivation been to instruct or amuse?

CC: To amuse. I never wanted to instruct. I've never had any message. People themselves will instruct.

RM: Was *Monsieur Verdoux* based on an actual man?

CC: Well, not exactly. I had the idea that Landru was a matter of two separate lives—a schizophrenic. He was one then the other. At home my character of Verdoux was very good, staid, a moral father with a beautiful wife, and he's just come from an abattoir where he's been putting women in his little stove! He would come home from a murder like a father having done a hard day's work.

RM: Did you explore the motivation for a murderer, the killing of somebody?

CC: Oh, no. That's purely inventive and imaginative and has nothing to do with murder. It was purely my conception of it. It just occurred to me that it would make a very funny comedy. I had a great desire when I started that picture. First of all, I was seeking my way and became lost a little bit in it. When I finished it there was no identification to the audience. And that was a mistake. Of course, some liked it, and now, as time goes on, I like it less. I was terrifically influenced by the public because they unconsciously were aggravated, and I have a profound respect for that. They don't know why, but it's our business to know why.

RM: How do you feel about *A King in New York* now?

CC: Well, as I said, the public influenced me a great deal. And I think, well, I wouldn't want to do anything like that now. Although genuinely I had what I thought was a comic notion. Frankly, I got a good opening. I didn't know where the hell the story was going, but the opening was very good. I think perhaps I went overboard a little bit, because I got into politics and so forth. And that was the time of McCarthy. But I see nothing anti-American in it.

RM: And this was never seen in America.

CC: No. It was shown in Europe, but the people didn't really understand it. There were certain things that were excellent. It's a very funny idea to do a comedy on honesty. As I say, I am influenced a great deal by the public. Not that they're completely right, but if something goes wrong, if they show the slightest indifference, that's me. And you've got to play to the public.

RM: Do you think critics influence the public in films?

CC: Well, I suppose they do to a certain amount, but it's very minor. It's not like the theater where they can just cut your throat.

Motion pictures are too popular, it's too much for the people. They go for entertainment, and they see something they like, of course, and it may be something that's very obvious. But you must take an audience seriously because their rebuffs are very gentle—they merely don't go. A critic gets furious, foams, and writes a column about how horrible a man is, but the public is not concerned that way—they merely don't go. I think that's terrifying—indifference.

RM: There were many wonderful lines in *Limelight* when you're trying to encourage Claire Bloom's character of Terry. That was a very personal film, wasn't it?

CC: In some sense yes, it was. It was generally what I felt and thought at that time. I made it believable and rational. If you rationalize a situation so that you can make the audience believe that people are happy, which I think on the whole they are—I think people are happy in a way, in spite of all these damn atomic bombs.

RM: This film is so different from what I'd been seeing, and I think partly it was the simplicity of the whole thing.

CC: Oh, yes. The camera is seeing the performance, and nothing can compete with the human equation, in my estimation. Nothing is more interesting.

RM: A line from *Limelight* I wrote down is "that's the trouble with the world, we all despise ourselves."

CC: Yes, I sincerely believe that. I try to be sincere about my feelings on the matter. I think men of great power are trying to get away from the fact that they really do despise themselves. They think they can exalt themselves without the average man. I think that's the psychology of half of our dictators.

RM: Do you think ordinary people despise themselves?

CC: No, not to that extent. I think they do to a degree. They feel they couldn't be leaders, but I think any man can be a leader. If they take the trouble and the responsibility, there's a great deal of so-called courage about it. I think we're all pretty lazy, but if somebody had to do it, they can do it. It's hard work to face problems, and who wants to face problems?

RM: In *Limelight* you have the background in one scene totally different from the scene which you have just seen, as sort of a joke on the people. That you feel that nobody cares whether things change from scene to scene.

CC: Well, I don't do those things deliberately. I don't have any joke on the public. They're not to be joked with, in my estimation. But I do know that if I've done a very good scene and a pillow may be out place in the background and the [continuity] girls will say that's no good, well, to hell with the pillow in the background. It's a good scene and that's more important. In *Shoulder Arms* I had a gun in one scene and in the other I didn't have it, but it was a good scene. So I used it.

RM: I was aware in some of your films that instead of a real city there would be a painting. It was rather charming.

CC: Yes. What I enjoy with pictures is to create something that looks as though it's a lot of money and do it for the sake of intention. Not because it's cheap, but because it's creative. To do it cleverly without spending a lot of money. People would build train platforms just for a simple scene of somebody going away. What a waste of money. In *A Woman of Paris* when a woman gets on the train, she has a shadow of a train that comes into the station pass her face, and it was done with just a piece of cardboard. People said it was beautiful, poetic.

RM: Your most recent film is *A Countess from Hong Kong.* A big question that's going to be on everybody's mind when they look at it is, is he going to be old-fashioned? What is it about the film that they might consider old-fashioned?

CC: Well, they all have an idea that I'm terribly conservative and I'm not. We don't twist the camera upside down. Personality, people, the human equation transcend any acrobatics that the camera might do. I don't think there is such a word as being old-fashioned, in the deepest sense, because we don't understand the past, the present; we're conscious of the future. I like the misty mysticism of that. Time is something that is there, and we pretend that everything is modern and new, but it's not. So I'm never bothered about being old-fashioned.

RM: I heard the comment that the script seemed terribly simple.

CC: Well, that's something as a director one has to overcome, and you tell them this is essentially a romantic love story in a realistic situation. And you just play it straightforward, without nonsense.

RM: And you wrote the music for this?

CC: Yes—well, you see, I don't write music, so I have to have another man there, but I can play. I have no technique, but I know what I want to do. I'm not very good. I will say, I want the flutes and nothing but the woodwinds here, and doing something, with a little brass here, French horns coming in here, and the climax there—something like that. I would play the tune—I always want the tune first, because my tunes are lyrical, then you can go into the violins and all of that afterwards, but I want to hear the tune clean.

RM: Is writing music like writing words in any way?

CC: No, because you have command in your words. You can go over them and rewrite and rearrange. But music is always in the hands of somebody else, and if you make a mistake, with forty-five musicians, and they're pretty well paid, it means you have to bring them back.

RM: This was your first movie in color. Did you enjoy that?

CC: Yes. Of course, one is so insecure, because you never know what the hell is coming out. It was very fine, very discreet. I rather liked the idea of it. It's like any picture—the only nervous qualms I had was starting. The moment we took the first scene I knew what I wanted.

RM: If a person walked into the cinema not knowing anything about it or what was being shown, would I know that you had a hand in it? Would it have something that I would recognize as having your stamp on it?

CC: I think so. The situations are crazy enough. And the thing is so absolutely logical; so right, and completely truthful. It's a sort of mad thing which has the pretense of being absolutely real. It's screamingly funny. It's treated so real and so mad.

RM: Did you have any different kinds of nervousness about this than previous films?

CC: Oh, slightly. My one desire was to please the actors, and I found that I wanted their respect more than anything else. It wasn't a question of nerves. I knew I'd got a good thing, I wasn't too sure whether it would come off or not.

RM: Do you have a film that's a favorite?

CC: Well, I think I liked *City Lights*. I think it's solid, well done. *City Lights* is a real comedy.

RM: That is a powerful film. What impressed me is how close tragedy and comedy are.

CC: Well, that has never interested me. That's been the feeling, I suppose, of subjectivity. I've always felt that, and it has more or less been second nature with me. That may be due to environment also. And I don't think one can do humor without having great pity and a sense of sympathy for one's fellow man.

RM: Is it that we want relief from tragedy?

CC: No, I think life is much more. If that were the reason I think there would be more suicides. People would want to get out of life. I think life is a very wonderful thing, and must be lived under all circumstances, even in misery. I think I would prefer life. Prefer the experience, for nothing else but the experience. I think humor does save one's sanity. We can go overboard with too much tragedy. Tragedy is, of course, a part of life, but we're also given an equipment to offset anything, a defense against it. I think tragedy is very essential in life. And we are given humor as a defense against it. Humor is a universal thing, which I think is derived from more or less pity.

RM: What keeps you from directing a play and keeps you fascinated with the film?

CC: Well, you can fix permanently the artistry in a film, but you cannot in a play. People fall off after the repetition of playing a part, they get into bad habits, and that's one aspect, although I enjoy the theater, and I would like to put a play on. But you would have to be a caretaker or watchdog. We have an expression— "that's in the can"—you've done that. And that's forever—as long as film lasts.

RM: Do you think there is such a thing as a genius?

CC: I've never known quite what a genius was. I think it's somebody with a talent, who's highly emotional about it, and is able to master a technique. Everybody is gifted in some way. The average man has to differentiate between doing a regular sort of unimaginative job, and the fellow who's a genius doesn't. He does something different, but does this very well. Many a jack-of-all-trades have been mistaken for a genius.

RM: Well, you have done something in your life that nobody did before, and nobody will do again. That's absolutely unique.

CC: Unique, yes, but genius is such a pretentious word, and you come to find it doesn't mean anything. You see genius all over the world, in beautiful paintings . . . I think they do their job well, and they're artists, and how far the genius goes, some are better artists than others.

RM: What do you think has kept you sustained all these years? Kept you from running away?

CC: Oh, I think it's my vitality. I'm an optimist within my own self. At my age, I enjoy it very much because there are a lot of things that one gives up, especially if you've been successful and in your success you've been sensible.

RM: What sort of fears did you have?

CC: I've never had any fears when I was young. If I had five dollars a week, I could go around and play my violin in a pub and make it.

RM: *Limelight* is a reflection of that, isn't it?

CC: A lot of that, yes. One is sort of haunted with the fact that you want to settle and be happy. And those things didn't come until very late. As I say, age is very gratifying, because you shed yourself of a lot of fears. Death doesn't have any fear for you. It did when I was young. I always thought I was going to die in the cold or something. And then, one doesn't want the social things so much. One doesn't want to go out and stand around with their back against the wall and talk to somebody you don't know. One gets lazy. It's nice to stay home and have a good meal. Put your feet up by the fire and have a drink, or read a book, and that's it.

RM: Is there anything in the world now that fires your imagination?

CC: There's a lot that fires my imagination, but I wouldn't make a story about it. But there is an optimistic note here. There is a lot of sorrow to life, there's plenty of trouble in the world, and I think to make a picture showing the possibility that there is another aspect to life is very charming. It's not the question of what life is, it's the question of what the possibilities are.

Notes

The Early Years

1. Charles Chaplin, *My Autobiography* (London, 1964), 8.
2. Ibid., 11.
3. Ibid., 15.
4. Ibid., 16.
5. Chaplin, "What People Laugh At," *American Magazine* 86 (Nov. 1918): 34.
6. Chaplin, *My Autobiography*, 22.
7. Chaplin, "A Comedian Sees the World," *Woman's Home Companion* 60, no. 9 (Sept. 1933): 89.
8. Chaplin, *My Autobiography*, 27.
9. Ibid., 29.
10. Ibid., 35.
11. Claire Bloom, in an interview with the author, 2002.
12. Chaplin, *My Autobiography*, 73.
13. Ibid., 77.
14. Fred Karno in an essay originally published in April 1931 and reprinted in Peter Haining, ed., *The Legend of Charlie Chaplin* (Secaucus, N.J. 1982), 25–26.
15. John McCabe, *Charlie Chaplin* (New York, 1978), 28.
16. Ibid., 34.
17. Chaplin, *My Autobiography,* 105.
18. Ibid., 111.
19. Chaplin, "A Comedian Sees the World," 8.
20. Chaplin, *My Autobiography*, 88.
21. Ibid., 86–87.
22. Ibid., 123.
23. Sigmund Freud to Yvette Guilbert, from Harry Crocker, "Charlie Chaplin: Man and Mime," chap. 14, pp. 2–3; unpublished typescript, Harry Crocker Collection, Margaret Herrick Library, Academy of Motion Picture Arts and Sciences.

Keystone: The Tramp is Born

1. Chaplin, *My Autobiography*, 145.
2. Chaplin's contract with the Keystone Film Company, signed Sept. 25, 1913, Chaplin Archives.
3. Chaplin, *My Autobiography*, 146.
4. Ibid., 151.
5. Ibid., 153.
6. "Comments on the Films: *Making a Living*," *Moving Picture World* 19, no. 6 (Feb. 7, 1914): 678.
7. Chaplin, *My Autobiography*, 154.
8. Ibid., 154.
9. Ibid., 154.

10. Ibid., 155.
11. Walter Kerr, *The Silent Clowns* (New York, 1975), 22.
12. In *My Autobiography*, Chaplin writes that *Caught in the Rain* was the first film he directed. However, in August 1914 Chaplin sent to his brother Sydney a list of twenty films in which he had appeared indicating six of them as "my own." The earliest of the six was *Twenty Minutes of Love*, suggesting it as his directorial debut. The letter survives in the Chaplin Archives and is reproduced in David Robinson, *Chaplin: His Life and Art* (London, 2001), 128. Chaplin's 1924 article "Does the Public Knows What it Wants?" also suggests *Twenty Minutes of Love* was his directorial debut. Chaplin, "Does the Public Know What it Wants?" *Adelphi* 1, no. 8 (Jan. 1924): 702.
13. Chaplin, *My Autobiography*, 164.
14. Ibid., 165.
15. Ibid., 168.
16. Ibid., 167.
17. Ibid., 163.
18. Ibid., 169.
19. Lewis Jacobs, *The Rise of the American Film* (New York, 1939), 226.
20. Gilbert Seldes, *The Seven Lively Arts* (New York, 1924), 41.
21. Chaplin, *My Autobiography*, 169.
22. Mack Sennett (as told to Cameron Shipp), *King of Comedy* (Garden City, N.Y., 1954), 180.

Essanay-Chaplin Brand

1. Chaplin, *My Autobiography*, 176.
2. Charles J. McGuirk, "Chaplinitis," *Motion Picture Magazine*. 9, no. 6 (July 1915): 121–24.
3. Chaplin, *My Autobiography*, 186.

Mutual-Chaplin Specials

1. Terry Ramsaye in *Reel Life*, the Mutual Film Corporation's publicity magazine, March 4, 1916, preserved in one of Chaplin's Mutual scrapbooks, Chaplin Archives.
2. "Chaplin Signs with Mutual," *Moving Picture World* 27, no. 10 (Mar. 11, 1916): 1622.
3. Chaplin, *My Autobiography*, 162.
4. Richard Roud, "The Baggy-Trousered Philanthropist," *The Guardian*, Dec. 28, 1977, 3.
5. Lady Chaplin to Robinson, in Robinson, *Chaplin: His Life and Art*, xix and 664.
6. Chaplin's working method was explored in Kevin Brownlow and David Gill's three-part

documentary *Unknown Chaplin* (1983), which analyzed some of the surviving Chaplin outtakes and devoted the first episode to the Mutual films.
7. Roland Totheroh, "Roland H. Totheroh Interviewed: Chaplin Films," in Timothy J. Lyons, ed., *Film Culture* 53–55 (spring 1972): 239–41.
8. Ramsaye, "Chaplin—and How He Does It," *Photoplay* 22, no. 4 (Sept. 1917): 22.
9. Chaplin, *My Autobiography*, 219.
10. Ibid., 221.
11. Minnie Maddern Fiske, "The Art of Charlie Chaplin," *Harper's Weekly* 62 (May 6, 1916): 494.
12. T. S. Eliot, quoted in Seldes, *The Seven Lively Arts*, 361.
13. Letter from Chaplin's attorney Nathan Burkan to Bobbs Merrill's attorneys Lockwood and Jeffery, Oct. 1, 1916, Chaplin Archives.
14. Seldes, *Movies for the Millions* (London, 1937), 37.
15. Chaplin, *My Autobiography*, 222.
16. Ibid., 201.
17. Chaplin, "Does the Public Know What it Wants?" 705. Chaplin vividly recalled the letter fifty years later in a 1966 interview with Richard Meryman.
18. Theodore Huff, *Charlie Chaplin* (New York, 1951), 71.
19. Four hundred twenty-three reels (approximately seventy hours) of Chaplin outtakes, visitors to the studio, and tests—most from the Mutual-Chaplin Specials—have been preserved by the British Film Institute. Although Chaplin never owned the films he made for Mutual, he nevertheless acquired the Mutual outtakes as a result of an injunction Chaplin secured against the Sales Corporation and Ralph Spence, who were making new Chaplin films from the Mutual outtakes. Chaplin bought the footage, thereby stopping the "new" films from being made. He had ordered the material—as well as the outtakes he did not specifically ask to retain from the later films he did own—to be destroyed in 1953 with the closing of the Chaplin Studios. These orders were not carried out, and film collector Raymond Rohauer acquired the material the following year. Rohauer subsequently gave some of the non-Mutual material back to Chaplin's Roy Export Company Establishment (which promptly destroyed it). After Rohauer's death in 1987, the Chaplin material he had retained was moved to the British Film Institute for preservation.

20. Huff, 71.

21. Chaplin, "What People Laugh At," 136.

22. Harvey O'Higgins, "Charlie Chaplin's Art,"
    The New Republic 10, no. 118 (Feb. 3, 1917): 17.

23. Kerr, *The Silent Clowns*, 95.

24. Sergei M. Eisenstein, "Charlie the Kid," *Sight
    and Sound* 15, no. 57 (spring 1946): 14.

25. Chaplin, *My Trip Abroad* (New York, 1922), 22.

26. Chaplin, *My Autobiography*, 202.

27. Chaplin, "What People Laugh At," 136.

28. Carlyle T. Robinson, *La vérité sur Charlie
    Chaplin: Sa vie, ses amours, ses déboirs*,
    translation by René Lulu (Paris, 1935), 18.

29. Julian Johnson, "The Shadow Stage" (review
    of *The Immigrant*), *Photoplay* 12, no. 4 (Sept.
    1917): 99–100.

30. Chaplin, *My Autobiography*, 225.

31. Chaplin, *My Life in Pictures* (London, 1974),
    150.

32. Chaplin, "What People Laugh At," 134.

33. Chaplin, *My Autobiography*, 202.

34. Sydney Chaplin, in an interview with the
    author, 1998, and corroborated by Jerry
    Epstein, in an interview with the author, 1991.

First National and First Marriage

1. Chaplin, *My Autobiography*, 318.

2. Ibid., 224.

3. Chaplin Studios Daily Production Report,
   February 26, 1918, Chaplin Archives.

4. Ibid, Apr. 29, 1918.

5. Chaplin, *My Autobiography*, 225.

6. Ibid., 227.

7. Louis Delluc, *Charlie Chaplin*, English translation by Hamish Miles (London, 1922), 92.
   Delluc's praise for the film was written before
   D. W. Griffith's masterworks *A Birth of a Nation*
   (1915) and *Intolerance* (1916) had been shown
   in France.

8. Chaplin, *My Autobiography*, 235.

9. Ibid., 236.

10. Theodore Dreiser, *Theodore Dreiser: American
    Diaries, 1902–1926* (Philadelphia, 1982), 350.

11. Chaplin, *My Autobiography*, 245.

12. Ibid., 247.

13. Huff, 90.

14. Chaplin, *My Autobiography*, 255.

15. Ibid., 248.

16. Huff, 288.

17. James Quirk, "A Letter to a Genius,"
    Photoplay 17, no. 5 (Apr. 1920): 27.

18. Chaplin, *My Autobiography*, 251.

19. Ibid., 253.

20. Ibid., 252.

21. Ibid., 293, and also Chaplin, *My Life in
    Pictures*, 188.

22. Francis Hackett, "The Kid," *The New Republic*
    26 (Mar. 30, 1921): 136–37.

23. James, in an interview with the author, 2000.

24. Chaplin, *My Life in Pictures*, 188.

25. Jackie Coogan, in an interview with Brownlow,
    1977.

26. Kerr, *The Silent Clowns*, 177–78.

27. Stephen M. Weissman, "What Made Charlie
    Run?" *Los Angeles Times*, Apr. 16, 1989, 18.

28. Totheroh, 267.

29. Chaplin, *My Autobiography*, 240.

30. Francis Wyndham, "Chaplin on the Critics, the
    Beatles, the Mood of London," *The Sunday
    Times*, Mar. 26, 1967, 10.

31. "Charlie Chaplin: A Doubt," *The New
    Statesman* 17, no. 440 (Sept. 17, 1921): 644.

32. James Agate, *Alarums and Excursions*
    (London, 1922), 180–82.

33. Anthony Coogan, in an interview with the
    author, 1996.

34. Carol Matthau, *Among the Porcupines* (New
    York, 1992), 233–34.

35. Chaplin, *My Autobiography*, 104.

36. Thomas Burke, "A Comedian," in *City of
    Encounters: A London Divertissement* (London,
    1932), 130–67.

37. Chaplin, *My Autobiography*, 318.

38. Norman Lloyd, in an interview with the author,
    1996, and Lloyd, *Stages of Life in Theatre, Film
    and Television* (New York, 1993), 121.

39. Chaplin, *My Life in Pictures*, 202.

40. Dean Riesner, in an interview with the author,
    2000, and Riesner and Jeffrey Vance, "Remem-
    bering *The Pilgrim*," unpublished typescript,
    2000.

41. Robert Sherwood, ed., *The Best Moving
    Pictures of 1922–23* (Boston, 1923), 62.

42. Chaplin, *My Autobiography*, 318.

United Artists

1. Tino Balio, *United Artists: The Company Built
   by the Stars* (Madison, Wis., 1976), 14.

2. Balio, "Charles Chaplin, Entrepreneur: A
   United Artist," in "Chaplin and Sound,"
   Journal of the University Film Association 31,
   no. 1 (winter 1979): 11.

3. Mary Pickford, *Sunshine and Shadow* (New
   York, 1955), 236.

A Woman of Paris

1. Chaplin, *My Autobiography*, 320.

2. Ibid., 322.

3. Ibid., 321.

4. Sutherland, in an interview with Bob and Joan
   Franklin, 1959, 46–47.

5. Adolphe Menjou and M. M. Musselman, *It
   Took Nine Tailors* (New York, 1948), 114.

6. Victor Saville visited the set for a day and
   observed that Chaplin did the fadeout himself,
   instructing Jack Wilson, who was operating the
   second camera, to follow his timing. Chaplin
   maintained that the timing of fadeouts was crucial. Victor Saville, unpublished manuscript, p.
   27. Victor Saville Collection, British Film
   Institute.

7. Sutherland, in an interview with Bob and Joan
   Franklin, 1959, 48.

8. Menjou and Musselman, 112–13.

9. Chaplin, *My Autobiography*, 322.

10. Totheroh, 270.

11. Menjou and Musselman, 117–18.

12. Chaplin, *My Autobiography*, 273.

13. Beyond the current German productions, sev-
    eral Cecil B. DeMille films of the late 1910s and
    early 1920s that featured marital infidelity—
    Old Wives for New (1918) in particular—influ-
    enced *A Woman of Paris*, but their wit derives
    more from felicitous intertitles rather than from
    the action. The direction by indirection and
    characterization by suggestion of Mauritz
    Stiller's *Thomas Graul's First Child* (1918) and
    Erotikon (1920) also influenced Chaplin's film.

14. Chaplin, *My Life in Pictures*, 217.

15. Chaplin's *A Woman of Paris* work papers,
    including *Public Opinion*, a play in two scenes
    written by Chaplin, Chaplin Archives. In the
    final film, only a portion of this text was used as
    an introductory title (removed by Chaplin for
    his 1976 reissue version), which reads: "All of
    us are seeking good—We sin only in blindness.
    The ignorant condemn our mistakes—But the
    wise pity them."

16. *Motion Picture Magazine* (Dec. 1923): 9.

17. Laurence Reid, "The Movie of the Month,"
    Motion Picture Classic 18, no. 5 (Jan. 1924): 92.

18. Edwin and Elza Schallert, "Hollywood High
    Lights," *Picture Play* 19, no. 5 (Jan. 1924): 66.

19. Menjou and Musselman, 120.

20. Ibid., 110–11.

21. Sutherland, in Brownlow, *The Parade's Gone
    By . . .* (New York, 1968), 498–99. The quota-
    tion is interposed from Brownlow's 1964 inter-
    view with Sutherland and Bob and Joan

Franklin's 1959 interview with Sutherland.

22. Lady Chaplin to Robinson, in Robinson, *Chaplin: His Life and Art*, 332.

23. Robinson, *Chaplin: His Life and Art*, 338.

24. *Exceptional Photoplays* review of *A Woman of Paris*, reprinted in Stanley Hochman, ed., *A Library of Film Criticism: American Film Directors* (New York, 1974), 147–48.

25. Totheroh, 270.

26. Chaplin, *My Autobiography*, 322.

27. Scott Eyman, *Lubitsch: Laughter in Paradise* (New York, 1993), 106.

28. Edwin Schallert, "A Forecast for 1925," *Picture Play Magazine* 21, no. 6 (Feb. 1925): 19.

29. Rex Ingram, "Art Advantages of the European Scene," *Theatre Magazine* (Jan. 1928): 24.

30. Eisenstein, "The New Language of Cinematography," *Close-Up* (May 1929): 11.

31. Robinson, *"A Woman of Paris," Sight and Sound* 48, no. 4 (autumn 1980): 223.

32. Martin Scorcese, in a conversation with the author, 2003.

33. Herman G. Weinberg, *The Lubitsch Touch* (New York, 1968), 51–57.

34. James, in an interview with the author, 1999. See also James, *Making Music with Charlie Chaplin* (Lanham, Md., 2000), 111–12.

35. Jack Kroll, "Voluptuous Silence," *Newsweek* (Jan. 10, 1977): 65.

The Gold Rush

1. Chaplin, *My Autobiography*, 327.

2. *The Gold Rush* pressbook, 13.

3. Chaplin, *My Autobiography*, 327.

4. Georgia Hale, *Charlie Chaplin: Intimate Close-Ups* (Metuchen, N.J., 1995), 62.

5. Sutherland, in an interview with Bob and Joan Franklin, 1959, 65.

6. Lita Grey Chaplin, in an interview with the author, 1995.

7. Chuck Jones, in an interview with the author, 1999.

8. Chaplin, *My Autobiography*, 235.

9. Based on Schallert, "Trick Photography in *The Gold Rush*," *Science and Invention* (Dec. 1925): 714–15; Grey Chaplin, in an interview with the author, 1995; and the *The Gold Rush* production records in the Chaplin Archives.

10. Totheroh's recollections regarding his double exposure work on *The Gold Rush* reveal that Chaplin relied completely on his crew to achieve the film's visual effects: "Well, first of all I take the main foundation, or the perspective shot. I had that made in miniature, maybe about ten feet long. Then I photographed the same contour that the stage would be after I painted it white. Then I had to figure out the dimensions of his [Chaplin's] height and the cabin's, and everything, where it was, and then

we got a special lens for this, and told him exactly where to jump and what to do and so forth. He [Chaplin] was dubious. He didn't know what he was doing. He couldn't see ahead what I intended to do. When he saw it in the morning, he said, 'It's perfect.' He went nuts about it, and called up Doug Fairbanks, brought Doug over there and anybody he could get a hold of to come and look at this." Totheroh, in a 1964 interview with his family.

11. Alexander Woolcott, "Charlie—As Ever Was," in *While Rome Burns* (New York, 1934), 270.

Marriage to Lita Grey

1. See Grey Chaplin and Jeffrey Vance, *Wife of the Life of the Party* (Lanham, Md., 1995). For a detailed history of Grey Chaplin's Spanish ancestry, see Esther Boulton Black, *Rancho Cucamonga and Dona Merced* (Redlands, Calif., 1975).

2. Grey Chaplin in an interview with the author, 1995.

3. Totheroh in a 1964 interview with his family.

4. Charles Chaplin Film Corporation continuity reports from Mar. 24, 1924, Chaplin Archives.

5. Chaplin and Vance, *Wife of the Life of the Party*, 43–45.

6. Lillita Louise Chaplin vs. Charles Spencer Chaplin et al. complaint of divorce, reprinted in *Wife of the Life of the Party*, 139.

7. Ibid.

8. Grey Chaplin, in an interview with the author, 1993.

9. One such effort to hide Chaplin's wealth during his divorce from Lita was recalled by Wyn Ritchie Evans, who worked at the Chaplin Studios along with her mother, who hid $50,000 of Chaplin's fortune at the instruction of Alf Reeves. Wyn Ritchie Evans, in an interview with the author, 1998.

10. Lillita Louise Chaplin vs. Charles Spencer Chaplin et al. complaint of divorce, reprinted in *Wife of the Life of the Party*, 136.

11. Ibid.

12. The complete divorce complaint filed by Grey Chaplin in the matter of Chaplin vs. Chaplin, Charles Chaplin's answer, Charles Chaplin's cross-complaint, Grey Chaplin's answer, and various court orders are reprinted in *Wife of the Life of the Party*.

13. Sydney Chaplin, in an interview with the author, 2002.

14. Tetrick, in an interview with the author, 2000, and corroborated by Pamela Paumier, in an interview with the author, 2002.

15. Chaplin, *My Autobiography*, 328.

16. Chaplin, *My Life in Pictures*, 228.

17. Grey Chaplin, in an interview with the author, 1995.

The Circus

1. "To Be, or Not to Be," *New York Times*, Nov. 29, 1925, sect. 8, p. 5. See also L'Estrange Fawcett, *Films: Facts and Forecast* (London, 1930), 156, for another contemporary reference to Chaplin's *The Suicide Club*. According to Alistair Cooke, Chaplin's *The Suicide Club* "was to be a revue, a film with six episodes. The most bizarre of which was to be the crucifixion performed as a night club act, with all sorts of rich people applauding wildly. . . . It was an interesting idea to be sure, but I don't think he could have gotten away with it in those days." Cooke, in an interview with the author, 1996.

2. Unsourced clipping of interview with Henry Bergman in Charles Chaplin scrapbook, Chaplin Archives.

3. Grey Chaplin, in a letter to the author, Nov. 29, 1993.

4. Robinson, *Chaplin: His Life and Art*, 383.

5. Charles Chaplin Film Corporation document certifying the destruction of the original negative, dated June 21, 1933, survives in the Chaplin Archives and is reproduced in Robinson, *Chaplin: His Life and Art,* 480. However, the Chaplin Studios projection log book indicates a 35mm print of *A Woman of the Sea* was retained and screened by Chaplin as late as Feb. 16, 1939. No print or preprint element of the film has survived.

6. See *New York Times*, Jan. 8, 1927, sect. 1, p. 19; Jan. 9, 1927, sect. 1, p. 8; Jan. 14, 1927, sect. 1, p. 15; and Jan. 15, 1927, sect. 1, p. 11 for an account of the *Pictorial Review* dispute. The Tully articles were published in *Pictorial Review* in four installments (Jan.–Apr. 1927 issues) under the title "Charlie Chaplin: His Real Life Story."

7. See *New York Times*, Jan. 18, 1927, sect. 1, p. 1; Jan. 26, 1927, sect. 1. p. 9; Jan. 28, 1927, sect. 1, p. 7 regarding Chaplin's difficulties with the Internal Revenue Service. Chaplin finally settled with the IRS on Jan. 12, 1928. See *New York Times*, Feb. 10, 1928, sect. 1, p. 26.

8. "Chaplin Among Clowns," *New York Times*, Jan. 1, 1928, sect. 8, p. 5.

9. M. Willson Disher, *Clowns and Pantomimes* (London, 1925), 34.

10. Chaplin must have also seen Max Linder's last film, *Der Zirkusköing* (*The King of the Circus*, 1924). The second half of the picture concerns Max, in love with a circus rider, becoming an animal trainer.

11. Fawcett, "Chaplin at Work on Comic Scenes Described by British Journalist," *New York Times,* Sept. 5, 1926, sect. 7, p. 5.

12. Ibid.

13. Ibid.

14. Robinson, *Chaplin: His Life and Art*, 392–93.
15. Crocker, chap. 12, p. 14.
16. Fawcett, "Chaplin at Work . . . ," 5.
17. Unsourced clipping of interview with Henry Bergman in Charles Chaplin scrapbook, Chaplin Archives.
18. Crocker, chap. 11, p. 18.
19. Ibid., chap. 10, p. 3.
20. Huff, 211.
21. Unsourced clipping in Charles Chaplin scrapbook, Chaplin Archives.
22. James, 86.
23. Ibid., 87.

City Lights

1. Chaplin, *My Autobiography*, 353.
2. Virginia Cherrill Martini, in an interview with the author, 1995.
3. Chaplin, in an interview with Richard Meryman, 1966.
4. Guinness World Records, in a letter to the author, May 20, 2002.
5. Robert Parrish, in an interview with the author, 1991.
6. Chaplin, *My Autobiography*, 354.
7. Martini, in an interview with the author, 1995.
8. Chaplin, quoted in Francis Wyndham's introduction to Chaplin, *My Life in Pictures*, 28.
9. Dan James, in an interview with Robinson, 1983. See also Robinson, *Chaplin: His Life and Art*, 523.
10. Martini, in an interview with the author, 1995.
11. Ibid.
12. Betty Chaplin Tetrick, in an interview with the author, 2000.
13. James Agee, "Comedy's Greatest Era," *Life* 27, no. 10 (Sept. 5, 1949): 77.
14. Henry Bergman interview in the *Boston Globe*, Feb. 22, 1931, in a *City Lights* scrapbook, Chaplin Archives.
15. The daily and periodical press on both sides of the Atlantic generally praised *City Lights*. However, the film did receive a few negative notices, the most notable of which was written by erstwhile Chaplin supporter Alexander Bakshy, whose review appeared in *The Nation*. Bakshy criticized the film for being serious and sentimental, two of the very qualities that modern audiences celebrate in the film. Alexander Bakshy, "Charlie Chaplin Falters," *The Nation* 132, no. 3426 (Mar. 4, 1931): 250–51.
16. "Movie of the Week: City Lights," *Life* (May 8, 1950), reprinted in *City Lights* 1950 reissue pressbook, 3.

Modern Times

1. Chaplin, *My Autobiography*, 415.
2. Ibid., 395.
3. Ibid., 415.
4. Goddard, in a telephone conversation with the author, 1986.
5. Totheroh, 275–76.
6. Chaplin, *My Autobiography*, 59.
7. Robinson, *Chaplin: His Life and Art*, 505.
8. Graham Greene, "*Modern Times*," *The Spectator*, Feb. 14, 1936, p. 254.
9. Otis Ferguson, "Hallelujah, Bum Again," *The New Republic* (Feb. 19, 1936), reprinted in Cooke, ed., *Garbo and the Night Watchman* (London, 1971), 273–75.
10. Roland Barthes, *Mythologies* (New York, 1972), 39.

Paulette Goddard

1. Chaplin, *My Autobiography*, 412–13.
2. Ibid., 414.
3. Charles Chaplin Jr. (with N. and M. Rau), *My Father, Charlie Chaplin* (New York, 1960), 58, and Sydney Chaplin, in an interview with the author, 1998.
4. Goddard, in a telephone conversation with the author, 1986.
5. Chaplin, *My Autobiography*, 425.
6. Chaplin Jr., 243.
7. Ibid., 258.
8. See Chaplin, *My Autobiography*, 418, in which he claims he married Goddard in 1936. Tetrick, in an interview with the author, 2000, and Epstein, in an interview with the author, 1991, claim Chaplin told them that he and Goddard were never married.
9. Chaplin, *My Autobiography*, 440.
10. Julie Gilbert, *Opposite Attraction: The Lives of Erich Maria Remarque and Paulette Goddard* (New York, 1995), 285.
11. Chaplin Jr., 367.
12. Gilbert, 125.

The Great Dictator

1. "An Old Friend Leaves Us," *New York Times*, Sept. 20, 1937, sect. 1, p. 22.
2. Chaplin, *My Autobiography*, 424.
3. Ivor Montagu, *With Eisenstein in Hollywood* (New York, 1969), 94.
4. Ibid. See also Lady Chaplin, quoted in Epstein, *Remembering Charlie: The Story of a Friendship* (London, 1988), 221. Chaplin told Richard Meryman in 1966, "I'm not Jewish . . . I would like to say 'yes.' They're fine people."
5. Huff, 263.
6. Chaplin, *My Autobiography*, 426.
7. Ibid., 424.
8. "The World Crisis in Dumb Show," *New York Times*, Apr. 15, 1932, 20.
9. Robert Van Gelder, "Chaplin Draws a Keen Weapon," *New York Times Magazine*, Sept. 8, 1940, sect. 7, p. 8.
10. Jack L. Warner of Warner Bros., in a letter to Chaplin dated March 23, 1939, wrote: "Ann [Mrs. Jack L. Warner] and I had a very lovely visit with the President last Friday and during our conversation the President brought up your picture *The Dictator*. He said he hoped you had not put it aside and would make it . . . President Roosevelt is very keen on seeing it made . . . I hope you do [go ahead with the film], Charlie, for if the President of our country is interested in your making the picture it certainly has merit." Jack L. Warner Collection, Box 58, Folder 5, USC Cinema-Television Library. Dan James, in an interview with Robinson, 1983, corroborates Roosevelt's enthusiasm for *The Great Dictator*.
11. Jack Oakie, *Jack Oakie's Double Takes* (San Francisco, 1980), 75.
12. Karl Struss remembered, "Charlie Chaplin's brother, Sydney, called me. His usual cameraman, Rollie Totheroh, couldn't handle *The Great Dictator*, which Charlie was about to make, and so Sydney asked me to do it. Later, on *Limelight*, they did start out with Rollie Totheroh and a top crew, but Rollie still didn't know how to light. So they called me in on that one, too." Charles Higham, *Hollywood Cameramen: Sources of Light* (Bloomington, Ind., 1970), 130.
13. Chaplin Jr., 204. Similarly, Tim Durant in an interview with Brownlow, 1980, recalled that Chaplin said to him after viewing footage of Hitler, "This guy is one of the greatest actors I've ever seen."
14. Dan James, in an interview with Robinson, 1983. See also Robinson, *Chaplin: His Life and Art*, 528.
15. Chaplin, *My Autobiography*, 426.
16. Chaplin, *My Life in Pictures*, 272. See also Epstein, 134.
17. Bosley Crowther, "*The Great Dictator*," *New York Times*, Oct. 16, 1940, sect. 1, p. 29.
18. Paul Goodman, "Chaplin Again Again and Again," *Partisan Review* 7, no. 6 (Nov.–Dec. 1940): 458.
19. Chaplin, "Mr. Chaplin Answers His Critics," *New York Times*, Oct. 27, 1940, sect. 9, p. 5.
20. Sydney Chaplin, in an interview with the author, 1998.
21. Peter Steffens, "Chaplin: The Victorian Tramp," *Ramparts* 3, no. 6 (Mar. 1965): 21. Screenwriter Budd Schulberg corroborated what Chaplin was told in Brownlow and Michael Kloft's documentary *The Tramp and the Dictator* (2002). Soon after World War II, Schulberg examined Hitler's projection log book, which recorded that he had ordered *The Great Dictator* be shown to him twice.
22. Robinson, *Chaplin: His Life and Art*, 518.

Joan Barry Scandal

1. Chaplin, My Autobiography, 449.
2. Ibid., 450.
3. See Charles J. Maland, Chaplin and American Culture: The Evolution of a Star Image (Princeton, N.J., 1989), 208–13, for a complete account of Hedda Hopper's involvement in the Barry scandal.
4. FBI documents relating to Chaplin available through the Freedom of Information Act and examined by the author. Robinson neatly outlines Hoover's role in the Barry debacle in Chaplin: His Life and Art, 565–67.
5. Ibid., 568.

Marriage to Oona O'Neill

1. Tetrick, in an interview with the author, 2000.
2. Chaplin, My Autobiography, 456.
3. Carol Matthau, 253.
4. Frederick Sands, "Oona," The American Weekly (June 19, 1960): 7. Oona Chaplin granted English journalist Frederick Sands her permission to publish his interview with her, although she later claimed in a letter to Louis Sheaffer that she had never been formally interviewed by Sands and took exception to much of what he wrote. Oona Chaplin to Louis Sheaffer, Sheaffer-O'Neill Collection, Connecticut College. See Jane Scovell, Oona: Living in the Shadows (New York, 1998), 249–51.
5. Sophia Loren, in an interview with the author, 1996.
6. Chaplin, My Autobiography, 528.
7. Tetrick, in an interview with the author, 2002, and Epstein, in interview with the author, 1991. See also Bloom, Limelight and After: The Education of an Actress (New York, 1982), 99; Epstein, 220; and James, 111.
8. Bloom, Leaving a Doll's House (New York, 1996), 73.

Monsieur Verdoux

1. Chaplin and Eisler were very good friends. Eisler, who once worked for the Comintern in Moscow, was assigned to Hollywood owing to his skills for cultural infiltration. After he was deported for perjury in 1948—a procedure Chaplin vehemently fought—Eisler claimed that he and Brecht had "radicalized" Chaplin. See Maland, 221–26.
2. Letter of agreement between Charles Chaplin Film Corporation and Orson Welles, dated July 24, 1941, Chaplin Archives. The document is reproduced in Paumier and Robinson, Chaplin: 100 Years, 100 Images, 100 Documents (Pordenone, Italy, 1989), 42.
3. Chaplin always denied Welles's claims of having supplied more than just the germinal idea for Monsieur Verdoux. See George Wallach, "Charlie Chaplin's Monsieur Verdoux Press Conference," Film Comment 5 (winter 1969), 35, and Chaplin, My Autobiography, 454. Welles maintained that he had written an entire script, which he gave to Chaplin. (According to Welles, his own copy of his script was later lost in a fire.) However, Welles himself conceded, in regard to Chaplin's final script, that, "An awful lot was his [Chaplin's]." Orson Welles and Peter Bogdanovich, This is Orson Welles (New York, 1998), 135. As virtually none of Chaplin's drafts and working notes from the film survive (only three handwritten notes are extant from a late stage in the writing process), it is not possible to examine the script's evolution.
4. Chaplin, My Autobiography, 473.
5. Lloyd, in an interview with the author, 1996.
6. Martha Raye, in a conversation with the author, 1988.
7. Marilyn Nash, in an interview with the author, 1997.
8. Florey's writings on Chaplin include Charlie Chaplin: Ses debuts, ses films, ses aventures (Paris, 1927), and, with coauthor Maurice Bessy, Monsieur Chaplin, ou le rire dans la nuit (Paris, 1952).
9. Nash, in an interview with the author, 1997.
10. Jean Renoir, in an article originally published in Screenwriter in July 1947 and reprinted in Haining, ed., The Legend of Charlie Chaplin, 175.
11. When Chaplin was asked at the Monsieur Verdoux press conference if it was his intention to create sympathy for the Verdoux character, Chaplin replied, "No," but went on to explain: "I intended to create pity for all humanity under certain drastic circumstances—in times of stress, I think—in catastrophe—conditions bring out the worst in humanity. . . . My motive—if there is any sympathy for Verdoux, it is to understand crime and the nature of crime. I'd sooner understand it and the nature of it than condemn it." Wallach, 37–38.
12. The famous Chaplin quotation is actually a revival of "One murder made a villain/Millions a hero," from British clergyman and writer Beilby Porteus (1731–1808).
13. Robert Lewis, in an interview with the author, 1997.
14. Ibid.
15. Agee, "Monsieur Verdoux—I," The Nation (May 31, 1947); "Monsieur Verdoux—II," The Nation (June 14, 1947); "Monsieur Verdoux—III," The Nation (June 21, 1947); reprinted in James Agee, Agee on Film: Reviews and Comments by James Agee (New York, 1958), 252–62.
16. Agee, "Comedy's Greatest Era," 70–82, 85–86, 88.
17. Charles Chaplin telegram to Gradwell Sears, Sept. 17, 1947.
18. Robert Warshow, "Charles Chaplin," in The Immediate Experience (Garden City, N.Y., 1962), 221.
19. Chaplin, My Autobiography, 490.
20. Chaplin, My Life in Pictures, 34.

Limelight

1. "To Be, or Not to Be," New York Times, Nov. 29, 1925, sect. 7, p. 5.
2. Ira S. Jaffe, "Chaplin's Labor of Performance: The Circus and Limelight," Literature/Film Quarterly 12, no. 3 (1984): 202–10.
3. Chaplin, "Footlights," unpublished novel, 1948 (with annotations), Chaplin Archives.
4. Chaplin, My Autobiography, 279.
5. Richard E. Lauterbach, "The Whys of Chaplin's Appeal," New York Times Magazine, May 21, 1950, p. 33.
6. Chaplin, My Autobiography, 279.
7. Lloyd, in an interview with the author, 1996.
8. Chaplin, My Autobiography, 494.
9. See Bloom, Limelight and After: The Education of an Actress, 85, and Bloom, Leaving a Doll's House, 54.
10. Bloom, in an interview with the author, 2002.
11. Ibid.
12. Sydney Chaplin, in an interview with the author, 2002.
13. Bloom, Limelight and After: The Education of an Actress, 107–8.
14. Ibid., 91.
15. Bloom, Leaving a Doll's House, 58.
16. Sydney Chaplin, in an interview with the author, 1997.
17. Lloyd, in an interview with the author, 1996.
18. Sydney Chaplin, in an interview with the author, 1997.
19. Epstein, in an interview with the author, 1991.
20. Sydney Chaplin, in an interview with the author, 1997. In fact, Lloyd performed his speech an additional thirty times on the May 5, 1952 retakes before Chaplin was satisfied.
21. Sydney Chaplin, in an interview with the author, 2002.
22. Sydney Chaplin, in an interview with the author, 1997.
23. Tetrick, in an interview with the author, 2000. See also Scovell, 114, and Patrice Chaplin, Hidden Star: Oona O'Neill Chaplin (London, 1995), 103.
24. Lloyd, in an interview with the author, 1996.
25. Bloom, Sydney Chaplin, Epstein, Melissa Hayden, Lloyd, Julian Ludwig, and Tetrick, in interviews with the author.
26. Lloyd, in an interview with the author, 1999.
27. Epstein, in an interview with the author, 1991. See also Epstein, 84.

28. Bloom, in an interview with the author, 2002.

29. Higham, 130–31.

30. Eugene Lourié, *My Work in Films* (New York, 1985), 221.

31. Chaplin, *My Autobiography*, 494.

32. Thomas M. Pryor, "How Mr. Chaplin Makes a Movie," *New York Times Magazine*, Feb. 17, 1952, p. 22.

33. Ibid.

34. *Limelight* pressbook.

35. Epstein, in an interview with the author, 1991. See also Epstein, 96.

36. Sydney Chaplin, in an interview with the author, 1999.

37. Eleanor Keaton, in an interview with the author, 1998. See also Keaton and Jeffrey Vance, *Buster Keaton Remembered* (New York, 2001), 202.

38. Although Chaplin could not have known that *Limelight* would be his last American film, a letter from Chaplin's representative Tim Durant to United Artists president Arthur Krim dated Aug. 23, 1951 (more than a year prior to Chaplin's departure to England) conveys Chaplin's desire to sell his studio. Chaplin's asking price was $1.3 million.

39. Chaplin, *My Autobiography*, 495. Chaplin did, however, have misgivings about one sequence in *Limelight* involving the character Claudius (Stapleton Kent), a man without arms. Following the premiere, Chaplin gave the order to have the sequence removed. The Chaplin Studios production report for the week of November 10–15, 1952, notes: "Cutting 'Claudius' sequence out of *Limelight* (in accordance with C. C.'s instructions) and inserting new 'Fade Out' and 'Fade In.'"

40. Kerr, "The Lineage of *Limelight*," *Theatre Arts* 36 (Nov. 1952): 75.

41. Balio, *United Artists: The Company that Changed the Film Industry* (Madison, Wis., 1987), 59.

42. It is generally believed that the reason *Limelight* never played in Los Angeles in 1953 was because of the American Legion's picketing of the film and exhibitor resistance. However, this is not the case. A letter written to United Artists by Chaplin's representative Arthur Kelly, dated Aug. 17, 1953, indicates that United Artists proposed the film be shown at the Las Palmas Theatre in Hollywood. Chaplin, however, did not want the film to go into the Las Palmas. According to Arthur Kelly, Chaplin wanted to "wait until [Spyros] Skouras [of Twentieth Century-Fox] gives us a decent theatre."

43. Chaplin, *My Autobiography*, 494.

Chaplin and Politics

1. Chaplin, *My Autobiography*, 376.

2. Al Hirschfeld, in an interview with the author, 2001.

3. Unsourced clipping of a 1921 interview with Chaplin in Charles Chaplin scrapbook, Chaplin Archives.

4. In 1922 the Federal Bureau of Investigation was called the "Bureau of Investigation." The name Bureau of Investigation was not changed to Federal Bureau of Investigation until 1935.

5. A. A. Hopkins FBI file report from 1922 relating to Chaplin, available through the Freedom of Information Act and examined by the author.

6. Wyndham, "Introduction," in Chaplin, *My Life in Pictures*, 31.

7. Chaplin, *My Autobiography*, 354.

8. Ibid., 383.

9. Hirschfeld, in an interview with the author, 2001.

10. Chaplin, *My Autobiography*, 410–11.

11. Cooke, "Charles Chaplin: The One and Only," in *Six Men* (New York, 1977), 27.

12. Chaplin, *My Autobiography*, 425.

13. Ibid., 432.

14. Ibid., 439.

15. Robinson, *Chaplin: His Life and Art*, 569. Chaplin also granted a request made directly from Brigadier-General Lord Croft, Under Secretary of State for War, for 16mm prints of the film for British expeditionary troops (Alfred Reeves in letter to Carl Leserman, April 2, 1942, in the Chaplin Archives).

16. Chaplin, *My Autobiography*, 443.

17. Hirschfeld, "A Man with Both Feet in the Clouds," *New York Times Magazine*, July 26, 1942, p. 12.

18. Chaplin, *My Autobiography*, 423.

19. Douglas Fairbanks Jr., in an interview with the author, 1993.

20. Lloyd, in an interview with the author, 1996.

21. Wallach, 36.

22. Chaplin, *My Autobiography*, 484.

23. Ibid., 504.

24. FBI, INS, CIA, Office of the Attorney General, Bureau of the Budget, Department of State, and Criminal Division, Department of Justice records relating to Chaplin, available through the Freedom of Information Act and examined by the author.

25. Lloyd, in an interview with the author, 1996.

26. Bloom, *Leaving a Doll's House*, 57.

27. Robinson, *Chaplin: His Life and Art*, 622.

28. "Chaplin Must Prove Case," *New York Times*, Oct. 29, 1952.

29. Ella Winter, "But It's Sad, Says Chaplin, It's Me," *The Observer*, Sept. 13, 1957, p. 4.

30. Chaplin, quoted in "Sayings of the Week," *The Observer*, July 17, 1960, p. 6.

31. Harold Clurman, "Oona, Oxford, America and the Book." *Esquire* LVIII, no. 5 (Nov. 1962): 182.

32. William A. McWhirter, "Grand Rerun for Charlie Chaplin," *Life* 71, no. 23 (Dec. 3, 1971): 95.

Exile

1. "McGranery Starts a Drive to Deport Alien Racketeers," *New York Times*, Oct. 3, 1952, p. 1.

2. In a memorandum from the FBI documents pertaining to Chaplin, dated September 29, 1952, A. N. Belmont of the FBI, at a meeting with three INS officers, advises: "Mr. Farrell stated bluntly that at the present INS does not have sufficient information to exclude Chaplin from the United States if he attempts to reenter. Mr. Mackey interposed that INS could, of course, make it difficult for Chaplin to reenter, but in the end, there is no doubt Chaplin would be admitted. Mr. Mackey pointed out that if INS attempted to delay Chaplin's reentry into the United States, it would involve a question of detention which might rock INS and the Department of Justice to its foundations." FBI documents pertaining to Chaplin, available through the Freedom of Information Act and examined by the author.

3. Christopher Chaplin, in an interview with the author, 2002.

4. Josephine Chaplin, in an interview with the author, 2002.

5. Michael Chaplin, in an interview with the author, 1997.

6. Geraldine Chaplin, in an interview with the author, 2002. Chaplin elaborated on his lack of religious convictions to Richard Meryman in 1966: "I was full of religion until about the age of twelve. My brother got rid of all that for me. He said, 'There's no God. If there was a God, why would he let your father die like an animal?' He convinced me."

A King in New York

1. Michael Chaplin, in an interview with the author, 1997.

2. Ibid.

3. Epstein, in an interview with the author, 1991. See also Epstein, 137.

4. Phil Brown, in an interview with the author, 1999.

5. Epstein, in an interview with the author, 1991. See also Epstein, 129.

6. Paumier, in an interview with the author, 2002.

7. Paul Dehn, "It's All There in Chaplin's Museum," *News Chronicle*, Sept. 13, 1957, p. 6.

8. John Osborne, "Chaplin Aims a Kick at America," *The Evening Standard*, Sept. 12, 1957, p. 6.

9. Kenneth Tynan, "Looking Back in Anger," *The Observer*, Sept. 15, 1957, p. 13.

10. Chaplin, *My Life in Pictures*, 306.

A Countess from Hong Kong

1. The notes and only pages of the original script for *Stowaway* survive in the Chaplin Archives. There were very few changes to the original *Stowaway* story.
2. Sydney Chaplin, in an interview with the author, 1998.
3. Lloyd, in an interview with the author, 1996.
4. Tippi Hedren, in an interview with the author, 1994.
5. Epstein, in an interview with the author, 1991. See also Epstein, 179.
6. Sydney Chaplin, in an interview with the author, 1998.
7. Chaplin, in an interview with Richard Meryman, 1966.
8. John Russell Taylor, "In the Studios with Charlie Chaplin," *The Times,* Mar. 17, 1966, p. 18, and Brownlow, "Watching Chaplin Direct *A Countess from Hong Kong,*" *Film Culture* 40 (spring 1966): 2–4, are two of the best reports of Chaplin at work on the film. See also Brownlow, *The Parade's Gone By . . . ,* 504–7.
9. Hedren, in an interview with the author, 1994.
10. Loren, in an interview with the author, 1996.
11. Ibid.
12. Epstein, in an interview with the author, 1991. See also Epstein, 186.
13. Sydney Chaplin, in an interview with the author, 1998.
14. Epstein, in an interview with the author, 1991. See also Epstein, 186.
15. Marlon Brando (with Robert Lindsey), *Brando: Songs My Mother Taught Me* (New York, 1994), 316, 319.
16. Josephine Chaplin, in an interview with the author, 2002.
17. Sydney Chaplin, in an interview with the author, 2002. See also Chaplin, *My Autobiography*, 303, for Chaplin's abhorrence of color photography.
18. Epstein, in an interview with the author, 1991.
19. Robinson, *Chaplin: His Life and Art*, 673.
20. Alexander Walker, "Sad Verdict on *A Countess*—Charlie Is Let Down by Words," *The Evening Standard,* Jan. 5, 1967, p. 14.
21. Taylor, "A Disappointing Film from Chaplin," *The Times,* Jan. 6, 1967, p. 14.
22. "An Irked Chaplin Calls Critics 'Bloody Idiots,'" *New York Times*, Jan. 7, 1967, p. 22.
23. Crowther, "*A Countess from Hong Kong,*" *New York Times*, Mar. 17, 1967, sect. 1, p. 35, and "How Hath the Mighty?" *New York Times*, Mar. 26, 1967, sect. 2, pp. 1, 7.
24. "Time to Retire," *Time* 89, no. 13 (Mar. 31, 1967): 95.
25. Wyndham, "Chaplin on the Critics, the Beatles, the Mood of London," p. 10.
26. "Big Rental Films of 1967," *Variety* 249, no. 7 (Jan. 3, 1968): 25.
27. Loren, in an interview with the author, 1996.
28. Chaplin, *My Autobiography*, 271–72.
29. Wyndham, p. 10.
30. Ibid.

Chaplin and Music

1. Chaplin, *My Trip Abroad*, 62.
2. Ibid.
3. BBC Light Programme interview with Chaplin, Oct. 15, 1953.
4. Chaplin, *My Autobiography*, 243.
5. Fawcett, *Films: Facts and Forecasts*, 153.
6. Apart from his own original compositions, Chaplin employs "The Star-Spangled Banner," quotes several musical standards (e.g. "I Hear You Calling Me" and "How Dry I Am"), and utilizes José Padilla's "La Violetera" as the theme of the blind flower girl.
7. Unsourced Chaplin interview clipping from the *New York Telegram*, 1931, in a *City Lights* scrapbook, Chaplin Archives.
8. Chaplin, *My Autobiography*, 355.
9. David Raksin, "Life with Charlie," *The Quarterly Journal of the Library of Congress* 40, no. 3 (summer 1983): 241.
10. Ibid., 242–43.
11. Ibid., 242.
12. Carl Davis, in an interview with the author, 1996.
13. Petula Clark, in an interview with the author, 2000.
14. Eric James, in an interview with the author, 1999.
15. Ibid.
16. Ibid.
17. James, *Making Music with Charlie Chaplin*, 111–12.

The Final Years

1. Robinson, *Chaplin: His Life and Art*, 641.
2. Chaplin, *The Freak*, unproduced script, c. 1974 (with annotations), 11, Chaplin Archives.
3. "*The Times* Diary: Stand-In." *The Times,* Nov. 10, 1969, p. 10.
4. Victoria Chaplin, in an interview with the author, 2002. Victoria Chaplin's account of why *The Freak* was not made was corroborated by Epstein, in an interview with the author, 1991. See also Epstein, 203.
5. Ibid.
6. Mo Rothman, in an interview with the author, 1998.
7. Ibid.
8. Stefan Kanfer, "Re-enter Charlie Chaplin, Smiling and Waiving." *Time* 99, no. 15 (Apr. 10, 1972): 65.
9. Forty-fourth annual Academy Awards presentation, Apr. 10, 1972.
10. Cooke, "Charles Chaplin: The One and Only," 44.
11. Wyndham to Jane Scovell, in Scovell, 255.
12. Chaplin, *My Autobiography*, 502.
13. Geraldine Chaplin, in an interview with the author, 2002.
14. Paumier, in an interview with the author, 2002.
15. Richard Patterson, in an interview with the author, 2002, and in a memorandum to the author, Aug. 29, 2002.
16. Paumier, in an interview with the author, 2002.
17. Patterson, in an interview with the author, 2002.
18. British Foreign Office documents pertaining to Chaplin's knighthood, 1956–71, declassified and released by the Public Record Office, London, and Epstein, in an interview with the author, 1991.
19. Philip Howard, "Sir Charles Silenced by Solemnity," *The Times,* Mar. 5, 1975, p. 1.
20. Epstein, in an interview with the author, 1991. See also Epstein, 209.
21. Christopher Chaplin, in an interview with the author, 2002.

Bibliography

Books

Adeler, Edwin, and Con West. *Remember Fred Karno? The Life of a Great Showman.* London: John Long, 1939.

Agate, James. *Alarums and Excursions.* London: Grant Richards Ltd., 1922.

Agee, James. *Agee on Film: Reviews and Comments by James Agee.* New York: McDowell, Oblensky, 1958.

Alemendros, Nestor. *A Man with a Camera.* New York: Farrar, Straus and Giroux, Inc., 1984.

Asplund, Uno. *Chaplin's Films.* English translation by Paul Britten Austin. New York: A.S. Barnes and Company, 1973.

Balio, Tino. *United Artists: The Company Built by the Stars.* Madison, Wis.: University of Wisconsin Press, 1976.

_____. *United Artists: The Company that Changed the Film Industry.* Madison, Wis.: University of Wisconsin Press, 1987.

Barry, Iris. *Let's Go to the Pictures.* London: Chatto & Windus, 1926.

Barthes, Roland. *Mythologies.* Selected and translated from the French by Annette Lavers. New York: Hill and Wang, 1972.

Bazin, Andre. *Essays on Chaplin.* Edited and translated by Jean Bodon. Preface by François Truffaut. New Haven: Conn.: University of New Haven Press, 1985.

Bercovici, Konrad. *It's the Gypsy in Me.* New York: Prentice-Hall, 1941.

Bergson, Henri. "Laughter" (1900), in *Comedy.* Edited by Wylie Sypher. Garden City, N.Y.: Doubleday and Company, 1956.

Bessy, Maurice. *Charlie Chaplin.* English translation by Jane Brenton. New York: Harper & Row, 1985.

_____, and Robert Florey. *Monsieur Chaplin, ou le rire dans la nuit.* Paris: Jacques Damase, 1952.

Bloom, Claire. *Leaving a Doll's House.* New York: Little, Brown and Company, 1996.

_____. *Limelight and After: The Education of an Actress.* New York: Harper & Row, 1982.

Booth, Charles. *Life and Labour of the People in London.* 7 vols. London: Macmillan, 1902.

Bowman, W. Dodgson. *Charlie Chaplin: His Life and Art.* Introduction by Douglas Fairbanks Jr. New York: The John Day Company, 1931.

Brando, Marlon (with Robert Lindsey). *Brando: Songs My Mother Taught Me.* New York: Random House, 1994.

Brownlow, Kevin. *The Parade's Gone By . . .* New York: Alfred A. Knopf, 1968.

_____. *The War, the West, and the Wilderness.* New York: Alfred A. Knopf, 1978.

Burke, Thomas. "A Comedian." In *City of Encounters: A London Divertissement.* London: Constable, 1932.

Capp, Al. *The World of Li'l Abner.* Introduction by John Steinbeck. Foreword by Charles Chaplin. New York: Farrar, Straus & Young, 1952.

Chaplin, Charles. *A Comedian Sees the World.* New York: Crowell, 1933.

_____. "The Fool." Reprinted in *The Best of Rob Wagner's Script.* Edited by Anthony Slide. Metuchen, N.J.: Scarecrow Press, 1985.

_____. *My Autobiography.* London: The Bodley Head, 1964.

_____. *My Life in Pictures.* Introduction by Francis Wyndham. London: The Bodley Head, 1974.

_____. *My Trip Abroad.* New York: Harper & Brothers, 1922.

_____. *My Wonderful Visit.* London: Hurst & Blackett, 1922. (British edition of *My Trip Abroad*).

_____. "Rhythm." Reprinted in Peter Cotes and Thelma Niklaus. *The Little Fellow: The Life and Work of Charles Spencer Chaplin.* London: Paul Elek, 1951.

Chaplin, Charles, Jr. (with N. and M. Rau). *My Father, Charlie Chaplin.* New York: Random House, 1960.

Chaplin, Lita Grey (with Morton Cooper). *My Life With Chaplin.* New York: Bernard Geis Associates, 1966.

Chaplin, Lita Grey, and Jeffrey Vance. *Wife of the Life of the Party.* Foreword by Sydney Chaplin. Landham, Md.: Scarecrow Press, 1998.

Chaplin, Michael. *I Couldn't Smoke the Grass on My Father's Lawn.* London: Leslie Frewin, 1966.

Chaplin, Patrice. *Hidden Star: Oona O'Neil Chaplin.* London: Richard Cohen Books, 1995.

Cocteau, Jean. *My Contemporaries.* Edited and introduced by Margaret Crosland. Philadelphia: Chilton Book Company, 1968.

_____. *Tour du Monde en 80 Jours (Mon Premier Voyage).* Paris: Editions Gallimard, 1936.

Codd, Elsie. "Charlie Chaplin's Methods." In *Cinema: Practical Course in Cinema Acting in Ten Complete Lessons.* Vol. II, Lesson 2. London: Standard Art Book Company, 1920.

Collier, Constance. *Harlequinade: The Story of My Life.* Preface by Noel Coward. London: John Lane, 1929.

Comte, Michel, and Sam Stourdzé. *Charlie Chaplin: A Photo Diary.* Gottingen, Germany: Steidl, 2002.

Cooke, Alistair. "Charles Chaplin: The One and Only." In *Six Men.* New York: Alfred A. Knopf, 1977.

_____, ed. *Garbo and the Night Watchman.* London: Secker & Warburg, 1971.

Cotes, Peter and Thelma Niklaus. *The Little Fellow: The Life and Work of Charles Spencer Chaplin.* Foreword by W. Somerset Maugham. London: Paul Elek, 1951.

Davies, Marion. *The Times We Had.* Edited by Pamela Pfau and Kenneth S. Marx. Foreword by Orson Welles. Indianapolis/New York: The Bobbs-Merrill Company, Inc., 1975.

Delage, Christian. *Chaplin: La Grande Histoire.* Paris: Jean-Michel Place, 1998.

Delluc, Louis. *Charlie Chaplin.* English translation by Hamish Miles. London: John Lane/The Bodley Head, 1922.

Disher, M. Willson. *Clowns and Pantomimes.* London: Constable, 1925.

_____. *Winkles and Champagne: Comedies and Tragedies of the Music Hall.* London: Batsford, 1938.

Dreiser, Theodore. *Theodore Dreiser: American Diaries, 1902–1926.* Edited by Thomas P. Riggio. Philadelphia: University of Pennsylvania Press, 1982.

Dressler, Marie (as told to Mildred Harrington). *My Own Story.* Foreword by Will Rogers. Boston: Little, Brown, and Company, 1934.

Eastman, Max. *Great Companions: Critical Memoirs of Some Famous Friends.* New York: Farrar, Straus and Cudahy, 1959.

_____. *Love and Revolution: My Journey Through an Epoch.* New York: Random House, 1964.

Epstein, Jerry. *Remembering Charlie: The Story of a Friendship.* London: Bloomsbury, 1988.

Eyman, Scott. *Lubitsch: Laughter in Paradise.* New York: Simon & Schuster, 1993.

Fairbanks, Douglas, Jr. *The Salad Days.* New York: Doubleday, 1988.

Faure, Elie. *The Art of Cine-Plastics.* English translation by Walter Pach. Boston: The Four Seas Company, 1923.

Fawcett, L'Estrange. *Films: Facts and Forecasts.* Foreword by Charlie Chaplin. London: Geoffrey Bles, 1930.

Fiaccarini, Anna, Peter von Bagh, and Cecilia Cenciarelli. *Limelight: Documents and Essays.* Genova, Italy: Le Mani, 2002.

_____, and Michela Zegna. *The Great Dictator.* Genova, Italy: Le Mani, 2002.

Flom, Eric L. *Chaplin in the Sound Era: An Analysis of the Seven Talkies.* Jefferson, N.C.:

McFarland & Company, 1997.

Florey, Robert. *Charlie Chaplin: Ses debuts, ses films, ses aventures*, Preface by Lucien Wahl. Paris: Jean-Pascal, 1927.

_____. *Hollywood d'Hier et d'Aujourd'hui*. Paris, 1948.

Fowler, Gene. *Father Goose: The Story of Mack Sennett*. New York: Covici Friede, 1934.

Gallagher, J. P. *Fred Karno: Master of Mirth and Tears*. London: Robert Hale, 1971.

Geduld, Harry M. *Chapliniana Volume I: The Keystone Films*. Bloomington and Indianapolis: Indiana University Press, 1987.

Gehring, Wes D. *Charlie Chaplin: A Bio-Bibliography*. Westport, Conn.: Greenwood Press, 1983.

Giesler, Jerry (as told to Pete Martin). *The Jerry Giesler Story*. New York: Simon & Schuster, 1960.

Gifford, Denis. *Chaplin*. London: Macmillan, 1974.

Gilbert, Julie. *Opposite Attraction: The Lives of Erich Maria Remarque and Paulette Goddard*. New York: Pantheon, 1995.

Goldwyn, Samuel. *Behind the Screen*. New York: George H. Doran Company, 1923.

Grobel, Lawrence. *Conversations with Brando*. New York: Hyperion, 1991.

Haining, Peter, ed. *Charlie Chaplin: A Centenary Celebration*. Foreword by Dilys Powell. London: W. Foulsham & Company, 1989.

_____. *The Legend of Charlie Chaplin*. Secaucus, New Jersey: Castle, 1982.

Hale, Georgia. *Charlie Chaplin: Intimate Close-Ups*. Edited with an introduction and notes by Heather Kiernan. Metuchen, N.J.: Scarecrow Press, 1995.

Harris, Frank. *Contemporary Portraits*. Freeport, N.Y.: Brentano's, 1924.

Higham, Charles. *Hollywood Cameramen: Sources of Light*. Bloomington: Indiana University Press, 1970.

Hochman, Stanley, ed. *A Library of Film Criticism: American Film Directors*. New York: Ungar, 1974.

Hotchner, A. E. *Sophia, Living and Loving*. New York, Morrow, 1979.

Hoyt, Edwin P. *Sir Charlie*. London: Robert Hale Limited, 1977.

Huff, Theodore. *Charlie Chaplin*. New York: Henry Schuman, 1951.

Jacobs, David. *Chaplin, The Movies and Charlie*. New York: Harper & Row, 1975.

Jacobs, Lewis. *The Rise of the American Film*. New York: Harcourt, Brace & Company, 1939.

James, Eric. *Making Music With Charlie Chaplin*. Introduction by Jeffrey Vance. Lanham, Md: Scarecrow Press, 2000.

Kamin, Dan. *Charlie Chaplin's One-Man Show*. Introduction by Marcel Marceau. Metuchen, N.J.: Scarecrow Press, 1984.

Karney, Robyn and Robin Cross. *The Life and Times of Charlie Chaplin*. London: Greenwood, 1992.

Keaton, Buster (with Charles Samuels). *My Wonderful World of Slapstick*. New York: Doubleday, 1960.

Keaton, Eleanor, and Jeffrey Vance. *Buster Keaton Remembered*. New York: Harry N. Abrams, 2001.

Kerr, Walter. *The Silent Clowns*. New York: Alfred A. Knopf, 1975.

Kimber, John. *The Art of Charlie Chaplin*. Sheffield, England: Sheffield Academic Press, 2000.

Lahue, Kalton C., and Terry Brewer. *Kops and Custards: The Legend of Keystone Films*. Norman: University of Oklahoma Press, 1966.

Lane, Rose Wilder. *Charlie Chaplin's Own Story*. Edited and with an introduction by Harry M. Geduld. Bloomington and Indianapolis: Indiana University Press, 1985.

Laurents, Arthur. *Original Story By: A Memoir of Broadway and Hollywood*. New York: Alfred A. Knopf, 2000.

Leprohon, Pierre. *Charles Chaplin*. Paris: Editions Jacques Melot, 1946.

Lewis, Robert. *Slings and Arrows: Theater in My Life*. New York: Stein and Day, 1984.

Lloyd, Norman. *Stages of Life in Theatre, Film and Television*. New York: Limelight Editions, 1993.

Lourié, Eugene. *My Work in Films*. New York: Harcourt Brace Jovanovich, 1985.

Lynn, Kenneth S. *Charlie Chaplin and His Times*. New York: Simon & Schuster, 1997.

Lyons, Timothy J. *Charles Chaplin: A Guide to References and Resources*. Boston: G. K. Hall & Company, 1976.

McCabe, John. *Charlie Chaplin*. New York: Doubleday & Company, 1978.

McCaffrey, Donald W. *4 Great Comedians: Chaplin, Lloyd, Keaton, Langdon*. New York: The Tantivy Press/A.S. Barnes & Company, 1968.

_____, ed. *Focus on Chaplin*. Englewood Cliffs, N.J.: Prentice-Hall, 1971.

McDonald, Gerald D. *The Picture History of Charlie Chaplin*. New York: Nostalgia Press, 1965.

_____, Michael Conway, and Mark Ricci. *The Complete Films of Charlie Chaplin*. Secaucus, N.J.: Citadel Press, 1988.

_____. *The Films of Charlie Chaplin*. New York: Citadel Press, 1965.

Maland, Charles J. *Chaplin and American Culture: The Evolution of a Star Image*. Princeton, N.J.: Princeton University Press, 1989.

Manvell, Roger. *Chaplin*. Introduction by J. H. Plumb. Boston: Little, Brown and Company, 1975.

Mast, Gerald. *The Comic Mind: Comedy and the Movies*. Indianapolis: The Bobbs-Merrill Company, 1973.

Matthau, Carol. *Among the Porcupines*. New York: Turtle Bay/Random House, 1992.

Maugham, W. Somerset. *A Writer's Notebook*. London: William Heinemann, Ltd., 1949.

Menjou, Adolphe, and M. M. Musselman. *It Took Nine Tailors*. Foreword by Clark Gable. New York: Whittlesey House/McGraw-Hill Book Company, 1948.

Minney, R. J. *Chaplin: The Immortal Tramp*. London: George Newnes, 1954.

Mitchell, Glenn. *The Chaplin Encyclopedia*. London: B. T. Batsford, 1997.

Milton, Joyce. *Tramp: The Life of Charlie Chaplin*. New York: HarperCollins, 1996.

Mitry, Jean. *Tout Chaplin*. Paris: Editions Seghers, 1972.

Montagu, Ivor. *With Eisenstein in Hollywood*. New York: International Publishers, 1969.

Moss, Robert F. *Charlie Chaplin*. New York: Pyramid Publications, 1975.

Negri, Pola. *Memoirs of a Star*. Garden City, N.Y.: Doubleday & Company, 1970.

Nysenholc, Adolph, ed. *Charlie Chaplin: His Reflection in Modern Times*. New York: Mouton de Gruyter, 1991.

Oakie, Jack. *Jack Oakie's Double Takes*. San Francisco: Strawberry Hill Press, 1980.

Oleksy, Walter. *Laugh, Clown, Cry—The Story of Charlie Chaplin*. Milwaukee, Wis.: Raintree Editions, 1976.

Paris, Barry. *Louise Brooks*. New York: Alfred A. Knopf, 1989.

Parrish, Robert. *Growing Up in Hollywood*. New York: Harcourt Brace Jovanovich, 1976.

Payne, Robert. *The Great God Pan*. New York: Hermitage House, 1952.

Pepper, Terence. *Limelight: Photographs by James Abbe*. London: National Portrait Gallery Publications, 1995.

Pickford, Mary. *Sunshine and Shadow*. New York: Doubleday, 1955.

Pratt, George C. *Spellbound in Darkness: A History of the Silent Film*. Greenwich, Conn.: New York Graphic Society, 1973.

Quigley, Isabel. *Charlie Chaplin, Early Comedies*. London: Studio Vista/Dutton, 1968.

Ramsaye, Terry. *A Million and One Nights*. 2 vols. New York: Simon & Schuster, 1926.

Reeves, May, and Claire Goll. *The Intimate Charlie Chaplin*. Translation, editing, and introduction by Constance Brown Kuriyama. Jefferson, N.C.: McFarland & Company, 2001.

Robinson, Carlyle T. *La vérité sur Charlie Chaplin: Sa vie, ses amours, ses déboirs*. Translation by René Lulu. Paris: Société Parisienne d'Édition, 1935.

Robinson, David. *Chaplin: His Life and Art*. London: Penguin Books, 2001.

_____. *Chaplin: The Mirror of Opinion*. London: Secker & Warburg, 1983.

_____. *Charlie Chaplin: The Art of Comedy*. London: Thames and Hudson, 1996.

_____. Introduction to reprint of Charles

Chaplin, *My Autobiography*. London: Penguin Books, 2003.

Ross, Lillian. *Moments with Chaplin*. New York: Dodd, Mead & Company, 1980.

Rutherford, Margaret (as told to Gwen Robyns). *Margaret Rutherford: An Autobiography*. London: W. H. Allen, 1972.

Sadoul, Georges. *Vie de Charlot: Charles Spencer Chaplin, ses films et son temps*. Foreword by Aragon. Paris: Pierre L'Herminier, 1978.

Sarris, Andrew. *The American Cinema: Directors and Directions, 1929–1968*. New York: Dutton, 1968.

Schroeder, Alan. *Charlie Chaplin: The Beauty of Silence*. New York: Franklin Watts, 1997.

Scovell, Jane. *Oona: Living in the Shadows*. New York: Warner Books, 1998.

Seldes, Gilbert. *Movies for the Millions*. Preface by Charlie Chaplin. London: B. T. Batsford, 1937.

———. *The Seven Lively Arts*. New York: Harper & Brothers, 1924.

Sennett, Mack (as told to Cameron Shipp). *King of Comedy*. Garden City, N.Y.: Doubleday & Company, 1954.

Sheridan, Clare. *My American Diary*. New York: Boni and Liveright, 1922.

———. *Naked Truth*. New York: Harper & Brothers, 1928.

Sherwood, Robert, ed. *The Best Moving Pictures of 1922–23*. Boston: Small, Maynard & Company, 1923.

Silver, Charles. *Charles Chaplin: An Appreciation*. New York: Museum of Modern Art, 1989.

Sinclair, Upton. *Autobiography*. New York: Harcourt, Brace & World, 1962.

Smith, Julian. *Chaplin*. Boston: Twayne Publishers, 1984.

Smolik, Pierre. *Chaplin apres Charlot: 1952–1977*. Preface by Federico Fellini. Paris: Honore Champion Editeur, 1995.

Sobel, Raoul, and David Francis. *Chaplin: Genesis of a Clown*. London: Quartet Books, 1977.

Stewart, Donald Ogden. *By a Stroke of Luck! An Autobiography*. New York: Paddington Press, 1975.

Taylor, Robert Lewis. *W. C. Fields: His Follies and Fortunes*. Garden City, N.Y.: Doubleday & Company, 1949.

Tyler, Parker. *Chaplin: Last of the Clowns*. New York: Vanguard Press, 1948.

von Sternberg, Josef. *Fun in a Chinese Laundry*. New York: Macmillan, 1965.

von Ulm, Gerith. *Charlie Chaplin: King of Tragedy*. Caldwell, Id.: Caxton Printers, 1940.

Wagenknecht, Edward. *The Movies in the Age of Innocence*. Norman, Okla.: University of Oklahoma Press, 1962.

Warshow, Robert. "Charles Chaplin." In *The Immediate Experience*. Garden City, N.Y.: Doubleday, 1962.

Weinberg, Herman G. *The Lubitsch Touch*. New York: E. P. Dutton & Co., 1968.

Weissman, Stephen M. "Chaplin's *The Kid*." In *Images in Our Souls: Cavell, Psychoanalysis, and Cinema*. Edited by Joseph H. Smith and William Kerrigan. Baltimore, Md.: Johns Hopkins University Press, 1987.

Welles, Orson, and Peter Bogdanovich. *This is Orson Welles*. Edited by Jonathan Rosenbaum. Introduction by Peter Bogdanovich. New York: Da Capo Press, 1998.

Willson, Meredith. *And There I Stood with My Piccolo*. Garden City, N.Y.: Doubleday, 1948.

Woollcott, Alexander. "Charlie—As Ever Was." In *While Rome Burns*. New York: Grosset & Dunlap, 1934.

———. "Mr. Chaplin." In *Enchanted Aisles*. New York: G. P. Putnam's Sons, 1924.

Periodicals

Agee, James. "Comedy's Greatest Era." *Life* 27, no. 10 (Sept. 5, 1949): 70–82, 85–86, 88.

———. "*Monsieur Verdoux*." *Time* 49, no. 18 (May 5, 1947): 98, 100, 102.

Anderson, Gillian. "The Music of *The Circus*." *Library of Congress Information Bulletin* 52, no. 17 (Sept. 20, 1993): 340–49.

"An Irked Chaplin Calls Critics 'Bloody Idiots.'" *New York Times*. Jan. 7, 1967, p. 22.

Baker, Peter. "Clown with a Frown." *Films and Filming* 3, no. 11 (Aug. 1957): 7–9.

Bakshy, Alexander. "A Knight-Errant." *Dial* 84, no. 5 (May 1928): 413–14.

———. "Charlie Chaplin Falters." *The Nation* 132, no. 3426 (Mar. 4, 1931): 250–51.

Bercovici, Konrad. "Charlie Chaplin: An Authorized Interview." *Collier's* (Aug. 15, 1925).

———. "A Day with Charlie Chaplin." *Harper's Monthly Magazine* 158 (Dec. 1928): 42.

Bergen, Candice. "I Thought They Might Hiss." *Life* 72, no. 15 (Apr. 21, 1972): 90.

Berglund, Bo. "The Day the Tramp Was Born." *Sight and Sound* 58, no. 2 (spring 1989): 106–12.

Bentley, Eric. "Chaplin's Mea Culpa." *New Republic* 127, no. 20 (Nov. 17, 1952): 30–31.

———. "Charlie Chaplin and Peggy Hopkins Joyce: A Comment on *A Woman of Paris*." *Moviegoer* (summer 1966): 10–18.

———. "*Monsieur Verdoux* as Theatre." *Kenyon Review* 10 (1948): 705–16.

Biby, Edward Allan. "How Pictures Found Charlie Chaplin." *Photoplay* 15, no. 4 (Apr. 1919): 70–71, 105.

"Big Rental Films of 1967." *Variety* 249, no. 7 (Jan. 3, 1968): 25.

Bonheur, Gaston. "Charlot." *Paris Match* (Jan. 6, 1978): 52–73.

Brooks, Louise. "Charlie Chaplin Remembered." *Film Culture* 40 (spring 1966): 5–6.

Brownlow, Kevin. "The Early Days of Charlie Chaplin." *Film* 40 (1964): 12–15.

———. "On the Trail of the Unknown Chaplin." *American Film* 9, no. 10 (Sept. 1984): 24–26, 28.

———. "Watching Chaplin Direct *A Countess from Hong Kong*." *Film Culture* 40 (spring 1966): 2–4.

———. "When Cinema Left the Nursery." *Time Out* 548 (Oct. 17–23, 1980): 45.

Capp, Al. "The Comedy of Charlie Chaplin." *Atlantic Monthly* 185 (Feb. 1950): 25–29.

Chaplin, Charles. "A Comedian Sees the World." *Woman's Home Companion* 9–12, 1, nos. 60–61 (Sept.–Dec. 1933; Jan. 1934).

———. "Does the Public Know What it Wants?" *Adelphi*. 1, no. 8 (Jan. 1924): 702–10.

———. "How I Made My Success." *The Theatre* 22 (Sept. 1915): 120–21,142.

———. "In Defense of Myself." *Collier's* 70, no. 2 (Nov. 11, 1922): 8,18.

———. "Mr. Chaplin Answers His Critics." *New York Times*. Oct. 27, 1940, sect. 9, p. 5.

———. "Nocturne." *Rob Wagner's Script*. 12, no. 292 (Nov. 10, 1934): 3.

———. "Pantomime and Comedy." *New York Times*. Jan. 25, 1931, sect. 8, p. 6.

Chaplin, Charlie. "What People Laugh At." *American Magazine*. 86 (Nov. 1918): 34, 134–37.

Chaplin, Sydney. "The Truth About My Father." *Sunday Chronicle*. Sept. 21, 1952, p. 7.

———. "Father Makes a Film." *Everybody's Weekly*. Oct. 18, 1952, pp. 22–23.

"Chaplin Signs with Mutual." *Moving Picture World* 27, no. 10 (Mar. 11, 1916): 1622.

"Charlie Chaplin: A Doubt." *The New Statesman* 17, no. 440 (Sept. 17, 1921): 643–44.

"Charlie Chaplin: Comic Genius of the Cinema Screen" (obituary). *The Times*. Dec. 28, 1977, p. 10.

Churchill, Winston. "Everybody's Language." *Collier's* 96, no. 17 (Oct. 26, 1935): 24, 37–38.

Clurman, Harold. "Oona, Oxford, America and the Book." *Esquire* LVIII, no. 5 (Nov. 1962): 86, 181–84.

"Comments on the Films: *Making a Living*." *Moving Picture World* 19, no. 6 (Feb. 7, 1914): 678.

Cooke, Alistair. "Charlie Chaplin." *The Atlantic Monthly* 164 (Aug. 1939): 176–85.

Crowther, Bosley. "*A Countess from Hong Kong*." *New York Times*. Mar. 17, 1967, p. 35.

———. "*The Great Dictator*." *New York Times*. Oct. 16, 1940, sect. 1, p. 29.

———. "How Hath the Mighty?" *New York Times*. Mar. 26, 1967, sect. 2, pp. 1, 7.

———. "The Modern—Mellower—Times of Mr. Chaplin." *New York Times Magazine*. Nov. 6, 1960, pp. 52–60.

Darnton, Charles. "The Woman Who Found Charlie Chaplin." *Photoplay* 46, no. 3 (Aug. 1934): 27, 110–11.

Davis, Victor. "Charlie—Shattering That Chaplin Myth . . ." *Daily Express*. Jan. 11, 1972, p. 8.

De Jongh, Nicholas. "Clown Who Would Not

Conform." *The Guardian*. Dec. 28, 1977, pp. 1, 4.

Dehn, Paul. "It's All There in Chaplin's Museum." *News Chronicle*. Sept. 13, 1957, p. 6.

_____. "Little Tramp Judges the Modern World." *News Chronicle*. Sept. 11, 1957, p. 7.

Dyer, Peter John. "The True Face of Man." *Films and Filming* 4, no. 12 (Sept. 1958): 13–15, 32–33.

Eisenstein, Sergei M. "Charlie the Grown Up." *Sight and Sound* 15, no. 58 (summer 1946): 53–55.

_____. "Charlie the Kid." *Sight and Sound* 15, no. 57 (spring 1946): 12–14.

_____. "The New Language of Cinematography." *Close-Up* (May 1929): 10–12.

Fiske, Minnie Maddern. "The Art of Charles Chaplin." *Harper's Weekly* LXII (May 6, 1916): 494.

Francke, Linda Bird. "Life with Charlie." *Interview* (Sept. 1989): 83–86.

Frank, Waldo. "Charles Chaplin: A Portrait." *Scribner's Magazine* LXXXVI, no. 3 (Sept. 1929): 237–45.

Gardiner, Reginald. "The Pleasure of Meeting a Dictator." *New York Herald Tribune*. Sept. 16, 1940.

Gill, David. "*The Gold Rush*: 1925–1942–1993." *Griffithiana* 18, no. 54 (Oct. 1995): 123–31.

Gittelson, Natalie. "My Father, Charlie Chaplin." *McCall's* CV, 6 (Mar. 1978): 80, 82,187–88.

Goodman, Paul. "Chaplin Again Again and Again." *Partisan Review* 7, no. 6 (Nov.–Dec. 1940): 456–59.

Greene, Graham. "*Modern Times*." *The Spectator*. Feb. 14, 1936, p. 254.

Hackett, Francis. "*The Kid*." *The New Republic* 26 (Mar. 30, 1921): 136–37.

Hall, Gladys. "Charlie Chaplin Attacks the Talkies." *Motion Picture Magazine* 37 (May 1929): 29.

Hall, Mordaunt. "A Chat with Chaplin." *New York Times*. July 14, 1929, sect. 9, p. 4.

_____. "Charlie Chaplin's New Comedy." *New York Times*. Aug. 17, 1925.

_____. "Shy Charlie Chaplin Opens His Heart." *New York Times*. Aug. 9, 1925.

Hamblin, Dora Jane. "The Passionate Clown Comes Back." *Life* 60, no. 13 (Apr. 1, 1966): 80–86.

Hamilton, Jack. "Charlie and His Countess." *Look* 30, no. 8 (Apr. 19, 1966): 96–100, 103–4.

Hinxman, Margaret. "An Interview with Chaplin." *Sight and Sound* 27, no. 2 (autumn 1957): 76–78.

Hirschfeld, Al. "A Man with Both Feet in the Clouds." *New York Times Magazine*. July 26, 1942, pp. 12, 29.

Houston, Penelope. "*A King in New York*: A Review." *Sight and Sound* 27, no. 2 (autumn 1957): 78–79.

Howard, Philip. "Sir Charles Silenced by Solemnity." *The Times*, Mar. 5, 1975, p. 1.

Huff, Theodore. "*Limelight*." *Films in Review* 3, no. 9 (Nov. 1952): 466–70.

Ingram, Rex. "Art Advantages of the European Scene." *Theatre Magazine* (Jan. 1928): 24.

Irwin, Bill. "How a Classic Clown Keeps Inspiring Comedy." *New York Times*. Apr. 9, 1989, sect. 2, pp. 1, 20.

Jaffe, Ira S. "Chaplin's Labor of Performance: *The Circus* and *Limelight*." *Literature/Film Quarterly* 12, no. 3 (1984): 202–10.

Johnson, Julian. "The Shadow Stage" (review of *The Immigrant*). *Photoplay* 12, no. 4 (Sept. 1917): 99–100.

Kanfer, Stefan. "Re-enter Charlie Chaplin, Smiling and Waiving." *Time* 99, no. 15 (Apr. 10, 1972): 65–66.

Kauffmann, Stanley. "Chaplin's *The Gold Rush*." *Horizon* XV, no. 3 (summer 1973): 40–47.

Keaton, Buster. "Chaplin." *La revue du cinema* no. 265 (Nov. 1972): 26–27.

_____. "Me gusta destruirlo todo." *Griffith* no. 2 (Nov. 1965): 15–21.

Kerr, Walter. "The Lineage of *Limelight*." *Theatre Arts* 36 (Nov. 1952): 73–75.

_____. "Spinning Reels of Memory on a Master's Centenary." *New York Times*. Apr. 9, 1989, sect. 2, pp. 1, 20–21.

Kroll, Jack. "Voluptuous Silence." *Newsweek* (Jan. 10, 1977): 65.

Kuriyama, Constance Brown. "Chaplin's Impure Comedy: The Art of Survival." *Film Quarterly* 45, no. 3 (spring 1992): 26–38.

Lambert, Gavin. "The Elegant Melancholy of Twilight." *Sight and Sound* 22, no. 3 (Jan.–Mar. 1953): 123–27.

Lane, John Francis. "My Life as Chaplin's Leading Lady" (interview with Dawn Addams). *Films and Filming* 3, no. 11 (Aug. 1957): 12–13, 15.

Lauterbach, Richard E. "The Whys of Chaplin's Appeal." *New York Times Magazine*. May 21, 1950, pp. 24–25, 32–33.

Lee, Raymond. "I Was a Chaplin Kid." *Movie Digest* (Sept. 1972): 36–47.

"*Limelight*: Mr. Chaplin's New Film." *The Times*. Oct. 15, 1952, p. 8.

Lyons, Timothy J. "The United States v. Charlie Chaplin." *American Film* 9, no. 10 (Sept. 1984): 29–30, 32–34.

_____, et al. "Chaplin and Sound." *Journal of the University Film Association* 31, no. 1 (winter 1979): 1–50.

McGuirk, Charles J. "Chaplinitis." *Motion Picture Magazine* 9–10, nos. 6–7 (July–Aug. 1915): 121–24, 85–89.

McWhirter, William A. "Grand Rerun for Charlie Chaplin." *Life* 71, no. 23 (Dec. 3, 1971): 93–96.

Malcolm, Derek, and Richard Roud. "The Baggy-Trousered Philanthropist." *The Guardian*. Dec. 28, 1977, p. 3.

Maltin, Leonard. "Silent-film Buffs Stalk and Find a Missing Tramp." *Smithsonian* 17, no. 4 (July 1986): 46–57.

Manning, Harold (edited with notes by Timothy J.

Lyons). "Charlie Chaplin's Early Life: Fact and Fiction." *Historical Journal of Film, Radio and Television* 3, no. 1 (Mar. 1983): 35–41.

Mathieu, Thierry Georges. *La Naissance de Charlot: Keystone 1914* nos. 1–11 (1999–2003).

Meryman, Richard. "Ageless Master's Anatomy of Comedy." *Life* 62, no. 10 (Mar. 10, 1967): 80–84, 86, 89–94.

_____. "Love Feast for Charlie." *Life* 72, no. 15 (Apr. 21, 1972): 86–89.

Morgan, Gene. "Where Are Chicago's Big Shoes? Charlie Chaplin, Movie Laugh Maker, Asks You." *The Chicago Herald*. Jan. 10, 1915.

Morgenstern, Joe. "The Custard Pie of Creation." *Newsweek* LXVII, no. 23 (June 6, 1966): 90–94.

Mulchrone, Vincent. "Meet Sir Charles, the Knight in Blue Suede Shoes." *Daily Mail*, Mar. 5, 1975, p. 3.

O'Donnell, James P. "Charlie Chaplin's Stormy Exile." *Saturday Evening Post*. Mar. 8, 15, and 21, 1953.

O'Higgins, Harvey. "Charlie Chaplin's Art." *The New Republic* 10, no. 118 (Feb. 3, 1917): 16–18.

Osborne, John. "Chaplin Aims a Kick at America." *The Evening Standard*. Sept. 12, 1957, p. 6.

"Playing Golf with Charlie Chaplin." *Toronto Star Weekly*. May 7, 1921.

Pryor, Thomas M. "How Mr. Chaplin Makes a Movie." *New York Times Magazine*. Feb. 17, 1952, pp. 18–19, 22.

Quirk, James. "A Letter to a Genius" (editorial). *Photoplay* 17, no. 5 (Apr. 1920): 27.

Raksin, David. "Life with Charlie." *The Quarterly Journal of the Library of Congress* 40, no. 3 (summer 1983): 234–53.

Ramsaye, Terry. "Chaplin—and How He Does It." *Photoplay* 12, no. 4 (Sept. 1917): 19–23, 138–39.

Reid, Laurence. "The Movie of the Month." *Motion Picture Classic* 18, no. 5 (Jan. 1924): 47, 92–93.

Robinson, Carlyle T. "The Private Life of Charlie Chaplin." Originally published in *Liberty* July 29, 1933. Reprinted in *Liberty* 1, no. 7 (winter 1972): 23–49.

Robinson, David. "Chaplin Meets the Press." *Sight and Sound* 35, no. 1 (winter 1965–1966): 20.

_____. "The Clown for All Times." *The Times*. Feb. 28, 1976, p. 6.

_____. "Entrance of a Movie Legend." *The Times*. Jan. 9, 1989, p. 14.

_____. "The Film That Chaplin Hid for Fifty Years." *Sunday Times Magazine*. Oct. 5, 1980, pp. 28–32, 35.

_____. "*A Woman of Paris*." *Sight and Sound* 48, no. 4 (autumn 1980): 221–23.

Roemer, Michael. "Chaplin: Charles and Charlie." *Yale Review* 64 (1974): 158–84.

Rothwell, Bruce. "Chaplin Tells Film Secret." *News Chronicle*. Sept. 23, 1952, pp. 1, 5.

_____. "One Big Day in 3 Reels." *News Chronicle*. Sept. 24, 1952, p. 3.

Rubin, Jay. "Jay Rubin Interviews Jackie Coogan." *Classic Film Collector* no. 52 (fall 1976): 6–9.

Sandilands, John. "The Clown of the Century." *Radio Times* (Dec. 14–21, 1972): 16–17.

Sands, Frederick. "Oona." *The American Weekly* (June 19, 1960): 7–10.

———. "Why I Love Oona." *Daily Herald.* Apr. 16, 1959, p. 6.

Schallert, Edwin. "A Forecast for 1925." *Picture Play Magazine* 21, no. 6 (Feb. 1925): 19.

———. "Trick Photography in *The Gold Rush.*" *Science and Invention* (Dec. 1925): 714–15.

———, and Elza Schallert. "Hollywood High Lights." *Picture Play* 19, no. 5 (Jan. 1924): 66–68.

Schickel, Richard. "Hail Chaplin—The Early Chaplin." *New York Times Magazine,* Apr. 2, 1972, pp. 12–13, 47–48.

Seldes, Gilbert. "A Chaplin Masterpiece." *The New Republic* 66, no. 847 (Feb. 25, 1931): 46–47.

Shivas, Mark. "The Kid from Kennington." *The Guardian,* Feb. 8, 1972, p. 10.

Silver, Charles, et al. "Charlie Chaplin: Faces and Facets." *Film Comment* 8, no. 3 (Sept.–Oct. 1972): 8–28.

Slide, Anthony. "The American Press and Public versus Charles Spencer Chaplin." *Cineaste* (winter 1984): 6–9.

Smith, Edward H. "Charlie Chaplin's Million Dollar Walk." *McClure's* 47 (July 1916): 26.

Smith, Frederick James. "The Tragic Comedian." *Shadowland* 5, no. 3 (Nov. 1921): 51, 76.

Smith, Tom, and John South. "Charlie Chaplin a Sad and Helpless Cripple at 88." *National Enquirer* 52, no. 16 (Nov. 29, 1977): 28.

Smith, W. Eugene. "Chaplin at Work" (photographic essay with unsigned text). *Life* 32, no. 11 (Mar. 17, 1952): 117–27.

Steffens, Peter. "Chaplin: The Victorian Tramp." *Ramparts* 3, no. 6 (Mar. 1965): 16–24.

Taves, Brian. "Charlie Dearest." *Film Comment* 24, no. 2 (Mar.–April 1988): 63–66, 68–69.

Taylor, John Russell. "A Disappointing Film from Chaplin." *The Times.* No. 56,832. January 6, 1967, 14.

———. "In the Studios with Charlie Chaplin." *The Times.* Mar. 17, 1966, p. 18.

"*The Times* Diary: Stand-In." *The Times.* Nov. 10, 1969, p. 10.

"Time to Retire." *Time* 89, no. 13 (Mar. 31, 1967): 95.

"To Be, or Not to Be." *New York Times.* Nov. 29, 1925, sect. 7, p. 5.

Totheroh, Roland. "Roland H. Totheroh Interviewed. Chaplin Films." Timothy J. Lyons, ed. *Film Culture* 53–55 (spring 1972): 230–85.

Tully, Jim. "Charle Chaplin: His *Real* Life Story." *Pictorial Review* XXVIII, nos. 4–7 (Jan.–Apr. 1927).

Tynan, Kenneth. "Looking Back in Anger." *The Observer.* Sept. 15, 1957, p. 13.

Van Gelder, Robert. "Chaplin Draws a Keen Weapon." *New York Times Magazine.* Sept. 8, 1940, sect. 7, pp. 8–9, 22.

Vance, Jeffrey. "*The Circus*: A Chaplin Masterpiece." *Film History* 8, no. 2 (1996): 186–208.

Wagner, Rob. "Charles Spencer Chaplin: The Man You Don't Know." *Ladies Home Journal* (Jan. 1918).

Walker, Alexander. "Sad Verdict on *A Countess*—Charlie is Let Down by Words." *The Evening Standard.* Jan. 5, 1967, p. 14.

Wallach, George. "Charlie Chaplin's *Monsieur Verdoux* Press Conference." *Film Comment* 5 (winter 1969): 34–42.

Weddle, David, et al. "Charlie Chaplin: Cinema's First Genius." *Variety* (Special Supplement) (Apr. 28–May 4, 2003): 1–24.

Weissman, Stephen M. "Charlie Chaplin's Film Heroines." *Film History* 8, no. 4 (1996): 439–44.

———. "What Made Charlie Run?" *Los Angeles Times.* Apr. 16, 1989, pp. 18, 88.

"What Chaplin Thinks." *New York Times.* Oct. 7, 1923, sect. 9, p. 4.

Whitaker, Alma. "The New Edna Purviance." *Los Angeles Times.* Oct. 21, 1923.

Whitman, Alden. "Charlie Chaplin Dead at 88; Made the Film an Art Form." *New York Times.* Dec. 26, 1977, pp. 1, 28–29.

Wilson, Edmund. "The New Chaplin Comedy." *The New Republic* 44, no. 561 (Sept. 2, 1925): 45–46.

Winter, Ella. "But It's Sad, Says Chaplin, It's Me." *The Observer.* Sept. 15, 1957, p. 4.

———. "Charles Chaplin." *Labour Monthly* 60, no. 2 (Mar./Apr. 1978): 118–19,122–26.

"The World in Crisis in Dumb Show." *New York Times.* Apr. 15, 1932, p. 20.

Wyndham, Francis. "Chaplin on the Critics, the Beatles, the Mood of London." *The Sunday Times.* Mar. 26, 1967, p. 10.

Interviews

Berle, Milton. Interviewed by Jeffrey Vance, 1998.

Blanke, Henry. Interviewed by Sue McConachy, 1976.

Bloom, Claire. Interviewed by Jeffrey Vance, 1993, 1999, 2002.

Boardman, True, Jr. Interviewed by Jeffrey Vance, 2002.

Brown, Phil. Interviewed by Jeffrey Vance, 1999.

Brownlow, Kevin and David Gill. Interviewed by Jeffrey Vance, 1991, 1995.

Chaplin, Annette. Interviewed by Jeffrey Vance, 2002.

Chaplin, Charles. Interviewed by Richard Meryman, 1966, 1972.

Chaplin, Christopher. Interviewed by Jeffrey Vance, 2002.

Chaplin, Eugene. Interviewed by Jeffrey Vance, 2002.

Chaplin, Geraldine. Interviewed by Jeffrey Vance, 2002.

Chaplin, Jane. Interviewed by Jeffrey Vance, 2000.

Chaplin, Josephine. Interviewed by Jeffrey Vance, 2002.

Chaplin, Lita Grey. Interviewed by Jeffrey Vance, 1993–95.

Chaplin, Michael. Interviewed by Jeffrey Vance, 1997–98.

Chaplin, Sydney. Interviewed by Jeffrey Vance, 1995–2002.

Chaplin, Victoria. Interviewed by Jeffrey Vance, 2002.

Clark, Petula. Interviewed by Jeffrey Vance, 2000.

Coghlan, Frank. Interviewed by Jeffrey Vance, 1998.

Coogan, Anthony. Interviewed by Jeffrey Vance, 1996.

Coogan, Jackie. Interviewed by Kevin Brownlow, 1977.

Cooke, Alistair. Interviewed by Jeffrey Vance, 1993, 1996.

Davis, Carl. Interviewed by Jeffrey Vance, 1996.

DeHaven, Gloria. Interviewed by Jeffrey Vance, 2002.

Durant, Tim. Interviewed by Kevin Brownlow, 1980.

Epstein, Jerry. Interviewed by Jeffrey Vance, 1991.

Evans, Wyn Ritchie. Interviewed by Jeffrey Vance, 1998.

Fairbanks, Douglas, Jr. Interviewed by Jeffrey Vance, 1993–95.

Flowers, Bess. Interviewed by Kevin Brownlow, 1981.

Gish, Lillian. Interviewed by Jeffrey Vance, 1991.

Hale, Georgia. Interviewed by Kevin Brownlow, 1981.

Hathaway, Silas. Interviewed by Jeffrey Vance, 2002.

Hayden, Melissa. Interviewed by Jeffrey Vance, 2002.

Hedren, Tippi. Interviewed by Jeffrey Vance, 1994.

Hirschfeld, Al. Interviewed by Jeffrey Vance, 2001.

James, Dan. Interviewed by David Robinson, 1983.

James, Eric. Interviewed by Jeffrey Vance, 1998–2002.

Jones, Chuck. Interviewed by Jeffrey Vance, 1999.

Keaton, Eleanor. Interviewed by Jeffrey Vance, 1998.

Lloyd, Norman. Interviewed by Jeffrey Vance, 1996, 1999, 2002.

Loren, Sophia. Interviewed by Jeffrey Vance, 1996.

Ludwig, Julian. Interviewed by Jeffrey Vance, 1997.

Marceau, Marcel. Interviewed by Jeffrey Vance, 2002.

Martini, Virginia Cherrill. Interviewed by Jeffrey Vance, 1995–96.

Nash, Marilyn. Interviewed by Jeffrey Vance, 1997–98.

Parrish, Robert. Interviewed by Jeffrey Vance, 1991.

Patterson, Richard. Interviewed by Jeffrey Vance, 2002.

Paumier, Pamela. Interviewed by Jeffrey Vance, 2002.

Raksin, David. Interviewed by Jeffrey Vance, 1995–2001.

Riesner, Dean. Interviewed by Jeffrey Vance, 1995–2000.

Roach, Hal. Interviewed by Jeffrey Vance, 1991.

Robinson, David. Interviewed by Jeffrey Vance, 1998, 2002.

Rogers, Charles "Buddy," Interviewed by Jeffrey Vance, 1997.

Rothman, Mo. Interviewed by Jeffrey Vance, 1998

Schallert, William. Interviewed by Jeffrey Vance, 1996.

Self, William. Interviewed by Jeffrey Vance, 1997.

Sutherland, A. Edward. Interviewed by Bob and Joan Franklin, 1959.

Tetrick, Betty Chaplin. Interviewed by Jeffrey Vance, 2000–02.

Tetrick, Paul Drew (Ted). Interviewed by Jeffrey Vance, 1993.

Totheroth, R. Jack. Interviewed by Jeffrey Vance, 1996.

Wallis, Shani. Interviewed by Jeffrey Vance, 1994.

Miscellaneous

Agreement between Charles Chaplin and Essanay Film Manufacturing Company, 1914.

Agreement between Charles Chaplin and First National Exhibitors' Circuit, Inc. June 17, 1917, and Amended agreement between Charles Chaplin and Associated First National Picture Company, Dec. 3, 1920.

Agreement between Charles Chaplin and Fred Karno, Feb. 21, 1908. David Robinson Collection.

Agreement between Charles Chaplin and Keystone Film Company, Sept. 25, 1913.

Agreement between Charles Chaplin and Lone Star Film Corporation, Mar. 9, 1916.

BBC Programme with Charles Chaplin, Oct. 15, 1952, BBC Sound Archives.

BBC Radio transatlantic telephone broadcast by Charles Chaplin, Mar. 5, 1943.

Berry v. Chaplin, 169 P.2d 442 (1946).

Biby, Edward Allen. "Charlie Chaplin was Framed." Unpublished typescript, c. 1921, Seaver Center for Western History Research, Natural History Museum of Los Angeles County.

British Foreign Office documents pertaining to Chaplin's knighthood, 1956–71, Public Record Office, London.

Brownlow, Kevin. "The Search for Charlie Chaplin." Unpublished typescript.

Chaplin, Charles. "Between You & Me." Criterion Theatre souvenir program for A Woman of Paris, Sept. 26, 1923.

———. Bound Scripts. Chaplin Archives.

———. "Footlights." Unpublished novel, 1948 (with annotations). Chaplin Archives.

———. The Freak. Unproduced script, c. 1974 (with annotations). Chaplin Archives.

———. A Woman of Paris program notes. Lyric Theatre souvenir program for A Woman of Paris, Oct. 1, 1923.

Chaplin Studios Daily Production Reports. Chaplin Archives.

Chaplin Studios Inventory of Vaults, April 1, 1946. Chaplin Archives.

Chaplin Studios Projection Log Book. Chaplin Archives.

Chaplin v. Vitagraph-Lubin-Selig-Essanay, Inc., and the Essanay Film Manufacturing Company, 1916.

Charles Chaplin Clipping Books. Chaplin Archives.

Charles Chaplin Notes. Chaplin Archives.

Charles Chaplin Unrealized Projects. Chaplin Archives.

Charlie Chaplin Research Foundation, British Film Institute.

Lita Grey Chaplin Collection (Jeffrey Vance Collection).

A Countess from Hong Kong documents and agreements. Chaplin Archives.

Crocker, Harry. "Charlie Chaplin: Man and Mime." Unpublished typescript. Harry Crocker Collection, Margaret Herrick Library, Academy of Motion Picture Arts and Sciences.

Jerry Epstein Collection, British Film Institute.

Eriksson, Lennart. "Books on/by Chaplin: An International Bibliography." Lennart Eriksson: Vasteras, Sweden, 1989.

Federal Bureau of Investigation, Immigration and Naturalization Service, Office of the Attorney General, Bureau of the Budget, and Criminal Division, Department of Justice records pertaining to Charles Chaplin, available through the Freedom of Information Act.

Robert Florey Collection, Margaret Herrick Library, Academy of Motion Picture Arts and Sciences.

Gehring, Wes D. "Charlie Chaplin's World of Comedy." Ball State University, monograph no. 30. Munice, Indiana: Ball State University, 1980.

Paulette Goddard Collection, Tisch School of the Arts, Film Studies Program, and Paulette Goddard Remarque Estate Collection, New York University.

Huff, Theodore. "The Early Work of Charles Chaplin." London: British Film Institute, 1961 (first published by the British Film Institute in 1945 in the periodical Sight and Sound).

Inman Hunter Collection, British Film Institute.

Fred Karno Companies brochure. Jeffrey Vance Collection.

Stan Laurel Collection, Seaver Center for Western History Research, Natural History Museum of Los Angeles County.

London Metropolitan Archives.

Edward Manson Collection, Margaret Herrick Library, Academy of Motion Picture Arts and Sciences.

Metro-Goldwyn-Mayer Archives (post-1952 United Artists Collection).

Ivor Montagu Collection, British Film Institute.

Richard Patterson memorandum to Jeffrey Vance, Aug. 29, 2002.

Paumier, Pamela, and David Robinson. "Chaplin: 100 Years, 100 Images, 100 Documents." Pordenone, Italy: Le Giornate del Cinema Muto, 1989.

Mary Pickford Collection, Margaret Herrick Library, Academy of Motion Picture Arts and Sciences.

Pressbooks for The Chaplin Revue, The Circus, City Lights, City Lights (1950 reissue), A Countess from Hong Kong, The Gold Rush, The Great Dictator, A King in New York, Limelight, Modern Times, Monsieur Verdoux, A Woman of Paris.

Dean Riesner scrapbook, 1934.

Riesner, Dean, and Jeffrey Vance. "Remembering The Pilgrim." Unpublished typescript, 2000.

Jess Robbins Collection, Cinema-Television Library, University of Southern California.

Robinson, David. "Charlie Chaplin: 100 Years." London: Museum of the Moving Image, 1989.

Victor Saville Collection, British Film Institute.

Mack Sennett Collection, Margaret Herrick Library, Academy of Motion Picture Arts and Sciences.

Sheaffer-O'Neill Collection, Connecticut College.

Rollie Totheroh Collection, Seaver Center for Western History Research, Natural History Museum of Los Angeles County.

Jim Tully Papers (collection 250). Department of Special Collections, Young Research Library, University of California, Los Angeles.

United Artists Collection, Wisconsin Center for Film and Theater Research, Wisconsin State Historical Library, Madison.

Rob Wagner Papers (collection 690). Department of Special Collections, Young Research Library, University of California, Los Angeles.

Jack L. Warner Collection, Cinema-Television Library, University of Southern California.

Filmography

The Keystone Films

MAKING A LIVING
Released: Feb. 2, 1914 (Finished and shipped: Jan. 14, 1914). Distributed by: Mutual Film Corporation. Produced by: Keystone Film Company. Length: one reel. Photography: E. J. Vallejo. Producer: Mack Sennett. Director: Henry Lehrman. Cast: Charles Chaplin (Sharper), Henry Lehrman (Reporter), Virginia Kirtley (Girl), Alice Davenport (Mother), Chester Conklin (Police officer)

KID AUTO RACES AT VENICE
Released: Feb. 7, 1914 (Finished and shipped: Jan. 17, 1914). Distributed by: Mutual Film Corporation. Produced by: Keystone Film Company. Length: split reel (released with an interest film, *Olives and Their Oil*). Photography: Frank D. Williams. Scenario: Henry Lehrman. Producer: Mack Sennett. Director: Henry Lehman. Cast: Charles Chaplin (Tramp), Henry Lehrman (Film director), Frank D. Williams (Cameraman)

MABEL'S STRANGE PREDICAMENT
Released: Feb. 9, 1914 (Finished and shipped: Jan. 20, 1914). Distributed by: Mutual Film Corporation. Produced by: Keystone Film Company. Length: one reel. Photography: Hans Koenekamp. Scenario: Reed Heustis. Producer: Mack Sennett. Director: Mabel Normand. Cast: Charles Chaplin (Tramp), Mabel Normand (Mabel), Chester Conklin (Husband), Alice Davenport (Wife), Harry McCoy (Lover), Al St. John (Hotel manager), Billy Gilbert (Bellman)

BETWEEN SHOWERS
Released: Feb. 28, 1914 (Finished and shipped: Feb. 7, 1914). Distributed by: Mutual Film Corporation. Produced by: Keystone Film Company. Length: one reel. Scenario: Henry Lehrman. Producer: Mack Sennett. Director: Henry Lehrman. Cast: Charles Chaplin (Masher), Ford Sterling (Rival masher), Chester Conklin (Police officer), Emma Clifton (Girl), Sadie Lampe (Police officer's lady friend)

A FILM JOHNNIE
Released: Mar. 2, 1914 (Finished and shipped: Feb. 11, 1914). Distributed by: Mutual Film Corporation. Produced by: Keystone Film Company. Length: one reel. Scenario: Craig Hutchinson. Producer: Mack Sennett. Director: George Nichols. Cast: Charles Chaplin (Film johnnie), Roscoe Arbuckle (Fatty), Edgar Kennedy (Director), Virginia Kirtley (Key-stone girl), Minta Durfee (Cinema patron), Ford Sterling (Ford), Harry McCoy (Belligerent cinema patron), Hank Mann (Stagehand), Mack Sennett (Himself), Henry Lehrman (Himself), George Nichols (Older man on screen), Billy Gilbert (Usher)

TANGO TANGLES
Released: Mar. 9, 1914 (Finished and shipped: Feb. 17, 1914). Distributed by: Mutual Film Corporation. Produced by: Keystone Film Company. Length: one reel. Scenario: Mack Sennett. Producer: Mack Sennett. Director: Mack Sennett. Cast: Charles Chaplin (Drunk), Ford Sterling (Band leader), Roscoe Arbuckle (Musician), Edgar Kennedy (Dance-hall manager), Chester Conklin (Dancer in police-officer costume), Minta Durfee (Dancer), Alice Davenport (Dancer), Al St. John (Guest in convict uniform), Glen Cavender (Drummer and Dancer in pointed hat), Hank Mann (Dancer), Billy Gilbert (Guest in cowboy hat)

HIS FAVORITE PASTIME
Released: Mar. 16, 1914 (Finished and shipped: Feb. 19, 1914). Distributed by: Mutual Film Corporation. Produced by: Keystone Film Company. Length: one reel. Scenario: Craig Hutchinson. Producer: Mack Sennett. Director: George Nichols. Cast: Charles Chaplin (Drunk), Roscoe Arbuckle (Drunk), Peggy Pearce (Wife), Edgar Kennedy (Drinking friend), Harry McCoy (Man at bar), Gene Marsh (Member of household), Billy Gilbert (Shoeshine man)

CRUEL, CRUEL LOVE
Released: Mar. 26, 1914 (Finished and shipped: Mar. 5, 1914). Distributed by: Mutual Film Corporation. Produced by: Keystone Film Company. Length: one reel. Scenario: Craig Hutchinson. Producer: Mack Sennett. Director: George Nichols. Cast: Charles Chaplin (Mr. Dovey), Minta Durfee (Minta), Edgar Kennedy (Butler), Glen Cavender (Doctor), Billy Gilbert (Ambulance attendant)

THE STAR BOARDER
Released: Apr. 4, 1914 (Finished and shipped: Mar. 19, 1914). Distributed by: Mutual Film Corporation. Produced by: Keystone Film Company. Length: one reel. Scenario: Craig Hutchinson. Producer: Mack Sennett. Director: George Nichols. Cast: Charles Chaplin (Boarder), Minta Durfee (Landlady), Edgar Kennedy (Landlord), Gordon Griffith (Son), Alice Davenport (Boarder), Harry McCoy (Boarder assisting magic lantern show), Billy Gilbert (Boarder)

MABEL AT THE WHEEL
Released: Apr. 18, 1914 (Finished and shipped: Mar. 31, 1914). Distributed by: Mutual Film Corporation. Produced by: Keystone Film Company. Length: two reels. Scenario: Mabel Normand, Mack Sennett. Producer: Mack Sennett. Directors: Mabel Normand, Mack Sennett. Cast: Charles Chaplin (Villain), Mabel Normand (Mabel), Harry McCoy (Mabel's boyfriend, a car racer) Chester Conklin (Mabel's father), Mack Sennett (Rube), Edgar Kennedy (Man in stands), Bill Hauber (Mabel's co-driver), Mack Swain (Spectator), Alice Davenport (Spectator)

TWENTY MINUTES OF LOVE
Released: Apr. 20, 1914 (Finished and shipped: Mar. 28, 1914). Distributed by: Mutual Film Corporation. Produced by: Keystone Film Company. Length: one reel. Editor: Charles Chaplin. Scenario: Charles Chaplin. Producer: Mack Sennett. Director: Charles Chaplin. Cast: Charles Chaplin (Tramp), Minta Durfee (Woman), Chester Conklin (Lover who pickpockets), Edgar Kennedy (Lover), Josef Swickard (Victim)

CAUGHT IN A CABARET
Released: Apr. 27, 1914 (Finished and shipped: Apr. 11, 1914). Distributed by: Mutual Film Corporation. Produced by: Keystone Film Company. Length: two reels. Scenario: Mabel Normand, Charles Chaplin. Producer: Mack Sennett. Director: Mabel Normand. Cast: Charles Chaplin (Waiter), Mabel Normand (Mabel), Harry McCoy (Lover), Chester Conklin (Waiter), Edgar Kennedy (Café proprietor), Minta Durfee (Dancer), Josef Swickard (Father), Alice Davenport (Mother), Mack Swain (Man in park and Cabaret tough), Gordon Griffith (Boy), Hank Mann (Dancer with eye patch), Glen Cavender (Piano player), Gene Marsh (Chambermaid), Billy Gilbert (Cabaret patron)

CAUGHT IN THE RAIN
Released: May 4, 1914 (Finished and shipped: Apr. 18, 1914). Distributed by: Mutual Film Corporation. Produced by: Keystone Film Company. Length: one reel. Editor: Charles Chaplin. Scenario: Charles Chaplin. Producer: Mack Sennett. Director: Charles Chaplin. Cast: Charles Chaplin (Inebriated hotel guest), Mack Swain (Husband), Alice Davenport (Wife), Alice Howell (Woman)

A BUSY DAY
Released: May 7, 1914 (Finished and shipped: Apr. 18, 1914). Distributed by: Mutual Film Corporation.

Produced by: Keystone Film Company. Length: split reel (released with an interest film, *The Morning Paper*). Editor: Charles Chaplin. Scenario: Charles Chaplin. Producer: Mack Sennett. Director: Charles Chaplin. Cast: Charles Chaplin (Wife), Mack Swain (Husband), Mack Sennett (Film director), Billy Gilbert (Police officer)

THE FATAL MALLET

Released: June 1, 1914 (Finished and shipped: May 16, 1914). Distributed by: Mutual Film Corporation. Produced by: Keystone Film Company. Length: one reel. Scenario: Mack Sennett. Producer: Mack Sennett. Director: Mack Sennett. Cast: Charles Chaplin (Suitor), Mabel Normand (Mabel), Mack Sennett (Mabel's suitor), Mack Swain (Rival suitor), Gordon Griffith (Boy)

HER FRIEND THE BANDIT

Released: June 4, 1914 (Finished and shipped: May 22, 1914). Distributed by: Mutual Film Corporation. Produced by: Keystone Film Company. Length: one reel. Editor: Charles Chaplin. Scenario: Charles Chaplin. Producer: Mack Sennett. Director: Charles Chaplin. Cast: Charles Chaplin (The bandit), Mabel Normand (Miss De Rock), Charles Murray (Count De Beans)

THE KNOCKOUT

Released: June 11, 1914 (Finished and shipped: May 29, 1914). Distributed by: Mutual Film Corporation. Produced by: Keystone Film Company. Length: two reels. Producer: Mack Sennett. Director: Charles Avery. Cast: Charles Chaplin (Referee), Roscoe Arbuckle (Fatty), Minta Durfee (Girl), Edgar Kennedy (Cyclone Flynn), Al St. John (Gang leader), Hank Mann (Tough), Mack Swain (Gambler), Mack Sennett (Spectator), George "Slim" Summerville (Spectator), Billy Gilbert (Singer)

MABEL'S BUSY DAY

Released: June 13, 1914 (Finished and shipped: May 30, 1914). Distributed by: Mutual Film Corporation. Produced by: Keystone Film Company. Length: one reel. Scenario: Mabel Normand. Producer: Mack Sennett. Director: Mabel Normand. Cast: Charles Chaplin (Pest), Mabel Normand (Mabel), Chester Conklin (Cop), George "Slim" Summerville (Cop), Billie Bennett (Spectator), Gene Marsh (Spectator), Harry McCoy (Hot-dog thief), Edgar Kennedy (Tough hot-dog eater), Mack Sennett (Spectator), Glen Cavender (Customer), Al St. John, Charles Parrot [Charley Chase]

MABEL'S MARRIED LIFE

Released: June 20, 1914 (Finished and shipped: June 6, 1914). Distributed by: Mutual Film Corporation. Produced by: Keystone Film Company. Length: one reel. Editor: Charles Chaplin. Scenario: Charles Chaplin, Mabel Normand. Producer: Mack Sennett. Director: Charles Chaplin. Cast: Charles

Chaplin (Mabel's husband), Mabel Normand (Mabel), Mack Swain (Philanderer), Eva Nelson (Philanderer's wife), Hank Mann (Man in bar), Charles Murray (Man in bar), Al St. John (Delivery boy), Alice Davenport (Neighbor)

LAUGHING GAS

Released: June 9, 1914 (Finished and shipped: June 26, 1914). Distributed by: Mutual Film Corporation. Produced by: Keystone Film Company. Length: one reel. Editor: Charles Chaplin. Scenario: Charles Chaplin. Producer: Mack Sennett. Director: Charles Chaplin. Cast: Charles Chaplin (Dentist's assistant), Fritz Schade (Dentist), Joseph Sutherland (Assistant), George "Slim" Summerville (Patient), Gene Marsh (Patient), Josef Swickard (Patient), Mack Swain (Bystander)

THE PROPERTY MAN

Released: Aug. 1, 1914 (Finished and shipped: July 20, 1914). Distributed by: Mutual Film Corporation. Produced by: Keystone Film Company. Length: two reels. Editor: Charles Chaplin. Scenario: Charles Chaplin. Producer: Mack Sennett. Director: Charles Chaplin. Cast: Charles Chaplin (Property man), Jess Dandy (Garlico), Phyllis Allen (Hamlena Fat), Charles Bennett (Hamlena's husband), Josef Swickard (Old stagehand), Mack Sennett (Man in audience and Spectator), Frank Opperman (Man in audience), George "Slim" Summerville (Man in audience), Joe Bordeaux (Old actor), Harry McCoy (Drunk), Vivian Edwards (Goo Goo sister), Gene Marsh (Garlico's assistant)

THE FACE ON THE BAR ROOM FLOOR

Released: Aug. 10, 1914 (Finished and shipped: July 20, 1914). Distributed by: Mutual Film Corporation. Produced by: Keystone Film Company. Length: one reel. Editor: Charles Chaplin. Scenario: Charles Chaplin, after the poem "The Face on the Bar Room Floor" (1887) by Hugh Antoine D'Arcy. Producer: Mack Sennett. Director: Charles Chaplin. Cast: Charles Chaplin (Artist), Cecile Arnold (Madeline), Jess Dandy (Lover who stole her), Fritz Schade (Drinker), Vivian Edwards (Model), Charles Bennett (Sailor), Harry McCoy (Drinker), Chester Conklin (Drinker), Josef Swickard (Drinker)

RECREATION

Released: Aug. 13, 1914 (Finished and shipped: July 21, 1914). Distributed by: Mutual Film Corporation. Produced by: Keystone Film Company. Length: split reel (released with an interest film, *The Yosemite*). Editor: Charles Chaplin. Scenario: Charles Chaplin. Producer: Mack Sennett. Director: Charles Chaplin. Cast: Charles Chaplin (Tramp), Gene Marsh (The girl), Charles Bennett (Sailor)

THE MASQUERADER

Released: Aug. 27, 1914 (Finished and shipped: Aug. 12, 1914). Distributed by: Mutual Film Corporation. Produced by: Keystone Film Company. Length: one reel. Editor: Charles Chaplin. Scenario: Charles Chaplin. Producer: Mack Sennett. Director: Charles Chaplin. Cast: Charles Chaplin (Film actor), Roscoe Arbuckle (Film actor), Chester Conklin (Film actor), Charles Murray (Film director), Mabel Normand (Actress), Minta Durfee (Leading lady), Cecile Arnold (Actress), Vivian Edwards (Actress), Gene Marsh (Actress), Harry McCoy (Actor), Charles Parrot [Charley Chase] (Actor), Billy Gilbert (Cameraman)

HIS NEW PROFESSION

Released: Aug. 31, 1914 (Finished and shipped Aug. 14, 1914). Distributed by: Mutual Film Corporation. Produced by: Keystone Film Company. Length: one reel. Editor: Charles Chaplin. Scenario: Charles Chaplin. Producer: Mack Sennett. Director: Charles Chaplin. Cast: Charles Chaplin (Charlie), Minta Durfee (Woman), Charles Parrot [Charley Chase] (Nephew), Gene Marsh (Nephew's girlfriend), Jess Dandy (Uncle), Cecile Arnold (Girl), Roscoe Arbuckle (Bartender), Bill Hauber (Cop), Glen Cavender (Drinker), Charlie Murray (Drinker), Vivian Edwards (Nurse)

THE ROUNDERS

Released: Sept. 7, 1914 (Finished and shipped: Aug. 21, 1914). Distributed by: Mutual Film Corporation. Produced by: Keystone Film Company. Length: one reel. Editor: Charles Chaplin. Scenario: Charles Chaplin. Producer: Mack Sennett. Director: Charles Chaplin. Cast: Charles Chaplin (Mr. Full), Roscoe Arbuckle (Mr. Fuller), Phyllis Allen (Mr. Full's wife), Minta Durfee (Mr. Fuller's wife), Al St. John (Bellman and Waiter), Charles Parrot [Charley Chase] (Diner), Dixie Chene (Diner), Jess Dandy (Diner), Gene Marsh (Diner), Cecile Arnold (Guest), Eddie Cline (Man in lobby), Billy Gilbert (Doorman)

THE NEW JANITOR

Released: Sept. 24, 1914 (Finished and shipped Sept. 3, 1914). Distributed by: Mutual Film Corporation. Produced by: Keystone Film Company. Length: one reel. Editor: Charles Chaplin. Scenario: Charles Chaplin. Producer: Mack Sennett. Director: Charles Chaplin. Cast: Charles Chaplin (Janitor), John Francis "Jack" Dillon (Clerk), Gene Marsh (Secretary), Jess Dandy (Bank president), Al St. John (Elevator attendant), Glen Cavender (Luke Connor)

THOSE LOVE PANGS

Released: Oct. 10, 1914 (Finished and shipped: Sept. 19, 1914). Distributed by: Mutual Film Corporation. Produced by: Keystone Film Company. Length: one reel. Editor: Charles Chaplin. Scenario: Charles Chaplin. Producer: Mack Sennett. Director: Charles

Chaplin. Cast: Charles Chaplin (Masher), Chester Conklin (Rival), Cecile Arnold (Girl), Vivian Edwards (Girl), Fred Fishback (Boyfriend), Harry McCoy (Police officer), Fritz Schade (Cinema patron), George "Slim" Summerville (Cinema patron), Billy Gilbert (Cinema patron)

DOUGH AND DYNAMITE
Released: Oct. 26, 1914 (Finished and shipped: Sept. 18, 1914). Distributed by: Mutual Film Corporation. Produced by: Keystone Film Company. Length: two reels. Editor: Charles Chaplin. Scenario: Charles Chaplin. Producer: Mack Sennett. Director: Charles Chaplin. Cast: Charles Chaplin (Waiter), Chester Conklin (Waiter), Fritz Schade (Bakery proprietor), Norma Nichols (Proprietor's wife), Cecile Arnold (Waitress), Vivian Edwards (Customer), Phyllis Allen (Customer), Charles Bennett (Customer), Glen Cavender (Striking baker), George "Slim" Summerville (Striking baker), Charles Parrot [Charley Chase] (Customer)

GENTLEMEN OF NERVE
Released: Oct. 29, 1914 (Finished and shipped: Oct. 7, 1914). Distributed by: Mutual Film Corporation. Produced by: Keystone Film Company. Length: one reel. Editor: Charles Chaplin. Scenario: Charles Chaplin. Producer: Mack Sennett. Director: Charles Chaplin. Cast: Charles Chaplin (Mr. Wow-Wow), Mack Swain (Ambrose), Mabel Normand (Mabel), Chester Conklin (Walrus), Phyllis Allen (His wife), Glen Cavender (Cop), Alice Davenport (Waitress), George "Slim" Summerville (Spectator), Cecile Arnold (Spectator), Charles Parrott [Charley Chase] (Spectator), Gene Marsh (Spectator), Harry McCoy (Spectator), Vivian Edwards (Spectator), Joe Bordeaux (Spectator), Billy Gilbert (Spectator)

HIS MUSICAL CAREER
Released: Nov. 7, 1914 (Finished and shipped: Oct. 17, 1914). Distributed by: Mutual Film Corporation. Produced by: Keystone Film Company. Length: one reel. Editor: Charles Chaplin. Scenario: Charles Chaplin. Producer: Mack Sennett. Director: Charles Chaplin. Cast: Charles Chaplin (Piano mover), Mack Swain (Ambrose, his partner), Charles Parrott [Charley Chase] (Piano-shop manager), Billy Gilbert (Piano-shop salesman), Fritz Schade (Mr. Rich), Frank Hayes (Mr. Poor), Cecile Arnold (Mrs. Rich), Gene Marsh (Miss Poor), Bill Hauber (Servant)

HIS TRYSTING PLACE
Released: Nov. 9, 1914 (Finished and shipped: Oct. 1, 1914). Distributed by: Mutual Film Corporation. Produced by: Keystone Film Company. Length: two reels. Editor: Charles Chaplin. Scenario: Charles Chaplin. Producer: Mack Sennett. Director: Charles Chaplin. Cast: Charles Chaplin (Husband), Mabel Normand (Mabel, his wife), Mack Swain (Ambrose),

Phyllis Allen (Ambrose's wife), Gene Marsh (Clarice), Glen Cavender (Cook and Police officer), Nick Cogley (Bearded customer), Frank Hayes (Diner in bowler), Vivian Edwards (Woman outside restaurant), Billy Gilbert (Restaurant patron)

TILLIE'S PUNCTURED ROMANCE
Released: Dec. 14, 1914 (Finished and shipped: Dec. 4, 1914). Distributed by: Mutual Film Corporation. Produced by: Keystone Film Company. Length: six reels. Scenario: Mack Sennett, from the 1910 musical play *Tillie's Nightmare*, by A. Baldwin Sloane and Edgar Sloane. Producer: Mack Sennett. Director: Mack Sennett. Cast: Marie Dressler (Tillie Banks), Charles Chaplin (Charlie, a city slicker), Mabel Normand (Mabel), Mack Swain (John Banks and Man on street), Charles Bennett (Douglas Banks), Charles Murray (Detective), Charles Parrot [Charlie Chase] (Detective in cinema), Chester Conklin (Guest), Edgar Kennedy (Restaurant proprietor and Butler), Glen Cavender (Police officer and Pianist), Harry McCoy (Pianist), Gene Marsh (Maid), Fred Fishback (Servant), Phyllis Allen (Wardress and Guest), Alice Davenport (Guest), Frank Opperman (Reverend D. Simpson), George "Slim" Summerville (Police officer), Al St. John (Police officer), A. Edward Sutherland (Police officer), Joe Bordeaux (Police officer)

GETTING ACQUAINTED
Released: Dec. 5, 1914 (Finished and shipped: Nov. 22, 1914). Distributed by: Mutual Film Corporation. Produced by: Keystone Film Company. Length: one reel. Editor: Charles Chaplin. Scenario: Charles Chaplin. Producer: Mack Sennett. Director: Charles Chaplin. Cast: Charles Chaplin (Husband), Phyllis Allen (Wife), Mack Swain (Ambrose), Mabel Normand (Ambrose's wife), Harry McCoy (Flirt), Edgar Kennedy (Police officer), Glen Cavender (A passing Turk), Cecile Arnold (Flirty girl), Gene Marsh (Girl in park)

HIS PREHISTORIC PAST
Released: Dec. 7, 1914 (Finished and shipped: Oct. 31, 1914). Distributed by: Mutual Film Corporation. Produced by: Keystone Film Company. Length: two reels. Editor: Charles Chaplin. Scenario: Charles Chaplin. Producer: Mack Sennett. Director: Charles Chaplin. Cast: Charles Chaplin (Weakchin), Mack Swain (King Lowbrow), Gene Marsh (Lowbrow's favorite wife), Cecile Arnold (Cave woman), Vivian Edwards (Cave woman)

The Essanay Films

HIS NEW JOB
Released: Feb. 1, 1915. Distributed by: General Film Company. Produced by: Essanay Film Manufacturing Company. Length: two reels. Editor: Charles Chaplin. Scenario: Charles Chaplin. Producer: Jess Robbins. Director: Charles Chaplin.

Cast: Charles Chaplin (Film extra), Ben Turpin (assistant property man), Charlotte Mineau (Leading lady), Leo White (Receptionist and Actor), Gloria Swanson (Stenographer), Agnes Ayres (Extra in costume drama). Filmed at the Essanay Chicago Studio

A NIGHT OUT
Released: Feb. 15, 1915. Distributed by: General Film Company. Produced by: Essanay Film Manufacturing Company. Length: two reels. Photography: Harry Ensign. Editor: Charles Chaplin. Scenario: Charles Chaplin. Producer: Jess Robbins. Director: Charles Chaplin. Cast: Charles Chaplin (Drunk), Ben Turpin (His drinking companion), Bud Jamison (Head waiter), Edna Purviance (His wife), Leo White (Frenchman and Hotel receptionist), Fred Goodwins (Hotel receptionist). Filmed at the Essanay Niles Studio and in Oakland

THE CHAMPION
Released: Mar. 11, 1915. Distributed by: General Film Company. Produced by: Essanay Film Manufacturing Company. Length: two reels. Photography: Harry Ensign. Editor: Charles Chaplin. Scenario: Charles Chaplin. Producer: Jess Robbins. Director: Charles Chaplin. Cast: Charles Chaplin (Aspiring pugilist), Fred Goodwins (Spike Dugan), Edna Purviance (Trainer's daughter), Bud Jamison (Champion), Leo White (Villain), Lloyd Bacon (Sparring partner), Billy Armstrong (Sparring partner), Ben Turpin (Cigar vendor), G. M. ("Broncho Billy") Anderson (Spectator), Spike (Dog). Filmed at the Essanay Niles Studio

IN THE PARK
Released: Mar. 18, 1915. Distributed by: General Film Company. Produced by: Essanay Film Manufacturing Company. Length: one reel. Photography: Harry Ensign. Editor: Charles Chaplin. Scenario: Charles Chaplin. Producer: Jess Robbins. Director: Charles Chaplin. Cast: Charles Chaplin (Charlie), Edna Purviance (Nursemaid), Bud Jamison (Her beau), Leo White (Frenchman), Margie Reiger (His lady friend), Lloyd Bacon (Thieving tramp), Paddy McGuire (Thieving tramp), Ernest Van Pelt (Police officer), Fred Goodwins (Hot-dog vendor). Filmed on location in Niles and San Francisco

A JITNEY ELOPEMENT
Released: Apr. 1, 1915. Distributed by: General Film Company. Produced by: Essanay Film Manufacturing Company. Length: two reels. Photography: Harry Ensign. Editor: Charles Chaplin. Scenario: Charles Chaplin. Producer: Jess Robbins. Director: Charles Chaplin. Cast: Charles Chaplin (Suitor, the fake Count), Edna Purviance (The girl), Fred Goodwins (Her father), Leo White (Count Chloride de Lime), Lloyd Bacon (Butler and Police officer), Paddy McGuire (Elderly servant and Police

officer), Bud Jamison (Police officer). Filmed at the Essanay Niles Studio and on location in Niles and San Francisco

THE TRAMP

Released: Apr. 11, 1915. Distributed by: General Film Company. Produced by: Essanay Film Manufacturing Company. Length: two reels. Photography: Harry Ensign. Editor: Charles Chaplin. Scenario: Charles Chaplin. Producer: Jess Robbins. Director: Charles Chaplin. Cast: Charles Chaplin (The Tramp), Edna Purviance (Farmer's daughter), Fred Goodwins (Farmer), Lloyd Bacon (Edna's fiancé and Thieving tramp), Paddy McGuire (Farmhand), Leo White (Thieving tramp), Bud Jamison (Thieving tramp), Billy Armstrong (Effeminate man holding a book). Filmed at the Essanay Niles Studio and on location in Niles

BY THE SEA

Released: Apr. 29, 1915. Distributed by: General Film Company. Produced by: Essanay Film Manufacturing Company. Length: one reel. Photography: Harry Ensign. Editor: Charles Chaplin. Scenario: Charles Chaplin. Producer: Jess Robbins. Director: Charles Chaplin. Cast: Charles Chaplin (Tramp), Billy Armstrong (Visitor to beach), Margie Reiger (His wife), Bud Jamsion (Jealous husband), Edna Purviance (His wife), Paddy McGuire (Police officer), Harry Pollard (Ice-cream vendor). Filmed on location in Venice, California

WORK

Released: June 21, 1915. Distributed by: General Film Company. Produced by: Essanay Film Manufacturing Company. Length: two reels. Photography: Harry Ensign. Assistant director: Ernest Van Pelt. Editor: Charles Chaplin. Scenario: Charles Chaplin. Producer: Jess Robbins. Director: Charles Chaplin. Cast: Charles Chaplin (Paperhanger's assistant), Charles Insley (His boss), Edna Purviance (Maid), Billy Armstrong (Home owner), Marta Golden (His wife), Leo White (Secret lover), Paddy McGuire (Workman). Filmed at the Bradbury Mansion Studio and on location

A WOMAN

Released: July 12, 1915. Distributed by: General Film Company. Produced by: Essanay Film Manufacturing Company. Length: two reels. Photography: Harry Ensign. Assistant director: Ernest Van Pelt. Editor: Charles Chaplin. Scenario: Charles Chaplin. Producer: Jess Robbins. Director: Charles Chaplin. Cast: Charles Chaplin (Tramp), Edna Purviance (Daughter), Charles Insley (Father), Marta Golden (Mother), Margie Reiger (The flirt), Billy Armstrong (Father's friend and Police officer), Leo White (Frenchman), Jess Robbins (Soda vendor). Filmed at the former Majestic Studio and on location in Echo Park

THE BANK

Released: Aug. 9, 1915. Distributed by: General Film Company. Produced by: Essanay Film Manufacturing Company. Length: two reels. Photography: Harry Ensign. Assistant director: Ernest Van Pelt. Editor: Charles Chaplin. Scenario: Charles Chaplin. Producer: Jess Robbins. Director: Charles Chaplin. Cast: Charles Chaplin (Charlie, a janitor), Edna Purviance (Secretary), Carl Stockdale (Charles, a cashier), Billy Armstrong (Janitor), Charles Insley (Bank president), Lawrence A. Bowes (Rejected bond salesman), Leo White (Bank customer representative), Paddy McGuire (Cashier). Filmed at the former Majestic Studio

SHANGHAIED

Released: Oct. 4, 1915. Distributed by: General Film Company. Produced by: Essanay Film Manufacturing Company. Length: two reels. Photography: Harry Ensign. Assistant director: Ernest Van Pelt. Editor: Charles Chaplin. Scenario: Charles Chaplin. Producer: Jess Robbins. Director: Charles Chaplin. Cast: Charles Chaplin (Tramp), Edna Purviance (Edna, the ship owner's daughter), Wesley Ruggles (Ship owner), Lawrence A. Bowes (Captain), John Rand (Cook), Billy Armstrong (Sailor), Paddy McGuire (Sailor), Leo White (Sailor). Filmed at the former Majestic Studio and on location

A NIGHT IN THE SHOW

Released: Nov. 20, 1915. Distributed by: General Film Company. Produced by: Essanay Film Manufacturing Company. Length: two reels. Photography: Harry Ensign. Assistant director: Ernest Van Pelt. Editor: Charles Chaplin. Scenario: Charles Chaplin. Producer: Jess Robbins. Director: Charles Chaplin. Cast: Charles Chaplin (Mr. Pest and Mr. Rowdy), Edna Purviance (Lady in the stalls), Bud Jamison (Singer), Dee Lampton (Fat boy), Leo White (Black-faced man in gallery, Frenchman in stalls, and Assistant to La Belle Wienerwurst), Wesley Ruggles (Man in gallery), John Rand (Theater patron, Woman with baby in gallery, and Orchestra conductor), James T. Kelly (Shaky musician), Paddy McGuire (Theater attendant and Musician), May White (Fat lady in foyer and La Belle Wienerwurst), Charles Insley (Gentleman in audience), Carrie Clark Ward (Woman in audience). Filmed at the former Majestic Studio

POLICE

Released: Mar. 27, 1916. Distributed by: General Film Company. Produced by: Essanay Film Manufacturing Company. Length: two reels. Photography: Harry Ensign. Assistant director: Ernest Van Pelt. Scenario: Charles Chaplin. Producer: Jess Robbins. Director: Charles Chaplin. Cast: Charles Chaplin (Ex-convict), Edna Purviance (Daughter of the house), Wesley Ruggles (Crook), James T. Kelly (Drunk), Leo White (Fruit seller, Doss-house proprietor, and Police officer), John Rand (Police officer),

Billy Armstrong (Police officer), Bud Jamison (Doss-house tramp), Paddy McGuire (Doss-house tramp), Harry Pollard (Doss- house tramp). Filmed at the former Majestic Studio and on location

BURLESQUE ON "CARMEN"

Released: Apr. 10, 1916. Distributed by: V-L-S-E, Inc. Produced by: Essanay Film Manufacturing Company. Length: two reels. Photography: Harry Ensign. Production designer: Albert Couder. Assistant director: Ernest Van Pelt. Scenario: Charles Chaplin. Producer: Jess Robbins. Director: Charles Chaplin. Cast: Charles Chaplin (Darn Hosiery), Edna Purviance (Carmen), Leo White (Corporal Morales), John Rand (Escamillo), Jack Henderson (Pastia), May White (Frasquita), Bud Jamison (Soldier). In extended version: Ben Turpin (Don Remendado), Wesley Ruggles (Vagabond). Filmed at the former Majestic Studio and on location. (The film was expanded from two reels [approx. 1,794 feet] to four [approx. 3,489 feet], without Chaplin's authority, after he had left Essanay. The new version was assembled by Leo White, who also filmed new material for it. Chaplin unsuccessfully took legal action against Essanay.)

The Mutual-Chaplin Specials

THE FLOORWALKER

Released: May 15, 1916. Distributed by: Mutual Film Corporation. Produced by: Lone Star Film Corporation. Length: two reels. Technical director: Edward Brewer. Property master: George Cleethorpe. Photography: William C. Foster. Assistant photographer: Roland H. Totheroh. Editor: Charles Chaplin. Scenario: Charles Chaplin, Vincent Bryan, Maverick Terrell. Producer: Henry P. Caulfield. Director: Charles Chaplin. Cast: Charles Chaplin (Tramp), Eric Campbell (General manager), Edna Purviance (His secretary), Lloyd Bacon (Floorwalker), Albert Austin (Store clerk), Leo White (Shoplifter and French customer), Charlotte Mineau (Detective), James T. Kelly (Elderly elevator attendant), Frank J. Coleman (Janitor)

THE FIREMAN

Released: June 12, 1916. Distributed by: Mutual Film Corporation. Produced by: Lone Star Film Corporation. Length: two reels. Technical director: Edward Brewer. Property master: George Cleethorpe. Photography: William C. Foster. Assistant photographer: Roland H. Totheroh. Editor: Charles Chaplin. Scenario: Charles Chaplin, Vincent Bryan, Maverick Terrell. Producer: Henry P. Caulfield. Director: Charles Chaplin. Cast: Charles Chaplin (Firefighter), Edna Purviance (Girl), Lloyd Bacon (Her father and Cook), Eric Campbell (Fire chief), Leo White (Owner of burning house), Albert Austin (Firefighter), John Rand (Firefighter), James T. Kelly (Firefighter), Frank J. Coleman (Firefighter)

THE VAGABOND

Released: July 10, 1916. Distributed by: Mutual Film Corporation. Produced by: Lone Star Film Corporation. Length: two reels. Technical director: Edward Brewer. Property master: George Cleethorpe. Photography: William C. Foster. Assistant photographer: Roland H. Totheroh. Editor: Charles Chaplin. Scenario: Charles Chaplin, Vincent Bryan, Maverick Terrell. Producer: Henry P. Caulfield. Director: Charles Chaplin. Cast: Charles Chaplin (Street musician), Edna Purviance (Gypsy drudge), Eric Campbell (Gypsy chief), Lloyd Bacon (Artist and Gypsy), Charlotte Mineau (Mother), Albert Austin (Musician), Leo White (Musician, Jew, and Old gypsy woman), John Rand (Musician and Gypsy), James T. Kelly (Musician and Gypsy), Frank J. Coleman (Musician and Gypsy)

ONE A.M.

Released: Aug. 7, 1916. Distributed by: Mutual Film Corporation. Produced by: Lone Star Film Corporation. Length: two reels. Technical director: Edward Brewer. Property master: George Cleethorpe. Photography: William C. Foster. Assistant photographer: Roland H. Totheroh. Editor: Charles Chaplin. Scenario: Charles Chaplin, Vincent Bryan, Maverick Terrell. Producer: Henry P. Caulfield. Director: Charles Chaplin. Cast: Charles Chaplin (Drunk), Albert Austin (Taxi driver)

THE COUNT

Released: Sept. 4, 1916. Distributed by: Mutual Film Corporation. Produced by: Lone Star Film Corporation. Length: two reels. Technical director: Edward Brewer. Property master: George Cleethorpe. Photography: Roland H. Totheroh. Assistant photographer: George C. Zalibra. Editor: Charles Chaplin. Scenario: Charles Chaplin, Vincent Bryan, Maverick Terrell. Producer: Henry P. Caulfield. Director: Charles Chaplin. Cast: Charles Chaplin (Tailor's assistant), Edna Purviance (Miss Moneybags), Eric Campbell (Tailor), Leo White (Count Broko), Charlotte Mineau (Mrs. Moneybags), Eva Thatcher (Cook), Albert Austin (Guest), John Rand (Guest), James T. Kelly (Butler), Lloyd Bacon (Conductor), Leota Bryan (Young girl), May White (Large guest), Loyal Underwood (Small guest), Frank J. Coleman (Police officer and Guest in Pierrot costume)

THE PAWNSHOP

Released: Oct. 2, 1916. Distributed by: Mutual Film Corporation. Produced by: Lone Star Film Corporation. Length: two reels. Technical director: Edward Brewer. Property master: George Cleethorpe. Photography: Roland H. Totheroh. Assistant photographer: George C. Zalibra. Editor: Charles Chaplin. Scenario: Charles Chaplin, Vincent Bryan, Maverick Terrell. Producer: Henry P. Caulfield. Director: Charles Chaplin. Cast: Charles Chaplin (Pawnbroker's assistant), Henry Bergman (Pawnbroker), Edna Purviance (His daughter), John Rand (The other assistant), Albert Austin (Customer with alarm clock), Eric Campbell (Crook), James T. Kelly (Old bum and Lady with goldfish), Frank J. Coleman (Police officer)

BEHIND THE SCREEN

Released: Nov. 13, 1916. Distributed by: Mutual Film Corporation. Produced by: Lone Star Film Corporation. Length: two reels. Technical director: Edward Brewer. Property master: George Cleethorpe. Photography: Roland H. Totheroh. Assistant photographer: George C. Zalibra. Editor: Charles Chaplin. Scenario: Charles Chaplin, Vincent Bryan, Maverick Terrell. Producer: Henry P. Caulfield. Director: Charles Chaplin. Cast: Charles Chaplin (David, stagehand's assistant), Eric Campbell (Goliath, stagehand), Edna Purviance (Aspiring actress), Henry Bergman (Director of historical film), Lloyd Bacon (Director of comedy film), Albert Austin (Scene shifter and Actor), John Rand (Scene shifter), Leo White (Scene shifter), Frank J. Coleman (Producer), Charlotte Mineau (Actress), Leota Bryan (Actress), Tom Wood (Actor), James T. Kelly (Cameraman)

THE RINK

Released: Dec. 4, 1916. Distributed by: Mutual Film Corporation. Produced by: Lone Star Film Corporation. Length: two reels. Technical director: Edward Brewer. Property master: George Cleethorpe. Photography: Roland H. Totheroh. Assistant photographer: George C. Zalibra. Editor: Charles Chaplin. Scenario: Charles Chaplin, Vincent Bryan, Maverick Terrell. Producer: Henry P. Caulfield. Director: Charles Chaplin. Cast: Charles Chaplin (Waiter and Sir Cecil Selzter), Edna Purviance (Girl), James T. Kelly (Her father), Eric Campbell (Mr. Stout), Henry Bergman (Mrs. Stout and Angry diner), Lloyd Bacon (Diner and Attendant at rink), Albert Austin (Cook and Skater), Frank J. Coleman (Restaurant manager), John Rand (Waiter), Charlotte Mineau (Edna's friend), Leota Bryan (Edna's friend)

EASY STREET

Released: Feb. 5, 1917. Distributed by: Mutual Film Corporation. Produced by: Lone Star Film Corporation. Length: two reels. Technical director: Edward Brewer. Property master: George Cleethorpe. Photography: Roland H. Totheroh. Assistant photographer: George C. Zalibra. Editor: Charles Chaplin. Scenario: Charles Chaplin, Vincent Bryan, Maverick Terrell. Producer: Henry P. Caulfield. Director: Charles Chaplin. Cast: Charles Chaplin (Tramp), Edna Purviance (Mission worker), Eric Campbell (Bully of Easy Street), Albert Austin (Minister and Police officer), James T. Kelly (Missionary), Henry Bergman (Anarchist), Loyal Underwood (Father and Police officer), Charlotte Mineau (Mother), Tom Wood (Chief of police), William Gillespie (Heroine addict), Lloyd Bacon (Drug addict), Frank J. Coleman (Police officer), John Rand (Drunk and Police officer), Erich von Stroheim Jr. (Baby)

THE CURE

Released: Apr. 16, 1917. Distributed by: Mutual Film Corporation. Produced by: Lone Star Film Corporation. Length: two reels. Technical director: Edward Brewer. Property master: George Cleethorpe. Assistant property man: Dan Allen. Photography: Roland H. Totheroh. Assistant photographer: George C. Zalibra. Editor: Charles Chaplin. Scenario: Charles Chaplin, Vincent Bryan, Maverick Terrell. Producer: Henry P. Caulfield. Director: Charles Chaplin. Cast: Charles Chaplin (Inebriate), Edna Purviance (Girl), Eric Campbell (Gentleman with gout), Henry Bergman (Masseur), Albert Austin (Spa attendant), John Rand (Spa attendant), James T. Kelly (Elderly bellman), Frank J. Coleman (Spa manager), Leota Bryan (Nurse), Tom Wood (Patient), Janet Miller Sully (Spa visitor), Loyal Underwood (Spa proprietor), William Gillespie (Man in shoe-throwing battle)

THE IMMIGRANT

Released: June 17, 1917. Distributed by: Mutual Film Corporation. Produced by: Lone Star Film Corporation. Length: two reels. Technical director: Edward Brewer. Property master: George Cleethorpe. Photography: Roland H. Totheroh. Assistant photographer: George C. Zalibra. Editor: Charles Chaplin. Scenario: Charles Chaplin, Vincent Bryan, Maverick Terrell. Producer: John Jasper. Director: Charles Chaplin. Cast: Charles Chaplin (Immigrant), Edna Purviance (Immigrant), Kitty Bradbury (Her mother), Albert Austin (Slavic immigrant and Diner), Henry Bergman (Slavic woman immigrant and Artist), Loyal Underwood (Small immigrant), Janet Miller Sully (Immigrant), Eric Campbell (Head waiter), William Gillespie (Café violinist), James T. Kelly (Crew member and shabby man in restaurant), John Rand (Crew member and Drunk diner who cannot pay), Frank J. Coleman (Gambler on ship, Ship's officer, and Café proprietor), Tom Harrington (Marriage registrar)

THE ADVENTURER

Released: Oct. 22, 1917. Distributed by: Mutual Film Corporation. Produced by: Lone Star Film Corporation. Length: two reels. Technical director: Edward Brewer. Property master: George Cleethorpe. Photography: Roland H. Totheroh. Assistant photographer: George C. Zalibra. Editor: Charles Chaplin. Scenario: Charles Chaplin, Vincent Bryan, Maverick Terrell. Producer: John Jasper. Director: Charles Chaplin. Cast: Charles Chaplin (Escaped convict posing as Commodore Slick), Edna Purviance (Girl), Henry Bergman (Her father, Judge Brown, and Docker), Marta Golden (Her mother), Eric Campbell (Her suitor), Albert

Austin (Butler), Toraichi Kono (Chauffer), John Rand (Guest), Frank J. Coleman (Police officer), Loyal Underwood (Small guest), May White (Stout lady), Janet Miller Sully

The First National Films

A DOG'S LIFE

Released: Apr. 14, 1918. Distributed by: First National Exhibitors Circuit. Produced by: Charlie Chaplin Film Company. Length: 2,674 feet (three reels). Production designer: Charles D. Hall. Assistant director: Charles F. Riesner. Photography: Roland H. Totheroh. Assistant photographer: Jack Wilson. Editor: Charles Chaplin. Scenario: Charles Chaplin. Producer: Charles Chaplin. Director: Charles Chaplin. Cast: Charles Chaplin (Tramp), Edna Purviance (Singer at the Green Lantern), Mutt (Scraps), Sydney Chaplin (Lunch wagon owner), Henry Bergman (Man in employment agency and Large woman in dance hall), Loyal Underwood (Small man in dance hall), Charles Riesner (Clerk in employment agency and Drummer), Albert Austin (Crook), Tom Wilson (Police officer), Granville Redmond (Proprietor of dance hall), M. J. McCarty (Unemployed man), Mel Brown (Unemployed man), James T. Kelly (Customer at hot-dog stand), Minnie Chaplin (Dramatic lady in dance hall), Alf Reeves (Man at bar), Bob Wagner (Man in dance hall). Reissue version: As part of *The Chaplin Revue* (see compilation)

SHOULDER ARMS

Released: Oct. 20, 1918. Distributed by: First National Exhibitors Circuit. Produced by: Charlie Chaplin Film Company. Length: 3,142 feet (three reels). Production designer: Charles D. Hall. Assistant director: Charles F. Riesner. Photography: Roland H. Totheroh. Assistant photographer: Jack Wilson. Editor: Charles Chaplin. Scenario: Charles Chaplin. Producer: Charles Chaplin. Director: Charles Chaplin. Cast: Charles Chaplin (Recruit), Edna Purviance (French woman), Sydney Chaplin (Charlie's pal and Kaiser Wilhelm), Jack Wilson (German crown prince), Henry Bergman (Fat German sergeant, Bartender, and Field Marshal von Hindenburg), Albert Austin (American soldier, German soldier, and Kaiser's chauffeur), Tom Wilson (Training camp sergeant and German soldier), Loyal Underwood (Small German officer), John Rand (American soldier), Alf Reeves (American soldier). Reissue version: As part of *The Chaplin Revue* (see compilation)

SUNNYSIDE

Released: June 15, 1919. Distributed by: First National Exhibitors Circuit. Produced by: Charlie Chaplin Film Company. Length: 2,769 feet (three reels). Production designer: Charles D. Hall. Assistant director: Charles F. Riesner. Photography: Roland H. Totheroh. Assistant photographer: Jack Wilson. Editor: Charles Chaplin. Scenario: Charles Chaplin. Producer: Charles Chaplin. Director: Charles Chaplin. Cast: Charles Chaplin (Farm hand), Edna Purviance (Village girl), Tom Wilson (Boss), Tom Terriss (City chap), Henry Bergman (Villager and Village girl's father), Loyal Underwood (Small father), Tom Wood (His big son), Albert Austin (Village doctor), Helen Kohn (Nymph), Olive Burton (Nymph), Willie Mae Carson (Nymph), Olive Alcorn (Nymph), Park Jones, Granville Redmond, Tom Harrington. Reissue version: Premiere: Oct. 23, 1974, Mayfair Hotel, London. General release: 1977. Distributed by: Black, Inc. Music by: Charles Chaplin. "When Other Lips" from *The Bohemian Girl* by Michael William Balfe. Arrangement by Eric Rogers. Music associate: Eric James. Music orchestrated and conducted by: Eric Rogers

A DAY'S PLEASURE

Released: Dec. 15, 1919. Distributed by: First National Exhibitors Circuit. Produced by: Charlie Chaplin Film Company. Length: 1,714 feet (two reels). Production designer: Charles D. Hall. Assistant director: Charles F. Riesner. Photography: Roland H. Totheroh. Assistant photographers: Jack Wilson, H. Wenger. Editor: Charles Chaplin. Scenario: Charles Chaplin. Producer: Charles Chaplin. Director: Charles Chaplin. Cast: Charles Chaplin (Father), Edna Purviance (Mother), Marion Feducha (Boy), Bob Kelly (Boy), Jackie Coogan (Youngest boy), Tom Wilson (Large husband and Police officer), Jean "Babe" London (His seasick wife), Henry Bergman (Man in car, Police officer and Captain), Loyal Underwood (Angry pedestrian), Toraichi Kono (Chauffeur). Reissue version: Released: 1974. Distributed by: Black, Inc. Music by: Charles Chaplin. Music associate: Eric James. Music orchestrated and conducted by: Eric Rogers. (The reissue version of *A Day's Pleasure* was tied with the general release of Black Inc.'s distribution of *The Circus* in 1974.)

THE KID

Premiere: Jan. 21, 1921, Carnegie Hall, New York City. Released: Feb. 6, 1921, Mark Strand Theatre, New York City. Distributed by: First National Exhibitors Circuit. Produced by: Charlie Chaplin Film Company. Length: 5,250 feet (six reels). Production designer: Charles D. Hall. Assistant director: Charles F. Riesner. Photography: Roland H. Totheroh. Assistant photographers: Jack Wilson, H. Wenger. Editor: Charles Chaplin. Scenario: Charles Chaplin. Producer: Charles Chaplin. Director: Charles Chaplin. Cast: Charles Chaplin (Tramp), Edna Purviance (Woman), Carl Miller (Man), Jackie Coogan (Kid), Silas Hathaway (Kid as a baby), Tom Wilson, (Police officer), Henry Bergman (Professor Guido, Slum dweller, and Night-shelter proprietor), Charles Riesner (Bully), Raymond Lee (His kid brother), Lillita MacMurray [Lita Grey] (Flirting angel), Jules Hanft (Country doctor), Frank Campeau (Welfare officer), F. Blinn (His assistant), Granville Redmond (The man's friend), May White (Police officer's wife), Edith Wilson (Lady with pram), Baby Wilson (Baby in pram), Nellie Bly Baker (Slum dweller), Albert Austin (Man in shelter), Jack Coogan Sr. (Pickpocket, Guest, and Devil), Edgar Sherrod (Priest), Beulah Bains (Bride), Robert Dunbar (Bridegroom), Kitty Bradbury (Bride's mother), Monta Bell, Elsie Codd, Esther Ralston. Reissue version: Premiere: Apr. 4, 1972, Philharmonic Hall, Lincoln Center, New York City. General release: 1973. Distributed by: Black, Inc.

THE IDLE CLASS

Released: Sept. 25, 1921. Distributed by: First National Exhibitors Circuit. Produced by: Charlie Chaplin Film Company. Length: 1,910 feet (two reels). Production designer: Charles D. Hall. Assistant director: Charles F. Riesner. Photography: Roland H. Totheroh. Assistant photographer: Jack Wilson. Editor: Charles Chaplin. Scenario: Charles Chaplin. Producer: Charles Chaplin. Director: Charles Chaplin. Cast: Charles Chaplin (Tramp and Absent-minded husband), Edna Purviance (Edna, the lonely wife), Mack Swain (Her father), Henry Bergman (Sleeping tramp and Guest), John Rand (Golfer), Lillita MacMurray [Lita Grey] (Maid and Party guest), Lillian Parker [Lillian Grey] (Maid and Party guest), Rex Storey (Pickpocket and Party guest), Loyal Underwood (Golfer), Allan Garcia (Golfer and Police officer), Edward Knoblock, Granville Redmond, Carlyle Robinson, Joe Van Meter (Party guests). Reissue version: Premiere: Apr. 4, 1972, Philharmonic Hall, Lincoln Center, New York City. General release: 1973. Distributed by: Black, Inc.

PAY DAY

Released: Apr. 2, 1922. Distributed by: First National Exhibitors Circuit. Produced by: Charlie Chaplin Film Company. Length: 1,950 feet (two reels). Production designer: Charles D. Hall. Assistant director: Charles F. Riesner. Photography: Roland H. Totheroh. Assistant photographer: Jack Wilson. Editor: Charles Chaplin. Scenario: Charles Chaplin. Producer: Charles Chaplin. Director: Charles Chaplin. Cast: Charles Chaplin (Worker), Phyllis Allen (His wife), Mack Swain (Foreman), Edna Purviance (Foreman's daughter), Sydney Chaplin (Worker and Lunch-wagon proprietor), Henry Bergman (Worker), John Rand (Worker), Loyal Underwood (Worker), Allan Garcia (Worker and Police officer). Reissue version: Released: 1974. Distributed by: Black, Inc. Music by: Charles Chaplin. Music associate: Eric James. Music orchestrated and conducted by: Eric Rogers. (The reissue version of *Pay Day* was tied with the general release of Black Inc.'s distribution of Chaplin's 1942 reissue version of *The Gold Rush* in 1973.)

THE PILGRIM

Premiere: Feb. 25, 1923, Mark Strand Theatre, New York City. Distributed by: First National Exhibitors Circuit. Produced by: Charlie Chaplin Film Company. Length: 3,647 feet (four reels). Production designer: Charles D. Hall. Assistant director: Charles F. Riesner. Photography: Roland H. Totheroh. Assistant photographer: Jack Wilson. Editor: Charles Chaplin. Scenario: Charles Chaplin. Producer: Charles Chaplin. Director: Charles Chaplin. Cast: Charles Chaplin (Escaped convict), Edna Purviance (Ms. Brown), Kitty Bradbury (Her mother, Mrs. Brown), Mack Swain (Deacon), Loyal Underwood (Elder), Charles Riesner (Howard Huntington alias "Nitro Nick" alias "Picking Pete"), "Dinky" Dean Riesner (Brat kid), Mai Wells (His mother), Sydney Chaplin (Her husband and Eloper and Train conductor), Tom Murray (Sheriff Bryan), Henry Bergman (Sheriff on train), Monta Bell (Police officer), Jack Wilson (Natatorial clergyman), Raymond Lee (Boy in congregation), Frank Antunez (Bandit), Joe Van Meter (Bandit), Phyllis Allen (Member of congregation), Marion Davies (Member of congregation), Carlyle Robinson. Reissue version: As part of The Chaplin Revue (see compilation)

The United Artists Films

A WOMAN OF PARIS

Premiere: Sept. 26, 1923, Criterion Theatre, Hollywood. Distributed by: United Artists Corporation. Produced by: Regent Film Company. Length: 8,432 feet (eight reels). Production manager: Alfred Reeves. Art director: Arthur Stibolt. Assistant director: A. Edward Sutherland. Photography: Roland H. Totheroh. Assistant photographer: Jack Wilson. Research: Jean de Limur, Henri d'Abbadie d'Arrast. Editor: Charles Chaplin. Literary editor: Monta Bell. Written by: Charles Chaplin. Producer: Charles Chaplin. Director: Charles Chaplin. Cast: Edna Purviance (Marie St. Clair), Clarence Geldert (Her stepfather), Carl Miller (Jean Millet), Lydia Knott (His mother), Charles French (His father), Adolphe Menjou (Pierre Revel), Betty Morrissey (Fifi), Malvina Polo (Paulette), Henry Bergman (Head waiter), Nellie Bly Baker (Masseuse), Harry Northrup (Revel's secretary), Karl Gutman (Orchestra conductor), Bess Flowers (Model at party), Frank Coghlan, Jr. (Boy), A. Edward Sutherland (cook), Arthur Stibolt (cook), Granville Redmond (Party guest), Henri d'Abbadie d'Arrast (Party guest), Phil Sleeman (Gigolo), James Marcus (Tramp), Charles Farrell (Man dancing in nightclub), Charles Chaplin (Porter). Reissue version: Premiere: Dec. 23, 1976, Museum of Modern Art, New York City. U.S. general release: 1978. U.K. premiere: Oct. 9, 1980, Gate Three Cinema, Camden Town, London. Distributed by: Black, Inc. Length: 7,559 feet (eight reels). Music: Charles Chaplin. Music associate: Eric James. Music orchestrated and conducted by: Eric Rogers

THE GOLD RUSH

Premiere: June 26, 1925, Grauman's Egyptian Theatre, Hollywood. Distributed by: United Artists Corporation. Produced by: Charles Chaplin Film Corporation. Length: 8,555 feet (nine reels). Production manager: Alfred Reeves. Art director: Charles D. Hall. Assistant directors: Henri d' Abbadie d'Arrast, A. Edward Sutherland. Photography: Roland H. Totheroh. Assistant cinematographers: Jack Wilson, Mark Marlatt. Editor: Charles Chaplin. Scenario: Charles Chaplin. Producer: Charles Chaplin. Associate director: Charles F. Riesner. Director: Charles Chaplin. Cast: Charles Chaplin (Lone prospector), Mack Swain (Big Jim McKay), Tom Murray (Black Larsen), Malcolm Waite (Jack Cameron), Georgia Hale (Georgia), Henry Bergman (Hank Curtis), Betty Morrissey (Georgia's friend), Joan Lowell (Georgia's friend), John Rand (Prospector), Heinie Conklin (Prospector), Albert Austin (Prospector), Allan Garcia (Prospector), Tom Wood (Prospector), Stanley J. Sandford (Bartender), Barbara Pierce (Manicurist), A. J. O'Connor (Officer), Art Walker (Officer), Daddy Taylor (Ancient dancing prospector), Fred Karno Jr., Sid Grauman, Lita Grey (extra in Chilkhoot Pass climb), Lillian Grey (extra in Chilkhoot Pass climb). (Shooting began with Lita Grey as leading lady. Georgia Hale took over the role in Dec. 1924.) Reissue version: Premiere: Apr. 17, 1942, Globe Theatre, New York City. Distributed by: United Artists Corporation. Length: 7,100 feet (seven reels). Production manager: Alf Reeves. Original compositions: Charles Chaplin. Musical direction: Max Terr. Photography: Roland H. Totheroh. Sound recording: Pete Decker, W. M. Dalgleish. Film editor: Harold McGhan. Narrative written and spoken by: Charles Chaplin

THE CIRCUS

Premiere: Jan. 6, 1928, Mark Strand Theatre, New York City. Distributed by: United Artists Corporation. Produced by: Charles Chaplin Film Corporation. Length: 6,500 feet (seven reels). Production manager: Alfred Reeves. Settings: Charles D. Hall. Assistant director: Harry Crocker. Photography: Roland H. Totheroh. Laboratory supervision: William E. Hinkley. Cameramen: Jack Wilson, Mark Marlatt. Editor: Charles Chaplin. Written by: Charles Chaplin. Producer: Charles Chaplin. Director: Charles Chaplin. Cast: Charles Chaplin (Tramp), Allan Garcia (The Circus Proprietor/Ring Master), Merna Kennedy (Merna, his stepdaughter, a circus rider), Harry Crocker (Rex, a tight rope walker; Disgruntled property man; and Clown), George Davis (Magician), Henry Bergman (Old clown), Stanley J. Sandford (Head property man), John Rand (Assistant property man and Clown), Steve Murphy (Pickpocket), Doc Stone (Prizefighter in cut sequence), Betty Morrissey (Vanishing lady), Armand Triller (Clown), Bill Knight (Police officer), Jack Pierce (Man operating

ropes), Numi (Lion), Bobby (Monkey), Josephine (Monkey), Jimmy (Monkey). Reissue version: Premiere: Apr. 16, 1969, Gaumont Colisée, Paris. Presented by: Roy Export Company Establishment. Prerelease engagement: Dec. 15, 1969, 72 Street Playhouse, New York City. General release: 1970. Distributed by: United Artists Corporation. Length: 6,300 feet (seven reels, released with the short subject The National Flower of Brooklyn). Music: Charles Chaplin. Music arranged by Lambert Williamson. Music associate: Eric James. Song "Swing, Little Girl," music and lyrics by Charles Chaplin. Sung by Charles Chaplin

CITY LIGHTS

Premiere: Jan. 30, 1931, Los Angeles Theater, Los Angeles. Distributed by: United Artists Corporation. Produced by: Charles Chaplin Film Corporation. Length: 8,093 feet (nine reels). Production manager: Alfred Reeves. Settings: Charles D. Hall. Assistant directors: Harry Crocker, Henry Bergman, Albert Austin. Photographers: Roland H. Totheroh, Gordon Pollock. Music: Charles Chaplin. Musical arrangement: Arthur Johnston. Music direction: Alfred Newman. Editor: Willard Nico. Written by: Charles Chaplin. Producer: Charles Chaplin. Director: Charles Chaplin. Cast: Charles Chaplin (Tramp), Virginia Cherrill (Blind girl), Florence Lee (Her grandmother), Harry Myers (Eccentric millionaire), Allan Garcia (His butler), Hank Mann (Prizefighter), Henry Bergman (Mayor and Tenant), Albert Austin (Street cleaner and Burglar), Joe Van Meter (Burglar), Eddie Baker (Referee), Robert Parrish (Newsboy), Austin Jewell (Newsboy), Tom Dempsey (Boxer), Eddie McAuliffe (Eddie Mason, boxer), Willie Keeler (Boxer), Victor Alexander (Superstitious boxer), Tony Stabeman (Victorious boxer, later knocked out), Joe Van Meter (Burglar), John Rand (Tramp), Stanley J. Sandford (Man on lift), T. S. Alexander (Doctor), James Donnelly (Foreman), Granville Redmond (Artist), Florence Wicks (Woman who sits on cigar), Jean Harlow (Extra in night club scene). Reissue version: Premiere: Apr. 8, 1950, Globe Theatre, New York City. Distributed by: United Artists Corporation

MODERN TIMES

Premiere: Feb. 5, 1936, Rivoli Theatre, New York City. Distributed by: United Artists Corporation. Produced by: Charles Chaplin Film Corporation. Length: 8,126 feet (nine reels). Production manager: Alfred Reeves. Assistant production manager: Jack Wilson. Settings: Charles D. Hall, Russell Spencer. Assistant director: Carter De Haven. Photography: Roland H. Totheroh, Ira Morgan. Assistant cameramen: Mark Marlatt, Morgan Hill. Music: Charles Chaplin. Conducted by: Alfred Newman. Arranged by: Edward Powell, David Raksin. Recorded by: Paul Neal, Frank Maher. Editor: Willard Nico. Scenario: Charles Chaplin. Producer: Charles Chaplin. Director: Charles Chaplin. Cast:

Charlie Chaplin (Factory worker), Paulette Goddard (Gamine), Henry Bergman (Café proprietor), Stanley Sandford (Big Bill), Chester Conklin (Mechanic), Hank Mann (Burglar), Stanley Blystone (Sheriff Couler), Allan Garcia (President of Electro Steel), Dick Alexander (Convict), Cecil Reynolds (Minister), Myra McKinney (Minister's wife), Murdoch McQuarrie, Wilfred Lewis, Edward Le Sainte, Fred Malatesta, Sam Stein, Juana Sutton (Woman with a large-buttoned bosom), Ted Oliver, Jack Low (Worker), Walter James (Foreman), Lloyd Ingraham (Café patron), Heinie Conklin (Worker), John Rand (Waiter), Edward Kimball. Reissue version: General release: Aug. 28, 1954. U.K. premiere: Oct. 7, 1954, London Pavilion. Distributed by: United Artists Corporation. Length: 8,100 feet (nine reels)

THE GREAT DICTATOR

Premiere: Oct. 15, 1940, Capitol and Astor Theatres, New York City. Distributed by: United Artists Corporation. Produced by: Charles Chaplin Film Corporation. Length: 11,625 feet. Production manager: Alfred Reeves. General assistant: Henry Bergman. Art director: J. Russell Spencer. Set decorations: Ed Boyle. Props: Clem Widrig. Electrical chief: Frank Testera. Construction foreman: William Bogdanoff. Special effects: Ralph Hammeras, Jack Cosgrove. Makeup: Ed Voight. Assistant directors: Dan James, Wheeler Dryden, Bob Meltzer. Directors of photography: Karl Struss, Roland H. Totheroh. Sound: Percy Townsend, Glenn Rominger. Music: Charles Chaplin. Musical direction: Meredith Willson. Assistant to Mr. Willson: Max Terr. Musical librarian: Al Kaye. Film editor: Willard Nico. Written by: Charles Chaplin. Producer: Charles Chaplin. Director: Charles Chaplin. Cast: Charles Chaplin (Adenoid Hynkel, Dictator of Tomania; and Jewish barber), Paulette Goddard (Hannah), Jack Oakie (Benzino Napaloni, Dictator of Bacteria), Reginald Gardiner (Schultz), Henry Daniell (Garbitsch), Billy Gilbert (Herring), Grace Hayle (Madame Napaloni), Carter De Haven (Bacterian ambassador), Maurice Moscovich (Mr. Jaeckel), Emma Dunn (Mrs. Jaeckel), Bernard Gorcey (Mr. Mann), Paul Weigel (Mr. Agar), Chester Conklin (Customer in barber shop), Esther Michelson, Hank Mann (Storm trooper), Florence Wright, Eddie Gribbon (Storm trooper), Robert O. Davis, Eddie Dunn, Nita Pike, Peter Lynn, Leo White (Hynkel's barber), Lucien Prival (Officer), Stanley J. Sandford (1918 soldier), Pat Flaherty, Harry Semels, Jack Perrin, Max Davidson, Nellie V. Nichols

MONSIEUR VERDOUX

Premiere: Apr. 11, 1947, Broadway Theatre, New York City. Distributed by: United Artists Corporation. Produced by: The Chaplin Studios, Inc. Length: 11,132 feet. Production manager: John McFadden. Art director: John Beckman. Assistant director: Rex Bailey. Director of photography: Roland H. Totheroh. Operative cameraman: Wallace

Chewning. Artistic supervision: Curtis Courant. Sound: James T. Corrigan. Wardrobe: Drew Tetrick. Makeup: William Knight. Hair stylist: Hedvig Mjorud. Music: Charles Chaplin. Music arranged and directed by: Rudolph Schrager. Film editor: Willard Nico. Original story: Charles Chaplin, based on an idea by Orson Welles. Producer: Charles Chaplin. Associate directors: Wheeler Dryden, Robert Florey. Director: Charles Chaplin. Cast: Charles Chaplin (Henri Verdoux, alias Varnay, alias Bonheur, alias Floray), Mady Correll (Mona, his wife), Allison Roddan (Peter, their son), Robert Lewis (Maurice Bottello, Verdoux's friend), Audrey Betz (Martha, his wife), Martha Raye (Annabella Bonheur), Ada-May (Annette, her maid), Isobel Elsom (Marie Grosnay), Marjorie Bennett (Her maid), Helen Heigh (Yvonne, Marie's friend), Margaret Hoffman (Lydia Floray), Marilyn Nash (Girl), Irving Bacon (Pierre Couvais), Edwin Mills (Jean Couvais), Virginia Brissac (Carlotta Couvais), Almira Sessions (Lena Couvais), Eula Morgan (Phoebe Couvais), Bernard J. Nedell (Prefect of police), Charles Evans (Detective Morrow), William Frawley (Jean La Salle), Arthur Hohl (Estate agent), Barbara Slater (Girl at flower shop), Fritz Leiber (Priest), Vera Marshe (Vicki, friend of Annabella), John Harmon (Joe, friend of Annabella), Christine Ell (Maid), Lois Conklin (Flower girl), Fred Karno Jr. (Mr. Karno), Barry Norton (Guest), Wheeler Dryden (Salesman), Joseph Granby (Court clerk), William Self (Reporter), Herb Vigran (Reporter), Julius Cramer (Executioner)

LIMELIGHT

Premiere: Oct. 16, 1952, Odeon Theatre, Leicester Square, London. U.S. premiere: Oct. 23, 1952, Astor and Trans-Lux Theatres, New York City. Released: Feb. 6, 1953. Distributed by: United Artists Corporation. Produced by: Celebrated Films Corporation. Length: 12,266 feet. Production manager: Lonnie D'Orsa. Art director: Eugene Lourié. Assistants to Mr. Chaplin: Jerome Epstein, Wheeler Dryden. Assistant director: Robert Aldrich. Director of photography: Karl Struss. Photographic consultant: Roland H. Totheroh. Makeup: Ted Larsen. Hair stylist: Florence Avery. Wardrobe designed by: Riley Thorne. Wardrobe: Drew Tetrick. Sound: Hugh McDowell. Sound editor: Harold E. McGhan. Choreography: Charles Chaplin, André Eglevsky, Melissa Hayden. Corps de ballet: Carmelita Maracci. Music: Charles Chaplin. Music arranged by: Ray Rasch and Charles Chaplin. Conducted by: Keith Williams. Assistant film editor: Edward Phillips. Editor: Joe Inge. Original story and screenplay: Charles Chaplin. Producer: Charles Chaplin. Director: Charles Chaplin. Cast: Charles Chaplin (Calvero), Claire Bloom (Thereza), Nigel Bruce (Postant), Buster Keaton (Calvero's partner), Sydney Chaplin (Neville), Norman Lloyd (Bodalink), André Eglevsky (Harlequin), Melissa Hayden (Columbine), Marjorie Bennett (Mrs.

Alsop), Wheeler Dryden (Thereza's Doctor and Clown), Barry Bernard (John Redfern), Stapleton Kent (Claudius), Mollie Glessing (Maid), Leonard Mudi (Calvero's doctor), Loyal Underwood (Musician), Harry "Snub" Pollard (Musician), Julian Ludwig (Musician), Charles Chaplin Jr. (Clown), Geraldine Chaplin (Child in street), Michael Chaplin (Child in street), Josephine Chaplin (Child in street), Harry Crocker (Music-hall patron), Tim Durant (Music-hall patron), Oona O'Neill Chaplin (Double for Claire Bloom, in two brief shots)

The British Productions

A KING IN NEW YORK

Premiere: Sept. 12, 1957, Leicester Square Theatre, London. Distributed by: Archway Film Distributors. U.S. premiere engagement: Dec. 19, 1973, Playboy Theatre, New York City. Produced by: Attica Film Company. Length: 9,891 feet. Production manager: Eddie Pike. Production controller: Mickey Delamar. Art director: Allan Harris. Assistant: Tony Bohy. Special effects: Wally Veevers. Continuity: Barbara Cole. Makeup: Stuart Freeborn. Hair stylist: Helen Penfold. Wardrobe supervisor: J. Wilson-Apperson. Furs: Deanfield. Assistant director: Rene Dupont. Director of photography: Georges Perinal. Camera operator: Jeff Seaholme. Sound supervisor: John Cox. Sound Recording: Bert Ross, Bob Jones. Sound editor: Spencer Reeve. Sound system: Westrex. Music: Charles Chaplin. Arranged by: Boris Sarbek. Conducted by: Leighton Lucas. Editor: John Seabourne. Written by: Charles Chaplin. Associate producer: Jerome Epstein. Producer: Charles Chaplin. Director: Charles Chaplin. Cast: Charles Chaplin (King Shahdov), Maxine Audley (Queen Irene), Jerry Desmonde (Prime Minister Voudel), Oliver Johnston (Ambassador Jaume), Dawn Adams (Ann Kay, TV specialist), Sidney James (Johnson, TV advertiser), Joan Ingram (Mrs. Cromwell, hostess), Michael Chaplin (Rupert Macabee), John McLaren (Macabee senior), Phil Brown (Headmaster), Harry Green (Lawyer), Robert Arden (Elevator attendant), Alan Gifford (School superintendent), Robert Cawdron (U.S. marshal), George Woodbridge (Member of Atomic Commission), Clifford Buckton (Member of Atomic Commission), Vincent Lawson (Member of Atomic Commission), Shani Wallis (Singer), Joy Nichols (Singer), Nicholas Tannar (Butler), George Truzzi (Comedian), Laurie Lupino Lane (Comedian), Macdonald Parke. Produced at Shepperton Studios, England. Reissue version: Released: 1973. Distributed by: Black, Inc./Classic Entertainment. Editor: Freddie Wilson

A COUNTESS FROM HONG KONG

Premiere: Jan. 5, 1967, Carlton Cinema, Haymarket, London. U.S. premiere: Mar. 15, 1967, Sutton Theatre, New York City. Distributed by: Universal Pictures. Produced by: Universal Pictures. Length: